Women's Studies for the Future

DATE DUE

Women's Studies for the Future

Foundations, Interrogations, Politics

EDITED BY

ELIZABETH LAPOVSKY KENNEDY

AGATHA BEINS

Rutgers University Press
New Brunswick, New Jersey, and London

Library of Congress Cataloging-in-Publication Data

Women's studies for the future : foundations, interrogations, politics / Elizabeth Lapovsky
Kennedy and Agatha Beins, [editors] .
    p. cm.
    Includes bibliographical references and index.
    ISBN 0-8135-3618-9 (hardcover : alk. paper) — ISBN 0-8135-3619-7 (pbk. : alk. paper)
    1. Women's studies. 2. Women's studies—United States. I. Kennedy, Elizabeth Lapovsky,
1939– II. Beins, Agatha, 1976–
    HQ1180.W6765 2005
    305.4'072—dc22

2004025318

A British Cataloging-in-Publication record for this book is available from the British Library.

Manufactured in the United States of America

We dedicate this book to the researchers, teachers, administrators, and students who have built women's studies and to those who will continue to do so into the future.

CONTENTS

PREFACE

This anthology grew out of a conference held to celebrate the twenty-fifth anniversary of Women's Studies, the twentieth anniversary of the Southwest Institute for Research on Women (SIROW) and the fifteenth anniversary for the Women's Studies Advisory Council (WOSAC) at the University of Arizona in October 2000. One of the editors, Elizabeth Lapovsky Kennedy, had arrived at the University of Arizona in 1998 to assume the headship of the Department of Women's Studies. Coming from an embattled women's studies program at the University of Buffalo, she was impressed by the support women's studies had at the University of Arizona. She was also aware that there was no cogent plan for future directions and that there was a great deal of internal dissension about appropriate focus. The beginning discussions of the state of women's studies in journals, such as *differences* and *Feminist Studies,* were not yet part of the planning process for women's studies at the University of Arizona, nor for most women's studies programs, judging by the presentations at the National Women's Studies Association.[1] Kennedy was nervous that women's studies was going to undercut its past accomplishments by not thinking through the challenges at hand. In addition, as a good citizen, she felt compelled to forge a workable vision for women's studies, rather than squander away taxpayers' monies or faculty and student time. Holding a working conference at the University of Arizona to discuss future directions for the field of women's studies, as part of the department's anniversary celebration, seemed a sensible intervention. The department agreed, wanting to create a vital space for reflection on the past, evaluation of the present, and planning for the future.

The key factor in shaping the success of the conference and its ability to generate this collection of essays was the decision early on by the conference organizers to engage the oppositions that have been the site of contentious and sometimes bitter struggles locally and nationally. They wanted a conference that encompassed the exciting scholarship that both deconstructs the categories of women and gender and analyzes the concrete systems of gender that oppress women daily around the world, limiting women's ability to earn money, create art, and even to live. Similarly, they wanted a conference that could recognize the strength of feminist scholarship in the disciplines but also the unique contributions of interdisciplinary women's studies. The conference was a great success. *Women's Studies for the Future: Foundations, Interrogations, Politics* aims to bring these discussions to a larger audience.

In the year following the conference, Kennedy, with the assistance of a research assistant, Meredith Trauner, worked to create a Web publication, "The Future of Women's Studies: Foundations, Interrogations, Politics," at http://w3.arizona.edu/~ws/future/. When Trauner completed her MA, Agatha Beins replaced her, putting the finishing touches on the online publication and taking on more and more work for the print publication. She had a talent for the work and in time she became the coeditor.

The composition of this collection of essays is shaped primarily by the design of the original conference, along with the visions of the editors and editorial board. The majority (thirteen) of the papers were originally either plenary or workshop presentations at the conference. The coeditors also recruited specific articles. In the end there was too much material and two excellent essays had to be cut in order to keep the book a manageable size. All articles were reviewed by the coeditors and a two-person editorial board consisting of Trauner, even though she was no longer a student, and Diane Wiener, a PhD student in comparative cultural and literary studies who had also been involved in the original planning of the conference. In addition, each article was also read by at least one outside reader drawn from faculty around the country, although the majority came from the University of Arizona. Final decisions were taken by the coeditors in consultation with the board.

Women's Studies for the Future is, therefore, part of the process of building women's studies, not an isolated project. It represents the collaboration of students and faculty in grappling with the institutionalization of women's studies. We offer it as a modest tribute to all the women's studies anniversaries of this first decade of the twenty-first century.

Notes

1. See *differences: A Journal of Feminist Cultural Studies* 9, no. 3 (1997); and *Feminist Studies* 24 no. 2 (1998).

ACKNOWLEDGMENTS

Since the conceptual framework for the book was largely shaped by the University of Arizona Women's Studies anniversary conference in 2000, we are indebted to all of the more than twenty-five people who served on the conference planning committee over a period of two years, and particularly to Karen Anderson, Susan Aiken, and Miranda Joseph, who forged the original conference vision, and to the late Jo Ann Troutman, the department business manager, who made sure that we had the resources necessary to attempt this publication. We also thank the Spencer Foundation, which was the primary funder of the conference and supported the beginning work on this collection.

We are very grateful to Diane Wiener and Meredith Trauner for their commitment to this anthology through service on the editorial board for more than two years; their careful and thorough evaluation of articles, informed by their probing questions about the field of women's studies, unquestionably shaped this collection. In addition, we thank the more than twenty anonymous outside readers for their insightful comments that helped us evaluate and recommend revisions for articles. Thanks also to Jan Monk and Theda Perdue, who generously shared their editing experience and guided us through the rough spots, and to Lauren Johnson and Philip Baron, who offered help with the computing difficulties that are inevitable with a collection this size. Melanie Halkias, our editor at Rutgers, has been extremely supportive of this project and has patiently encouraged its completion.

Engaging the present and imagining a future for women's studies is not an easy task. Kennedy thanks her colleagues in the Women's Studies Department at the University of Arizona for creating an environment that encourages analysis of the issues facing women's studies, and her long time friends Ellen DuBois, Carolyn Korsmeyer, Lillian Robinson, and Sheila Slaughter for always being willing to discuss the institutionalization of women's studies. But ideas alone do not make a book. Kennedy was able to finish the project in a timely fashion due to a National Humanities Center Fellowship for the year 2003–2004 that not only gave her time for editing and writing, but also provided excellent technical and library services.

Beins would like to thank the Women's Studies Department at the University of Arizona for giving her the tools to look at the world in a more complicated and compassionate way. She is especially grateful to have worked with Kari McBride and Sandra Soto, whose mentorship has been invaluable, and with her peers, Anne Bonds, Jessica Pabon, David Rubin, Kat Sabine, and Joy Wilcox, whose academic work has helped her understand the vast relevance of feminist scholarship throughout academia. Also, Beins gives many thanks to her parents and brother for their consistent and unconditional encouragement. We both thank Florence Babb, Jordanna Bailkin, Ellen Dubois, Frances Ferguson, Bonita Hampton, Barbara Harris, Carolyn Korsmeyer, Kari McBride, Joan Nestle, Catherine Raissiguier, Margaret Randall, Carol Summers, Meredith Trauner, and Diane Wiener for their generosity in reading drafts of the Introduction and offering invaluable feed back.

We learned a great deal in editing this book, primarily due to the contributors' passionate thinking about women's studies, and we thank them heartily for this and for their patience in the long editorial process. We particularly appreciate Beverly Guy-Sheftall, Evelynn Hammonds, and Chandra Talpade Mohanty for agreeing to have their articles reprinted in this collection and Duke University for granting the permission. In addition, we are grateful to Monica Brown for introducing us to the paintings by her mother, Isabel Brown, one of which we use for the cover of the book. And special thanks to Sandra Soto for sharing her ideas about what constitutes a good cover, to Kari McBride for advice on questions of grammar and style, and to Laura Madeline Wiseman for assistance in the final preparation of the manuscript.

We also thank one another for the grace, generosity, and intellectual rigor that make team work possible. Lastly, we want to thank our significant others, Bobbi and Mike, whose continuing emotional support for our intellectual work allows us to be full human beings.

Women's Studies for the Future

Introduction

ELIZABETH LAPOVSKY KENNEDY AND AGATHA BEINS

In the early twenty-first century, women's studies is at a critical point for establishing future directions. Not only have the numbers of programs and the students that are served on campuses continued to grow nationally and internationally, but women's studies has also become more completely institutionalized, offering graduate degrees and taking on departmental status. In keeping with this growth, the subject matter has shifted, no longer adhering to a unitary understanding of woman. At the same time women's studies finds itself in an increasingly conservative political environment and in a society that is often called "post-feminist." This situation raises difficult and challenging questions for faculty, students, and administrators. How does the field need to adjust its goals and methods to respond to and effect change in the contemporary world and thrive into the future? *Women's Studies for the Future: Foundations, Interrogations, Politics* addresses these questions.

There is surprisingly little written that grapples with the institutionalization of women's studies while looking toward the future. Academic feminists have amply questioned the histories, values, and visions of women's studies programs; however, at this point in history this self-reflexivity has primarily focused on revealing the supposed failures of women's studies—its lack of a coherent or defensible subject or method of study, its abandonment of the original project of activism and social change, its politicizing of research and teaching—rather than grappling with the implications of successful institutionalization.[1] This collection of essays recognizes the strengths as well as the limitations of institutionalization and faces the challenge of envisioning successful departments that are also voices for change.[2]

The lack of unanimity about the success of women's studies, despite what it has accomplished in terms of institutionalization, indicates the complex nature of the field. Participants in women's studies today come from most traditional disciplines in the modern university as well as from interdisciplinary fields and from professional schools. They have varied theoretical trainings, political perspectives, and cultural backgrounds. They are located in a variety of institutions, from community colleges to research universities, with widely varying resources and degrees of administrative support and acceptance, as well as in educational institutions throughout the world. They also belong to different generations of scholars entering the university under radically different social conditions. This collection, while focused on embracing and building upon success, aims to encompass and make explicit this variety of perspectives and therefore asks authors to situate themselves in relation to their essays.

Recognizing our locations has been fruitful to Kennedy and Beins as editors. It has helped us develop a perspective that is historically situated, yet also focuses on the present and the future, with Kennedy having been a founder of women's studies in 1970 and Beins having just finished her MA in women's studies in 2003.

In Kennedy's words: My perspective on women's studies is formed by helping to build women's studies at the University of Buffalo from 1969 to 1997; in turn this work has shaped the scholar and teacher I have become. I had been trained as a social anthropologist, but after inhabiting interdisciplinary programs for thirty years, I now consider myself an interdisciplinary scholar. Most importantly, I was only an incipient feminist when I became a sponsor of women's studies, but I rapidly became a socialist feminist, melding my antiwar activism and my new contacts with women's liberation. During my long-term relationship with women's studies, I have witnessed extraordinary changes in social, economic, and political conditions in the field, in the university, and in society at large. I have struggled in these contexts to keep feminist education and scholarship radical, critical, and contributing to social change and to refine continually the meaning of a socialist feminist perspective. Perhaps the most important thing I have learned in this process is that history is ruthless; it keeps moving ahead; social movements, institutions, and individuals (even radical ones) either engage it or quickly become ineffective.

In Beins's words: Women's studies has always been a part of post-secondary education for me, from my BA in classical languages, through my MA in women's studies, and continuing into the MFA in creative writing I am currently pursuing. As an undergraduate, my understanding of feminism was primarily rooted in identity politics, but I realize that my education has taken place in an era influenced by postmodernism, poststructuralism, and other theories that work to deconstruct and disrupt traditional ideas about identity. Thus, I have been able to take women's studies for granted, as I take for granted more traditional disciplines, while contemporary scholars have given me the language to presuppose the fluidity and incoherency of identity, even that identity upon which women's studies is supposed to be based. Working on my MA, and now this anthology, has helped me understand how the tension between coherency and incoherency can affect women's studies' relationships with other academic programs and shape its struggles to institutionalize as an interdisciplinary field in a disciplinary university.

Reflecting upon women's studies as a field, as an academic department, and as a set of practices that scholars in other fields have adopted, we—Kennedy and Beins—have realized that neither of us could imagine a university without women's studies and that we are both hopeful about further institutional successes. However, we have also confronted the differences in our educational histories, the amount of time we each have spent as feminist scholars, and our future plans. Thus, Kennedy is tired of the self-reflective criticism that predominates in women's studies. To her, the endless criticisms sound like a Greek chorus, locking women into failure and victimhood and preventing feminist scholars from analyzing the nature of the social institutions that they inhabit. In contrast, for Beins this emphasis on self-reflection is one of the field's strengths. It enables feminist scholars to interrogate and theorize identities, ideas, and systems, while also being aware of their own institutional complicity. We have learned in working together that it is useful to understand that we are both right. Women's studies' vitality as a field comes from its ability to encompass contradiction. Our differences and similarities have been equally fundamental in the way we have related to and developed this anthology—broadening what is included but staying focused on the challenges of successful institutionalization.

Accepting various perspectives on women's studies has led us to understand that this book cannot be about prescriptions for how women's studies can best proceed. Rather it is about exploring the ideas and issues that are shaping the field of women's studies. As editors, we share a set of questions, not answers. Such an approach should allow readers to find useful insights for furthering their work as teachers, researchers, administrators, and/or students, whatever their locations geographically, theoretically, or institutionally.

Toward this end, the essays are organized around five issues. First, what is the subject of women's studies? Second, how does women's studies negotiate the politics of alliance and the politics of difference? Third, how can women's studies fulfill the promise of interdisciplinarity? Fourth, what is the continuing place of activism in women's studies? Fifth, how has feminist pedagogy responded to changing social conditions? Although these are certainly not all of the questions one could pose to assess the contemporary situation of women's studies, we are confident that grappling with these questions will give the reader a good overview of challenges and directions in the field. We will end the introduction with some of our own thoughts on the future.

What Is the Subject of Women's Studies?

Despite the substantial increase in the number of women's studies MA and PhD programs, the core and boundaries of the field are not clear. In its early history women's studies was consistently defined as the study of the history and culture of women, or education for and about women to end the oppression of, or the discrimination against, women. These simple definitions are no longer possible due to feminist scholarship's deconstruction of the category "woman" in the context of a society-wide challenge to identity politics. Yet no new definition has gained widespread acceptance. From our reading and experience at conferences, it seems that some definitions focus on women, some on gender, and some on multiple identities and interlocking systems of hierarchy, and that often these are all in tension with one another in the same program/department.

Problematizing identity, and therefore the subject of women's studies, grows out of two strong traditions, the analytical frameworks of feminists of color and of feminist poststructuralists. Although several good intellectual histories of women's studies exist, we revisit the subject here in order to remind the reader of the multiple frameworks shaping definitions of women's studies today.[3] It is certainly true that all women's studies programs in the early 1970s were based in an understanding that women share a common experience of oppression/discrimination that needs to be studied in order to eliminate it. At the same time many were also aware that analyses of this experience were usually based in the white upper middle class and did not reveal connections between multiple systems of oppression. The founders of women's studies came from different racial/ethnic groups, different classes, and different sexual orientations. They had participated in the old and new left, in the civil rights and antiwar movements as well as in the feminist and gay liberation movements, so many were aware of differences among women as well as the systems of power that shape those differences. In addition, the validation of experience, so central to consciousness-raising groups, opened spaces for "minority" positions to be heard.[4]

It was through the practices and writing of feminists of color that Kennedy first learned of the need to problematize identity in the early 1970s. At the University of Buffalo, where she taught, this was perhaps apparent earlier than in other places around the country because women's studies was located within the Department of American Studies, which also housed Native American studies and Puerto Rican studies, a structure that challenged segregated work relations at the university. These three identity studies programs had regular contact in department meetings, offering the possibility for women of color and white women to associate with both women's studies and ethnic studies. Kennedy remembers the women's studies governing committee being pushed to develop an introductory course that focused on all women, not simply white middle-class women.

But this was not simply a local phenomenon; nationally, feminists of color were raising similar issues about racism in women's studies, indicating that there were not only differences but also hierarchies of power between and among women. In the early 1980s, three landmark books were published, Angela Davis's *Woman, Race, and Class,* Cherríe Moraga and Gloria Anzaldúa's *This Bridge Called My Back: Writings by Radical Women of Color,* and bell hooks's *Ain't I a Woman: Black Women and Feminism,* that changed the shape of feminist scholarship, making it intellectually irresponsible to talk about "woman" as an undifferentiated universal category.[5] Throughout the 1970s and 1980s lesbians also complicated the notion of a unitary woman's identity, exploring the distinct conditions of lesbian lives; in the path-breaking works of Cherríe Moraga, Gloria Anzaldúa, and Audre Lorde, the critiques of women of color and lesbians were brought together.[6] By the mid–1980s it was no longer just feminists of color and lesbians writing about the challenges of understanding the complexity of the category of woman and of woman's identity. Elizabeth Spelman's 1988 book, *Inessential Woman: Problems of Exclusion in Feminist Thought,* made a strong philosophical argument for the compound nature of identity and the impossibility of understanding black women through a single lens either of blackness or of femaleness.[7]

Although the writings of feminists of color and lesbians complicated understandings of identity, they did not necessarily challenge the concept of identity itself. In the mid-1980s poststructuralist and postmodernist theoretical approaches came to play a prominent role in the academy, particularly in the humanities. In women's studies, it became as important a theoretical approach as historical materialism had been in earlier years. Poststructuralism offered convincing critiques of building a field of study around identity questions and analyses of systems of oppression, critiques that resonated well with problems the field was already struggling with due to the cogent criticisms of feminists of color. This intellectual framework approached identities and experience as constructed narratives.[8] As Beins indicated earlier, to those entering women's studies after poststructuralism became the dominant tradition, "woman" was understood as an endlessly shifting signifier. This intellectual framework had a freeing effect, offering new ways of thinking about the complexity of subjectivity, identity, and experience and, therefore, new approaches for thinking through the connections of antiracist, queer, and feminist scholarship and the meaning of multiple identities. Furthermore, by disassociating women from femininity and gender from bodies, it opened up new possibilities for thinking about female masculinity and transgendered persons.[9]

In the process of deconstructing identities, poststructuralism began to shift the field from looking at women to looking at gender. This is not to say that early feminist scholars did not use the concept of gender; they did, but mainly as a descriptive term to convey the constructed differences between men and women. By the 1980s some social scientists in their effort to analyze work and family began to understand gender as a hierarchical system of social relations, a development that dovetailed with the frameworks of poststructuralism.[10] However, this convergence of materialist and empirical analyses of institutions and systems—patriarchy, racism—which had predominated in early women's studies, with poststructuralist analyses of gender as discourse was more apparent than real. Tensions developed between the two approaches and often one approach was given priority over the other in particular departments and journals.[11] Although as early as 1986 Sandra Harding called for the need both to deconstruct women's identity and to analyze systems of oppression, suggesting that feminist scholarship needs to integrate cultural theory and material analysis of institutions, many women's studies practitioners have not yet moved through this binary.[12]

The changing definition of the subject of women's studies is perhaps best evidenced by the field's move in the 1990s to internationalize its curriculum, revealing the hierarchical relations among nations and, therefore, among women. Previously, international studies of women were often called women and development and were a subfield of women's studies rather than at its core. In the introduction to their new text book, *An Introduction to Women's Studies: Gender in a Transnational World,* Inderpal Grewal and Caren Kaplan write: "When the world changes, a field such as women's studies must engage these changes and lead the way in analyzing and discussing women and gender in new ways."[13] Advertisements for jobs and conference topics as well as publications suggest this has begun to happen.[14] Some scholars embracing this new focus for women's studies have consciously attempted to bring together material analyses of globalization under late capitalism with poststructuralist/postcolonial critiques of discourses of domination.[15]

Reflecting the lack of fixed definitions for the core and boundaries of women's studies, women's studies programs have been exploring alternate names. Some women's studies programs are changing their name to gender studies or to gender and sexuality studies or to women's and gender studies. However, program naming turns out to be as much about tactics for reaching a particular student body as it is about defining the focus of the field. For some the change is a way to broaden the audience of women's studies, to make it inclusive of the construction of masculinity and of the analysis of sexuality, including lesbian and gay studies, as for instance in Nan Alamilla Boyd's article in this collection.[16] Others want to move beyond the narrow basis of identity politics, although Robyn Wiegman has recently argued that gender itself is an identity-based category.[17] Yet others advocate the change to gender studies as a way to disassociate women's studies from a political movement.[18] Usually, those who want to hold onto "woman" as in "women's studies" or "women's and gender studies" do so in an explicit attempt to keep the field connected to a political tradition to end the oppression of women. Shirley Yee has argued that by maintaining the name women's studies, the field at least indicates a connection to a social movement and is therefore hospitable to the concerns of feminists of color for social justice.[19] In contrast, Boyd's article in this collection suggests that the concepts of gender and queer make women's studies more hospitable to students of color.

Living with conflicting definitions of women's studies is made more complicated by the fact that the process is not simply about evaluating interesting ideas, but also about building a program or department and, therefore, about the allocation of resources. Those pursuing one direction of scholarship have used their power as gatekeepers to jobs and publication to exclude others. People are turned down for jobs in women's studies, denied promotion, denied admission into graduate programs, labeled by other feminists as neoliberal, racist, or divisive, or judged intellectually uninteresting, irrelevant.[20] Unquestionably, at this point in history women's studies is riddled with this ill-feeling and lack of trust, perhaps contributing to the dominant trope of failure mentioned at the beginning of this introduction. Bitterness still exists today, with each group feeling more wronged than the other, creating intellectual arguments that are polarized and fraught with emotion. Definitions of women's studies cannot escape these painful struggles. In some senses this anthology is shaped by these divisions while trying to heal them by pointing in more inclusive directions and by suggesting that these tensions are central to the vitality of the field.

In the early twenty-first century, the ferment about the focus and definition of women's studies has crystallized around the publication of "The Impossibility of Women's Studies," by feminist political theorist Wendy Brown; the articles in this collection are no exception, many discussing her ideas in detail.[21] Brown brilliantly articulates the many potential problems raised by institutionalizing a field that is based on social identity, thereby strengthening the field's self-critical edge. Yet she also maddeningly ignores the field's long-term history of grappling with these problems and the many partial solutions offered. It is as if she articulates a feminist intellectual's worst fears about the risks involved in creating a new field.

While informed and inspired by Brown's work, this anthology most definitely asserts the possibility of women's studies. Some contributors draw on the more than twenty-five years of practice for guidelines about the subject matter, arguing that contested questions about identity have been at the core of the field. Others are less convinced by past practice and suggest that women's studies needs to respond to the present conditions—its successful institutionalization, the deconstruction of gender, sex, and the body, and the globalization of the economy—that offer the possibility of imagining new forms of feminist knowledge production. Unquestionably, the subject of women's studies remains a challenging question with multiple answers. *Women's Studies for the Future* makes no attempt to come up with a single definition for women's studies but assumes the complexity of the question and is comfortable with this.

"Beyond Dualisms: Some Thoughts about the Future of Women's Studies," by Bonnie Zimmerman, distills the subject of women's studies from the actual practice of programs nationally. She understands the subject matter as a cluster of concepts centering around woman as a category of analysis, gender as a system of power relations, interlocking systems of power, feminism, and social change. She also acknowledges the many complicated questions that this definition raises but argues that women's studies is the site where these questions have been debated since its beginning, pointing out that it is one of the few places in the modern university to value these questions. Based in her own experience with functioning and thriving women's studies programs, she finds it hard to believe Brown's point that faculty in women's studies could not come up with a subject for women's studies and could not grasp that the debates raised by definition are part of the field. Zimmerman helpfully locates disagreements about the subject of women's studies in the differences between the intellectual traditions of materialism and poststructuralism. She identifies herself as part of the materialist tradition and argues that, although women's studies has learned a great deal from poststructuralism, a self-critical materialism can continue to produce knowledge about systems of oppression, "inspire students, . . . and change the world."

"The Possibility of Women's Studies," by Robyn Wiegman, is a useful complement to Zimmerman's essay. Like Zimmerman, she agrees that the debates and complications of building a field around a social identity are central to women's studies; but, from a poststructuralist perspective, she is concerned that the process of institutionalizing such a field inevitably restricts if not eradicates such intellectual work. Wiegman makes at least two important interventions in discussions of the subject of women's studies. First, she identifies the trope of failure that is prominent in discussions of women's studies today and analyzes its role in limiting women's studies to a narrow vision based in the past. Second, she argues that feminist theory and women's studies need to imagine new possibilities commensurate with the significance of feminist intellectual work in the contemporary university and not limited by the subject "woman." Toward this end, she agrees with Brown's analysis that it is impossible to maintain the vitality of a field based on a heritage of identity politics while disagreeing with her recommendation to abandon women's studies and relocate its courses throughout the university. She argues that Brown fails to recognize the identitarian base of the traditional disciplines to which women's studies will be dispersed and that the affect of racial guilt that Brown emphasizes is broader than women's studies; it is symptomatic of the way the university and U.S. political life has managed social difference. (For further discussion of this point, see Janet Jakobsen and Sandra Soto in this volume.) Wiegman's unique contribution is her forceful and convincing argument that we don't yet know the future shape of women's studies and that we need to be very careful not to reproduce old models in new situations. Women's studies has shifted from the margin to the center of contemporary knowledge production; minimally, our visions of the future need to begin here.

Evelynn Hammonds's interview with Beverly Guy-Sheftall, "Whither Black Women's Studies: An Interview, 1997 and 2004," demonstrates the wisdom and problems in both Zimmerman's and Wiegman's perspectives: women's studies is potentially a place of ferment about questions of women, gender, power, and social change, but it also can become rigidified in limited identitarian structures such as whiteness. Although Zimmerman's framework for the subject of women's studies is theoretically open to looking at racial hierarchy among other systems of power, it does not necessarily center around these questions; therefore, Guy-Sheftall and Hammonds, like many other feminists of color, in some contexts designate such a framework as one for white women's studies. "Whither Black Women's Studies" explores the specific accomplishments and challenges of black women's studies—a field that focuses on both gender and race—centering their examination on women's studies in historically black colleges. Though few in number, these are the only organized sites for black women's studies in the United States. They discuss the ways that women's studies at Spelman College has grown with support from the administration and outside foundations; the program thrives today, offering a curriculum that gives black women tools to understand and resist daily oppression. But such programs have not been fostered and encouraged in very many places, neither within women's studies nor within African American studies. Guy-Sheftall and Hammonds implicitly recognize the limitations of identity-based fields, but also their fluidity and ability to change. Although they see black women's studies as distinct, they never see it as separate from women's studies; rather they see it as having had a deep effect on women's studies by broadening its understanding of feminism, by pushing for the hiring of people of color, by working to establish black feminist courses.

Chandra Talpade Mohanty's "'Under Western Eyes' Revisited: Feminist Solidarity through Anticapitalist Struggles" is a revaluation of her 1986 article "Under Western Eyes" in the light of changes in global capital, women's studies, and the women's movement, as well as in her own career. By example, she shows that feminism and historical materialism need not lock women's studies into reproducing the past. Rather she uses them to provide tools for embracing the present; they lead her to give urgent priority to developing an anticapitalist transnational feminist practice. Just as she argued in her 1986 article for bringing the material complexities of Third World women's lives into Western feminist theory, she now argues for bringing this complexity into the production of knowledge about globalization. She proposes to do this by anchoring her analyses in the poorest of women's communities, arguing that their standpoint helps reveal the totality of power relations in global capitalism. She focuses on two sites where feminist projects can make effective interventions in the production of knowledge about globalization: the internationalizing of the women's studies curriculum and the growing anti-globalization movement. In regard to the former, she argues that the frameworks we use and the stories we tell in the classroom have profound implications; she explores ways to create a new comparative feminist pedagogy, one that challenges colonial relations and fosters feminist solidarity across difference. In regard to the latter, she aims to use the growing body of feminist anti-globalization scholarship to disrupt the increasingly masculinist discourse of anti-globalization movements. Since poor women and girls are by and large the hardest hit by the changes wrought by global capitalism and have taken leading roles in the resistance, feminism is essential for addressing the injustices of capitalism. Mohanty envisions that anti-capitalist feminist projects have the potential to become the basis of a liberatory politics for this century.

"What Does Queer Studies Offer Women's Studies? The Problem and Promise of Instability," by Nan Alamilla Boyd, offers yet another perspective on the limitations of identity-based definitions of women's studies. She argues that both women's studies and lesbian and gay studies are based on a predictable connection between gender, sex, and the body, while queer studies' unique contribution is to disrupt that assumption of seamless continuity. Looking at the development of women's studies' intellectual frameworks, Boyd discusses how in at least some women's studies programs the original identity-based framework remained primary through the 1990s and did not foster the debate and discussion that Zimmerman indicates; but rather it worked to exclude poststructuralist frameworks—gender studies, queer studies, and critical race theory. From her experience in women's studies, Boyd judges that identity politics often valued difference by simply counting "different bodies" to demonstrate inclusiveness rather than by transforming the intellectual perspectives that create exclusion. Her analysis shows that disagreements about identity can produce bitterness and exclusion that also need to be acknowledged as part of women's studies' history. In this context queer studies in conjunction with other deconstructive approaches helps to counter these identity forces, with queer studies having the particularly important position of critically examining gendered and sexualized bodies. In addition, Boyd suggests that queer studies further expands the possibilities of women's studies by offering the potential for new intersectional analyses of race/ethnicity with gender and sex.

How Does Women's Studies Negotiate the Politics of Alliance and the Politics of Difference?

How does women's studies develop and maintain a research agenda and a curriculum that explore and analyze the imbrication of gender with race, ethnicity, class, disability, sexuality, and nation in history and culture? Although women's studies has been asking some variation of this question for a long time, it has not yet found answers that transform the field. Thus, in 1998, Beverly Guy-Sheftall still found it necessary to urge that PhD programs make serious attempts to grapple with difference in the core of their curriculum.[22] As a result, many women's studies scholars and students have become frustrated with the lack of progress, some leaving women's studies completely, others deciding the goal of an inclusive curriculum is inappropriate or even a distraction for the field because it generates guilt and dissension.[23] The vision of women's studies fostered in this book is one that puts questions of intersecting differences right at the center of the field, undermining the hegemony of whiteness, heterosexuality, and class privilege. This is a vision articulated in the mission statement of women's studies at the University of Arizona; it is our guess that some variation of this mission exists for many programs.[24] In our view the mission is worth fostering, given that women are found in all social formations and feminism arises in multiple sites.

Recognizing their anomalous position in a university divided by identity programs, women of color have taken leadership in keeping issues of multiple oppression and, therefore, of difference and of alliance on the women's studies agenda.[25] In the 1980s their work was helped by a number of foundations that supported faculty development and curriculum transformation programs.[26] Over the course of thirty years teachers and students have offered exceptionally thoughtful and creative approaches for transforming research and curriculum to illuminate the interconnections of gender, race, ethnicity, class, disability, nation, and sexuality.[27] To name a few, Elsa Barkley Brown and Elizabeth Higginbotham introduced ideas about decentering whiteness in courses, ideas which have since been criticized for reproducing a dichotomy between margin and center.[28] Others introduced the idea of teaching about interlocking systems of oppression.[29] Kimberlé Crenshaw offered the framework of intersecting incommensurate social systems, and Gloria Anzaldúa contributed the idea of border crossings.[30] Adrienne Rich and Donna Haraway introduced the idea of situated knowledge.[31] Evelyn Brooks Higgenbotham drew attention to the way that difference is produced through metalanguages such as that of race.[32] The 1990s also saw pioneering attempts by feminist disability studies to expand the focus of women's studies research and teaching.[33]

Partly in response to the difficulties in developing research and teaching that is based in the interconnections of hierarchical systems of power, scholars began to ask the meta-question about what makes this task so difficult. Mohanty offered a powerful critique about how the university under the rubric of diversity recast struggles against oppression as simple appreciation of difference, thereby containing change—ideas that are explored further in essays by Wiegman and Jakobsen in this volume.[34] Janet R. Jakobsen's *Working Alliances and the Politics of Differ-*

ence analyzes the problematic use of difference in women's studies and the feminist movement, revealing how the women's studies narrative of steady progress toward inclusiveness always assigns resolution to the future rather than encouraging action in the present.[35] These analyses draw scholarship away from experience and identity and toward the social processes that create difference, recommending that this be a focus for women's studies. Thus, questions of research and teaching on the imbrication of gender with race, nation, ethnicity, class, disability, and sexuality are transformed into questions about the politics of difference and alliance. How can programs/departments such as women's studies, LGBT studies, Africana studies, American Indian studies, Judaic studies, Mexican American studies, disability studies, Latin American studies, ad infinitum, constituted as discrete in the modern university, build the interconnections necessary for the fields to encompass the vital questions required for complex understandings of identity and social processes of oppression?

While directly criticizing the concept of "inclusion," the critique of "difference" cannot override it. Rather the two seem to have a dialectical relationship with one another. The demand for inclusion came out of social movements asking that the history of lesbians, of people of color, of people with disabilities be part of women's studies; a demand that cannot be easily set aside even if the response reproduces "difference." The articles in this section build on this past work to forge a scholarship and practice centered in difference and alliance.

Sandra K. Soto, in "Where in the Transnational World Are U.S. Women of Color," speaks to the recurring erasure of ethnic studies within women's studies. She argues that the recent move to reconceive women's studies as a transnational endeavor has the potential to devalue ethnic studies. Analyzing several current feminist transnational texts, such as that by Grewal and Kaplan, she criticizes their tendency to discount ethnic studies, seeing it as "co-opted multiculturalism." She suggests this devaluing is not just an anomaly of their work, or an issue of simple competition for scarce resources, but rather is implicit in their analytical frameworks, showing how this same problem was identified in the internationalizing of the field of American studies. She argues that this devaluation is not based on a serious evaluation of ethnic studies but on uncritical acceptance of the way women's studies and, by implication, the academy have tended to reify, exoticize, and tokenize people of color and the scholarship they produce. In an attempt to change the shape of women's studies, she cogently argues for analytical perspectives and teaching methods that challenge the assumption that Third World feminist experiences are unitary and discrete and that explore the social processes that create difference. Soto's perspective resonates with and furthers that of Guy-Sheftall and Hammonds and Boyd, suggesting that women's studies needs to create more spaces for the serious examination of ethnic studies while cultivating skepticism about intellectual structures that devalue such scholarship.

Janet Jakobsen, in "Different Differences: Theory and the Practice of Women's Studies," contextualizes women's studies in the broader university in order to illuminate past practice around difference and develop future strategies. She argues that women's studies participants need to recognize that the field is not an isolated island but part of a university that is organized to foster exploration of difference in order to maintain, not to challenge, hierarchy. In this situation, women's studies cannot lose sight of the interlocking nature of systems of oppression by focusing only on their autonomy, or of the different operations of these systems by focusing exclusively on their simultaneity. From this perspective, it will not help to abolish programs like women's studies, built around difference and identity; nor can we create a women's studies that fully explores the imbrication of gender with race, class, ethnicity, sexuality, disability, and nation because it makes a difference analytically that the curriculum starts with gender. By not dealing with these contradictions feminist scholars keep multiplying sites of difference while struggling to integrate our understanding of them without changing the hierarchical system. This leads to frustration and defensiveness because we become invested in all the hard work we have done and become oriented toward achieving the perfect yet impossible future instead of intervening in the hierarchy of differences in the present. Jakobsen offers concrete strategies such as being prepared to consciously explain particular decisions to include some differences rather than others in a course or research and finding ways for women's studies to become what she calls "interstructed with" other interdisciplinary units focused around difference. She orients us gently toward this task by suggesting it is larger than we imagine because it involves changing not only women's studies, but also the university, and smaller because we can start with our current syllabi and departmental policies and expand on that.

The remaining three articles in this section start from the assumption of the autonomous effects of difference and examine the process and politics of alliance, building the relationship between women's studies and Chicana studies, between women's studies and Jewish feminist studies, and between women's studies and American Indian studies. Monica Brown and Miroslava Chávez-García, in "Women's Studies and Chicana Studies: Learning from the Past, Looking to the Future," document the development of Chicana studies from the Chicano nationalist movement and from women's liberation, thereby indicating the depth of its differences from and commonalities with women's studies. They demonstrate Chicana feminist leadership in formulating analyses that integrate studies of race, class, gender, and sexuality and also in articulating criticism of the racism, classism, and sexism in women's studies in the 1970s and 1980s. Nevertheless, they argue that by the late 1990s tokenization rather than change was the dominant practice, generating increased criticism of women's studies by Chicana and women of color scholars and defensiveness on the part of women's studies scholars. Brown and Chávez-García suggest a multifaceted program to improve relationships and transform the field of women's studies. Their suggestions come from many sources and work on many levels, cumulatively indicating the complexity of change needed and very much in keeping with Jakobsen's recommendations of working in the here and now. Some recommendations continue to heighten difference while others work on building alliance, suggesting that the tension between the two will be ongoing in women's studies.

In "Feminism, Anti-Semitism, Politics: Does Jewish Women's Studies Have a Future?" Esther Fuchs addresses the ambivalent relationship between women's studies and Jewish feminist scholarship. Recognizing that some have argued this is due to anti-Semitism, Fuchs suggests that this explanation is too simple, looking for explanations in the explosive politics of the Israeli-Palestinian conflict and in the different paradigms each field uses for studying race and class. To understand the complexity of the issues, Fuchs urges reconsideration of a debate about anti-Semitism that occurred in the 1980s in the women's movement between Jewish feminist scholars Elly Bulkin and Jenny Bourne. The issues include identity versus class politics; anti-Semitism as a real force or as a memory; the rightness of the Palestinian position versus support of both sides in a search for peace; understanding of Jews as a homogenous, privileged group versus Jews as a diverse group. Although these issues should be vital to both women's studies and Jewish feminist studies, Fuchs points out with regret that the analyses of anti-Semitism in women's studies put forth by feminist Judaic studies scholars in the 1990s did not even mention these issues. Thus, although Fuchs would agree that women's studies' categories of analysis that center on race, class, gender, sexuality, and nation are too limited in their exclusion of anti-Semitism, she is also arguing that the complex issues raised by Bulkin and Bourne need to be fully discussed. She calls for dialogue and begins by suggesting that Jewish feminist studies reconsider the concept of "the Jewish woman," thinking carefully of the class and race contexts of texts and sources. She also asks for a greater integration of scholarship with ethical and activist questions. Recognizing the volatility of this approach, she calls for an intellectual atmosphere that bridges playfulness and responsibility, creativity and planning, academic vision and activist agendas.

Writing from what they call a tribal perspective, one that recognizes the continuing influence of tribal culture on contemporary American Indian peoples, Mary Jo Tippeconnic Fox and Sheilah E. Nicholas, in "Beyond Pocahontas, Princess, and Squaw: Investigating Traditional Feminism," aim to give visibility to American Indian women's voices. They call for more research that illuminates the role of women in tribal societies, cutting through stereotypes about the past to focus on the respect and influence accorded women because of their leading roles in the family, the economy, and ritual. This research reveals tribal cultures with balanced and reciprocal relationships among community members in general and between men and women in particular. Fox and Nicholas question whether contemporary feminist concepts that are located in the Western state-based legal system of equal rights can be used to analyze and evaluate the significance of tribal women. Their position is counter to existing dominant paradigms in women's studies, which assume that gender roles and gender hierarchy are socially constructed, but that male dominance has existed throughout history.[36] In contrast Fox and Nicholas are using a paradigm in which an element of sex roles is natural while gender hierarchy and oppression are socially constructed, arguing that many tribal societies do not have a tradition of gender hierarchy. Their analysis demonstrates yet again that part of alliance building means being open to the epistemologies and methodologies of other academic programs and disciplines.

How Can Women's Studies Fulfill the Promise of Interdisciplinarity?

The creation of women's studies departments and the offering of women's studies graduate degrees have reinvigorated discussion about the interdisciplinary nature of women's studies, bringing to the fore such questions as these: What is the nature of the interdisciplinary training that women's studies gives to graduate students? How does women's studies build an interdisciplinary department and what is the relationship between that department and feminist scholars in the disciplines? At the moment there are many answers to these questions, as is demonstrated by even a casual look at the structures of the existing women's studies PhD programs. Some, like that at the University of Michigan, hold onto a disciplinary-based education, requiring students to do a double PhD, in women's studies and English or in women's studies and psychology. Others, like Rutgers University, are the opposite extreme, envisioning a completely interdisciplinary educational program. And many are somewhere in between, like the University of Iowa, requiring that students do a minor in a discipline.[37]

Most writing about interdisciplinarity in women's studies today is framed by the debates about the possibility and value of interdisciplinary graduate degrees. Sally Kitch and Judith Allen's article "Disciplined by the Disciplines?" has been a catalyst for this discussion, urging departments to work through the contradictions in the PhD and the challenges of "true" interdisciplinarity to further the institutional promise of the field.[38] In their view, "interdisciplinarity" refers to scholarship that synthesizes different disciplinary traditions; and it is this synthesis that does the important and difficult work of revisioning knowledge production. Recognizing that feminist scholars have worked to deconstruct disciplines as natural divisions of knowledge and method, they also judge that interdisciplinarity has been produced unevenly in women's studies programs.[39] Kitch and Allen argue that women's studies has until now primarily produced multidisciplinary research, collaboration with little integration, because of the academic pressure to have a disciplinary "home" and the disciplinary training of most women's studies faculty. To remedy this situation, Bonnie Zimmerman suggests that the National Women's Studies Association, which by definition is not allied with a specific discipline, can be useful for working through the challenges of interdisciplinarity.[40]

Other scholars are less sanguine about the possibilities of interdisciplinary research for the PhD, arguing that the "too muchness" of the field prevents students and faculty from being proficient in women's studies' epistemologies and methodologies, which extend across the humanities, social sciences, and hard sciences.[41] Furthermore, others argue that it is unethical to develop graduate degree programs in women's studies when the academy cannot absorb the graduates. In a 2002 article, Vivian M. May points out that even women's studies departments are ambivalent about interdisciplinarity, with job advertisements seeming to prefer disciplinary training.[42] For students, the decision about whether to pursue a women's studies PhD is not only intellectual but also political and emotional. Beins, who plans to pursue a doctorate, fears that choosing a literature program over women's studies could represent lack of confidence in the women's studies PhD.

The vision of interdisciplinary women's studies program development raises yet another set of questions. In pursuing interdisciplinarity, is women's studies on the path to becoming a discipline in its own right? And, if so, how will it relate to other disciplines? Although there are different ideas about what defines a discipline, some common factors are shared discourses/vocabularies, shared areas of inquiry and methodologies, a definitive institutional and professional presence, and a collective past, present, and future, all of which women's studies can claim.[43] An aspect of this process of becoming a discipline, one that has received little attention in the literature but one that the editors feel is important for the future, is the relationship of women's studies departments with other departments, disciplines, and professional schools. In its early years, women's studies was dependent on the faculty in traditional departments for its survival; in fact, most faculty were located in traditional departments. But today many women's studies departments are doing their own hiring, making feminist scholars in other departments less essential to the day-to-day running of the department. Delineating the role of feminist scholars in other disciplines and the professional schools is nevertheless important as these scholars offer graduate courses for women's studies students and also train students who take women's studies courses. Building relationships across departments seems particularly important in the recent trend toward a market-driven university that tends to devalue and underfund the humanities.[44] Links to professional schools—particularly law and public health, which are essential for the development of social policy—and to science seem pragmatically sound.[45] Also interconnections with the traditional humanities and social science disciplines seem well advised in order to build allies for influencing the university's priorities.

The articles in this section further discussions about the ongoing challenges of institutionalizing interdisciplinarity by focusing on these questions: What new visions do we need in order to encourage interdisciplinarity? What can be gained by bringing together the methods of cultural theory and historical materialism? How can women's studies continue to develop it relationship with other fields/disciplines, such as the sciences? In "Disciplining Feminist Futures? 'Undisciplined' Reflections about the Women's Studies PhD," May uses the paradoxes made visible by the debates about the women's studies PhD to assess the current state and future directions of the field. She is concerned with the ways that the larger university system, which has been built upon Enlightenment epistemologies, is reproducing women's studies as a discipline. She argues that, "despite the wide range of feminist theorists who affirm difference, discontinuity, and unruly multiplicity, women's studies' sense of self and origin narrative continue to be framed in problematic ways that reinvoke ruly ways of thinking and being." She identifies this inability to imagine a field that is based on multiple and contested frameworks, methods, and bodies as the basis of the resistance to the PhD. Realizing that women's studies programs and departments cannot exist "outside" academia's system for organization of knowledge into disciplines, May identifies distinct approaches of feminist theory and methodology that can lead toward a productive interdisciplinarity for the women's studies PhD. Besides calling for a bold intellectual vision based in feminist theory, her approach also suggests modest changes in the way we envision the field of women's studies: for instance, the traits that are often taken as its weaknesses—such as lack of sameness from program to program, marginality, uneven development—can be sources of vital energy and potential. She suggests that working with feminist theories that celebrate multiplicity and fluidity can promote an institutionalization that is both respectful of boundaries and committed to boundary crossing.

"Toward a New Feminist Internationalism," by Miranda Joseph, Priti Ramamurthy, and Alys Eve Weinbaum, offers an example of why it is valuable for women's studies to bring together scholars using diverse methodologies such as cultural theory and materialist analyses. Building on the work of Inderpal Grewal and Caren Kaplan, they effectively argue for more attention to economic analyses in the study of culture internationally, in order to reveal the interconnections of the local and the global and begin to solve the problematic feminist polarization between universalizing the situation of women and relativizing each unique situation. In the first section Ramamurthy provides a map of the integrated global economy, showing that the same processes of late capitalism that generate wealth and poverty in the United States generate uneven development and gendered inequality throughout the world. Like Mohanty in this volume, Ramamurthy argues that to study women internationally is not simply about looking at women in a variety of different social and cultural situations, but about understanding the social and economic systems that link them into the world economy. In the second section Weinbaum offers a detailed criticism of current feminist thinking about transnationalism, focusing particularly on the problems in universalist and relativist approaches. She identifies the U.S.-centered nature of these approaches, showing that their inability to engage the hierarchical relations of the economy and world politics leads either to the erasure or reification of difference. Using the theoretical tools of a feminist, poststructuralist Marxism, Joseph situates women's studies and the modern university in late capitalism and globalization, identifying the ways women's studies is both complicit with and resistant to these processes. Challenging the commonly articulated opposition between community and capital, which she identifies in the women's studies ideal of autonomous community, she argues that we need to understand community as produced by and inextricably related to capital. As we develop women's studies, we need to pay particular attention to the ways that feminist knowledge production is affected by such oppositions as community and capital, culture and the economy.

Banu Subramaniam's "Laboratories of Our Own: New Productions of Gender and Science" provides insight into the necessity, difficulties, and excitement of cultivating a relationship between women's studies and more traditional disciplines. Subramaniam believes that feminist scholarship is important for looking at disciplinary knowledge in a new way, but also that "the difficulty of the project of feminism and science is as much a failure of women's studies as it is about the sciences." While many feminists critique the patriarchal and Enlightenment traditions that allow scientific studies to reproduce oppressions and structural inequalities based upon identity, Subramaniam observes that science has been unevenly integrated into the ontological space of women's studies. These boundaries reflect not only the insistent disciplinarity of the university but also the ambivalence with which feminists often approach science. Subramaniam writes, "On the one hand, we critique Western feminism for its Eurocentric, masculinist biases and yet we want to embrace that very monster to save women's lives." Thus, in order to more effectively synthesize the projects of women's studies and science studies, Subramaniam explores the ways that feminists can move beyond merely deconstructing science to effect a reconstruction of both science and women's studies, clearing space for a new study of "nature" and "culture."

What Is the Continuing Place of Activism in Women's Studies?

The increasing institutionalization of women's studies has brought to the fore questions of the relationships of theory to practice and activism to scholarship. Although the majority of women's studies participants take for granted that feminism, a desire to change the world, is central to women's studies and that they see practice as part of women's studies, there is little agreement about what that means.[46] At one extreme is the position of Daphne Patai and Noretta Koertge, which criticizes women's studies as dogmatic rather than a serious scholarly undertaking.[47] Focusing on the political excesses of women's studies, the book does not portray a women's studies that Beins and Kennedy recognize. Although we assume such excesses exist, they must be the exception rather than the rule; all women's studies programs we are familiar with work consciously to promote serious scholarship and avoid propaganda and indoctrination.

Ironically, four years before the 2003 edition of *Professing Feminism,* feminist theory was accused of not being political enough, of betraying its activist goals, by Martha Nussbaum in a widely read article, "The Professor of Parody." She argues that feminist theory, particularly that of Judith Butler and other cultural theorists, does nothing for the "real problems" faced by "real women." She writes, "Many feminists in America are still theorizing in a way that supports material change and responds to the situation of the most oppressed. Increasingly, however, the academic and cultural trend is toward the pessimistic flirtatiousness represented by the theorizing of Butler and her followers." And she ends with a powerfully moralistic statement about this work: "But it is a bad response. It collaborates with evil. Feminism demands more and women deserve better."[48] Although she does not directly mention women's studies, the condemnation is implied, since Butler is taught in the majority of women's studies programs nationally. Thus, Nussbaum catapulted to center stage the issue of academic feminism and, therefore, women's studies failing their original promise of activism.

The frame of the critique, one that opposes "real women" and "theory," resonates with the opposition between theory and practice, the academic and the political, cultural theory and empirical analysis that predominates in American culture and in the university. This opposition reflects some of the tensions in women's studies today among students, faculty, and also the educated public. Nussbaum, after all, published her article in the *New Republic,* intending to reach a wide audience. At the University of Arizona many of our graduate students come in wanting to improve women's lives and are fed up with the theory we require them to learn. Others come in, trained in theory in their undergraduate days, and are disdainful of the modest activist projects undertaken through internships to improve women's lives. The heatedness of this debate is related to divisions in women's studies faculty. People doing more empirically oriented work are suspicious of the poststructuralist theorists, and those doing cultural criticism are condescending toward empirical work. As mentioned earlier, these are not simply verbal disagreements for they have repercussions for what is published and who is hired. Nussbaum's article furthers these oppositions, inflaming their emotional bases rather than moving forward to see beyond them.

As a whole this collection does not agree with the implications of Nussbaum's analysis that women's studies has left its original mission by focusing on theory instead of the real world. Rather it focuses on the challenge of finding a viable relationship between theory and practice, one that can learn from the past but does not hold the 1970s as the golden age of activism. Social conditions change, so that a practice that was good twenty years ago might be ineffective today. Robyn Wiegman suggests that this nostalgia for the past disciplines women's studies and prevents us from grappling with the political and institutional challenges of the present. The collection implies other critiques as well: Is the idyllic image of the 1970s marriage of theory and practice accurate? Doesn't historical materialism assume that social conditions change and therefore each generation needs to develop new theory and practice? Why single out feminism's failure to develop an effective politics when other social movements of the 1970s are having similar problems, indicating the drastically changed political conditions? This debate over women's studies' betrayal of its heritage has served as a wake-up call for women's studies to seriously examine the place of activism. In this section the articles explore ways for women's studies to integrate theory and practice in the twenty-first century, grappling with the changing conditions of the world and women's studies; for instance, the increasing institutionalization of women's studies, the expanding presence of neoliberal globalization; the decrease in power of a radical women's movement in the United States.

Building on the work of Wiegman, David Rubin's "Women's Studies, Neoliberalism, and the Paradox of the 'Political'" aims to challenge the common opposition between theory and practice and the academic and the political. Toward this end, he offers a critique of Ellen Messer Davidow's *Disciplining Feminism: From Social Activism to Academic Discourse,* querying the analysis that institutionalization in academia has caused women's studies to focus on theory rather than engage in changing the "real" world. Rubin argues that the same bureaucratization that occurred in women's studies took place in other feminist projects such as international non-governmental organizations (NGOs) and points to larger social forces such as neoliberalism as leading to this process. He also argues for the importance of theory in guiding practice, drawing on his own experience as an activist in the anti–World Trade Organization (WTO) movement. Most importantly, he criticizes Messer Davidow's recommendations for feminist political action, suggesting that they will not achieve her goals of social justice. Because her analysis lacks attention to neoliberalism and changing forms of late capitalism, Rubin argues that her vision of feminism is unable to challenge the disciplining forces of contemporary institutions. Her suggestion of adopting the political strategies of conservatives will likely lead to reproducing the global inequalities against which women's studies is fighting. Rubin concludes by arguing for deconstruction of the political as part of women's studies, in order to reveal both its freeing and limiting aspects.

Lorenia Parada-Ampudia's "The Institutionalization of Women's and Gender Studies in Mexico: Achievements and Challenges" offers a crystal-clear example of what it might mean to analyze women's studies in the context of larger social forces. The article provides a historical overview of the development of women's and gender studies in Mexico, showing how possibilities and constraints emerge in the context of changing social conditions. The analysis is a model of comparative feminist studies by showing connections between gender and nation and the ways that the local and global constitute one another. While analyzing the goals and desires of the activists creating women's studies, she also documents the impact of international funding agencies in shaping women's studies' agendas. During the 1990s the numbers of women's studies programs continued to expand while feminism became primarily located in NGOs. Collaboration with international agencies and political parties was no longer subject to critical reflection even though it influenced the agenda of women's studies. Tensions between marginalization and legitimization characterize contemporary women's studies as feminist scholars search for ways to transform education and society while also being part of its institutions. Today's feminist agenda aims not only to make women and gender part of all levels of the educational system, but also to improve critical thinking about the constraints of institutions and to create more satisfying and less hierarchical social relationships.

Julia Balén's "Practicing What We Teach" complements Parada-Ampudia's essay by exploring the administrative paradoxes that can accompany the institutionalization of feminism in higher education. Working and teaching in universities puts feminists in the position of supporting the hegemonies of academia while also critiquing them. However, the awareness that one can never be entirely outside systems of power does not mean that change is impossible, but that feminists can utilize knowledge about their positions of power and privilege to more effectively resist oppressive practices. Balén utilizes her experience as a former administrator in a relatively large women's studies department in a research institution to illustrate the ways that feminist knowledge production can intervene in administrative practices. She focuses in detail on two concrete challenges faced by women's studies programs: the development of a Chicana studies concentration as part of the major and the development of fair graduate admissions policies. She suggests ways to negotiate these and other administrative challenges while moving toward greater social justice.

How Has Feminist Pedagogy Responded to Changing Social Conditions?

Trends in higher education and in women's studies have combined to blur the definition of feminist pedagogy, making the distinction between feminist and mainstream educational approaches and between feminist and other critical pedagogies less obvious. Some research universities, like the University of Arizona, have come to call themselves student-centered, supporting students' active learning. Many of the techniques they use for encouraging discussion, collaboration, and practice on the surface resemble those of feminist pedagogy, although feminism is rarely given credit. Feminists disagree about whether student centered and collaborative approaches as adopted throughout the university are akin to feminism, asking: If the core of feminist pedagogy is to challenge systems of power, do these techniques manage that when appropriated by institutions of higher education? Or, in fact, might they be easily used to maintain hierarchy, as suggested by Jakobsen's article in this volume?[49]

At the same time the trend toward poststructuralist theoretical frameworks in the university and in women's studies has led feminist pedagogy to envision itself as challenging all systems of power thereby becoming similar to other critical pedagogies.[50] Maralee Mayberry and Ellen Cronan Rose define the common goal of the contributors to their volume on feminist pedagogy as this: "to empower our students to understand and ultimately transform the interlocking systems of oppression that deform contemporary life."[51] This definition does not distinguish feminist pedagogies from other pedagogies that are challenging hierarchical systems of power. Nevertheless, feminist pedagogy is not made irrelevant because it makes a difference whether gender is the entry point for discussing systems of oppression.[52]

The blurring of the boundaries of what constitutes feminist pedagogy has not led to a decrease in writing about the topic. Contemporary writings about feminist/critical pedagogy, what Mayberry and Rose designate as the scholarship of teaching, are extremely rich, with new collections being published regularly.[53] The vitality of reflection on transformative education is likely related to teaching being one aspect of women's studies that is not substantially affected by the uneven development of the field; a feminist scholar can realize innovative teaching no matter if she is located in a small elective or a large degree-granting program. The contributors to this volume all pursue relatively unexplored areas of feminist pedagogy. The essays are heterogeneous, only unified by grappling with the tensions between students' lives inside and outside the classroom. Like the essays in the previous section, they attempt to consider pedagogy in the context of social issues of the twenty-first century.

In "Antifeminism and the Classroom," Lise Gotell and Barbara Crow state that there is not one feminist pedagogy, distinguishing between an emancipatory feminist pedagogy and a "pedagogy of difference." The former is invested in the idea that there is a truth that can be produced through one's position as a female in a patriarchal culture, and that a feminist classroom should provide a safe space for students to do this. The latter reflects the belief that a feminist classroom is not free from power dynamics and can benefit from conflicting perspectives, even though these perspectives might not resolve into one seamless truth. Aligning with a pedagogy of difference, the authors understand the classroom as a public space, one in which instructors are working with groups of students who all have different relationships to the content/texts of a class. The essay aims to distinguish student resistance to and disagreement with course content from antifeminism that shuts down a feminist intellectual environment. They discuss Gotell's experience with antifeminism in an introductory women's studies class, making visible the tension between their pedagogical practices and the way that a feminist classroom is situated within the North American social and political culture. They argue that antifeminist attitudes emerge in response to the direct gains of the feminist movement in regard to such matters as reproductive freedom or workplace equity and need to be addressed as such, rather than be cloaked under the guises of freedom of speech or disruption of a classroom, which, although important, do not direct attention to the public foreclosure of feminist intellectual spaces.

Inez Martinez, in "Imagining Our Way Together," also makes connections between a feminist education and its political and social context. Structuring her argument as a critique of Western epistemology, Martinez uses her somewhat frustrating experience as a graduate student in literature to discuss the disconnect between knowledge produced through "the head," and that produced through "the heart" or imagination. For her, a head-based education can successfully inform, but she is advocating for education that also transforms, that contributes to ending the injustices of racism and the atrocities of war. Although women's studies programs have worked toward a goal of transformation through the attention to activism and instructors' pedagogical practices, the pivotal question is whether or not women's studies, as it becomes more institutionalized through degree programs, will uncritically reify Western epistemology. Thus, Martinez's argument articulates another layer in the relationship between theory and practice, both of which need to include emotion and be "accompanied by hope and by imagination, seeking alternatives." She offers some suggestions about how to achieve this, such as studying art, reflecting on dreams, and giving students more time to "integrate their feelings and sensations with their ideas."

In "Distance Education: A Manifesto for Women's Studies," Laura Briggs and Kari Boyd McBride invoke a transformative pedagogy through an e-certificate in women's studies and Internet computing that would be accessible to nontraditional students, such as people who are homebound, live in rural areas, or are incarcerated. Re-envisioning the physical and ideological structures of education, this program questions who is able to produce and consume knowledge, whose lives and experiences an academic curriculum reflects, as well as what physically constitutes a classroom. While some feminist educators see the Internet as a masculine arena that does not allow for the creation of "woman friendly" spaces, others take advantage of the forums for communication that the Internet allows. Briggs and McBride navigate this tension, pointing to the ways in which both visions are accurate. They argue that Third World educators have been using transgressive and effective models of distance education, overcoming individual, geographical, and systemic barriers that prevent access to educational resources. Drawing particularly on the work of Guillermo Gomez-Peña, they propose to implement a program that takes into account students' place-specific bodies while also breaking down the barriers produced by their (geographical and identitarian) locations. Instead of merely fitting students' education into the current economic system, Briggs and McBride hope to increase student employability in a way that enlarges the control students have over their education.

Thoughts for the Future

In editing this volume, we have come to understand that questions about the future are really questions about the relations between the past, present, and future, with the question of history being critical. Wiegman has asked us to recognize the conditions of the present in order to imagine the future. She is wary of understandings of history that claim to determine the future, such as the popular narratives of women's studies as progressive perfection or as failure. Is history a helpful lens through which to theorize the present and future of women's studies? As editors, our different locations in the academy give us different reactions to this question. Beins agrees with Wiegman that it is not useful to think of the present and future as the culmination of past experiences and events. For Kennedy, Zimmerman's and Mohanty's call for historical materialism is not for the kind of history that aims to determine the future; it is an analysis of changing social conditions and social institutions, an analysis that illuminates the present. As in other aspects of our editing of this anthology, we have come to understand both our approaches to history as right and try to draw on them in our discussion of the future—encouraging bold new thinking while understanding the social conditions that have shaped the present.

With these perspectives, we can envision possible futures for the issues discussed in this anthology. In terms of the future subject of women's studies, it seems indisputable that it will be based on a complex multivocal core with porous and messy boundaries both within the field itself and in relation to other fields. One challenge will be keeping this openness in the hierarchical and discipline-bounded institutions of higher education. In severe competition for resources, it is unclear whether this openness will be honored within departments and programs and in building alliances with programs across institutions. Another challenge will be whether we want to systematize or regulate the content and degrees of women's studies as suggested by Sally Kitch.[54] Whatever we decide, will women's studies be required to systematize in an increasingly market-driven university?

Judging by the current vitality of research and teaching about the interconnections between gender, race, sexuality, disability, nation, anti-Semitism, and class, this concern will continue to occupy women's studies into the future. The field seems to be moving toward a radical break with a past that has tended to hold out the future as a time when women's studies will resolve ways to theorize and practice gender's connection to other social formations, rather than envisioning these issues as a part of the daily concerns of women's studies. The possibility of transforming women's studies to include analyses of multiple systems of power has now broadened its scope to focus on the forces that make this goal so difficult, such as the establishment of separate identity programs organized around difference rather than relations of hierarchy and the concomitant processes of tokenism that exoticize difference. In this context, remedies are not simply focused on research proposals and course syllabi, but in changing policies and practices of the entire university. More of this multidimensional work seems on the agenda for the future, particularly with the possibility of women's studies using its institutional success to effect change. We can begin to imagine a future where the structures of the university and women's studies might even encourage research on interconnecting social formations rather than work against it. Although we glimpse the possibility of these changes, this volume also indicates the active forces working against them. Changing the hierarchical systems created and reproduced by transnational capital will require a society-wide movement for social justice.

The increasing numbers of women's studies graduate programs, particularly PhDs, will foster the fields' interest in interdisciplinarity. With its own intellectual space, women's studies has the radical potential for revisioning the field in terms of epistemology, theory, and method. It is asking, "What are the knowledge traditions, critical vocabularies and methodological presumptions that attach to women's studies and differentiate it from feminist scholarship in the disciplines."[55] Unquestionably, the field is embarking on an uncharted future of feminist knowledge production. As women's studies pursues interdisciplinarity, further questions about the nature of the field emerge: Will it be a discipline? A transdiscipline? An interdiscipline? What is the relationship between women's studies and feminist scholarship in the disciplines? Can there be interdisciplinarity without an ongoing relationship with the disciplines?

From the centrality of activism in these essays, it seems safe to assume that struggles to combine theory and practice will remain important to women's studies into the future; this integration takes on increasing difficulty with women's studies' mandate to pursue new forms of knowledge, not necessarily having immediate relevance to contemporary political issues. Cumulatively, these essays lead women's studies away from modeling activism on the past and toward responding to contemporary social conditions: successful institutionalization, the disappearance of a radical mass women's movement in the United States, and the expansion of global capitalism and transnational feminist movements, among other issues. In doing this they set the parameters for research and activism in the near future. Bridging the division between the economy and feminism by meshing feminist practices with anti-globalization movements seems an important priority for challenging suffering and exploitation in the world as well as for cultivating the long-term health of feminism. Attention to the paradoxes of administering successful women's studies programs also seems a key issue for the immediate future; if women's studies is to keep a multivocal core and amorphous boundaries, it will need to develop governance structures that encourage this. Negotiating paradox can often lead to ill will and division if not handled with clearly articulated procedures. In addition, to capitalize on success while offering a critical perspective on higher education and society will require sophisticated administrative leadership.

The steady production of thoughtful and engaged writing about feminist pedagogy is an impressive aspect of the field. Feminist pedagogy, like the field of women's studies as whole, has developed porous boundaries while expanding its focus. This allows it to engage critical issues of our time while keeping issues of gender and feminism central: dissent versus disruption, education to transform, technology for social justice. The prominent place of the theory and practice of good teaching in women's studies bodes well for the field's continued vitality. High-quality education of students—one that analyzes systems of power and recognizes the specificity of students' locations—encourages the discussion of issues of feminism and social justice in the society at large.

Cumulatively, the essays in this book suggest that in thinking about the future of women's studies, the goal is not to find definitive answers to some of the issues that keep occupying our scholarship and practice. Instead, as the field explores questions that have emerged from previous feminist work, it also needs to understand how these questions have shaped feminist scholarship and created meta-narratives about the institutionalization of women's studies, that limit our abilities to keep formulating new questions and practices. While demanding this self-critical openness, the essays also push the field to actively engage the present rather than long for an ideal future. The exceptional productivity of women's studies scholars over the last thirty-five years and, concomitantly, the field's increased institutionalization point toward at least three guideposts for women's studies: to explore the complex factors shaping the construction of identity, community, and nation-state while analyzing the history of women/gender, feminism, and women's studies as they interact with other systems of power, social movements, and fields of study, respectively; to develop policy and activist programs, grounded in changing social conditions and institutions, that will work toward a more just social order in the university, the local community, the nation, and the world; to create bold visions for the future that are not linear continuations of the present and can encompass the local and global contexts that shape people's lives and dreams. These guideposts will keep the core of women's studies vital and its boundaries flexible in the present and, therefore, into the future.

Notes

1. See, for instance, Wendy Brown, "The Impossibility of Women's Studies," *differences* 9 no. 3 (1997): 79–101; Martha Nussbaum, "The Professor of Parody," *New Republic* (February 22, 1999): 37–45; and Daphne Patai and Noretta Koertge, *Professing Feminism: Education and Indoctrination in Women's Studies* (Lanham, Md.: Lexington Books, 2003). This is a new and expanded version of their *Professing Feminism: Cautionary Tales from the Strange World of Women's Studies* (New York: Basic Books, 1994). See also Ellen Messer Davidow, *Disciplining Feminism: From Social Activism to Academic Discourse* (Durham: Duke University Press, 2002). For a discussion of this tendency to focus on failure see Robyn Wiegman, this volume.
2. It builds on Biddy Martin, "Success and Its Failures," *differences* 9, no. 3 (1997): 102–

132; Marilyn Boxer, *When Women Ask the Questions* (Durham: Duke University Press, 2001); Sally L. Kitch, "Claiming Success: From Adversity to Responsibility in Women's Studies," *NWSA Journal* 14, no. 1 (2002): 160–181; and Robyn Wiegman, ed., *Women's Studies on Its Own* (Durham: Duke University Press, 2003).

3. See Leora Auslander, "Do Women's + Feminist + Men's + Lesbian and Gay + Queer Studies = Gender Studies?" *differences* 9, no. 3 (1997): 1–30; Robyn Wiegman, "The Progress of Gender: Whither 'Women'?" in *Women's Studies on Its Own*, ed. Wiegman, 106–140.

4. Elizabeth Lapovsky Kennedy, "Dreams of Social Justice," in *The Politics of Women's Studies: Testimony from Thirty Founding Mothers*, ed. Florence Howe (New York: Feminist Press, 2000), 243–264.

5. Angela Davis, *Women, Race, and Class* (New York: Random House, 1981); Cherríe Moraga and Gloria Anzaldúa, eds., *This Bridge Called My Back: Writings by Radical Women of Color* (Watertown, Mass.: Persephone Press, 1981); bell hooks, *Ain't I a Woman: Black Women and Feminism* (Boston: South End Press, 1983).

6. See, for instance, Monique Wittig, *Les Guérillères* (London: Owen, 1971); Adrienne Cecile Rich, *On Lies, Secrets, and Silence: Selected Prose, 1966–1978* (New York: Norton, 1979); Margaret Cruikshank, *Lesbian Path: 37 Lesbian Writers Share Their Personal Experiences, Viewpoints, Traumas, and Joys* (Monterrey, Calif.: Angel Press, 1980); Susan J. Wolfe and Julia Penelope, *Coming Out Stories* (Watertown, Mass.: Persephone Press, 1980); Joan Nestle, *A Restricted Country* (Ithaca, N.Y.: Firebrand Books, 1987); Monique Wittig, *The Straight Mind and Other Essays* (Boston: Beacon Press, 1992); Cherríe Moraga, *Loving in the War Years: Lo que nunca pasó por sus labios* (Boston: South End Press, 1983); Gloria Anzaldúa, *Borderlands/La Frontera: The New Mestiza* (San Francisco: Spinsters/Aunt Lute Press, 1987); Audre Lorde, *Zami: A New Spelling of My Name* (Trumansburg, N.Y.: Crossing Press, 1982).

7. Elizabeth Spelman, *Inessential Woman: Problems of Exclusion in Feminist Thought* (Boston: Beacon, 1988).

8. Judith Butler, *Gender Trouble: Feminism and the Subversion of Identity* (New York: Routledge, 1990); Teresa de Lauretis. *Technologies of Gender: Essays on Theory, Film, and Fiction* (Bloomington: Indiana University Press, 1987); Linda L. Nicholson, ed., *Feminism/Postmodernism* (New York: Routledge, 1990); and Trinh T. Minh-ha, *Woman, Native, Other: Writing Postcoloniality and Feminism* (Bloomington: Indiana University Press, 1989).

9. See Wiegman, "The Progress of Gender." For further discussion of female masculinity, see Judith Halberstam, *Female Masculinity* (Durham: Duke University Press, 1998).

10. For a helpful discussion of gender in feminist scholarship, see Joan Wallach Scott, "Gender: A Useful Category of Historical Analysis," in *Gender and the Politics of History*, ed. Joan Wallach Scott (New York: Columbia University Press, 1988), 28–50.

11. This tension is nicely expressed in the reviews Joan Wallach Scott and Linda Gordon give to one another's books and their responses, which are brought together in *Signs:* Joan W. Scott, book review, *Heroes of Their Own Lives: The Politics and History of Family Violence* by Linda Gordon; Linda Gordon, "Response to Scott"; Linda Gordon, book review, *Gender and the Politics of History* by Joan Wallach Scott; Joan W. Scott, "Response to Gordon," *Signs* 15, no. 4 (1990): 853–860.

12. Sandra Harding, "The Instability of the Analytical Categories of Feminist Theory," *Signs* 11, no. 4 (1986): 645–664.

13. Inderpal Grewal and Caren Kaplan, *An Introduction to Women's Studies: Gender in a Transnational World* (New York: McGraw Hill, 2002), xviii.

14. In addition to the Grewal and Kaplan text cited in the previous note, there are earlier collections of essays: Chandra Talpade Mohanty, Ann Russo, and Lourdes Torres, eds., *Third World Women and the Politics of Feminism* (Bloomington: Indiana University Press, 1991); Inderpal Grewal and Caren Kaplan, eds., *Scattered Hegemonies: Postmodernity and Transnational Feminist Practices* (Minneapolis: University of Minnesota Press, 1994); M. Jacqui Alexander and Chandra Talpade Mohanty, *Feminist Genealogies, Colonial Legacies, Democratic Futures* (New York: Routledge, 1997); and Caren Kaplan, Norma Alarcón, and Minoo Moallem, *Between Woman and Nation: Nationalism, Transnational Feminism, and the State* (Durham: Duke University Press, 1999).

15. Inderpal Grewal and Caren Kaplan, "Transnational Feminist Cultural Studies: Beyond the Marxism/Poststructuralism/Feminism Divides," in *Between Woman and Nation*, ed. Kaplan et al., 349–363; and Chandra Talpade Mohanty, *Feminism without Borders: Decolonizing Theory, Practicing Solidarity* (Durham: Duke University Press, 2003).

16. Kaye Trimburger, "What's in a Name: Why Women's and Gender Studies?" National Women's Studies Association meetings, Albuquerque, June 15, 1999.

17. Wiegman, "The Progress of Gender."

18. Auslander, "Do Women's + Feminist + Men's + Lesbian and Gay + Queer Studies = Gender Studies?"

19. Shirley Yee, "The 'Women' in Women's Studies," *differences* 9, no. 3 (1997): 46–64.

20. For a discussion of the pain experienced by a poststructuralist scholar, see Boyd in this volume; for pain experienced by a historical, materialist scholar, see Berencie Malka Fisher, *No Angel in the Classroom: Teaching through Feminist Discourse* (Lanham, Md.: Rowman and Littlefield, 2001), 15–16.

21. Wendy Brown, "The Impossibility of Women's Studies."

22. Beverly Guy-Sheftall, "Engaging Difference: Racial and Global Perspectives in Graduate Women's Studies Education," *Feminist Studies* 24 no. 2 (1998): 327–332.

23. Brown, "The Impossibility of Women's Studies"; Davidow, *Disciplining Feminism;* Patai and Koertge, *Professing Feminism.*

24. Patai quotes a section of the University of Arizona mission statement in order to label it foolish for its grandiose goals: Patai and Koertge, *Professing Feminism*, 259.

25. Women of color's anomalous position is beautifully encapsulated in the titles of two classic books: Moraga and Anazaldúa, *This Bridge Called My Back*; and Gloria Hull, Barbara Smith, and Patricia Bell Scott, *All the Women Are White, All of the Men Are Black, but Some of Us Are Brave* (New York: Feminist Press, 1952); and in Patricia Hill Collins's naming of the black woman as "the outsider within." Patricia Hill Collins, *Black Feminist Thought: Knowledge, Consciousness, and the Politics of Empowerment* (Boston: Unwin Hyman, 1990).

26. Liza Fiol-Matta and Mariam K. Chamberlain, *Women of Color and the Multicultural Curriculum: Transforming the College Classroom* (New York: Feminist Press, 1994).

27. For a thoughtful commentary on this literature, see Erika Giesen, "Pedagogy, Process, and Practice in Introductory Women's Studies" (MA thesis, University of Arizona, 2001).

28. Elsa Barkley Brown, "African-American Women's Quilting: A Framework for Conceptualizing and Teaching African-American Women's History," *Signs* 14, no. 4 (1989): 921–929; Elizabeth Higginbotham, "Designing an Inclusive Curriculum: Bringing All Women into the Core," *Women's Studies Quarterly* 25, no. 1–2 (1997): 237–253; Patricia Hill Collins, "What's Going On? Black Feminist Thought and the Politics of Postmodernism," in *Working the Ruins: Feminist Poststructural Theory and Methods*

in Education, ed. Elizabeth A. St. Pierre and Wanda S. Pillow (New York: Routledge, 2000); Analouise Keating, "(De)Centering the Margins? Identity Politics and Tactical (Re)Naming," in *Other Sisterhoods: Literary Theory and U.S. Women of Color,* ed. Sandra Kumamoto Stanley (Urbana: University of Illinois Press, 1998).

29. Polly Pagenhart, "The Very House of Difference: Toward a More Queerly Defined Multiculturalism," in Linda Garber, ed., *Tilting the Tower: Lesbians Teaching Queer Subjects* (New York: Routledge, 1994), 177–185.

30. Kimberlé Crenshaw, "Mapping the Margins: Intersectionality, Identity Politics, and Violence against Women of Color," *Stanford Law Review* 43 (1991): 1241–1299; Anzaldúa, *Borderlands.*

31. Adrienne Rich, "Notes towards a Politics of Location," in *Blood, Bread, and Poetry: Selected Prose, 1979–1985* (New York: W. W. Norton & Co., 1986); and Donna Haraway, "Situated Knowledges: The Science Question in Feminism as a Site of Discourse on the Privilege of Partial Perspective," *Feminist Studies* 14, no. 3 (1988): 575–600.

32. Evelyn Brooks Higginbotham, "African-American Women's History and the Metalanguage of Race," *Signs* 17 no. 2 (1992): 251–274.

33. See, for instance, Rosemarie Garland Thompson, *Extraordinary Bodies: Figuring Physical Disability in American Culture and Literature* (New York: Columbia University Press, 1997); and Sharon L. Snyder, Brenda Jo Brueggeman, and Rosemarie Garland Thompson, eds., *Disability Studies: Enabling the Humanities* (New York: Modern Language Association of America, 2002).

34. Chandra Talpade Mohanty, "On Race and Voice: Challenges for Liberal Education in the 1990s," in *Between Borders: Pedagogy and the Politics of Cultural Studies,* ed. Henry Giroux and Peter McLaren (New York: Routledge, 1994), 145–166; see also Miranda Joseph, "Analogy and Complicity: Women's Studies, Lesbian/Gay Studies, and Capitalism," in *Women's Studies on Its Own,* ed. Wiegman, 267–292.

35. Janet R. Jakobsen, *Working Alliances and the Politics of Difference: Diversity and Feminist Ethics* (Bloomington: Indiana University Press, 1998).

36. This has not always been the dominant paradigm in women's studies. In the mid-1970s there was a lively debate in anthropology, which spilled over into women's studies, about whether women have always been oppressed. See, for instance, Rayna Reiter (Rapp), ed., *Toward an Anthropology of Women* (New York: Monthly Review Press, 1975); and Michelle Zimbalist Rosaldo and Louise Lamphere, *Women, Culture, and Society* (Stanford: Stanford University Press, 1974).

37. This overview of PhD programs comes from our reading of department brochures. For further discussion of institutionalizing the interdisciplinary PhD, see for instance, Laura E. Donaldson, Anne Donadey, and Jael Silliman, "Subversive Couplings: On Antiracism and Postcolonialism in Graduate Women's Studies, in *Women's Studies on Its Own,* ed. Wiegman, 438–456.

38. Judith A. Allen and Sally L. Kitch, "Disciplined by Disciplines? The Need for an Interdisciplinary Research Mission in Women's Studies," *Feminist Studies* 24, no. 2 (1998): 278.

39. Robyn Wiegman, Cindi Katz, and Banu Subramaniam, "Women's Studies: Interdisciplinary Imperatives, Again," *Feminist Studies* 27, no. 2 (2001): 514–532.

40. Bonnie Zimmerman, "Women's Studies, NWSA, and the Future of the (Inter)discipline," *NWSA Journal* 14, no. 1 (2002): viii–xviii.

41. See, for instance, Susan Stanford Friedman, "(Inter)Disciplinarity and the Question of the Women's Studies Ph.D." *Feminist Studies* 24, no. 2 (1998): 318; and Anke Finger

and Victoria Rosner, "Doing Feminism in Interdisciplinary Contexts," *Feminist Studies* 27, no. 2 (2001): 499–504.

42. Vivian May, "Disciplinary Desires and Undisciplined Daughters: Negotiating the Politics of a Women's Studies Doctoral Education," *NWSA Journal* 14, no. 1 (2002): 134–160.

43. See, for instance, Marilyn J. Boxer, "Remapping the University: The Promise of the Women's Studies Ph.D.," *Feminist Studies* 24, no. 2 (1998): 387–402; Elizabeth Lapovsky Kennedy, "Rethinking Women's Studies as an Interdisciplinary Field," *Journal of General Education* (Taiwan) 3 (2000):7–26; and Eloise Buker, "Is Women's Studies a Disciplinary or an Interdisciplinary Field of Inquiry?" *NWSA Journal* 15, no. 1 (2003): 73–93.

44. Sheila Slaugher and Larry Leslie, *Academic Capitalism: Politics, Policies, and the Entrepreneurial University* (Baltimore: Johns Hopkins University, 1997).

45. For a discussion of the productive ties between women's studies and laws schools around social policy issues, see Barbara Atwood, "The Impact of Women's Studies on Family Law Scholarship: Competing Feminist Visions of Child Custody Dispute Resolution," paper based on a presentation for the Future of Women's Studies conference, Tucson, Arizona, October 2000.

46. A good indication of the centrality of activism and practice to women's studies is the number of recent publications on teaching about activism. See, for instance, Karen Bojar and Nancy A. Naples, eds., *Teaching Feminist Activism: Strategies from the Field* (New York: Routledge, 2002).

47. Patai and Koertge, *Professing Feminism,* the 2003 edition.

48. Nussbaum, "The Professor of Parody," 44–45.

49. For different approaches to whether collaborative learning is part of feminist pedagogy, see Maralee Mayberry, "Reproductive and Resistant Pedagogies: The Comparative Roles of Collaborative Learning and Feminist Pedagogy in Science Education," in *Meeting the Challenge: Innovative Feminist Pedagogies in Action*, ed. Maralee Mayberry and Ellen Cronan Rose (New York: Routledge, 1999), 1–22; and Jane A. Rinehart, "Feminist Wolves in Sheep's Disguise: Learning Communities and Internships," in *Meeting the Challenge*, ed. Mayberry and Rose, 63–97.

50. For a comprehensive discussion of the interconnections of feminist pedagogy and critical pedagogy, see Carmen Luke and Jennifer Gore, eds., *Feminism and Critical Pedagogy* (New York: Routledge, 1992).

51. Maralee Mayberry and Ellen Cronan Rose, Introduction to *Meeting the Challenge*, ed. Mayberry and Rose, xvi.

52. Fisher, *No Angel in the Classroom.*

53. For a discussion of the scholarship of teaching, see Mayberry and Rose, *Meeting the Challenge*, vii–ix. For examples of recent books on pedagogy, other than those already cited in this section, see Bojar and Naples, *Teaching Feminist Activism*; and Amie A. MacDonald and Susan Sánchez-Casal, *Twenty-first Century Feminist Classrooms: Pedagogies of Identity and Difference* (New York: Palgrave Macmillan, 2002).

54. Kitch, "Claiming Success."

55. This question is from the brochure of the Women's Studies Department at Duke University, 2004.

Part I

What Is the Subject of Women's Studies?

Beyond Dualisms

Some Thoughts about the Future of Women's Studies

Bonnie Zimmerman

Since women's studies emerged as a fledgling field in the late 1960s, its development has been marked by constant interrogation, reflection, debate, and reinscription. Women's studies truly is and always has been a field in motion. One trajectory of its movement has been between the two poles we might identify roughly as materialism and poststructuralism. Along this trajectory, the debates that invigorate the field are those over how to shape and understand "woman" or "women," gender, and sexuality as categories of analysis.[1] It is possible to construct many histories of women's studies, one version of which might run like this. The first thirty years of women's studies falls into two very rough phases: the first dominated by the interplay between radical feminism and Marxism, the second marked by the ascendance of poststructuralist theories. The epistemological presupposition of the first phase was surely the famous (or notorious) slogan, "The personal is the political." In academic terms, we developed the knowledge base of early women's studies by collating our personal experiences in a fairly direct and uncomplicated fashion. I am not sure there is an equivalent phrase that sums up the presuppositions of the second phase, but one could surely point to the relationship between knowledge and power as articulated by Foucault. The first set of presuppositions leads to standpoint epistemology, the idea that experiences, identities, and social locations are productive of particular kinds of knowledge—that who I am shapes how and what I know. While poststructuralist theory has shifted some of the ground beneath our feet by showing how experience and identity are to some extent produced by the very knowledge they are supposed to be producing, I will still contend that standpoint epistemology has enabled women's studies for thirty years and that, carefully used and always self-critical, it can continue to inspire students, produce useful knowledge, and change the world.

The dynamic I identify here has been analyzed and debated in many venues, none more forthright and influential than in the 1997 special issue of *differences,* "Women Studies on the Edge," most particularly in articles by Wendy Brown and Shirley Yee.[2] Brown's provocative and controversial essay, "The Impossibility of Women's Studies," offers perhaps the most uncompromising poststructuralist, anti-essentialist position on identity-based academic fields like women's studies. She argues that women's studies "may be politically and theoretically incoherent, as well as tacitly conservative—incoherent because by definition it circumscribes uncircumscribable 'women' as an object of study, and conservative because it must resist all objections to such circumscription if it is to sustain that object of study as its raison d'être."[3] She depicts a women's studies that, in her words, must resist, restrict, or colonize theories that destabilize the category of women or identity formations that disrupt the unity or primacy of the category. According to Brown, these disruptive voices are "compelled to go elsewhere, while women's studies consolidates itself in the remains, impoverished by the lack of challenges from within, bewildered by its new ghettoization in the academy—this time by feminists themselves."[4]

Brown acknowledges that all academic fields of inquiry tend to consolidate their subject matter and police their borders, although she thinks there may be something especially vulnerable about a "field organized by social identity rather than by genre of inquiry." Without explaining exactly why, she suggests that it is "paradoxical" that "sustaining gender as a critical, self-reflexive category rather than a normative or nominal one, and sustaining women's studies as an intellectually and institutionally radical site rather than a regulatory one—in short, refusing to allow gender and women's studies to be disciplined—are concerns and refusals at odds with affirming women's studies *as* a coherent field of study."[5]

In place of this rigid, normative, regulatory model of women's studies—the border patrol of gender—Brown describes a non-unified, non-coherent, anti-foundational academic study that might, in her words, "allow us to take those powerful founding and sustaining impulses of women's studies—to challenge the seamless histories, theories, literatures, and sciences featuring and reproducing a Humanism starring only Man—and harness them for another generation or two of productive, insurrectionary work. However much it is shaped by feminism, this work will no longer have gender at its core and is in that sense, no longer women's studies."[6]

Brown's argument is a powerful one, although it is limited in two ways. First, the kind of work that Brown argues for is directed almost entirely toward the analysis of discourse and subject formation, an important but not exclusive concern of women's studies. She does not address institutionalized oppression and resistance or the material structures of society which constrain women's individual and collective actions. Second, her description of women's studies simply does not match the work that I, and thousands of others, have been doing for the past thirty years. While there certainly have been tendencies within women's studies (and feminism in general) toward a monolithic notion of gender and women, these tendencies have swiftly and regularly been challenged, reviewed, and transformed. It is true that many of us have been working strenuously toward an articulation of a coherent women's studies, but I do not accept that "coherence" is a dirty word or an illegitimate goal. Coherence does not necessarily mean sameness, exclusion, or distortion. It means that things hang together. And in my world—a world dominated by social totalities like heteropatriarchy, white racism, imperialism, and capital-ism—things do.

The other position, which we might call the *possibility* or *necessity* of women's studies, is articulated in the same issue of *differences* by Shirley Yee. She argues that "for both ethnic studies and women's studies, the terms 'ethnic' and 'women' are rooted in historically specific political moments that cannot be eas-ily discarded."[7] Positioning herself against those who would restructure women's studies as gender studies (which seems implied by, or at least congenial to, Brown's argument), Yee argues that the value of women's studies lies "in its capacity to keep 'woman' on the table as a contested, visible, and complex category of analy-sis that validates the existence of women as a group in society and addresses sex-ism and racism directly in the production of feminist scholarship." Thus, she argues, "women's studies should be retained both for its intellectual and for its political value, precisely because it enables explicit engagement with 'women' as an ad-mittedly unstable, fragmented term. Without the 'women' in women's studies, we stand to lose the focus of this intellectual and political endeavor."[8]

Like many who have found the anti-essentialist, postmodern critique of femi-nism suspicious, Yee wonders about the "timing of the debate over naming." She is especially concerned that just as the "women" in "women's studies" has finally begun to signify the full diversity of concrete, embodied females, a movement has emerged which "shifts the ground underneath those who have fairly recently found a place in the discourse."[9] For Yee, "the category 'women' not only exists as a con-tested *idea* about how best to study gender, but has concrete meanings in terms of *who* gets to do scholarship and who gets to enroll in colleges and universities where the work is being done."[10]

It might be argued that the visions of women's studies articulated by Brown and Yee are not so far apart, that both see women's studies as a strategic location within the university. One ostensible difference is that Brown is willing to give it only another generation or two, while Yee sets no limits on its existence. But a more significant difference of approach is this: Brown's argument is rooted in a theoretical and political analysis of the discursive construction of the subject, and Yee's in an equally theoretical and political analysis of the material structures by which subjectivity is constrained. Women's studies needs both these approaches and emphases, but for the past fifteen years or so, they have too often been at odds with each other.

It is not my intention to write another polemic for/against essentialism, for/against poststructuralism, for/against woman as a category of analysis. I have noth-ing to say that is new, nor do I have any insights that will resolve the question of Woman. At best, I can offer this observation. Much of the work in women's stud-ies and feminist theory in the late 1980s and 1990s focused on the notion of "woman" as a discursive construction, just as the work of the 1970s and early 1980s had emphasized the material base of women's oppression. I have found this em-phasis on discourse, language, and subjectivity to be healthy and clarifying; I be-lieve that my own work in women's studies and lesbian studies is better, stronger, and smarter because of it. But I think that at this point it is equally important to reassert the materiality of women's lives, experience, bodies, and oppression. As Suparna Bhaskaran argues, "In creating a crisis of subjectivity, a crisis is created for our bodies. Discourses that continue to deconstruct women or darker peoples directly participate in the material domination of the bodies of women and persons of color. It is therefore necessary for us to re-embody a revised notion of 'physical subjectivity.'"[11]

While individuals may differ on their investments in discursive or material analyses, I believe we can agree on one point: women's studies is the site for these questions, these debates, these antagonisms. Where else will they go on? In departments of sociology, literature, psychology, biology? Women's studies is both the location of new disciplinary thinking about women and gender and the point at which feminist scholarship and theorizing within these older disciplines intersect with those occurring within ethnic studies, area studies, sexuality studies, and cultural studies; with the work taking place in activist projects and organizations; and with the insights drawn from personal narratives and the creative arts. As such, women's studies offers the best opportunities for productive interdisciplinary theorizing about women, gender, knowledge, and society.

Unlike Wendy Brown, I think that women's studies is and always has been a contested site, not a stable location, and that instability, fluidity, and multiplicity is both its strength and weakness within the university system. The "women" in women's studies has always been conjectural, unfixed, slippery, and contested. Indeed, the phrase is awkward or downright ungrammatical, with that odd and unfelicitous "apostrophe *s*." As Marilyn Boxer points out, from the beginning there was no agreement over the meaning of the apostrophe that "blurs the difference between studies by, about, and belonging to women."[12] As much as we might prefer the more forthright "feminist studies" or the pseudo-scientific "feminology," it is the awkward, incorrect, indeterminate "women's studies" that survived and best describes the nature of our academic project. The structure of women's studies—department, center, program, discipline, interdiscipline, multidiscipline—has been equally difficult to pin down. Every attempt to limit women's studies has proven futile; every time one Hydra-head is cut off, ten more grow back.

Women's studies, therefore, is not only the place where women are studied, analyzed, researched, and taught about, but the place where multiple and changing meanings of "woman" (and femininity, feminism, gender, etc.) are constructed, deconstructed, debated, challenged, and revised. Or, to paraphrase Uma Narayan's anti-essentialist definition of culture, we might conclude that women's studies is not a "simple" description employed to single out an "already distinct" entity. Instead, it is an "arbitrary and shifting" designation "connected to various political projects" that have "different reasons for insisting upon the distinctiveness" of one gender from another and, within this gender, of different cultures and identifications from others. To continue this analogy, women's studies may be understood as an entity whose "individuation is not pre-discursively determined but dependent upon complex discursive processes linked to political agendas."[13]

So far I have focused this essay on epistemology, which is closely linked to methodology, since how we know is constrained and enabled by the tools we use to know. What is the methodology of women's studies? we are asked, and ask ourselves, constantly. Implicit in this question is the assumption that the lines of demarcation between disciplines are drawn by methodologies. In women's studies, we have inherited a compendium of methodologies—statistics, double-blind experiments, case studies, interviews, textual analysis, archival research—that are so associated with specific disciplines that these seem to constitute the only real divisions of the university. And we often stand in opposition to them, sometimes refusing to use tools that could advance our intellectual and political projects. So if women's studies has no unique methodology, it has no epistemology and therefore is not a discipline but rather a political activity cross-dressing as an intellectual endeavor. And feminist theory—what is that? Everybody else's theory—Marxism, psychoanalysis, poststructuralism—in drag.

Poor women's studies! No subject, no methodology, no theory. And to believe some of our critics, no more students or faculty either. Consequently, we have important theorists, like Wendy Brown, who find "the question of what constituted the fundamentals of knowledge in women's studies" more "elusive" than that of political science.[14] Having come up with a "contestable" list of subjects about which an undergraduate in political science should have a basic knowledge, Brown writes, "What concerns me here is the disconcerting fact of my inability, and my colleagues' inability, to even conjure a similar list for women's studies about which to begin arguing."[15]

What concerns me here is the disconcerting fact that this faculty in women's studies was unable to even imagine the intellectual foundations of their subject. Other practitioners in the field have found it easier to identify the fundamentals of women's studies knowledge. Marilyn Boxer refers to a group of faculty who identified five essential concepts:

> The systematic, interlocking oppression of women;
>
> Women's varied relations to patriarchy;
>
> The social construction of gender;
>
> The social construction of knowledge; and
>
> The redefining and reconceptualizing of women's power and empowerment.[16]

Like Boxer, I believe we ought to start with what we are doing, and build our theoretical constructs from our practice. That is how my department articulated our understanding of the foundations of knowledge in women's studies when faced with the need to do so for an academic review. We found that we had been doing so all along—in the lists of goals and objectives that most of us include in course syllabi. By collating our various descriptions of our courses, we were able to identify a set of student learning goals for the major in women's studies and another set for general education. I include the former here as one example of how we might conceptualize the intellectual presuppositions of our field, or discipline. A women's studies major should be able to do the following:

Demonstrate an understanding of the social construction of gender and sexuality;

Demonstrate an understanding of the ways that women's lives are shaped by large social structures and conventions of representation;

Demonstrate an understanding of the intersectionality of different dimensions of social organization (gender, race, class, culture, etc.) as concepts and as lived experience;

Identify mechanisms of oppression and resistance;

Analyze the role of social location and power in the production of ideas, theories, and representations (including their own);

Understand and appreciate multiple perspectives; and

Make connections between abstract knowledge and social activism.

As Brown notes in reference to political science, our list is "contestable," but, significantly, it is a list we generated from the practical work we were doing in the classroom, not an artificial or arbitrary list conjured up out of theoretical premises only.

Whatever its methodology or epistemology, women's studies, like all disciplines, is faced with defining its "subject." That is, if the subject of political science is politics and that of English is literature, what is the subject of women's studies? Thirty years ago, when we began the project of women's studies, we would have quickly and easily answered, "Women, of course." Today, the answer is more complicated, but I believe most practitioners would agree upon a cluster of concepts:

Woman as a category of analysis/metaphor;

Gender as a system of relations, power, oppression;

Women as concrete, material agents with lived experiences;

Women as nodal points at which multiple systems of power and oppression intersect;

Feminism as historical event/process; and

Social change as an essential element of education.

The subject of women's studies is still women, but the women who form the subject are not the same women who started the studies. Marilyn Boxer asks the question, "Who was this 'woman' for whom feminism presumed to speak?"[17] The hard struggles and genuine learning and growing that have occurred over thirty years have shown this woman to be multi-faceted, multi-situated, multi-lingual, and multivalent.

This leads me to address the question of gender studies, not a question I often wish to contemplate. If women's studies modulates into gender studies, as is happening in a number of institutions, and then into a gender and sexuality studies connecting women's studies to gay and lesbian studies, for which some argue, then what comes of the analyses of the past thirty years that have focused on the interconnections of gender, sexuality, *and* race and class? In the same issue of *differences* that includes the articles by Wendy Brown and Shirley Yee, Leora Auslander argues for the close institutional linkage of women's studies and gay studies under the rubric of gender and sexuality. She explains the "inconsistency" of her institution (the University of Chicago) keeping a separate center for the study of race: "The implications of this organization is that the study of sexuality and the study of gender are closely related and should be housed in the same research context, while the study of race is different enough to need its own."[18]

This argument seems profoundly, fatally flawed. Does this latest move not reorient gender (and sexuality) as somehow more central to the experiences of embodied women than race and class (or, for that matter, age, religion, nationality, and ability)? Even if this is a gender and sexuality studies that pays careful attention to race and class differences, is this enough (or any different than what women's studies has always been)? Have we not been moving toward a women's studies that understands that gender is always racialized and race always gendered? That race is not a "difference" among women, but a determining factor in the way women become women, and men become men?

"Difference studies," as even Auslander argues, is no alternative, for many reasons. One is that this notion reinscribes positions of power as central, with "difference" in the position of marginality and otherness. It is also impossible to imagine what would—and, more importantly, what would not—be included under such a rubric. But of most significance is that such a "studies" would essentialize difference in a way even more insidious than the most essentializing moves of women's studies. The difference of gender is not the difference of race is not the difference of sexuality is not the difference of class.

Another reason why I question the move away from *women's* studies is suggested by a question increasingly heard in the twenty-first century: What is the relationship between feminisms and women's studies? My answer to this is simple. There is no women's studies without feminism. Feminism is the theoretical and political foundation of women's studies. Without feminism, we can study "women" as we do any other object in any established discipline. Feminism is what turns the study of women into women's studies. Gender studies might or might not be feminist. Gay and lesbian, or sexuality, studies might or might not be feminist. Ethnic studies or cultural studies might or might not be feminist. But women's studies must be feminist or it is not women's studies.

I return then to the questions posed at the beginning of this essay: What is the current condition of women's studies, and how can we shape its future? I would suggest that one key enterprise we must undertake at this juncture is to deconstruct—and here I think I am using the word correctly—all the oppositions that have been at play within the project of women's studies and feminism from their very beginnings. They include the following:

Radical feminism/socialist feminism,

Activism/academics,

Women's studies programs/mainstreaming projects,

Standpoint epistemology/postmodernism,

Humanities/social sciences,

Women's studies/gender studies,

Women's studies/research on women,

Discourse/material reality,

Essentialism/social constructionism,

Sameness/difference, and

Disciplines/interdisciplines

Most of the humanities and social science disciplines are divided in some way or another: between micro and macro, qualitative and quantitative, empirical and abstract. Even literary studies has been torn between the authority of the text and the authority of the reader. The questions phrased at the beginning of my essay (Is woman a discursive construct or something real?) stand for one of our versions of this division: the conflict between discourse and material reality. I have seen this conflict illustrated by a hand inscribing circles in the air and a fist pounding the table—that is, Doctor Johnson refuting Bishop Berkeley. But you can't have the micro without the macro, the soft without the hard, discourse without reality— and vice versa. Why must we choose? Surely the answer is both/and, not either/or. Women exist. We exist as real, material creatures whose lives unfold within a complex, interlinked pattern of social forces or totalities that shape or limit us much as corsets shaped the bodies of Victorian women. But we are never just the product of social totalities; we are also the product of individual histories and agents who make choices and narrate our own stories. These stories are individual and unique; they are common to us as women; they are different in the way that social totalities cast the lights and shadows differently. Women's studies can incorporate all the different tools available to us in order to make sense of these multiple points of convergence and conflict.

What will it take for us to truly think outside binary oppositions? To really deconstruct dualisms? To revolutionize knowledge for and about women and gender? I cannot answer these questions here, but I believe that women's studies is the only location where they can and must be addressed. We have hardly yet begun to imagine the possibilities of the interdisciplinary study of women.

Notes

1. For example, the following questions were posed at the Future of Women's Studies Conference at the University of Arizona in October 2000: "Does 'Women's Studies'

beg the question of definition by assuming a stable object of investigation? I.e., Does it reify a conception of 'women,' 'woman,' gender, and sexuality that might more appropriately be understood as fluid or problematic? Conversely, given that the category 'woman' still has material, cultural, and psychic consequences throughout the world, what possibilities does an analytic focus on women offer to the intellectual and political project of women's studies?" Questions such as these continue to inform the development of women's studies as a discipline or field of study. See the essays in Robyn Wiegman, ed., *Women's Studies on its Own* (Durham: Duke University Press, 2002).

2. Shirley Yee, "The 'Women' in Women's Studies," *differences* 9, no. 3 (1997): 46–64; Wendy Brown, "The Impossibility of Women's Studies," *differences* 9, no. 3 (1997): 79–101.
3. Brown, "The Impossibility of Women's Studies," 86.
4. Ibid., 83.
5. Ibid., 86.
6. Ibid., 95.
7. Yee, "The 'Women' in Women's Studies," 56.
8. Ibid., 61–62.
9. Ibid., 48.
10. Ibid., 49.
11. Suparna Bhaskaran, "Physical Subjectivity and the Risk of Essentialism," in *Our Feet Walk the Sky: Women of the South Asian Diaspora,* ed. Women of South Asian Descent Collective (San Francisco: Aunt Lute Books, 1993), 199.
12. Marilyn Boxer, *When Women Ask the Questions: Creating Women's Studies in America* (Baltimore: Johns Hopkins University Press, 1998), 13.
13. Uma Narayan, "Essence of Culture and a Sense of History: A Feminist Critique of Cultural Essentialism," in *Decentering the Center: Philosophy for a Multicultural, Postcolonial, and Feminist World*, ed. Uma Narayan and Sandra Harding (Bloomington: Indiana University Press, 2000), 87.
14. Brown, "The Impossibility of Women's Studies," 82.
15. Ibid., 99.
16. Boxer, *When Women Ask the Questions,* 32.
17. Ibid., 137.
18. Leora Auslander, "Do Women's + Feminist + Men's + Lesbian and Gay + Queer Studies = Gender Studies?" *differences* 9, no. 3 (1997): 20.

The Possibility
of Women's Studies

ROBYN WIEGMAN

In the early 1970s, feminism in the U.S. academy was less an organized entity than a set of practices: an ensemble of courses listed on bulletin boards and often taught for free. Positioned outside disciplines and institutional economies, feminism was a renegade knowledge, one whose academic illegitimacy demonstrated the movement's central claim concerning women's systemic exclusion. Today, it is surely safe to say, things have greatly changed: general education courses across the United States routinely take up the study of women and gender, while a familiarity with feminist scholarship has become an established part of doctoral competency in many fields. Once fledgling women's studies programs have become departments and their tenure-line faculty are now engaged in a national movement to develop autonomous PhD degrees. From this perspective, academic feminism in general and women's studies in particular are doing quite well in the U.S. academy. And yet, since the early 1990s, there has been growing uneasiness, often overt despair, among feminist scholars about the agenda, languages, and political consequences of feminism's academic enterprise. That decade began, let us recall, with a tonal shift so significant—think of *Conflicts in Feminism* and *Feminism without Women*—that Carla Kaplan would describe it in 1992 as a burgeoning "language of crisis."[1] Kaplan's assessment grew more resonant across the decade, as scholars found *Feminism beside Itself* (1995) and at *Cross Purposes* (1997) before it was declared in *Critical Condition* (1999).[2] By the new century, academic feminism had gone apocalyptic, by which I mean that political optimism over its future disappeared beneath widespread anxiety, anger, and fear.

Who was to blame? Was it the villainy of the corporatism of "the university in ruins," as Bill Readings so evocatively called it?[3] Or the right's well-funded ideological dismantling of political movements on the left? Perhaps it was the backlash against identity-based claims to rights and knowledge in both the U.S. public and academic spheres? Critical attention to any of these would begin to measure the multiple and powerful assaults against leftist projects of all kinds, assaults that have radically transformed not only the meaning of political struggle in recent years but the very conditions under which alternative futures can be imagined and pursued. But rarely does apocalyptic narration, as I call this proliferating genre, turn to social or historical explanation as a means for deciphering recent transformations in the power and political presence of feminism as a world-building force. Instead it finds political failure in academic feminism's institutional success. The narrative routes to failure are by now commonplace: the theft of activism generated by the seductions of poststructuralist theory, the fragmentation of the unity of women created by the proliferation of identities, and the loss of collective commitments arising from the privatizing ambitions of professionalization. In each of these formulations, the apocalyptic narrates the academic *against* feminism, thereby establishing a history of the political present that views academic institutionalization as a betrayal of the political urgencies and critical vocabularies that inaugurated the project thirty years ago. Adrift from the political anchor of the past, academic feminism thus comes to figure the impossibility of a transformed and transformative feminist future.

Readers familiar with recent debates about the past and future of women's studies as a field understand the referential weight of the word *impossibility* used in the sentence above. No essay on the internal dynamics of women's studies has been more important and more controversial than Wendy Brown's 1999 "The Impossibility of Women's Studies."[4] Special panels have been organized to discuss it, and numerous scholars, many published in this volume, have thought it crucial to critique or defend. Not only the title, which bristles with negativity, but the special issue it appeared in, ominously called "Women's Studies on the Edge," make it a likely contribution to the apocalyptic archive. Add to this the fact that Brown's most provocative argument—against consolidating contests "for freedom and equality . . . in the form of new degree-granting programs"—arises from what she takes to be the failure of academic institutionalization, and one might be hard pressed *not* to view the essay as endemic of the dystopic bent of last century's final decade.[5] But while it raises the specter of a dramatic ending, "The Impossibility of Women's Studies" stakes out its critical position on far different terrain than that of apocalyptic narration: poststructuralist theory is not, for Brown, debilitating; differences among women have not robbed the field (or feminism) of an originary coherence; countering professionalization by returning to the agendas, discourses, and affects of social movement will resuscitate nothing. Indeed, the problem of women's studies is its conflation, in her words, of "the political with the academic," and she drives this point home by insisting at her essay's end that the time now is for sustained and deliberate "thinking."[6]

I want to follow Brown's lead and imagine how to transform her anti-apocalyptic negativity into the conditions that can generate, as my title proposes, the possibility of women's studies. This entails turning the apocalyptic narrative on its head: instead of lamenting the divergence between women's studies and feminism, I operate from the suspicion that contemporary feminism, in whatever formulation you name, is not adequate to the knowledge project built in its name. I also assume that any attempt to define feminism's future according to the modes of articulation arising from politics as we inherit them today does not forestall the forces of institutionalization. It simply institutionalizes—as object or method, value form or critical language—a truncated and presentist political order, one that casts our political imaginary as adequate to what the future will need to know. Beneath the arrogance of this perspective is a kind of desperation, borne no doubt from the difficulty of what I think of as the mean time: the time not of revolutionary beginnings or celebratory arrivals but of the endless demeaning of the ideals and grammar of left-leaning political change. Against this arrogance and desperation, I emphasize contingency and unknowability in order to begin to imagine women's studies as something other than compensation for the unrecoverable loss that the future, by definition, always is. Because the future never belongs to those who imagine it, we need curricular agendas, departmental cultures, and affective relationships to feminism that offer students institutional histories—along with the contingent futures they beget—that neither demand nor rehearse the shape of our own. This begins not in the resolution of the problems that arise from the non-identicality of women's studies and feminism, but in developing our ability to sustain, interrogate, and inhabit them.

Before showing how "The Impossibility of Women's Studies" helps us conceptualize these matters, I want to trace in more detail the plot lines of apocalyptic narration. To that end, I focus on another controversial essay from the end of the 1990s, Martha Nussbaum's "The Professor of Parody." For Nussbaum, U.S. academic feminism, influenced by poststructuralism and embodied in the work of Judith Butler, interrupts feminism's historical continuity by abandoning both practical politics and "the suffering of women" in order to luxuriate in theoretical pleasure.[7] To right this situation, Nussbaum seeks to return feminist theory to "concrete projects" aimed at transforming laws and institutions, which Janet Halley has critiqued in another context as a version of U.S. "governance feminism"[8] and which Nussbaum defends as the necessary means to ward off theoretical collaborations with "evil."[9] Brown, as we already know, deplores such privileging of the political over the academic and calls instead for feminist intellectual practice to grapple with the limitations of its inaugurating conceptions of both identity and power. She thus turns to law not, as does Nussbaum, to identify a proper destination for academic feminist commitments, but to trace the incoherence of subject formation that likewise haunts women's studies. By reading these essays together, I parse their idioms of failure in order to understand something about how U.S. academic feminism today can occupy such contradictory terrain, being too theoretical and not theoretical enough, too politicized or not political enough. In the end, I offer my own contingent positivity for women's studies by imagining it as the institutional site that simultaneously makes legible these contestations and provides the opportunity for their ongoing deliberation. I argue that the possibility of women's studies resides in generating the analytic perspective necessary for apprehending the most paradoxical features of U.S. academic feminist discourse today: its struggle with the forms and consequences of *academic feminism* itself.

I

By most political and historical definitions, feminism is a resistant force. It operates most generally as an argument *against* political systems, ideological discourses, and cultural practices that have organized not only the subordination of women and the feminine but all human activities, qualities, and potentials through narrow, often dimorphic, frameworks of various kinds, including but not always limited to gender. In this, its project remains temporally constrained: coming after, forging a response, being responsive to some kind of failure (called freedom or democracy or revolution or even, less ambitiously, women's equality). For academic feminism in the United States in general and for women's studies in particular, the reactivity of its origins has always strained against the desire to originate—to create new traditions, generate original theories, and inaugurate an autonomous field of study that goes beyond correcting the partialities of traditional disciplines. Feminist scholars have repeatedly cast the drive toward institutionalization as a consequence of feminism's original emergence in social movement, and it has ridden this self-defined insurgency until anxieties about the academy seemed impossible to ignore. Witness Biddy Martin's provocative title, "Success and Its Failures."[10] We might read the contradiction between error and achievement evoked here as the effect of discovering, somewhat after the fact, what institutionalization would extract. This would be one way of understanding the pain of revolutionary desire as it confronts the limitations that institutionalization materializes. Name it post-exuberant despair.

It is rarely a generous reading that is offered to account for the mood swing in academic feminism. More often, present worries are cast as the consequence of various avoidable errors: theory's abandonment of politics, or one generation's belligerent disregard of another, or the triumph of professional upward mobility over collective struggle. Regardless of the specifics, the point here is that narratives that explain the present regularly feature academic feminism's own coming to institutional power as a betrayal of the modes of political engagement identified with social movement. Martha Nussbaum's well-known lament against the work of poststructuralist feminism in general and Judith Butler's work in particular reiterates the ideal of an originary academic feminist project and demonstrates how the apocalyptic narrative is entangled with a geopolitical imaginary that symptomatically maintains the United States as its center. While Nussbaum does not link her critique of feminist theory to women's studies directly, her assumptions about how objects and protocols of study can guarantee a relation of justice to women reproduce many of the key characteristics of apocalyptic narration.

Written as a manifesto for a return to "old-style feminist politics," Nussbaum's "The Professor of Parody" takes Judith Butler's scholarship as symptomatic of a theoretical shift in feminist academic work, a shift that has profound generational dimensions. Readers familiar with it will have no trouble, I am sure, remembering the ferociousness of the critique whereby Butler, as representative of "the new feminism," is said to write in a "teasing, exasperating way," to use obscurity to create "an aura of importance," and to bully the reader "into granting that, since one cannot figure out what is going on, there must be something sig-nificant going on."[11] Beneath the obscurity, Nussbaum finds "shopworn notions" and a "narrow vision for the possibilities of social change."[12] Plato and John Stuart Mill, she asserts, already gave us Butler's main idea that "gender is a social arti-fice," and Catherine MacKinnon and Andrea Dworkin already gave feminist theory an understanding that "social forces go so deep that we should not suppose we have access to . . . 'nature.'"[13] Evincing a "dangerous quietism," Butler is said to lack a "sense of the texture of social oppression and the harm that it does."[14] The essay ends on this note: "Hungry women are not fed by [Butler's theory], battered women are not sheltered by it, raped women do not find justice in it, gays and lesbians do not achieve legal protections through it. . . . The big hope . . . for a world of real justice, where laws and institutions protect the equality and the dig-nity of all citizens, has been banished. . . . Judith Butler's hip quietism is a com-prehensible response to the difficulty of realizing justice in America. But it is a bad response. It collaborates with evil. Feminism demands more and women de-serve better."[15] In critiquing Butler's theoretical practice and political commitments (not to mention her sentence structure and rhetorical habits), Nussbaum's essay is a call to arms for a feminism driven by its political claim to the real: to "the mate-rial conditions of real women," "real bodies," "real struggles," and the "real issue of legal and institutional change."[16] To be trained on the real is, in her terms, feminism's historical inheritance and U.S. academic feminism's critical, at times distinctly moral, imperative.

In her contrast between old-style and new feminism, Nussbaum deploys the apocalyptic narrative's familiar temporal construction, defining the present as that which destroys the future and thereby privileging both the political projects and the theoretical discourses of the past. Like other authors of the apocalyptic narra-tive, she too pits the academic against feminism by writing the academy as other to the real. "Feminist theory has been understood . . . as not just fancy words on paper; theory is connected to proposals for social change. . . . Indeed, some theo-rists have left the academy . . . [to] address . . . urgent problems directly."[17] In this framework, the academy functions to interrupt feminism's political time by ex-changing a focus on legal routes of redress for theoretical and highly linguistic accounts of the social constitution of subjects. Under the auspices of this "sym-bolic" feminism, young feminists are led to believe that "one need not engage with messy things such as legislatures and movements in order to act daringly";[18] in-stead, they learn to "do politics in [the] safety of their campuses . . . making sub-versive gestures at power through speech."[19] Such a "self-involved feminism," which Nussbaum claims is "easier than the old feminism," is also distinctly Ameri-can: "It is not surprising," she writes, "that it has caught on here, where success-ful middle-class people prefer to focus on cultivating the self rather than . . . help[ing] the material condition of others."[20] Thus countering Butler's seemingly narcissistic entrapments in the self, "The Professor of Parody" cultivates a lan-guage for social change—"working for others who are suffering" and for "the pub-lic good"—that arises at the scene of women's disempowerment and loss.[21] Coupling these affective attachments to suffering with a definition of the public good as "building laws and institutions," Nussbaum not only gives to old-style feminism the authority and autonomy of an unquestioned relationship of justice to women, but privileges law as equivalent—and adequate—to feminism's pursuit of justice.[22]

As some of the quotations above indicate, "The Professor of Parody" links its lengthy critique of Butler to the specificities of feminism's development in the U.S. university. But beyond identifying Butler as a quintessentially narcissistic U.S. subject, Nussbaum does not go far in addressing the critical and political consequences of her own focus on the United States. She does criticize new feminism, however, for paying "relatively little attention to the struggles of women outside the United States," even as she must concede, though only parenthetically, that "this was always a dispiriting feature . . . of the earlier period."[23] But because new feminism is, in her account, indicative of "something more insidious than provincialism"—"the virtually complete turning from the material side of life"—she can suspend interrogating the way old-style feminism routinely focused on struggles within the U.S. nation-state.[24] In doing so, she resuscitates old feminism as adequate to the political imaginary of an increasingly global world. Hence, after delineating the kinds of concrete projects in legal reform and movement politics that the new feminism has abandoned, she can make this claim: "Feminist theory still looks like this in many parts of the world. In India, for example, . . . feminist theorizing is closely tethered to practical commitments such as female literacy . . . unequal land laws . . . rape law . . . sexual harassment and domestic violence. These feminists know that they live in . . . a fiercely unjust reality; they cannot live . . . without addressing [this] . . . in their theoretical writing and in their activities outside the seminar room.[25] Defining the project of Indian feminism as akin to the work of "the first generation of American feminists," Nussbaum produces the Third World woman of color as a referent for real U.S. feminist commitments *and* as the authenticating agent through which old feminism can replenish herself. In this dislocation from the United States to India, old feminism is made young again by rendering its activist agenda in the present time of the Third World. Geopolitical dislocation, in short, offers old feminism temporal continuity.

In claiming this continuity, Nussbaum must repress not only contradictions between U.S. feminism's formulation of state-based tactics of intervention and those in postcolonial sites, but also the ways in which postcolonial feminist agendas in the Third World continue to resist the globalizing discourses of U.S. feminism—issues that certainly raise the stakes of the discussion about old feminism's nationalism well beyond the problem that "provincialism" suggests.[26] As Gayatri Spivak counters in a letter to the editor, "This flag waving championship of needy women . . . [s]ounds good, from a powerful tenured academic in a liberal [U.S.] university. But how does she know?"[27] Nussbaum's essay does not offer an answer to this question. It builds its rhetorical power instead on a temporal order that organizes the present and future of feminism in the U.S. academy according to a narrative of fidelity to an implicitly U.S.-made past, which is to say a narrative that cannot account in any terms other than despair and chastisement for feminism's articulations of power, politics, and subject formation beyond the formulations of activist agencies and political discourse provided by interventions in (and projections of the perfection of) the U.S. nation-state. Ironically, Nussbaum's version of old feminism evinces no complicity with power—not even the power of its global dissemination as the original feminism—because its referential object, Third World "suffering women," exists as the public counter and missionary project to new feminism's purportedly privatized politics and narcissistic abandonment of the real.

For Nussbaum, then, old feminism is the authentic and authenticating project of social transformation, and it is precisely through its sentimental discourse that she sees it as serving as a foundation for global feminist agency. In this, "The Professor of Parody" reiterates a liberal tradition of social change connected to U.S. democratic nationalism and its universalizing affect, thereby resuscitating the Westernized liberal humanist subject that Butler and other poststructuralist feminists have been trying, pointedly, to think both against and without. At the same time, it banishes from consideration the late twentieth-century feminist tradition within the United States and outside it of critiquing the state as the end logic of political reform.[28] Certainly feminism's articulation of a geopolitical perspective through U.S. antiwar discourses or the Marxian International would lead any assessment of the present in different directions, as would an understanding of contemporary feminist theory that took into account the connections between poststructuralist, critical race, and postcolonial theoretical efforts to challenge the legal and institutional hegemonies of the nation-state as the sole means for political change. But for Nussbaum, the new discourses of feminist theory can only occupy an oppositional, if not antithetical relation to the political, given the ways in which the political is equated with a precise set of projects, analyses, and claims. Hence, she forfeits the opportunity to consider how feminism's entanglements with theory broadly conceived have given depth and texture to a difference previously unperceived between *feminism as a national political movement* with global desires and *feminism as a politicized knowledge project* in need of challenging its own imbrication in U.S. nationalism, Enlightenment modernity, and a sentimental geopolitics of missionary attachment.

My reading of "The Professor of Parody" is not a defense of Judith Butler per se, though readers no doubt sense my considerable lack of sympathy with Nussbaum's strategy for guaranteeing old feminism's futurity. *That* future of feminism as a monotheistic globalizing politic, narratively equipped with theory as its own fallen angel, is finally too allergic to the possibility of any future that old feminism has not already imagined. By characterizing academic feminism as the force of feminism's depoliticization, Nussbaum reproduces one of the most paradoxical features of old feminism today: she defines it against the very project of institutional intervention it inaugurated in the United States and hence against those discourses through which feminist theorists have come to question, among other things, feminism's historical relationship to national politics, geopolitical imperialisms, and the gendered division of being and knowing (of materiality and theory) in the U.S. university more generally. To the extent that Nussbaum, like other authors of the apocalyptic narrative, reiterates a normative temporality for social change and feminism's own historical becoming, she forecloses all but (a highly condensed version of) old feminism's future. In the process, academic knowledge production and feminism's theoretical battles over the value and meaning of politics and social change are rendered not simply secondary to the real, but the real's most traitorous and energetic enemy.

II

In her postulation of a referential real as the defining feature of feminist politics, Nussbaum tacitly establishes a model for feminist knowledge production that is familiar to anyone currently working in women's studies in the United States. It views feminism in the academy as fulfilling its political mission by reproducing social activism, which sets the standard of judging the success of the field according to a trajectory of movement (of knowledge, bodies, and practices) into and out of the academy, from the so-called ivory tower to the real. Women's studies thus garners its value by reproducing within the academy the social organization of *women* as a political sign outside of it, which not only defines the field as a site of belonging in the social identitarian sense but promises to guarantee for it a relation of justice to women. For many feminist scholars, belonging to women and belonging to women's studies are thus completely compatible, if not seemingly identical, as the field's object of study and the subjects who study "her" are (politically speaking) one.

The costs of this configuration of knowledge and politics—and the structure of belonging it has generated—are at the heart of Wendy Brown's "The Impossibility of Women's Studies," which critiques the institutionalization of identitarian political struggles not because such academic projects fail in their obligation to politics, as in Nussbaum's lament, but precisely because making politics the priority "renders dispensable a deep and rigorous [intellectual] basis for women's studies."[29] In making this critique, Brown emphasizes the "unimpeachable importance" of feminist interventions in university practices of all kinds: "Without doubt we are everywhere now, and without doubt, this 'we' was literally brought into being by the fight to establish and legitimate women's studies."[30] Nonetheless, she wants to question whether "the strategies and ambitions that produced this effect at one historical moment are . . . necessarily those that will sustain or enhance it at another," and hence she seeks to write the future as an open question.[31] "The process of watching women's studies falter in the 1990s," she writes, "does not tell us what to do instead. Perhaps the present moment is one . . . for thinking."[32] In arriving at her essay's final word, "thinking," Brown offers a striking reversal of the apocalyptic formulation by engaging feminism's generational battle at its temporal and epistemological core, refusing both to already know politics and to know it as linear narration. As Brown puts it, "What is needed is the practice of a historiography quite different from that expressed by notions of cause and effect, accumulation, [and] origin."[33]

Brown's critique of the institutionalization of feminism as a politics that subordinates the intellectual helps us take seriously what feminism has come to disavow: that feminism's proliferation in critical and political practice might actually *constitute* the possibility of generating and sustaining a knowledge project in its name. But while Brown nods repeatedly toward this possibility—toward research and curricula that could inhabit what I think of as the inexhaustibility, indeed, unknowability, of feminism's coherent relation to women, race, power, theory, politics, etc.—in the end she views such work as critically different from women's studies. When she calls for the field to engage postcolonial studies, queer theory, and critical race studies in order to take the "sustaining impulses of women's studies— to challenge the seamless histories, theories, literatures, and sciences featuring and reproducing a Humanism starring only Man—and harness them for another generation or two of productive, insurrectionary work," she understands that to do so would constitute a project rather distinct from women's studies.[34] Such work, she writes, "will add up neither to a unified and coherent notion of gender nor to a firm foundation for women's studies."[35] This is the case because the identity-based foundation of women's studies can only function to constrain and contain the problematic she so compellingly diagnoses. "Indisputably, women's studies . . . was politically important," she writes, but contemporary women's studies is "politically and theoretically incoherent, as well as tacitly conservative—incoherent because by definition it circumscribes uncircumscribable 'women' as its object of study, and conservative because it must resist all objections to such circumscription if it is to sustain that object of study."[36]

In launching this critique, Brown is not calling for already-existing women's studies programs and departments to be dissolved, as many of her readers have contended. Instead, she moves between three different but related claims: first, that we need to avoid "new degree-granting programs in the university," which means suspending the institutionalizing project that locates all aspiration for feminist knowledge production in women's studies as an autonomous baccalaureate (and, one assumes, doctoral) field;[37] second, that the core curriculum of the field needs to be taught in other disciplinary and interdisciplinary sites; and third, that existing curricular projects in women's studies need to be transformed "in name, content, and scope" by the recognition that their organization around singular identity rubrics inhibits their ability to account for the complexities of the subject.[38] "To the extent that women's studies programs can allow themselves to be transformed," she writes, "they will be renewed as sites of critical inquiry and political energy."[39] And yet, no matter how much they are "shaped by feminism," because they "will no longer have gender at [their] core . . . [they will] no longer [be] women's studies."[40]

While Brown acknowledges that "the definitions of all disciplines wobble," she finds that "there is something about women's studies, . . . and perhaps about any field organized by social identity rather than by genre of inquiry, that is especially vulnerable to losing its raison d'etre when the coherence or boundedness of its object of study is challenged."[41] She thus turns to law to trace the core intellectual problem that haunts all identity-based academic endeavors: their reduction of "the powers involved in the construction of subjects" into singular identitarian domains.[42] Where Nussbaum cites law as the political enterprise that, in linking gendered, racial, sexual, and class-based discriminations, can provide the answer for feminism as a project of justice, Brown finds law to reflect and inhabit the very paradox that women's studies encounters "in its simultaneous effort to center gender analytically and to presume gender's imbrication with other forms of social power."[43] Because "the injuries of racism, sexism, homophobia, and poverty . . . are rarely recognized or regulated through the same legal categories, or redressed through the same legal strategies, . . . legal theorists engage with different dimensions of the law depending on the identity category with which they are concerned."[44] Such fragmentation within the legal apparatus demonstrates for Brown two crucial points: first, that the social powers at work in subject formation are neither compatible nor evenly distributed across the social field, which means that "formations of socially marked subjects occur in radically different modalities, which themselves contain different histories and technologies, touch different surfaces and depths, form different bodies and psyches";[45] and, second, that this problem "can only be compounded by programs of study that feature one dimension of power—gender, sexuality, race, or class—as primary and structuring. And there is simply no escaping that this is what women's studies does, no matter how strenuously it seeks to compensate for it."[46] As a consequence, "the model of power developed to apprehend the making of a *particular* subject/ion will never accurately describe or trace the lines of a living subject."[47]

This last statement is one that would receive little rebuttal in contemporary academic feminism, as it defines the very problematic that has animated feminist theory inside and outside the United States for over a decade. Why, then, does Brown locate in the problematic that occupies the field the very substance that necessitates suspending its institutionalization in the present and future? Why does the theoretical difficulty of developing a complex model of power serve as evidence for moving the intellectual project from the institutional site that has most revealed this difficulty and which therefore might have a particular investment in sustaining its analytic pursuit? Why must critical content be compatible, if not coterminous, with modes of inquiry, objects of study, and field domain names; and, hence, why must we be inevitably, even irretrievably, bound to a relation of fidelity to women as our only or only legitimate object of study? Why can't we instead, following Brown's injunction for thinking, not only use the institutional site of women's studies to construct a knowledge project around our refusal to concede to the disciplinary demand now organized by and as *women,* but do so in an equally belligerent refusal to concede the field name to the inaugurating project of old feminism and its practices, methods, and modes of critical analysis and political judgment? Might we, in short, inhabit the possibility that it will be our failure to reproduce the historical project of women's studies within the field's institutional and degree-granting domain that most profoundly holds open the future?

To pursue these questions, we need to examine not only how women's studies comes to be inhabited, in Brown's account, by affect and not intellect, but how this inhabitation functions in the broader context of identity formation in the contemporary university. As I will discuss, Brown's solution to the problem of social identity's disciplinary demand—to disseminate the content and course work of women's studies across the university—is one viable option, but it obscures in the end the extent to which the traditional disciplines themselves are identity formations, though of the academic and intellectual, not social kind. My elaboration of this point will open discussion into another one, about the way Brown situates women's studies as the singular habitat for incubating the crisis of racial guilt and monotheistic identity that we might better understand as a symptomatic effect of the U.S. university's own management of national political life and the social forms of difference that erupted into political claims in the mid to late twentieth century. To the extent that Brown seeks to challenge the institution's capitulation to identity's social formation and to release the knowledge of women's studies into the disciplines, she wants to counter, in an almost utopian vein, the effects of the university's management of social difference in favor of a liberated epistemological project, one no longer bound to the project of supplementing, through identity categories, the elisions of U.S. democratic nationalism. But this strategy, as I will show, does not so much liberate the field as exchange one identity form for another, giving to the disciplines the seeming capaciousness to be unmarked by the problematic of affect and difference that for Brown condemns the project of women's studies to an anti-intellectual reproduction of *women* as a social form. From this perspective, the move to animate feminist intellectual inquiry outside women's studies in the disciplines can end up eliding the field with the problematic of identity that might more cogently be understood as inhabiting the U.S. university in multiple and contradictory ways.

To be sure, Brown does not situate her critique in the national context I am gesturing toward, nor does she address overtly how the impossibility of women's studies she cites is bound up with a history of national political struggle over higher education, state-sponsored knowledge production, and national subject formation. Only in her final paragraph does she identify the geopolitical location of her critical discussion as the U.S. university. But her rendering of the problematic of the field is implicitly predicated on the national political horizons of the inaugurating narrative that now circumscribes it, which I take as both underlying and inciting her desire to differentiate for academic feminism an intellectual project devoted to political thought from the distinctively political demand to defend identity's social coherence that she finds constraining women's studies. From this perspective, Brown might be seen as trying to escape precisely that which Nussbaum seeks to resuscitate: not just an affective tie to what Brown calls in another context "wounded attachments," but the nation-state as the implicit destination for and contestatory arena of feminism's contemporary political imaginary.[48] But why, let me ask again, must this desire to be delivered from wounded attachments and missionary nationalism close the book on the institutionalizing project of women's studies as a degree-granting site altogether? To get closer to some sustaining answer to this question, I want to delve more deeply into the problem of disciplinary identity and its relation to social identity in the broad organization of knowledge in the U.S. university.

III

To trace the complexity of competing forms of identity formation in the U.S. university, let us return to the departmental scene that Brown uses to open her essay—for it is here, in the difficulties of reforming the undergraduate curriculum in her own department (then University of California, Santa Cruz), that she initially locates the impossibility of women's studies. She writes, "We found ourselves completely stumped over the question of what a women's studies curriculum should contain. . . . Each approach . . . [we took] continued to beg the question of what a well-educated student in women's studies ought to know and with what tools she ought to craft her thinking. . . . Why, when we looked closely at this project for which we had fought so hard and that was now academically institutionalized, could we find no there there? That is, why was the question of what constituted the fundamentals of knowledge in women's studies so elusive to us?"[49] Brown lists a number of crucial issues that contributed to this impasse: the multiple divides that have emerged within women's studies between ethnic studies, feminist theory, and queer studies; the proliferation of feminist scholarship into methodologically incompatible domains of knowledge where no "single conversation" emerges; and the inability of gender to adequately configure the complexity of social identity.[50] "We were up against more than any one of these challenges," she writes, "because we were up against all of them."[51]

In describing her department's impulse to seek curricular reform, Brown reviews the incoherence that she finds at the heart of the women's studies major where students were asked to pursue both "generic" and "political" inquiries in their four-course set of core requirements: (the generic) Introduction to Feminism, Feminist Theory, and Methodological Perspectives in Feminism, and (the political) Women of Color in the United States.[52] The requirements thus made legible two animating desires for women's studies: "the desire for disciplinary status signified by the claim to a distinct theory and method . . . and the desire to conquer the racialized challenge to women's studies' early objects of study by institutionalizing that challenge in the curriculum."[53] While Brown views both of these desires as, in the end, impossible ones, she focuses most closely on the way that the women of color course functions as a compensatory strategy for the field's inescapably compromised relation to complex subject formation. As she puts it, the "compensatory cycle of guilt and blame" that accompanies the course is "structured by women's studies['] original, nominalist, and conceptual subordination of race (and all other forms of social stratification) to gender."[54] And further, "insofar as the superordination of white women within women's studies is secured by the primacy and purity of the category gender, guilt emerges as the persistent social relation of women's studies to race, a guilt that cannot be undone by any amount of courses, readings, and new hires focused on women of color." As such, no resignification, no performative rearticulation, indeed, no possible difference in the deployment of *women* is possible as gender is rendered "pure" and secure as the sole enabling analytic for the field. The critique launched by feminists of color against the reduction of women to white women can never hit its target, as the category of women remains structurally predetermined to yield an exclusionary result "insofar as the superordination of white women . . . is secured by the primacy . . . of . . . gender."[55]

Brown's response to this impasse, to the structural impossibility (in her terms) of rearticulating women to yield anything but an exclusionary effect, is to call for teaching the women's studies curriculum in something other than its own degree-granting site. Might we, she asks, move such "basic courses as 'Introduction to Feminisms,' 'Introduction to Feminist Theories,' and 'Histories and Varieties of Women's Movements' . . . into the general curriculum of other disciplinary and especially interdisciplinary programmatic sites"?[56] This solution is particularly interesting given her essay's rumination on the failure of the women's studies faculty to find the "there there" for a coherent women's studies undergraduate curriculum. "Our five core and three most closely affiliated faculty are trained respectively in American literature, American history, Chinese history, English literature, Renaissance Italian and French literature, Western political theory, European history, and molecular biology."[57] While Brown notes that all these scholars "have strayed from the most traditional boundaries of these fields," they nonetheless experience the women's studies classroom as the scene of intellectual disappointment as students are not simply unprepared in "the faculty's areas of expertise" but drawn to "some variant of feminist sociological or psychological analysis—experientially, empirically, and practically oriented—or in studies of popular culture. Yet not one of our core faculty worked in [these areas]."[58] The chasm thus created between student interest and faculty expertise might be interpreted as the profound difference between two forms of identity production: the social relation of identity that produces political belonging through the experiential and practical in women's studies and the intellectual formation of identity that proceeds from disciplinary training and the academic construction of "expertise."[59] Where Brown diagnoses the problems of installing the former as the faulty coherence of a women's studies curriculum, she does not detail how the latter identity structure of traditional disciplinarity operates. In this way, her essay relies, contradictorily, on the very distinction between intellectual and social identity that characterizes the impossibility of women's studies in the first place. In the process, the intellectual is implicitly aligned with disciplinary training and given priority in overcoming the limitations of social identity. Such a formulation reverses the value but not the organizing structure within which knowledge and bodies, identities and thought, in the university now move.

It is in this broader context that I want to resituate the impossibility of women's studies that Brown so cogently cites. For while identity studies in general have sought to intervene in the U.S. university by critiquing its practices of excluding particular groups of subjects, they have been less successful in establishing the study of identity as a knowledge project that distinctly challenges the identitarian form of the university's intellectual reproduction in the disciplines. This is the case, it seems to me, regardless of the earliest intentions of programs in identity studies which organized themselves as critical interruptions into disciplinary practices through a foregrounded discourse of interdisciplinarity. Through interdisciplinary frameworks, identity studies sought to overcome the professionalized divide between knowledge domains in the U.S. university (between, for instance, the study of literature and political economy).[60] And yet, given the academy's own political economy of knowledge production, identity studies have relied and continue to rely on faculty both trained and located in traditional disciplines, which means that intellectual subjective formation as well as intellectual belonging are predicated on the identity and authority conferred by disciplinary structures. This is not to say that scholars experience no abjection in their relation to disciplinary structures, but it is to foreground the fact that knowledge identity is today disciplinarily based, which often has the powerful effect of rendering identity studies solely as domains of belonging precisely in the corporeal identitarian sense that Brown rightly laments. In this dynamic where one may *be* a woman, one also *is* a literary critic, political scientist, sociologist, or critical theorist (and often most decidedly so in such interdisciplinary contexts as women's studies!), which means that the turn away from women's studies to escape identity delivers us once again up to it, but in its most powerful professional form. To the extent that knowledge production as we know it today is also an identitarian project, it too binds us to privileged objects of study and their equally privileged modes of inquiry, *and* it too requires an obligation to forms of coherence that are both arbitrary and contested, if not at times without any justification, other than historical precedent, at all. That these intellectual identities have come to rest in Enlightened modernity on their dis-establishment from the corporeal does not make them less identitarian; rather it reveals how profoundly shaped by practices of identity formation is the U.S. university on the whole.

Brown's notion that other academic sites are adequate to feminist knowledges in ways that women's studies is not does offer an escape from the affect-laden, wounded state that it has become, but it will not settle the problem of identity's incoherence or the affective dimensions of social difference in the U.S. university today. It is for this reason that the courses she lists for integration into the existent organization of the university by necessity omit Women of Color in the United States. That referent and the problematic of a "notoriously fraught relationship" it cannot help but bring are rendered wholly internal to women's studies; indeed, this seems to have no living trace in the dissemination of women's studies courses across the university.[61] While some of Brown's critics have taken this as evidence of her dismissal of race, it is important to distinguish, as she does, the difference between the women of color rubric and the analytic importance of race for feminist scholarship. I would argue, with Brown, against the course's placement in a core curriculum, but on the grounds of its intellectual displacements: how it reduplicates but does not reveal its complicity with the university's broader condescension of race with particularist bodies; how it reinscribes a national political horizon for thinking feminism's relation to race and racialization by constraining the question of "color" within the referential framework of the United States; and how this constraint produces both intellectual and political difficulties for thinking through the challenge of international/transnational/post-national knowledges in the field.[62] At the same time, I would argue, against Brown, that, in order to make race analytically significant, we cannot leave it to the disciplines, to the teaching of Introduction to Feminism in English, political science, or history—or any of the various underfunded interdisciplinary sites—to give complexity to the present that "The Impossibility of Women's Studies" so cogently charts. After all, it is precisely the existence of women's studies today, as an interdisciplinary institutional domain defined by but irreducible to identity, that could make the movement of courses from women's studies to other institutional arenas productive.

More importantly, the suggestion she offers will not rescue us from the difficult and problematical entanglements of social formation and knowledge production that affect women's studies as part of a national university system that has become increasingly intent on managing diversity. It is the importance of the field's continued grappling with the ease with which identity can be appropriated that allows us to interrogate the histories of national political life that inhabit, in uneven and often inexplicable ways, the university as a social and institutional form. Rather than move out of the site that brings us now to these difficult considerations, we need to rethink the ways in which national epistemologies of political change meet up with, contest, and transform the conception of what and who belongs to women's studies as a field. In other words, only by retaining the problematic within women's studies—that there might be "no there there"—is it possible to render a future of the field that can productively encounter identity as the complex subject production which Brown seeks—and that is predicated, as I have been arguing, on retaining as a political strategy of resignification the nomination of the field as women's studies.

This does not mean, however, that I think Brown is wrong to suggest that academic feminism mobilize itself by teaching what we think of as basic women's studies courses in various sites throughout the institution. To offer an introduction to feminism in a sociology or English department, instead of such discipline-based mainstay courses as Sociology of Gender or Women and Literature, does offer an important reconfiguration of feminist knowledge. It allows for a different kind of intellectual circulation and the displacement of the stable unity of *women* and gender in multiple domains. Such mobility, however, cannot be in lieu of the continued reshaping of objects and modes of inquiry within an ongoing project of institutionalizing women's studies, which is to say that the intellectual rigor that Brown calls for can be most productively sustained in relation to the continued function of women's studies as the resignified signature for an extra-disciplinary domain devoted to thinking about and against identitarian projects. The present that Brown calls into thinking as an interruption of the assumptions of the past provides the necessary first move in the reanimation of feminist knowledge production in the U.S. academy, but such a move begets another: a theoretical investigation of the organization of knowledge that structured the field's inaugurating understanding of its object of study and that continues to consign identity-based studies to their most reduced and realist referential function as affect and not intellect, as social particularity and not intellectual complexity. When Brown calls for thinking to interrupt the past's temporal determination of the future, it is this that must be interrupted as well: the particularist reduction whereby the U.S.

university's distillation of bodies from knowledge yields an understanding of identity studies as an institutional domain within which the complexity of power cannot possibly be thought.

To say that the study of identity needs more critical thinkers like Wendy Brown might seem inconsistent at this point, but it is precisely because "The Impossibility of Women's Studies" allows us to understand so much that I am compelled to labor over the possibilities of what it does not yet say. Women's studies does "need a combination of, on one hand, analyses of subject-producing power accounted through careful histories, psychoanalysis, political economy, and cultural, political, and legal discourse analysis, and, on the other, genealogies of particular modalities of subjection that presume neither coherence in the formations of particular kinds of subjects nor equivalences between different formations."[63] But this does not mean that, because "the work . . . will add up neither to a unified and coherent notion of gender nor to a firm foundation for women's studies," it will "no longer [be] women's studies."[64] Why refuse the possibility that attention to the issues she defines will productively contribute to the redefinition, resignification, and redeployment of the intellectual force, frame, and function of the field? If it is *women* that we must let go of, as along with Brown I believe it is, then we must also refuse the assumption that intellectual domains and their objects of study are referentially the same. The contingent positivity I seek begins here where we commit ourselves to the possibility that the disciplining work of the field's origins has no necessary claim on the future content, scope, and intellectual formation signified by the name.

In this present that is not possibly the same as the past nor a simple predictive platform for the future, academic feminism's attachment to the institution is decidedly insecure. Political failure haunts us on all sides, and we have very little vocabulary outside accusation, injury, and despair for understanding the institutionalizing process of feminism's transit from the street to the U.S. university. While Brown comes closest to offering us the object lessons that identity-based studies might be made to yield, she is finally, paradoxically, too optimistic, as the contemporary U.S. university offers quite literally "no there there" for the study "of the powers involved in the construction of subjects."[65] The present of *thinking* that Brown calls for needs to register *this* institutional failure, not as preamble to dismissing women's studies as an academic endeavor but in order to extend the critique of identitarian belonging to the disciplinary formations that structure not only women's studies' own internal practices of knowledge production, but the broader shape and scope of the university's organization of bodies and knowledge as well.

IV

In "The Impossibility of Women's Studies," Brown suggests that a mode of social belonging has been installed as the political rationale for the field, thereby rendering it an intellectually domesticated site. In doing so, she makes two central claims: first, that degree-granting projects formed around identity actually inhibit critical thought about power and the complexity of the living subject; and, second, that the future productivity of feminist knowledge will be possible, indeed, more probable, outside the institutionalizing project of women's studies as an autonomous curricular entity. I have sought to counter these two claims by positing that the critical diagnosis of the field offered by Brown is not intellectually possible from outside it, that, indeed, it is the productive disparity between the field's own critical horizons and its internal critique that have rendered "The Impossibility of Women's Studies" possible as a critical project. In addition, I have defined a second and equally formidable identitarian project in the U.S. academy, one whose effect of fragmentation is no less intense than the structural incommensurabilities that Brown finds in identity-based programs and departments: the disciplines. In doing so, I have tried to emphasize that within the disciplinary apparatus of knowledge production, one does not simply study literature, politics, or social organization. One is constituted as belonging on an identitarian basis, where the imperative to *be* a biologist, philosopher, political scientist, even a critical theorist is to participate in an identitarian project; and it is this project that has long been opposed to and in a management relation with notions of identity as a national social form. My purpose in these moves has been to interrupt Brown's determination of an end to the project of institutionalization by arguing that the intellectual transformations she calls for are possible, indeed necessary, for animating the possibility of women's studies, which entails a refusal to relinquish the institutional site to the disciplining presumptions of its inaugurating imperatives.

With institutionalization in the U.S. academy as part of and not antithetical to the future, I have also questioned, through my discussion of Martha Nussbaum, the status of the real and of justice as the twin frameworks within which we understand the critical value of academic feminism in general and women's studies in particular. This fetishization of a real world that exists elsewhere from the university has unfortunately made it difficult to train our attention on the specificities and force of the U.S. university as a political location and productive site for academic feminism's futurity. To say this does not mean that we should think about the world outside the U.S. academy less, but certainly we must stop thinking about it in place of or in simple opposition to thinking about the specific knowledge politics of the university. None of this should be taken to suggest that the U.S. academy is feminism's equivalent or that feminism as a political project can be reduced to its articulation in the academy, either in the United States or elsewhere. Academic feminism in any national scene can never stand for feminism as a whole, and the very notion of feminism as a whole must repeatedly be fractured by feminism's inability to remain identical to itself. At the same time, as I have argued through my discussion of Wendy Brown, feminism as an academic project bears a critical difference from the models of social movement that may have inaugurated it. To the extent that the idiom of failure laments this difference, as in Nussbaum's essay, it abandons the challenge of feminist engagement in the very institution that absorbs not only Nussbaum's but our own critical labors. To the extent that the idiom of failure turns the other way—lamenting the conflation of the academic with identity-based social struggle, as in Brown—it leaves unarticulated how women's studies might serve as the field domain for plumbing the theoretical and epistemological possibilities of the "no there there" that accompany our struggles against the institutionalized norms that inhibit us: not just of generational transmission and the incoherence of both social and disciplinary identity, but of the democratic elisions of national politics that permeate the organization of knowledge, bodies, and social life in the contemporary U.S. university.

The future of women's studies in the U.S. university that I seek stakes its contingent positivity on following the non-identical, which entails our own historical-national-temporal displacement: a refusal of the apocalyptic narrative's attachment to the idea that the past generates the future or that the future must always stand as a symbolic embodiment of the past. Cast in critical terms, it is a *non-identical feminism* that slips free of the conundrum of failure that currently encompasses both U.S. women's studies and academic feminism. It does this by offering the possibility that the knowledge that academic feminists will need in different futures is not "our" knowledge, that any particular future and our knowledge will have no necessarily productive relationship, no narrative that makes us live in the present of some future academic feminist time. A non-identical feminism will not be efficient; it will not have the clarity of productive order; it will not seek to guarantee that feminist struggle culminates in a future that we can already know from the vantage point of our present. This is the case because the future that we need is the excess of teleological time, elusive and unmanageable, certainly unable to be historically mandated, politically guaranteed, or subjectively owned. What this means for women's studies is that it is time to rearticulate the content and scope of the field by thinking, as Elizabeth Grosz puts it in another context, of "the radical openness of the future," which entails a turn away from "time, memory, and history" to "conceptions of duration and becoming."[66] Such concentration on the politics of what I call "the mean time" affirms the possibility that women's studies can exceed its contemporary emplottment as the critical container of U.S. feminism's twentieth-century political subjectivity. In the meantime is the space of duration for academic feminism's non-identical agency, which is to say the space from which its institutionalizing project in the university stands a chance to simultaneously outthink and outlive us all.

Notes

This paper incorporates and revises portions of three previously published works: "Academic Feminism against Itself," *NWSA Journal* 14, no. 2 (summer 2002): 18–37; "Feminism, Institutionalism, and the Idiom of Failure," *differences* 11 (fall 1999–2000): 107–136 (copyright Duke University Press); and "Feminism's Apocalyptic Futures," *New Literary History* 31, no. 4 (autumn 2000): 805–825 (copyright Johns Hopkins University Press). My thanks to Brian Carr and Jody Greene for productive engagements with earlier drafts.

1. See, respectively, Marianne Hirsch and Evelyn Fox Keller, eds., *Conflicts in Feminism* (New York and London: Routledge, 1990); Tania Modleski, *Feminism without Women: Culture and Criticism in a "Postfeminist" Age* (New York: Routledge, 1991); and Carla

Kaplan, "The Language of Crisis in Feminist Theory," *Bucknell Review*, special issue: "'Turning the Century': Feminist Criticism in the 1990s," ed. Glynis Carr (Lewisburg, Pa.: Bucknell University Press, 1992): 68–89.

2. Diane Elam and Robyn Wiegman, eds., *Feminism beside Itself* (New York: Routledge, 1995); Dana Heller, ed., *Cross Purposes: Lesbians, Feminists, and the Limits of Alliance* (Bloomington: Indiana University Press, 1997); and Susan Gubar, *Critical Condition* (New York: Columbia University Press, 1999).

3. Bill Readings, *The University in Ruins* (Cambridge, Mass.: Harvard University Press, 1996).

4. While Brown's essay appeared in the fall 1997 special issue of *differences,* "Women's Studies on the Edge," I am using 1999 as the publication date of the essay since that is when the volume actually appeared.

5. Wendy Brown, "The Impossibility of Women's Studies," *differences* 9, no. 3 (1997): 98.

6. Ibid.

7. Martha Nussbaum, "The Professor of Parody." *New Republic* 220, no. 16 (February 22, 1999): 44.

8. Ian (Janet) Halley, "Queer Theory by Men," *Duke Journal of Gender, Law, and Policy* 11 (spring 2004): 7–53.

9. Nussbaum, "Professor," 37, 45.

10. Biddy Martin, "Success and Its Failures," *differences* 9, no. 3 (1997): 102–131.

11. Nussbaum, "Professor," 46.

12. Ibid.

13. Ibid.

14. Ibid., 42.

15. Ibid., 45.

16. Ibid., 44, 37.

17. Ibid.

18. Ibid., 38.

19. Ibid., 38, 45.

20. Ibid., 46.

21. Ibid., 46, 44.

22. Ibid., 44.

23. Ibid., 38.

24. Ibid.

25. Ibid.

26. See Inderpal Grewal and Caren Kaplan, eds., *Scattered Hegemonies: Postmodernity and Transnational Feminist Practices* (Minneapolis: University of Minnesota Press, 1994); Inderpal Grewal and Caren Kaplan, "Warrior Marks: Global Womanism's Neo-Colonial Discourse in a Multicultural Context," *Camera Obscura* 39 (September 1996): 5–33; and Inderpal Grewal and Caren Kaplan, "Transnational Feminist Cultural Studies: Beyond the Marxism/Poststructuralism/Feminism Divides," in *Between Women and Nation: Transnational Feminisms and the State,* ed. Caren Kaplan, Norma Alarcón, and Minoo Moallem (Durham: Duke University Press, 1999), 349–363.

27. Gayatri Spivak, letter to the editor, *New Republic* 220, no. 16 (April, 19, 1999): 43.

28. This critique has been forwarded by a number of scholars, but given Nussbaum's listing of gays and lesbians as among those whom Butler abandons, it is especially important to cite the work of Janet Halley and Gayle Rubin, who trace—against Nussbaum's heroines Catherine MacKinnon and Andrea Dworkin—how feminist rem-

edies for sexual harassment and anti-pornography have become the means for policing non-normative sexualities. See Janet Halley, "Sexuality Harassment," in *Left Le-
galism/Left Critique*, ed. Wendy Brown and Janet Halley (Durham: Duke University
Press, 2002), 80–104; and three essays by Gayle Rubin: "Sexual Traffic," *differences*
6, nos. 2–3 (summer–fall 1994): 62–99; "Misguided, Dangerous, and Wrong: An Analysis of Anti-Pornography Politics," in *Bad Girls and Dirty Pictures: The Challenge to
Reclaim Feminism,* ed. Allison Assiter and Avedon Carol (London: Pluto, 1993), 18–
40; and "Thinking Sex: Notes for a Radical Theory of the Politics of Sexuality," in
Pleasure and Danger: Exploring Female Sexuality, ed. Carole S. Vance (New York:
Routledge, Kegan and Paul, 1984), 267–319.

29. Brown, "Impossibility," 98.
30. Ibid., 96.
31. Ibid.
32. Ibid., 98.
33. Ibid., 94.
34. Ibid., 95.
35. Ibid.
36. Ibid., 83.
37. Ibid., 98.
38. Ibid., 95.
39. Ibid.
40. Ibid.
41. Ibid., 85, 86.
42. Ibid., 86.
43. Ibid., 88.
44. Ibid.
45. Ibid., 92.
46. Ibid., 93.
47. Ibid., emphasis mine.
48. See chapter 3 of Wendy Brown's *States of Injury: Power and Freedom in Late Modernity* (Princeton, N.J.: Princeton University Press, 1995), 52–76.
49. Brown, "Impossibility," 81–82.
50. Ibid., 82–83.
51. Ibid., 83.
52. Ibid., 80.
53. Ibid., 81.
54. Ibid., 93.
55. Ibid.
56. Ibid., 97.
57. Ibid., 82.
58. Ibid., 81, 82.
59. Ibid., 92.
60. As Lisa Lowe has discussed in "The International within the National: American Studies and Asian American Critique" (*Cultural Critique* 40 [fall 1998]: 29–47), it is the
organization of the disciplines that bifurcates the realms of culture and political
economy, which in turn produces structural antagonisms for accounting for subject construction across various social domains.
61. Brown, "Impossibility," 93.
62. For recent critical work on the problems and complexities of the women of color course,

see both Rachel Lee, "The Prisonhouse of White Women's Exclusions: Now What? for Women of Color," in *Women's Studies on Its Own*, ed. Robyn Wiegman (Durham: Duke University Press, 2002), 82–105; and Minoo Moallem, "Women of Color in the US: Pedagogical Reflections on the Politics of the Name," in *Women's Studies on Its Own,* ed. Wiegman, 368–382.

63. Brown, "Impossibility," 95.
64. Ibid.
65. Ibid., 86.
66. Elizabeth Grosz, "Deleuze's Bergson: Duration, the Virtual, and a Politics of the Future," lecture delivered at University of California, Irvine, October 28, 1998.

Whither Black Women's Studies

An Interview, 1997 and 2004

Beverly Guy-Sheftall and Evelynn M. Hammonds

Evelynn Hammonds: I want to start with a set of questions about women's studies programs. Among the goals that informed the founding of women's studies programs was the integration of women into the existing curriculum. Whether that meant changing the disciplines, rethinking theoretical and analytic approaches, or adding new knowledge about women to ongoing research and teaching projects, the point was to have women included in every branch of knowledge. Has that been accomplished at historically black colleges? Are they operating on a different timeline at these institutions? Are there specific and different issues that women's studies has to address on these campuses versus predominantly white ones? How would you characterize the mission of women's studies at a black women's college? What are the barriers you've encountered in establishing your program? What are your successes?

Beverly Guy-Sheftall: The first thing that I would say is that Spelman has been fairly unique in the commitment that it's made to the establishment of the Women's Studies Program. It is still the case that we are the only historically black college with an undergraduate women's studies major. Atlanta University has a doctorate in Africana women's studies, but since its merger with Clark College it has kept the doctoral program without an undergraduate option. There are some historically black colleges with a smattering of women's studies courses here and there, but I don't think that there are any which have either a women's studies minor or major, which we at Spelman just passed in the fall of last year. It is still the case that women's studies with respect to coherent programs are just not cropping up at historically black colleges, despite thirty years of agitation on part of women's studies folk, and I think that there are a number of reasons for that. One, there is a paucity of interdisciplinary programs in general in these colleges, even, for example, with respect to African American studies. And there is still the assumption that women's studies is not critical to the education of students at historically black colleges. It is also the case that there just hasn't been a critical mass of faculty willing to struggle over a number of years to get a program going without adequate resources. Overall these efforts are really struggling. The advantages that we have had at Spelman are, first, administrative support and, secondly, external funding.

EVELYNN HAMMONDS: Do you think that there has been an integration of knowledge about women into the traditional disciplines at historically black colleges?

BEVERLY GUY-SHEFTALL: Not to any substantial extent. I'm making this assertion on the basis of my knowledge about curricula from examining catalogues, but also from anecdotal reports from faculty at historically black colleges. I have a number of contacts, including the people I met recently when I co-taught a comparative women's studies seminar at NYU this past summer with Professor Chandra Mohanty (of Hamilton College). Many faculty from historically black colleges were in that seminar and most of them acknowledged the absence of women's studies either as separate courses or in terms of mainstreamed courses. There are some pockets at particular places, for example, at Howard University in the history department you certainly have a women's studies presence and maybe to some extent in English, but I would say that probably it is still the case in 1997 that women's studies has not been mainstreamed into traditional disciplines in any significant way.

EVELYNN HAMMONDS: How would you characterize the mission of women's studies at a black women's college?

BEVERLY GUY-SHEFTALL: At a black women's college as opposed to a historically black college in general?

EVELYNN HAMMONDS: Well, both.

BEVERLY GUY-SHEFTALL: I believe that any undergraduate college in 1997, including historically black colleges, ought to have reflected in their curriculum important new scholarship on women that's been emerging in the last thirty years, particularly as it relates to women of African descent, women of color, and women in the diaspora (the Americas, the Caribbean, and Europe). This should be done at the most fundamental level in order to have students understand the entire range of human experience. I would also add that this is critical, perhaps even more critical, at historically black colleges because there's been such a preoccupation with race and not sufficient attention paid to gender. The addition of women studies in these colleges would be correcting an imbalance in the way that we transform curricula with respect to race at majority institutions. Dealing with race *and* gender issues at historically black colleges is extremely important.

EVELYNN HAMMONDS: Can you say something about the specific barriers that you encountered at Spelman in establishing the program and also from your experience in the NYU seminar this past summer?

BEVERLY GUY-SHEFTALL: The first barrier was the assumption that because we were and are a women's college, that we were already by definition doing this work—which, of course, would be incorrect. The second barrier, and this would have been clearer in 1981, almost fifteen years ago, there was tremendous discomfort about an explicitly feminist curriculum at historically black colleges. The assumption was that feminism was not relevant to black folk. There was also some resistance to what was perceived to be a radical political feminist agenda which was perceived to have nothing to do with traditional disciplinary scholarship. The assumption also was that women's studies would cripple black students by not providing them a traditional, acceptable education and that somehow we were disadvantaging them. In other words, I think there was even greater sensitivity at historically black colleges about providing students with something that was perceived to be "off color."

As a result, far too few black students have been exposed to women's studies courses. The situation has changed somewhat over the years; however, the fact that women's studies in general has paid inadequate attention to issues of race and class has also limited the participation of black students. In addition, in many women's studies courses white students express hostility in discussions about race and class in ways that black students find unsettling.

EVELYNN HAMMONDS: How would you characterize your successes then?

BEVERLY GUY-SHEFTALL: We were able to overcome these barriers because we had a friendly administration who recognized the importance of women's studies, particularly after President Johnetta Cole arrived in 1987. In addition, we always had supportive provosts both in Donald Stewart's administration and in Cole's with Barbara Carter, Ruth Simmons, and Glenda Price. So we didn't have administrative resistance, which is not the case in many historically black colleges where the leadership has been predominantly male. The other advantage we had from the very beginning was external funding, much of which came from the Ford Foundation, which meant that we had sufficient external financial support to really do the kind of faculty development on campus that I think was necessary for the curricular transformation. Finally, over time we began to get a critical mass of faculty and students who were very interested in women's studies courses as well.

EVELYNN HAMMONDS: There's been this fairly extensive critique about identity politics both within and outside of the academy. The argument is that programs like women's studies have institutionalized political agendas, which you referred to when you were talking about some of the barriers at historically black colleges. It has been suggested that this political agenda perpetuated rather than ended discriminatory treatment of women because the programs are often cast as victim studies. Is this a problem for black women's studies? Or is the problem somewhat different in that women's studies is perceived to be aligned with feminism and feminism is perceived as "white?" As a result is the question of identity politics posed in terms of "feminism" versus "nation/black community"—expressed in neonationalist rhetoric which argues that black women don't need to study, research, or critically interrogate their position as women separate from the concerns of the "race"?

BEVERLY GUY-SHEFTALL: I think that people who identify with black women's studies are aware of, and in opposition to, the victim studies orientation of traditional Western feminist approaches to understanding women's experience. Black women's studies, almost from its inception, wanted to theorize about the oppression of women of African descent but also wanted very much to talk about the ways that black women resisted. Black women's studies consciously and very explicitly wanted *not* to construct a discourse that primarily emphasized black women's victimhood. At the same time though, black women's studies advocates were up against the notion that black women were in fact not oppressed and had not been victimized. So we had to find a balance between the two premises because within African American communities there's the notion that black women have not been victimized at all, particularly vis-à-vis black men. This was the difficult balance that black women's studies had to negotiate. I think we have done a pretty good job of emphasizing the multiple oppressions that black women face, but also we have emphasized the issue of resistance and the need to interrogate the different ways black women experience patriarchy.

EVELYNN HAMMONDS: What about the question of feminism?

BEVERLY GUY-SHEFTALL: I think that black women's studies has as one of its main contributions its reconceptualization of feminism. It has not rejected feminism, but we have said that it needed to be expanded, broadened, and made more sensitive to the issues of race and to global questions with respect to constructions of womanhood outside the U.S., around the world. I think black women's studies really reinvigorated and reconceptualized feminism in such a way so that now it is not a narrow, culturally specific manifestation of one group of women's experiences.

EVELYNN HAMMONDS: I agree that black women's studies has been successful in pluralizing women's experiences, but do you still see a tension in talking about the need to critically interrogate the position of black women vis-à-vis the concerns of the race especially when it has been said, pejoratively perhaps, that "the race" really is a code for the concerns of black men?

BEVERLY GUY-SHEFTALL: I agree with your assessment of this persistent dilemma, which may also explain why it is that you don't have adequate women's studies curricula at historically black colleges, or in publications that black people produce. I still think that there's the assumption that teaching African American studies means primarily dealing with racial questions.

EVELYNN HAMMONDS: Yes, so do you think that identity politics and the whole question of difference as it's characterized in women's studies programs in predominantly white institutions is that the same kind of problem that women's studies faces in the historically black college context?

BEVERLY GUY-SHEFTALL: I don't think so. I think that one of the problems that women's studies faces at white colleges is an inability to deal with difference, and here I'm talking primarily about white faculty and white students. There's still tremendous reluctance on the part of women students of color, particularly African American women, to come into women's studies at white institutions, to literally bring their bodies to the court. That is not the same problem that you have at historically black colleges. In other words, we get students into women's studies courses at Spelman because they are not assuming that when they enter the courses they're going to be about white women or taught only by white faculty. The problem that we have at Spelman is that there are many students who are uncomfortable or hostile to feminism. They think our courses are about feminism, which they find uncomfortable because they see it as something that is going to make it difficult for them to have relationships with men.

EVELYNN HAMMONDS: What about the difference in terms of other women of color or the difference of sexuality or sexual preference?

BEVERLY GUY-SHEFTALL: With respect to those questions black women's studies is still dealing with a number of problems. In my experience in teaching women's studies at Spelman the questions of sexuality are probably the most contested and result in the most tension and the most difficulty in the classroom. I think that's because there's so little in the curriculum otherwise that helps students to understand sexuality beyond what they already know. They've had very little discourse which helps them to analyze sexuality in an intellectual and analytical manner so they're just coming at it with their personal belief systems, like most college students, with their personal values that haven't been subjected to any rigorous analysis. So this remains a big problem. With respect to other women of color, there is a lack of information or misinformation about other peoples of color, particularly in the U.S. We have to spend a lot of time discussing the fact that black people are not the only group of people who have had difficulties with race in this country or the world.

EVELYNN HAMMONDS: Now it's often talked about that women's studies in the U.S. has been successfully institutionalized, although everything you have just said about what has happened in historically black colleges suggests that is not the case in all institutions. Institutionalization of women's studies, as you've pointed out, is at a very different point in historically black colleges. Given that there's your program and others including the one at Howard, how are they perceived from abroad? I ask this because I think that American women's studies is perceived to be very well established, very well funded, very well supported. Do you think your program and Howard's are seen in this way? For example, I remember when a student of Philomena Essed's came over from Holland to do interviews for her dissertation on black feminism. When she visited me and Fran White at Hampshire College, she said she was looking for the black feminist institute. She believed from reading a number of anthologies and other books on black women's studies that have been widely translated that it must have had an institutional location here in the States. Fran and I laughed somewhat ruefully, but that exchange along with many others gave me the impression that there's this idea that black women's studies is as well established in the U.S. as women's studies more generally.

BEVERLY GUY-SHEFTALL: Let me say two things quickly. First of all, I think that even the question about the institutionalization of white women's studies is a complicated one. I think that in some ways, despite the fact that there are over six hundred women's studies programs in the U.S. academy, that women's studies is still institutionally fragile, in the sense that most women's studies programs are without their own faculty lines and have inadequate budgets and very little control over their curricula because they depend on departmental courses or joint appointments. There's also been in recent years a tremendous backlash and some tightening of resources so that, though women's studies is visible and has had a tremendous impact, it may not be the case that it is institutionally strong in the sense that we think about traditional departmental studies. It is still the case that even if they are fragile, black women's studies probably has almost no institutional strength.

EVELYNN HAMMONDS: Yours is still a program, not a department?

BEVERLY GUY-SHEFTALL: Yes, it's still a program. Ours functions more like a department, but the program is how it is instituted. Structurally, it is not quite as fragile for the reasons I discussed earlier. However, I think that could quickly change. It helps that our women's studies program is in an institutional home (the Women's Center) where it functions more like a department; we now have two faculty lines, in addition to mine. There are no prominent black women's studies programs in the U.S. And I think it's also fair to say that most well-established African American studies programs do not have even what I would call a serious black women's studies concentration.

You might assume that since the institutionalization of black women's studies has not happened within women's studies it is happening within African American studies. Yet, this is not the case. As you know, before Elsa Barkley Brown left the University of Michigan several years ago, she and other faculty there were working on a gender concentration within African American studies. If they had succeeded this would have been tantamount to mounting a black women's studies component within that program. Currently, there are no major African American studies programs with a focus on gender. On the other hand, another potential site for the institutionalization of black women's studies is within women's studies programs with a significant number of black women faculty. The University of Maryland's Women's Studies Program, because of the presence of so many black women faculty, certainly has this potential. If black women's studies has a future, in terms of institutionalization, I think it is in those women's studies programs like Maryland's because the difficulties in developing autonomous black women's studies programs are so severe.

EVELYNN HAMMONDS: I want to take that up in a second, but what about the question of perceptions from abroad?

BEVERLY GUY-SHEFTALL: Oh, I think that you're right. The assumption about the strength of black women's studies has no relationship to the reality. But you can also understand why there would be that perception because of the huge popularity of black women writers (mostly novelists) outside the U.S.—which prompts people to think that there's a cultural context that produces those writings—but it's not in women's studies or the academy by and large. The reception of these books also speaks to the popularity of black feminism outside the U.S., which supports the assumption that it is institutionalized within the American academy, which it's not.

EVELYNN HAMMONDS: Does the popularity of black feminist writings make a demand on black women's studies programmatically to try to address questions about women of color in the diaspora? In other words, when you engage in conversations with other women of color from around the world, as you do when you participate in Andrea McLaughin's International, Cross-Cultural Black Women's

Studies Institute, do you have to represent black women's studies as being engaged programmatically with the broader concerns of women in the diaspora?

BEVERLY GUY-SHEFTALL: Absolutely. Black women's studies can't be narrowly focused on the U.S.

EVELYNN HAMMONDS: I would argue that's somewhat different from white women's studies. It is not always forced to have that engagement.

BEVERLY GUY-SHEFTALL: Right—I think that black women's studies is much more inherently, or at least potentially, global because it is interested in black women's experiences all over the world. As early as 1981, with the publication of Filomena Steady's edited volume, *The Black Woman Cross-Culturally,* black women's studies has tried to address the experiences of women on the African continent and in the diaspora, especially in the Caribbean.[1]

EVELYNN HAMMONDS: Let's return to the question of integrating women's studies into the curriculum more broadly. There's a lot of debate going on right now about whether or not women's studies programs should change their names to feminist studies or gender studies . . . and people are talking about the advantages and disadvantages of such a change. You were just speaking about the integration of black women's studies into African American studies. Would an emphasis on gender rather than women make that integration more possible?

BEVERLY GUY-SHEFTALL: I'm one of the people who believe that women's studies ought to keep the name women's studies. I think the whole debate about gender studies is mostly a political one, and I also see a problem with the name feminist studies. If we change to feminist studies, we will face more problems among persons of color.

EVELYNN HAMMONDS: Well, a change to feminist studies also narrows women's studies.

BEVERLY GUY-SHEFTALL: It also narrows it. That's right. I think that women's studies is sufficiently generic and also keeps in the forefront that it emerged from a political movement that began twenty or thirty years ago, that's still in progress.

EVELYNN HAMMONDS: What about gender studies?

BEVERLY GUY-SHEFTALL: First of all, I think that women's studies is inherently gender studies. Women studies claims that it uses gender as a major category of analysis, so, therefore, to me it's already gender studies. Now that women's studies is moving more towards interrogating constructions of masculinity I don't think we have to change the name for gender to remain a primary focus. I believe women's studies has already been primarily interested in gender—which has been the major critique by women of color. It hasn't been sufficiently concerned about issues of race and class. I don't think the problem is gender.

EVELYNN HAMMONDS: I also wanted you to think about this question in light of the position taken by Mamphela Ramphele in her essay "Whither Feminism."[2] In the essay, Ramphele argues, quite persuasively I thought, that feminists need to outline a new vision of gender equity and to directly confront the oppression of men by patriarchy. I thought she specifically put this challenge to African American feminists to address and produce a theory of power.

BEVERLY GUY-SHEFTALL: I found her essay problematic, or maybe I could agree with her if she's mostly thinking about the South African context. I think it would be very difficult for me to argue that patriarchy has had as detrimental impact upon men as it has had on women, which I think she basically says. I could agree, and I think she is probably one of the people that noted early on, that racism has had a very profound impact on white people in ways that we don't think that much about. (James Baldwin also made this point, much earlier.)[3] I don't think, however, that it means racism has had the same impact or as devastating an impact as it has had on black people. And I think that she actually says that.

EVELYNN HAMMONDS: Well, I agree with you, but I also think that in the positive reading of it, from my perspective, it's her insistence that we need to think about the next step. I think she was speaking specifically to the South African context—now that they're in the place of making a new society they've got to think about gender equity in a new way and therefore take into account the oppression of black African men by white men.

BEVERLY GUY-SHEFTALL: What she does not mention in that essay is the oppression of black South African women by black South African men. I think that's the part that was missing. Her premise can be tested in the African American case, but African American feminists have also argued that black men have been complicit in the oppression of black women, and I don't see that in her equation. She also doesn't address the serious problem of violence against black women in South Africa by black men. That is one of the ways the patriarchy has also impacted South African men.

EVELYNN HAMMONDS: Yet, you don't think she goes far enough in her analysis.

BEVERLY GUY-SHEFTALL: No. I agree with her that it certainly is the case that women of African descent are as concerned about black men as they are about themselves.

EVELYNN HAMMONDS: Her point raised for me the ongoing difficulties that black feminists have had in confronting patriarchal attitudes within black communities. I think of the problems we encountered in the group of black feminists, largely academics, when we were drafting a black feminist response to the Million Man March—or earlier when we responded to the Anita Hill/Clarence Thomas hearings. We had real problems trying to talk about male power. And maybe we don't want to go so far as to call it patriarchy, but I felt there was an urgent need to figure out some way to theorize the power that men of color have over women of color. In other words, don't we as black feminists have to find a way to theorize race and gender at the same time?

BEVERLY GUY-SHEFTALL: I absolutely agree with that. One of the comments Ramphele makes is that black women want to understand the behavior of black men. I think that this should be a focus of black women's studies, to really look at issues of black masculinity. When we talk about black men, we usually discuss how they have been disempowered racially, but we don't talk about their gender. We race black men, but we don't gender them. This is a critical issue that black feminist scholarship has to address.

EVELYNN HAMMONDS: In a sense what you're saying is that black women's studies has fallen into the same trap that women's studies has more broadly, in conflating gender with women and thus failing to adequately theorize race *and* gender. As a result you are arguing that the issue of black male power has to be considered under the rubric of black masculinity.

BEVERLY GUY-SHEFTALL: Right. I put it under black masculinity and patriarchy, which, I think, speaking about the future, should be a key area within African American studies as well—which it currently is not.

EVELYNN HAMMONDS: But hopefully the integration of gender into African American studies might bring that conversation into being. What other issues do you most worry about in terms of the future of women's studies?

BEVERLY GUY-SHEFTALL: I continue to worry about the inability of women's studies to deal—in appropriate ways—with issues of race and difference, particularly difference in a cross-cultural context. I don't think women's studies does a good job of addressing women's issues outside the West. Those issues are not always related to race. It could be religion; it could be all kinds of issues, though race continues to be a problem. Also the persistent white face of women's studies in the U.S. continues to be a problem. There just are not enough faculty of color within women's studies. The problem is equally as dismal within African American studies. The hostility to feminism and to black feminism in black studies is as strong as it was ten years ago, I suspect, with a few exceptions of places where black women and a few black men in black studies are actually self-identified as people who use feminist frameworks. I continue to worry about the hostility to black feminism within African American studies and the continued domination of that field by men hostile to feminism.

EVELYNN HAMMONDS: What about affirmative-action rollbacks?

BEVERLY GUY-SHEFTALL: This is going to be devastating with respect to black students' access to white institutions. Think about the situation in Texas, where the affirmative-action guidelines in place at the University of Texas have been overturned by recent court orders. Also, the latest data from California show a decline in admissions of students of color as a result of affirmative-action rollbacks. The other thing is that the assault on affirmative action also confirms for many black people that race is still the primary problem that black people face, which provokes even more resistance to foregrounding gender.

EVELYNN HAMMONDS: You hear black people arguing that race is still primary because white conservatives are not going after programs to prevent gender discrimination.

BEVERLY GUY-SHEFTALL: And they also see white women as successful.

EVELYNN HAMMONDS: Yes, but I think that perception only highlights the way in which gender is misunderstood, if not ignored, by some black people. Affirmative efforts to end gender discrimination are seen as only benefiting white women, not black women or women of color. This is precisely why, as you've already suggested, it is critical for black women's studies to engage the intersection of gender and race.

EVELYNN HAMMONDS: Finally, can you comment on the successes you've had in women's studies at Spelman and their wider impact? Specifically, can you speak about the responses of Spelman students this spring to the quite misogynist video,

Tip Drill, by rap artist Nelly, which featured extremely negative images of young African American women? I saw the public response of these young college women, which garnered national attention and resulted in the cancelling of his appearance on campus, as one that was influenced by the kind of black feminist perspectives you teach in your classes.

BEVERLY GUY-SHEFTALL: As you know, Spelman remains the only historically black college with an undergraduate major in women's studies and a women's research center devoted to the concerns of women of African descent here and around the globe. Our recent (June 2004) conference, Women, Girls, and HIV/AIDS in Africa and the African Diaspora, which attracted delegations from South Africa, Senegal, and Brazil, was the first gathering at a black college to discuss both the racial and gendered dimensions of the pandemic. Because of the continued support of the Ford Foundation since 1983, we have been able to remain on the cutting edge of curriculum development in women's studies and feminist theory and have helped to transform the way women's studies is taught in the academy. Our evolving work on African feminisms (Associate Director M. Bahati Kuumba guest-edited a special issue of *Agenda,* a South African feminist journal, on African feminisms) will hopefully contribute to new research and curricular efforts in both women's studies and African diaspora studies.[4]

Perhaps what we're proudest about most recently is that the work of the women's studies program at Spelman attracted national attention because of a protest April 21, 2004, on the part of students (led mostly by women's studies majors and members of the campus-based Feminist Majority Leadership Alliance) against the negative portrayals of black women in the rap music industry. Rap star Nelly was scheduled to come to campus in connection with a bone-marrow drive, but after students saw his music video, *Tip Drill,* they demanded that he engage in a dialogue with students on campus about his pornographic portrayals of young black women. When he refused, they decided to hold a protest on campus anyway to bring attention to the more generic problems of misogyny in rap music. In her June 4, 2004, article in the *Chronicle of Higher Education,* "It's Gettin' Hot in Here," Elizabeth F. Farrell had this to say: "Why did students at Spelman have such a strong reaction to the video? One explanation is that the campus has a unique environment: Out of 105 historically black colleges in the United States, Spelman is the only one with a women's studies department."[5] We certainly believe that the work of our Women's Studies Program (this includes courses like Images of Women in the Media in the English Department and our own Women and Social Resistance Movements) and the feminist organizations on campus that it has spawned have been a major catalyst for the kind of feminist activism that the Nelly protest was all about. It is also the case that, were it not for our women's studies curriculum and the activities of the Women's Center, our students might not have responded to the misogyny of the Nelly video in the ways that they did. Two of the major organizers of the protest were actually in my Feminist Theory class when the issue of what to do about Nelly's video arose. What we would never have been able to anticipate, however, is the national attention that the student protest engendered, which included coverage by CNN, Fox News, *Sunday Morning News,*

USA Today, the *Washington Post,* an upcoming PBS documentary, and several financial contributions from Spelman graduates and other black women. Our students' willingness to take a courageous stand, even when other students on campus discouraged them, was quite refreshing and underscored for us the real value of women's studies with respect to its ability to help students bridge the disconnect between theory and practice. Several black scholars reminded us that spurring activism and feminism among black women students is rare in academe. We are convinced that teaching feminist theory has an important impact beyond the development of critical thinking skills—which the Nelly protest certainly underscored. It enables students to devise strategies that actually impact the lives of women and girls in the "real world." This is certainly what women's studies at Spelman has been attempting to do since 1983.

Notes

Beverly Guy-Sheftall's "Whither Black Women's Studies: An Interview with Evelynn Hammonds," is reprinted from *differences: A Journal of Feminist Cultural Studies* 9, no. 3, copyright 1997 by Brown University and *differences,* by permission of the publisher. The original interview took place on December 24, 1997; the authors added the last question in August 2004.

1. Filomena Chioma Steady, ed., *The Black Woman Cross-Culturally* (Cambridge: Schenkman Publishing Company, 1981).
2. Mamphela Ramphele, "Whither Feminism," in *Transitions, Environments, Translations: Feminisms in International Politics,* ed. Joan W. Scott, Cora Kaplan, and Debra Keates (New York: Routledge, 1997), 334–340.
3. James Baldwin, *The Fire Next Time* (New York: Dial Press, 1963).
4. M. Bahati Kuumba, ed., *Agenda* 58 (2003).
5. Elizabeth F. Farrell, "It's Gettin' Hot in Here," *Chronicle of Higher Education* 50, no. 39 (June 4, 2004): A27.

"Under Western Eyes" Revisited

Feminist Solidarity through Anticapitalist Struggles

Chandra Talpade Mohanty

I write this chapter at the urging of a number of sisters/comrades and with some trepidation, allowing myself the difficult and important challenge of revisiting an essay written some fifteen years ago. This is a complicated chapter to write, and I undertake it hesitantly and humbly, yet feeling that I must do so to take responsibility for my ideas and the influence they have had in debates in feminist theory.

"Under Western Eyes" was not only my very first "feminist studies" publication, it remains the one that marks my presence in the international feminist community.[1] I had barely completed my PhD when I wrote this essay—I am now a professor of women's studies. The "under" of Western eyes is now much more an "inside" in terms of my own location in the United States academy.[2] The site from which I wrote "Under Western Eyes" consisted of a very vibrant, transnational women's movement—the site I write from today is different. With the increasing privatization and corporatization of public life, it has become much harder to access such a women's movement from the United States (although women's movements are thriving around the world), and my site of access and struggle has increasingly come to be the U.S. academy. In the United States, women's movements have become increasingly conservative, and much radical, antiracist feminist activism occurs outside the rubric of such movements. Thus, much of what I say here is influenced by the primary site I occupy as an educator and scholar. It is time to revisit "Under Western Eyes" to clarify ideas that remained implicit and unstated in 1986 and to further develop and historicize the theoretical framework I crafted then. I also want to assess how this essay has been read (and misread) and to respond to its critiques and celebrations. And it is time for me to move explicitly from critique to reconstruction, to identify the urgent issues facing feminists at the beginning of the twenty-first century, to ask the question, How would "Under Western Eyes"—the Third World inside and outside the West—be explored and analyzed a decade later in 2001? What do I consider to be the urgent theoretical and methodological questions facing a comparative feminist politics at this time in history?

Given the apparent and continuing life of "Under Western Eyes" and my own travels through transnational feminist scholarship and networks, I begin with a summary of the central arguments of "Under Western Eyes," contextualizing them in intellectual, political, and institutional terms. Based on this discussion, I describe ways the essay has been read and situated in a number of different, often overlapping scholarly discourses. I engage with some useful responses to the essay in an attempt to further clarify and crystallize the very meanings of the West, Third World, etc., to re-engage questions of the relation of the universal and the particular in feminist theory, and to make visible some of the spaces left opaque or ambivalent in my earlier writing.

I look to see how my thinking has changed over the past fifteen years. What are the urgencies today for transnational feminist practice? How have the possibilities of feminist cross-cultural work developed and shifted? What is the intellectual, political, and institutional context which informs my own shifts and new commitments at the time of this writing? What categories of identification have changed in the past fifteen years? What has remained the same? What are the challenges facing transnational feminist practice in 2001? I wish to begin a dialogue between the intentions, effects, and political choices that underwrote "Under Western Eyes" some fifteen years ago and ones I would make today in 2001. I hope it provokes others to ask similar questions about our individual and collective projects in feminist studies.

Revisiting "Under Western Eyes"

Decolonizing Feminist Scholarship: 1986

I wrote "Under Western Eyes" to discover and articulate a critique of "Western feminist" scholarship on Third World women via the discursive colonization of Third World women's lives and struggles. I also wanted to expose the power/ knowledge nexus of feminist cross-cultural scholarship expressed through Eurocentrism, falsely creating universalizing methodologies that serve the narrow self-interest of Western feminism. As well, I thought it crucial to highlight the connection between feminist scholarship and feminist political organizing while drawing attention to the need to examine the "political implications of our analytic strategies and principles." And, I also wanted to chart the location of feminist scholarship within a global political and economic framework dominated by the "First World."[3]

My most simple concern was to make clear that cross-cultural feminist work must be attentive to the micro-politics of context, subjectivity, and struggle as well as to the macro-politics of global economic and political systems and processes. I discussed Maria Mies's study of the lace makers of Narsapur as a demonstration of how it is possible to do this kind of multilayered, contextual analysis such that it becomes evident how the particular is universally significant, without using the universal to erase the particular or posit a fundamental gap between the universal and the particular.[4] Implicit in this analysis was the use of historical materialism as a method and a definition of material reality in both its local and micro, as well as global, systemic dimensions. Also I articulated a framework of feminist solidarity across borders, a framework which is sometimes more implicit than explicit. I argued at this time for the definition and recognition of the Third World not just through oppression but in terms of complexities and struggles which actively work to change these oppressions. Thus, I argued for grounded, particularized analyses linked with larger economic and political frameworks. In a perceptive analysis of my argument of this politics of location, Sylvia Walby recognizes and refines the relation between difference and equality of which I speak.[5] She draws further attention to the need for a shared frame of reference among Western, postcolonial, Third World feminists in order to decide what counts as difference. She asserts, and rightly so, I think, that

> Mohanty and other postcolonial feminists are often interpreted as arguing only for situated knowledges in popularisations of their work. In fact, Mohanty is claiming, via a complex and subtle argument, that she is right and that (much) white Western feminism is not merely different, but wrong. In doing this she assumes a common question, a common set of concepts and, ultimately the possibility of, a common political project with white feminism. She hopes to argue white feminism into agreeing with her. She is not content to leave white Western feminism as a situated knowledge, comfortable with its local and partial perspective. Not a bit of it. This is a claim to a more universal truth. And she hopes to accomplish this by the power of argument.[6]

Walby's reading of the essay pushes others to engage my notion of a common political project, which critiques the effects of Western feminist scholarship on women in the Third World, but within a framework of solidarity and shared values. My insistence on the specificity of difference is anchored in a vision of equality attentive to power differences within and among the various communities of women. I did not argue against all forms of generalization, nor was I privileging the local over the systemic, difference over commonalities, or the discursive over the material.

I did not write "Under Western Eyes" as a testament to the impossibility of egalitarian and noncolonizing cross-cultural scholarship, nor did I define Western and Third World feminism in such oppositional terms that there would be no possibility of solidarity between Western and Third World feminists. Yet, this is often how the essay has been read and utilized.[7] I have wondered why this disjuncture has developed in this form. Perhaps mapping the intellectual and institutional context in which I wrote back then and the shifts that have affected its reading since would clarify the intentions and claims of the essay.

Intellectually, I was writing in reaction to the critique of Western humanism in terms of its universalizing, Eurocentric, masculinist assumptions. It was anchored in a firm belief in the importance of the particular in relation to the universal—a belief in the local as specifying and illuminating the universal—not in the univer-

sal erasing the particular or vice versa. My concerns drew attention to the dichoto-
mies embraced and identified with this universalized framework, the critique of
"white feminism" by women of color and the critique of "Western feminism" by
Third World feminists anchored in a paradigm of de-colonization. I was committed, both politically and personally, to building a noncolonizing feminist solidarity across borders. I believed in a larger feminist project than the colonizing,
self-interested one I saw emerging in much influential feminist scholarship and in
the mainstream women's movement.

My newly found faculty position at a primarily white U.S. academic institution also deeply affected my writing at this time. I was determined to make an
intervention into this space in order to create a location for Third World, immigrant, and other marginalized scholars like myself who saw themselves colonized
within the dominant Euro-American feminist scholarship and their communities.
It has been a source of deep satisfaction that I was able to begin to open an intellectual space to Third World/immigrant women scholars as was done at the international conference I helped organize, Common Differences: Third World Women
and Feminist Perspectives (held in Urbana, Illinois, in 1983). This conference allowed for the possibility of a de-colonized, cross-border feminist community and
cemented for me the belief that "common differences" can form the basis of deep
solidarity and that we have to struggle to achieve this in the face of unequal power
relations among ourselves.

There have also been many effects—personal and professional—in my writing this essay. These effects range from being cast as the "non-dutiful daughter"
of white feminists to being cast as a mentor for Third World/immigrant women
scholars, from being invited to address feminist audiences at various academic venues to being told I should focus on my work in early childhood education and not
dabble in feminist theory. Practicing active disloyalty has its price as well as its
rewards. Suffice it to say, however, that I have no regrets and only deep satisfaction in having written "Under Western Eyes."

I attribute some of the readings and misunderstandings of the essay to the
triumphal rise of postmodernism in the U.S. academy in the past three decades.
Although I have never called myself a postmodernist critic, some reflection on why
my ideas have been assimilated as such is important.[8] In fact, one reason to revisit
"Under Western Eyes" at this time is my desire to clarify this postmodernist appropriation.[9] I am misread when interpreted as being against all forms of generalization and as emphasizing difference over commonalities. This misreading occurs
in the context of a hegemonic postmodernist discourse that labels as "totalizing"
all systemic connections and emphasizes the fundamental instability of identities
and structures.

Yes, I did draw on Michel Foucault to craft an analysis of power/knowledge,
but I also drew on Anour Abdel Malek to show the directionality and material effects of a particular imperial power structure, and I drew too on Maria Mies to
argue for the need for a materialist analysis that linked everyday life and local
gendered contexts and ideologies to the larger transnational political and economic
structures and ideologies of capitalism.[10] What is interesting for me is to see how

and why difference has been embraced over commonality, and I realize that my writing leaves open this possibility. In 1986 I wrote to challenge the false universality of Eurocentric discourses, and maybe was caught in a pre-articulated valorization of difference over connectivity in postmodernist discourse. Now I find myself wanting to reemphasize the connections between local and universal. In 1986, my priority was on difference, but now I want to recapture and reiterate its fuller meaning, which was always there, and that is its connection to the universal. In other words, this discussion today allows me to reemphasize the way that differences are never just "differences." In knowing differences and particularities, we can better see the connections because no border is ever complete or rigidly determining. The challenge is to see how differences allow us to explain the connections and border crossings better and more accurately, more fully, how specifying difference allows us to theorize universal concerns. It is this intellectual move that allows for my concern for women of different communities and identities to build coalitions and solidarities across borders.

So what has changed and what remains the same for me? What are the urgent intellectual and political questions for feminist scholarship and organizing at this time in history? First, let me say that the terms "Western" and "Third World" retain a political and explanatory value in a world that appropriates and assimilates multiculturalism and "difference" through commodification and consumption. However, these would not be the only terms I would choose to use now. With the United States, the European Union, and Japan as the nodes of capitalist power in the early twenty-first century, the increasing proliferation of Third and Fourth Worlds within the national borders of these very countries, as well as the rising visibility and struggles for sovereignty by First Nations/indigenous peoples around the world, "Western" and "Third World" explain much less than the categorizations North/South or Two-Thirds World/One-Third World.[11]

I find the language of One-Third World versus Two-Thirds World as elaborated by Gustavo Esteva and Madhu Suri Prakash particularly useful, especially in conjunction with Third World/South and First World/North. These terms represent what Esteva and Prakash call social minorities and social majorities—categories based on the quality of life led by peoples and communities in both the North and the South.[12] The advantage of One-Third/Two-Thirds World in relation to terms like "Western/Third World" and "North/South" is that they move away from geographical and ideological binarisms.

By focusing on quality of life as the criteria for distinguishing between social minorities and majorities, One-Third/Two-Thirds World draws attention to the continuities as well as the discontinuities between the haves and have-nots within the boundaries of nations and between nations and indigenous communities. This designation also highlights the fluidity and power of global forces that situate communities of people as social majorities/minorities in disparate form. One-Third/Two-Thirds is a nonessentialist categorization, but it incorporates an analysis of power and agency which is crucial, yet what it misses is a history of colonization to which the terms Western/Third World draw attention. But as the above discussion serves to illustrate, we are still working with a very imprecise and inadequate analytic language.

Finally, I want to reflect on an important issue not addressed in "Under Western Eyes": the question of native or indigenous struggles.[13] Native or indigenous women's struggles which do not follow a postcolonial trajectory based on the inclusions and exclusions of processes of capitalist, racist, heterosexist, and nationalist domination cannot be addressed under the purview of categories like Western and Third World. But they become visible and even central to the definition of One-Third/Two-Thirds Worlds because indigenous claims for sovereignty, their life ways, and environmental and spiritual practices situate them as central to the definition of "social majority" (Two-Thirds World). While a mere shift in conceptual terms is not a complete response to this situation, I think it clarifies and addresses the limitations of my earlier use of "Western" and "Third World." Interestingly enough, while I would have identified myself as both "Western" and "Third World"—in all my complexities—in the context of "Under Western Eyes," in this new frame, I am clearly located within the One-Third World. Then again, now, as in my earlier writing, I straddle both categories. I am of the Two-Thirds World in the One-Third World. I am clearly a part of the social minority now, with all its privileges; however, my political choices, struggles, and vision for change place me alongside the Two-Thirds World. Thus, I am for the Two-Thirds World, but with the privileges of the One-Third World. I speak as a person situated in the One-Third World, but from the space and vision of, and in solidarity with, communities in struggle in the Two-Thirds World.

Under (and Inside) Western Eyes: At the Turn of the Century

There have been a number of shifts in the political and economic landscapes of nations and communities of people in the last two decades. The intellectual cartographies of disciplines and areas of study in the U.S. academy have shifted as well during this time. The advent and institutional visibility of postcolonial studies, for instance, is a relatively recent phenomenon—as is the simultaneous rollback of the gains made by race and ethnic studies departments in the 1970s and 1980s. Women's studies is now a well-established field of study with over eight hundred degree-granting programs and departments in the U.S. academy. Postmodernism is less and less the dominant intellectual phenomenon in the U.S. academy. Feminist theory and feminist movements across national borders have matured substantially since the early 1980s, and there is now a greater visibility of transnational women's struggles and movements, brought on in part by the United Nations world conferences on women held over the last two decades.

Economically and politically, the declining power of self-governance among certain poorer nations is matched by the rising significance of transnational institutions like the World Trade Organization and governing bodies like the European Union, not to mention for-profit corporations. Of the world's largest economies, fifty-one happen to be corporations, not countries, and Amnesty International now reports on corporations as well as nations.[14] Also, the hegemony of neoliberalism, alongside the naturalization of capitalist values, influences the ability to make choices on one's own behalf in the daily lives of economically marginalized as well as economically privileged communities around the globe.

The rise of religious fundamentalisms with their deeply masculinist and often racist rhetoric poses a huge challenge for feminist struggles around the world. Finally, the profoundly unequal, "information highway" as well as the increasing militarization (and masculinization) of the globe, accompanied by the growth of the prison industrial complex in the United States, pose profound contradictions in the lives of communities of women and men in most parts of the world. I believe these political shifts to the right, accompanied by global capitalist hegemony, privatization, and increased religious, ethnic, and racial hatreds, pose very concrete challenges for feminists. In this context, I ask what would it mean to be attentive to the micro-politics of everyday life as well as to the larger processes which recolonize the culture and identities of people across the globe. How we think of the local in/of the global and vice versa without falling into colonizing or cultural relativist platitudes about difference is crucial in this intellectual and political landscape. And for me this kind of thinking is tied to a revised race-and-gender-conscious historical materialism.

The politics of feminist cross-cultural scholarship from the vantage point of Third World/South feminist struggles remains a compelling site of analysis for me.[15] Eurocentric analytic paradigms continue to flourish and I remain committed to re-engaging in the struggles to criticize openly the effects of discursive colonization on the lives and struggles of marginalized women. My central commitment is to build connections between feminist scholarship and political organizing. My own present-day analytic framework remains very similar to my earliest critique of Eurocentrism. However, I now see the politics and economics of capitalism as a far more urgent locus of struggle. I continue to hold to an analytic framework that is attentive to the micro-politics of everyday life as well as to the macro-politics of global economic and political processes. The link between political economy and culture remains crucial to any form of feminist theorizing—as it does for my work. It isn't the framework that has changed. It is just that global economic and political processes have become more brutal, exacerbating economic, racial, and gender inequalities, and thus they need to be demystified, reexamined, and theorized.

While my earlier focus was on the distinctions between Western and Third World feminist practices, and while I downplayed the commonalities between these two positions, my focus now is on what I have chosen to call an anticapitalist transnational feminist practice—and on the possibilities, indeed, on the necessities of cross-national feminist solidarity and organizing against capitalism. While "Under Western Eyes" was located in the context of the critique of Western humanism and Eurocentrism, and of white, Western feminism, a similar essay written now would need to be located in the context of the critique of global capitalism (on antiglobalization), the naturalization of the values of capital, and the unacknowledged power of cultural relativism in cross-cultural feminist scholarship and pedagogies.

"Under Western Eyes" sought to make the operations of discursive power visible, to draw attention to what was left out of feminist theorizing, namely, the material complexity, reality, and agency of Third World women's bodies and lives. This is, in fact, exactly the analytic strategy I use to now draw attention to what is unseen, under-theorized, and left out in the production of knowledge about globalization. While globalization has always been a part of capitalism, and capitalism is not a new phenomena, at this time I believe the theory, critique, and activism around antiglobalization has to be a key factor for feminists. This does not mean that the patriarchal and racist relations and structures that accompany capitalism are any less problematic at this time, or that antiglobalization is a singular phenomenon. Along with many other scholars and activists, I believe capital as it functions now depends on as well as exacerbates racist, patriarchal, and heterosexist relations of rule.

Feminist Methodologies: New Directions

What kinds of feminist methodology and analytic strategy are useful in making power (and women's lives) visible in overtly non-gendered, non-racialized discourses? The strategy discussed here is an example of how capitalism and its various relations of rule can be analyzed through a transnational, anticapitalist, feminist critique, one that draws on historical materialism and centralizes racialized gender. This analysis begins from and is anchored in the place of the most marginalized communities of women—poor women of all colors in affluent and neocolonial nations: women of the Third World/South or the Two-Thirds World.[16] I believe that this experiential and analytic anchor in the lives of marginalized communities of women provides the most inclusive paradigm for thinking about social justice. This particularized viewing allows for a more concrete and expansive vision of universal justice.

This is the very opposite of "special interest" thinking. If we pay attention to and think from the space of some of the most disenfranchised communities of women in the world, we are most likely to envision a just and democratic society capable of treating all its citizens fairly. Conversely, if we begin our analysis from, and limit it to, the space of privileged communities, our visions of justice are more likely to be exclusionary because privilege nurtures blindness of those without the same privileges. Beginning from the lives and interests of marginalized communities of women, I am able to access and make the workings of power visible—to read up the ladder of privilege. It is more necessary to look upward—colonized peoples must know themselves and the colonizer. This particular marginalized location makes the politics of knowledge and the power investments that go along with it visible so that we can then engage in work to transform the use and abuse of power. The analysis draws on the notion of epistemic privilege as it is developed by feminist standpoint theorists (with their roots in the historical materialism of Marx and Lukacs) as well as postpositivist realists, who provide an analysis of experience, identity, and the epistemic effects of social location.[17] My view is thus a materialist and "realist" one and is antithetical to that of postmodernist relativism. I believe there are causal links between marginalized social locations and experiences and the ability of human agents to explain and analyze features of capitalist society. Methodologically, this analytic perspective is grounded in historical materialism. My claim is not that all marginalized locations yield crucial knowledge about power and inequity, but that within a tightly integrated capitalist system, the particular standpoint of poor indigenous and Third World/South women provides the most inclusive viewing of systemic power. In numerous cases of environmental racism, for instance, where the neighborhoods of poor communities of color are targeted as new sites for prisons and toxic dumps, it is no coincidence that poor black, Native American, and Latina women provide the leadership in the fight against corporate pollution. Three out of five Afro-Americans and Latinos live near toxic waste sites, and three of the five largest hazardous waste landfills are in communities with a population that is 80 percent people of color.[18] Thus it is precisely their critical reflections on their everyday lives as poor women of color that allow the kind of analysis of the power structure that has led to the many victories in environmental racism struggles. Herein lies a lesson for feminist analysis.

Feminist scientist Vandana Shiva, one of the most visible leaders of the antiglobalization movement, provides a similar and illuminating critique of the patents and intellectual property rights agreements sanctioned by the World Trade Organization (WTO) since 1995.[19] Along with others in the environmental and indigenous rights movements, she argues that the WTO sanctions biopiracy and engages in intellectual piracy by privileging the claims of corporate commercial interests, based on Western systems of knowledge in agriculture and medicine, to products and innovations derived from indigenous knowledge traditions. Thus, through the definition of Western scientific epistemologies as the only legitimate scientific system, the WTO is able to underwrite corporate patents to indigenous knowledge (as to the Neem tree in India) as their own intellectual property, protected through intellectual property rights agreements. As a result, the patenting of drugs derived from indigenous medicinal systems has now reached massive proportions. I quote Shiva: "Through patenting, indigenous knowledge is being pirated in the name of protecting knowledge and preventing piracy. The knowledge of our ancestors, of our peasants about seeds is being claimed as an invention of U.S. corporations and U.S. scientists and patented by them. The only reason something like that can work is because underlying it all is a racist framework that says the knowledge of the Third World and the knowledge of people of color is not knowledge. When that knowledge is taken by white men who have capital, suddenly creativity begins. . . . Patents are a replay of colonialism, which is now called globalization and free trade."[20] The contrast between Western scientific systems and indigenous epistemologies and systems of medicine is not the only issue here. It is the colonial and corporate power to define Western science and the reliance on capitalist values of private property and profit as the only normative system that result in the exercise of this immense power. Thus, indigenous knowledges, which are often communally generated and shared among tribal and peasant women for domestic, local and public use, are subject to the ideologies of a corporate Western scientific paradigm where intellectual property rights can only be understood in possessive or privatized form. All innovations that happen to be collective, to have occurred over time in forests and farms are appropriated or excluded. The idea of an intellectual commons where knowledge is collectively gathered and passed on for the benefit of all, not owned privately, is the very opposite of the notion of private property and ownership that is the basis for the WTO property rights agreements. Thus, this idea of an intellectual commons among tribal and peasant women actually excludes them from ownership and facilitates corporate biopiracy.

Shiva's analysis of intellectual property rights, biopiracy, and globalization is made possible by its very location in the experiences and epistemologies of peasant and tribal women in India. Beginning from the practices and knowledges of indigenous women, she "reads up" the power structure, all the way to the policies and practices sanctioned by the WTO. This is a very clear example, then, of a transnational, anticapitalist feminist politics.

However, Shiva says less about gender than she could. She is after all talking in particular about women's work and knowledges anchored in the epistemological experiences of one of the most marginalized communities of women in the world—poor tribal and peasant women in India.

These particular examples offer the most inclusive paradigm for understanding the motivations and effects of globalization as it is crafted by the WTO. Of course, if we were to attempt the same analysis from the epistemological space of Western corporate interests, it would be impossible to generate an analysis which values indigenous knowledge anchored in communal relationships rather than profit-based hierarchies. Thus, poor tribal and peasant women, and their knowledges and interests, would be invisible in this analytic frame because the very idea of an intellectual commons falls outside the purview of privatized property and profit that is a basis for corporate interests. The obvious issue for a transnational feminism without borders pertains to the visions of profit and justice embodied in these opposing analytic perspectives. The focus on profit versus justice illustrates my earlier point about social location and analytically inclusive methodologies. It is the social location of the tribal women as explicated by Shiva that allows this broad and inclusive focus on justice. Similarly, it is the social location and narrow self-interest of corporations that privatizes intellectual property rights in the name of profit for elites.

Shiva essentially offers a critique of the global privatization of indigenous knowledges. This is a story about the rise of transnational institutions like the WTO, the World Bank, and the International Monetary Fund (IMF), of banking and financial institutions and cross-national governing bodies like the MAI (Multinational Agreement on Investments). The effects of these governing bodies on poor people around the world have been devastating. In fundamental ways, it is girls and women around the world, and especially in the Third World/South, that bear the brunt of globalization. Poor women and girls are the hardest hit by the degradation of environmental conditions, wars, famines, privatization of services and deregulation of governments, the dismantling of welfare states, the restructuring of paid and unpaid work, increasing surveillance and incarceration in prisons, and so on. And this is why a feminism without and beyond borders is necessary to address the injustices of global capitalism.

Women and girls are still 70 percent of the world's poor and the majority of the world's refugees. Girls and women comprise almost 80 percent of displaced persons of the Third World/South in Africa, Asia, and Latin America.[21] It is especially on the bodies of women and girls from the Third World/South—the Two-Thirds World—that global capitalism writes its script, and it is by paying attention to and theorizing the contextual experiences of the bodies of these communities of women and girls that we demystify capitalism as a system of debilitating sexism and racism and envision anticapitalist resistance. Thus, any analysis of the effects of globalization needs to centralize the experiences and struggles of these particular communities of women and girls.

Drawing on Arif Dirlik's notion of "place consciousness as the radical other of global capitalism," Grace Lee Boggs makes an important argument for place-based civic activism that illustrates how centralizing the struggles of marginalized communities connects to larger antiglobalization struggles.[22] Boggs suggest that "place consciousness . . . encourages us to come together around common, local experiences and organize around our hopes for the future of our communities and cities. While global capitalism doesn't give a damn about the people or the natural environment of any particular place because it can always move on to other people and other places, place-based civic activism is concerned about the health and safety of people and places."[23] Since women are central to the life of neighborhoods and communities, they assume leadership positions in these struggles.

I do not wish to leave this discussion of capitalism as a generalized site without contextualizing its meaning in and through the lives it structures. Disproportionately, these are girls' and women's lives, although I am committed to the lives of all exploited peoples. However, the specificity of girls' and women's lives encompasses the others through their particularized and contextualized experiences. If these particular gendered, classed, and racialized realities of globalization are unseen and undertheorized, even the most radical critiques of globalization effectively render Third World/South women and girls as absent. Perhaps it is no longer simply an issue of Western eyes, but rather how the West is inside and continually reconfigures globally, racially, and in terms of gender. Without this recognition, a necessary link between feminist scholarship/analytic frames and organizing/activist projects is impossible. Faulty and inadequate analytic frames engender ineffective political action and strategizing for social transformation.

What does the above analysis suggest? That we—feminist scholars and teachers—must respond to the phenomenon of globalization as an urgent site for the recolonization of peoples, especially in the Two-Thirds World. Globalization colonizes women's as well as men's lives around the world, and we need an anti-imperialist, anticapitalist, and contextualized feminist project to expose and make visible the various overlapping forms of subjugation of women's lives. Activists and scholars must also identify and reenvision forms of collective resistance that women, especially, in their different communities enact in their everyday lives. It is their particular exploitation at this time as well as their particular forms of solidarity that can be the basis for re-imagining a liberatory politics for the start of this century.

Antiglobalization Struggles

Although the context for writing "Under Western Eyes" in the mid 1980s was a visible and activist women's movement, this radical movement no longer exists as such. Instead, I draw inspiration from a more distanced, but significant antiglobalization movement in the United States and around the world. Activists in these movements are often women, although the movement is not gender focused. So I wish to redefine the project of decolonization, not reject it. It appears more complex to me today given the newer developments of global capitalism. Given the complex interweaving of cultural forms, people of and from the Third World live not only under Western eyes, but within them. This shift in my focus from "under Western eyes" to "under and inside" the hegemonic spaces of the One-Third World necessitates re-crafting the project of decolonization.

My focus is thus no longer just the colonizing effects of Western feminist scholarship. This does not mean the problems I identified in the earlier essay do not occur now. But the phenomena I addressed then has been more than adequately engaged by other feminist scholars. While feminists have been involved in the antiglobalization movement from the start, this has not been a major organizing locus for women's movements nationally in the West/North. It has, however, always been a locus of struggle for women of the Third World/South because of their location. Again, this contextual specificity should constitute the larger vision. Women of the Two-Thirds World have always organized against the devastations of globalized capital, just as they have always historically organized anticolonial and antiracist movements. In this sense they have always spoken for humanity as a whole.

I have tried to chart feminist sites for engaging globalization, rather than providing a comprehensive review of feminist work in this area. I hope that this exploration makes my own political choices and decisions transparent and that it provides readers with a productive and provocative space to think and act creatively for feminist struggle. So today my query is slightly different although much the same as in 1986. I wish to better see the processes of corporate globalization and how and why they recolonize women's bodies and labor. We need to know the real and concrete effects of global restructuring on raced, classed, national, sexual bodies of women in the academy, in workplaces, streets, households, cyberspaces, neighborhoods, prisons, and social movements.

What does it mean to make antiglobalization a key factor for feminist theorizing and struggle? To illustrate my thinking about antiglobalization, let me focus on two specific sites where knowledge about globalization is produced. The first site is a pedagogical one and involves an analysis of the various strategies being used to internationalize (or globalize) the women's studies curriculum in U.S. colleges and universities.[24] I argue that this move to internationalize women's studies curricula and the attendant pedagogies that flow from this is one of the main ways we can track a discourse of global feminism in the United States. Other ways of tracking global feminist discourses include analyzing the documents and discussions flowing out of the Beijing United Nations conference on women and, of course, popular television and print discourses on women around the world. The second site of antiglobalization scholarship I focus on is the emerging, notably ungendered and deracialized discourse on activism against globalization.

Antiglobalization Pedagogies

Let me turn to the struggles over the dissemination of a feminist cross-cultural knowledge base through pedagogical strategies "internationalizing" the women's studies curriculum. The problem of "the (gendered) color line" remains, but is more easily seen today as developments of transnational and global capital. While I choose to focus on women's studies curricula, my arguments hold for curricula in any discipline or academic field that seeks to internationalize or globalize its curriculum. I argue that the challenge for internationalizing women's studies is no different from the one involved in racializing women's studies in the 1980s, for very similar politics of knowledge come into play here.

So the question I want to foreground is the politics of knowledge in bridging the local and the global in women's studies. How we teach the "new" scholarship in women's studies is at least as important as the scholarship itself in the struggles over knowledge and citizenship in the U.S. academy. After all, the way we construct curricula and the pedagogies we use to put such curricula into practice tell a story—or tell many stories. It is the way we position historical narratives of experience in relation to each other—the way we theorize relationality as both historical and simultaneously singular and collective—that determines how and what we learn when we cross cultural and experiential borders.

Drawing on my own work with U.S. feminist academic communities, I describe three pedagogical models used in internationalizing the women's studies curriculum and analyze the politics of knowledge at work. Each of these perspectives is grounded in particular conceptions of the local and the global, of women's agency, and of national identity, and each curricular model presents different stories and ways of crossing borders and building bridges. I suggest that a "comparative feminist studies" or "feminist solidarity" model is the most useful and productive pedagogical strategy for feminist cross-cultural work. It is this particular model that provides a way to theorize a complex relational understanding of experience, location, and history such that feminist cross-cultural work moves through the specific context to construct a real notion of universal and of democratization rather than colonization. It is through this model that we can put into practice the idea of "common differences" as the basis for deeper solidarity across differences and unequal power relations.

Feminist-as-Tourist Model.   This curricular perspective could also be called the "feminist as international consumer" or, in less charitable terms, the "white women's burden" or "colonial discourse" model.[25] It involves a pedagogical strategy in which brief forays are made into non-Euro-American cultures and particular sexist cultural practices addressed from an otherwise Eurocentric women's studies gaze—in other words, the "add women as global victims or powerful women and stir" perspective. This is a perspective in which the primary Euro-American narrative of the syllabus remains untouched, and examples from non-Western or

Third World/South cultures are used to supplement and add to this narrative. The story here is quite old. The effects of this strategy are that students and teachers are left with a clear sense of the difference and distance between the local (defined as self, nation, and Western) and the global (defined as other, non-Western, and transnational). Thus, the local is always grounded in nationalist assumptions—the United States or a western European nation-state provides a normative context. This strategy leaves power relations and hierarchies untouched since ideas about center and margin are reproduced along Eurocentric lines.

For example, in an introductory feminist studies course, one could include the obligatory day or week on dowry deaths in India, women workers in Nike factories in Indonesia, or precolonial matriarchies in West Africa, while leaving the fundamental identity of the Euro-American feminist on her way to liberation untouched. Thus, Indonesian workers in Nike factories or dowry deaths in India stand in for the totality of women in these cultures. These women are not seen in their everyday lives (as Euro-American women are)—just in these stereotypical terms. Difference in the case of non-Euro-American women is thus congealed, not seen contextually with all of its contradictions. This model is the pedagogical counterpart of the orientalizing and colonizing Western feminist scholarship of the past decades. In fact, it may remain the predominant model at this time. Thus, implicit in this pedagogical strategy is the crafting of the "Third World difference," the creation of monolithic images of Third World/South women. This contrasts with images of Euro-American women, who are vital, changing, complex, and central subjects within such a curricular perspective.

Feminist-as-Explorer Model.   This particular pedagogical perspective originates in area studies, where the "foreign" woman is the object and subject of knowledge and the larger intellectual project is entirely about countries other than the United States. Thus, here the local and the global are both defined as non-Euro-American. The focus on the international implies that it exists outside the U.S. nation-state. Women's, gender, and feminist issues are based on spatial/geographical and temporal/historical categories located elsewhere. Distance from "home" is fundamental to the definition of international in this framework. This strategy can result in students and teachers being left with a notion of difference and separateness, a sort of "us and them" attitude; but, unlike the tourist model, the explorer perspective can provide a deeper, more contextual understanding of feminist issues in discretely defined geographical and cultural spaces. However, unless these discrete spaces are taught in relation to one another, the story told is usually a cultural relativist one, meaning that differences between cultures are discrete and relative with no real connection or common basis for evaluation. The local and the global are here collapsed into the international that by definition excludes the United States. If the dominant discourse is the discourse of cultural relativism, questions of power, agency, justice, and common criteria for critique and evaluation are silenced.[26]

In women's studies curricula this pedagogical strategy is often seen as the most culturally sensitive way to internationalize the curriculum. For instance, entire courses on women in Latin America or Third World women's literature or postcolonial feminism are added on to the predominantly U.S.-based curriculum as a way to globalize the feminist knowledge base. These courses can be quite sophisticated and complex studies, but they are viewed as entirely separate from the intellectual project of U.S. race and ethnic studies. The United States is not seen as part of "area studies," as white is not a color when one speaks of people of color. This is probably related to the particular history of institutionalization of area studies in the U.S. academy and its ties to U.S. imperialism.[27]

The problem with the feminist-as-explorer strategy is that globalization is an economic, political, and ideological phenomenon that actively brings the world and its various communities under connected and interdependent discursive and material regimes. The lives of women are connected and interdependent, albeit not the same, no matter which geographical area we happen to live in.

Separating area studies from race and ethnic studies thus leads to understanding or teaching about the global as a way of not addressing internal racism, capitalist hegemony, colonialism, and heterosexualization as central to processes of global domination, exploitation, and resistance. Global or international is thus understood apart from racism—as if racism were not central to processes of globalization and relations of rule at this time. An example of this pedagogical strategy in the context of the larger curriculum is the usual separation of "world cultures" courses from race and ethnic studies courses. Thus, identifying the kinds of representations of (non-Euro-American) women mobilized by this pedagogical strategy and the relation of these representations to implicit images of First World/North women are important foci for analysis. What kind of power is being exercised in this strategy? What kinds of ideas of agency and struggle are being consolidated? What are the potential effects of a kind of cultural relativism on our understandings of the differences and commonalities among communities of women around the world? Thus, the feminist-as-explorer model has its own problems, and I believe this is an inadequate way of building a feminist cross-cultural knowledge base because in the context of an interwoven world with clear directionalities of power and domination, cultural relativism serves as an apology for the exercise of power.

The Feminist Solidarity or Comparative Feminist Studies Model.   This curricular strategy is anchored in the premise that the local and the global are not defined in terms of physical geography or territory, but exist simultaneously and constitute each other. It is then the links, the relationships, between the local and the global that are foregrounded, and these links are conceptual, material, temporal, contextual, and so on. This framework assumes a comparative focus and analysis of the directionality of power no matter what the subject of the women's studies course is—and it assumes both distance and proximity (specific/universal) as its analytic strategy.

Differences and commonalities thus exist in relation and tension with each other in all contexts. What is emphasized are relations of mutuality, coresponsibility, and common interests, anchoring the idea of feminist solidarity. For example, within this model, one would not teach a U.S. women of color course with additions on Third World/South or white women, but a comparative course which shows the interconnectedness of the histories, experiences, and struggles of U.S. women of color, white women, and women from the Third World/South. By doing this kind of comparative teaching that is attentive to power, each historical experience illuminates the experiences of the others. Thus, the focus is not just on the intersections of race, class, gender, nation, and sexuality in different communities of women, but on mutuality and coimplication, which suggest attentiveness to the interweaving of the histories of these communities. In addition the focus is simultaneously on individual and collective experiences of oppression and exploitation and of struggle and resistance.

Students potentially move away from the "add and stir" and the relativist "separate but equal" (or different) to the coimplication/solidarity perspective. This solidarity perspective requires understanding the historical and experiential specificities and differences of women's lives as well as the historical and experiential connections between women from different national, racial, and cultural communities. Thus it suggests organizing syllabi around social and economic processes and histories of various communities of women in particular substantive areas, like sex work, militarization, environmental justice, the prison/industrial complex, and human rights, and looking for points of contact and connection as well as disjuncture. It is important to always foreground not just the connections of domination, but those of struggle and resistance as well.

In the feminist solidarity model, the One-Third/Two-Thirds World paradigm makes sense. Rather than Western/Third World or North/South or local/global seen as oppositional and incommensurate categories, the One-Third/Two-Thirds World differentiation allows for teaching and learning about points of connection and distance among and between communities of women marginalized and privileged along numerous local and global dimensions. Thus, the very notion of inside/outside necessary to the distance between local/global is transformed through the use of a One-Third/Two-Thirds World paradigm, as both categories must be understood as containing differences/similarities, inside/outside and distance/proximity. Thus, sex work, militarization, human rights, and so on, can be framed in their multiple local and global dimensions using the One-Third/Two-Thirds World, social minority/social majority paradigm. I am suggesting, then, that we look at the women's studies curriculum in its entirety and that we attempt to use a comparative feminist studies model wherever possible.[28]

I refer to this model as the feminist solidarity model because, besides its focus on mutuality and common interests, it requires one to formulate questions about connection and disconnection between activist women's movements around the world. Rather than formulating activism and agency in terms of discrete and disconnected cultures and nations, it allows us to frame agency and resistance across the borders of nation and culture. I think feminist pedagogy should not simply expose students to a particularized academic scholarship, but that it should also envision the possibility of activism and struggle outside the academy. Political education through feminist pedagogy should teach active citizenship in such struggles for justice.

My recurring question is how pedagogies can supplement, consolidate, or resist the dominant logic of globalization. How do students learn about the inequities among women and men around the world? For instance, traditional liberal and liberal feminist pedagogies disallow historical and comparative thinking, radical feminist pedagogies often singularize gender, and Marxist pedagogy silences race and gender in its focus on capitalism. I look to create pedagogies that allow students to see the complexities, singularities, and interconnections between communities of women such that power, privilege, agency, and dissent can be engaged with and made visible.

In an instructive critique of postcolonial studies and its institutional location, Arif Dirlik argues that the particular institutional history of postcolonial studies as well as its conceptual emphases on the historical and local as against the systemic and the global permit its assimilation into the logic of globalism.[29] While Dirlik somewhat overstates his argument, deradicalization and assimilation should concern those of us involved in the feminist project. Feminist pedagogies of internationalization need an adequate response to globalization. Both Eurocentric and cultural relativist (postmodernist) models of scholarship and teaching are easily assimilated within the logic of late capitalism because this is fundamentally a logic of seeming decentralization and accumulation of differences. What I call the comparative feminist studies/feminist solidarity model, on the other hand, potentially counters this logic by setting up a paradigm of historically and culturally specific "common differences" as the basis for analysis and solidarity. Feminist pedagogies of antiglobalization can tell alternate stories of difference, culture, power, and agency. They can begin to theorize experience, agency, and justice from a more cross-cultural lens.[30]

After almost two decades of teaching feminist studies in U.S. classrooms, it is clear to me that the way we theorize experience, culture, and subjectivity in relation to histories, institutional practice, and collective struggles determines the kind of stories we tell in the classroom. If these varied stories are to be taught such that students learn to democratize rather than colonize the experiences of different spatially and temporally located communities of women, neither a Eurocentric nor a cultural pluralist curricular practice will do. In fact, narratives of historical experience are crucial to political thinking not because they present an unmediated version of the "truth" but because they can destabilize received truths and locate debate in the complexities and contradictions of historical life. It is in this context that postpositivist, realist theorizations of experience, identity, and culture become useful in constructing curricular and pedagogical narratives that address as well as combat globalization. These realist theorizations explicitly link a historical materialist understanding of social location to the theorization of epistemic privilege and the construction of social identity, thus suggesting the complexities of the narratives of marginalized peoples in terms of relationality rather than separation. These are the kinds of stories we need to weave into a feminist solidarity pedagogical model.

Antiglobalization Scholarship and Movements

Women's and girl's bodies determine democracy: free from violence and sexual abuse, free from malnutrition and environmental degradation, free to plan their families, free to not have families, free to choose their sexual lives and preferences.
Zillah Eisenstein, *Global Obscenities: Patriarchy, Capitalism, and the Lure of Cyberfantasy*

There is now an increasing and useful feminist scholarship critical of the practices and effects of globalization. Instead of attempting a comprehensive review of this scholarship, I want to draw attention to some of the most useful kinds of issues it raises. Let me turn, then, to a feminist reading of antiglobalization movements and argue for a more intimate, closer alliance between women's movements, feminist pedagogy, cross-cultural feminist theorizing, and these ongoing anticapitalist movements.

I return to an earlier question: What are the concrete effects of global restructuring on the "real" raced, classed, national, sexual bodies of women in the academy, in workplaces, streets, households, cyberspaces, neighborhoods, prisons, and in social movements? And how do we recognize these gendered effects in movements against globalization? Some of the most complex analyses of the centrality of gender in understanding economic globalization attempt to link questions of subjectivity, agency, and identity with those of political economy and the state. This scholarship argues persuasively for the need to rethink patriarchies and hegemonic masculinities in relation to present-day globalization and nationalisms, and it also attempts to retheorize the gendered aspects of the refigured relations of the state, the market, and civil society by focusing on unexpected and unpredictable sites of resistance to the often devastating effects of global restructuring on women.[31] And it draws on a number of disciplinary paradigms and political perspectives in making the case for the centrality of gender in processes of global restructuring, arguing that the reorganization of gender is part of the global strategy of capitalism.

Women workers of particular caste/class, race, and economic status are necessary to the operation of the capitalist global economy. Women are not only the preferred candidates for particular jobs, but particular kinds of women—poor, Third World and Two-Thirds World, working-class, and immigrant/migrant women—are the preferred workers in these global, "flexible," temporary job markets. The documented increase in the migration of poor, Third/Two-Thirds World women in search of labor across national borders has led to a rise in the international "maid trade" and in international sex trafficking and tourism.[32] Many global cities now require and completely depend on the service and domestic labor of immigrant and migrant women. The proliferation of structural adjustment policies around the world has reprivatized women's labor by shifting the responsibility for social welfare from the state to the household and to women located there. The rise of religious fundamentalisms in conjunction with conservative nationalisms, which are also in part reactions to global capital and its cultural demands, has led to the policing of women's bodies in the streets and in the workplaces.

Global capital also reaffirms the color line in its newly articulated class structure evident in the prisons in the One-Third World. The effects of globalization and deindustrialization on the prison industry in the One-Third World lead to a related policing of the bodies of poor, Third/Two-Thirds World, immigrant, and migrant women behind the concrete spaces and bars of privatized prisons. Angela Davis and Gina Dent argue that the political economy of U.S. prisons and the punishment industry in the West/North bring the intersection of gender, race, colonialism, and capitalism into sharp focus.[33] Just as the factories and workplaces of global corporations seek and discipline the labor of poor, Third World/South, immigrant/migrant women, the prisons of Europe and United States incarcerate disproportionately large numbers of women of color, immigrants, and noncitizens of African, Asian, and Latin American descent.

Making gender and power visible in the processes of global restructuring demands looking at, naming, and seeing the particular raced and classed communities of women from poor countries as they are constituted as workers in sexual, domestic, and service industries: as prisoners, household managers, and nurturers. In contrast to this production of workers, Patricia Fernández-Kelly and Diane Wolf focus on communities of black U.S. inner-city youth situated as "redundant" to the global economy.[34] This redundancy is linked to their disproportionate representation in U.S. prisons. There is also increased feminist attention to the way discourses of globalization are themselves gendered and the way hegemonic masculinities are produced and mobilized in the service of global restructuring. Marianne Marchand and Anne Runyan discuss the gendered metaphors and symbolism in the language of globalization whereby particular actors and sectors are privileged over others, naturalizing the hierarchies required for globalization to succeed.[35] Charlotte Hooper identifies an emerging hegemonic Anglo-American masculinity through processes of global restructuring.[36]

While feminist scholarship is moving in important and useful directions in terms of a critique of global restructuring and the culture of globalization, I want to ask some of the same questions I posed in 1986 once again. In spite of the occasional exception, I think that much of present-day scholarship tends to reproduce particular "globalized" representations of women. Just as there is an Anglo-American masculinity produced in and by discourses of globalization, it is important to ask what the corresponding femininities being produced are. Clearly, there is the ubiquitous global teenage girl factory worker, the domestic worker, and the sex worker. There is also the migrant/immigrant service worker, the refugee, the victim of war crimes, the woman-of-color prisoner who happens to be a mother and drug user, the consumer-housewife, and so on. There is also the mother-of-the-nation/religious bearer of traditional culture and morality.

Although these representations of women correspond to real people, they also often stand in for the contradictions and complexities of women's lives and roles. Certain images, such as that of the factory or sex worker, are often geographically located in the Third World/South, but many of the representations identified above are dispersed throughout the globe. Most refer to women of the Two-Thirds World, and some to women of the One-Third World. And a woman from the Two-Thirds World can live in the One-Third World. The point I am making here is that women are workers, mothers, or consumers in the global economy, but we are also all those things simultaneously. Singular and monolithic categorizations of women in discourses of globalization circumscribe ideas about experience, agency, and struggle. While there are other relatively new images of women that also emerge in this discourse—the human rights worker or the NGO advocate, the revolutionary militant, and the corporate bureaucrat—there is also a divide between false, overstated images of victimized and empowered womanhood, and they negate each other. We need to further explore how this divide plays itself out in terms of a social majority/minority, One-Third/Two-Thirds World characterization. The concern here is with whose agency is being colonized and who is privileged in these pedagogies and scholarship. These, then, are my new queries for the twenty-first century.[37]

Because social movements are crucial sites for the construction of knowledge, communities, and identities, it is very important for feminists to direct themselves toward them. The antiglobalization movements of the last five years have proven that one does not have to be a multinational corporation, controller of financial capital, or transnational governing institution to cross national borders. These movements form an important site for examining the construction of transborder democratic citizenship. But first a brief characterization of antiglobalization movements is in order.

Unlike the territorial anchors of the anticolonial movements of the early twentieth century, antiglobalization movements have numerous spatial and social origins. These include anticorporate environmental movements such as the Narmada Bachao Andolan in central India and movements against environmental racism in the U.S. Southwest, as well as the antiagribusiness small-farmer movements around the world. The 1960s consumer movements, people's movements against the IMF and World Bank for debt cancellation and against structural adjustment programs, and the antisweatshop student movements in Japan, Europe, and the United States are also a part of the origins of the antiglobalization movements. In addition, the identity-based social movements of the late twentieth century (feminist, civil rights, indigenous rights, etc.) and the transformed U.S. labor movement of the 1990s also play a significant part in terms of the history of antiglobalization movements.[38]

While women are present as leaders and participants in most of these antiglobalization movements, a feminist agenda only emerges in the post-Beijing "women's rights as human rights" movement and in some peace and environmental justice movements. In other words, while girls and women are central to the labor of global capital, antiglobalization work does not seem to draw on feminist analysis or strategies. Thus, while I have argued that feminists need to be anticapitalists, I would now argue that antiglobalization activists and theorists also need to be feminists. Gender is ignored as a category of analysis and a basis for organizing in most of the antiglobalization movements, and antiglobalization (and anticapitalist critique) does not appear to be central to feminist organizing projects, especially in the First World/North. In terms of women's movements, the earlier "sisterhood is global" form of internationalization of the women's movement has now shifted into the "human rights" arena. This shift in language from "feminism" to "women's rights" can be called the mainstreaming of the feminist movement— a (successful) attempt to raise the issue of violence against women on to the world stage.

If we look carefully at the focus of the antiglobalization movements, it is the bodies and labor of women and girls that constitute the heart of these struggles. For instance, in the environmental and ecological movements, such as Chipko in India, and indigenous movements against uranium mining and against breast-milk contamination in the United States, women are not only among the leadership: their gendered and racialized bodies are the key to demystifying and combating the processes of recolonization put in place by corporate control of the environment. My earlier discussion of Vandana Shiva's analysis of the WTO and biopiracy from the epistemological place of Indian tribal and peasant women illustrates this claim, as does Grace Lee Boggs's notion of "place-based civic activism."[39] Similarly, in the anticorporate consumer movements and in the small farmer movements against agribusiness and the antisweatshop movements, it is women's labor and their bodies that are most affected as workers, farmers, and consumers/household nurturers.

Women have been in leadership roles in some of the cross-border alliances against corporate injustice. Thus, making gender and women's bodies and labor visible and theorizing this visibility as a process of articulating a more inclusive politics are crucial aspects of feminist anticapitalist critique. Beginning from the social location of poor women of color of the Two-Thirds World is an important, even crucial, place for feminist analysis; it is precisely the potential epistemic privilege of these communities of women that opens up the space for demystifying capitalism and for envisioning transborder social and economic justice.

The masculinization of the discourses of globalization analyzed by Hooper and Marchand and Runyan seems to be matched by the implicit masculinization of the discourses of antiglobalization movements.[40] While much of the literature on antiglobalization movements marks the centrality of class and race and, at times, nation in the critique and fight against global capitalism, racialized gender is still an unmarked category.

On the other hand, many of the democratic practices and process-oriented aspects of feminism appear to be institutionalized into the decision-making processes of some of these movements. Thus, the principles of non-hierarchy, democratic participation, and the notion of the personal being political all emerge in various ways in this antiglobal politics. Making gender and feminist agendas and projects explicit in such antiglobalization movements thus is a way of crafting a more accurate genealogy as well as providing potentially more fertile ground for organizing. And, of course, to articulate feminism within the framework of antiglobalization work is also to begin to challenge the unstated masculinism of this work. The critique and resistance to global capitalism, and uncovering of the naturalization of its masculinist and racist values, begins to build a transnational feminist practice.

A transnational feminist practice depends on building feminist solidarities across the divisions of place, identity, class, work, belief, and so on. In these very fragmented times it is both very difficult to build these alliances and also never more important to do so. Global capitalism both destroys the possibilities and also offers up new ones.

Feminist activist teachers must struggle with themselves and each other to open the world with all its complexity to their students. Given the new multiethnic, racial student bodies, teachers must also learn from their students. The differences and borders of each of our identities connect us to each other, more than they sever. So the enterprise here is to forge informed, self-reflexive solidarities among ourselves.

I no longer live simply under the gaze of Western eyes. I also live inside it and negotiate it every day. I make my home in Ithaca, New York, but always as from Mumbai, India. My cross-race and cross-class work takes me to interconnected places and communities around the world—to a struggle contextualized by women of color and of the "Third World," sometimes located in the Two-Thirds World, sometimes in the One-Third World. So the borders here are not really fixed. Our minds must be as ready to move as capital is, to trace its paths and to imagine alternative destinations.

Notes

Chandra Talpade Mohanty's "'Under Western Eyes' Revisited: Feminist Solidarity through Anticapitalist Struggles," in *Feminism without Borders: Decolonizing Theory, Practicing Solidarity,* 221–251, copyright 2003 by Duke University Press, is used by permission of the publisher and has been edited. It also previously appeared in *Signs: Journal of Women in Culture and Society* 28, no. 2 (2002): 499–535.

This chapter in its present form owes much to many years of conversation and collaboration with Zillah Eisenstein, Satya Mohanty, Jacqui Alexander, Lisa Lowe, Margo Okazawa-Rey, Beverly Guy-Sheftall, and Ella Shohat. Zillah Eisenstein's friendship has been crucial in my writing this chapter—she was the first person to suggest I do so.

1. "Under Western Eyes" has enjoyed a remarkably multiple life, being reprinted almost every year since 1986, when it first appeared in the leftist journal *Boundary 2* 12, no. 3 (1986): 333–358. The essay has been translated into German, Dutch, Chinese, Russian, Italian, Swedish, French, and Spanish. It has appeared in feminist, postcolonial, Third World, and cultural studies journals and anthologies and maintains a presence in women's studies, cultural studies, anthropology, ethnic studies, political science, education, and sociology curricula. It has been widely cited, sometimes seriously engaged with, sometimes misread, and sometimes used as an enabling framework for cross-cultural feminist projects.

2. Thanks to Zillah Eisenstein for this distinction.

3. I use the terms "Western feminism," "First World," and "Third World" with full knowledge of their limitations, suggesting a critical rather than self-evident, monolithic, or non-questioning use of the terms.

4. Maria Mies, *The Lace Makers of Narsapur: Indian Housewives Produce for the World Market* (London: Zed Books, 1982).

5. See Sylvia Walby, "Beyond the Politics of Location: The Power of Argument," *Feminist Theory* 1, no. 2 (2000): 109–207.

6. Ibid., 199.

7. See Rita Felski, "The Doxa of Difference," *Signs* 23, no. 1 (1997): 1–21; and Radhika Mohanram, *Black Body: Women, Colonialism, and Space* (Minneapolis: University of Minnesota Press, 1999), 91.

8. Linda Nicholson and Steven Seidman, eds., *Social Postmodernism: Beyond Identity Politics* (Cambridge: Cambridge University Press, 1995); Robyn Warhol and Diane Price Herndal, eds., *Feminisms: An Anthology of Literary Theory and Criticism* (New Brunswick, N.J.: Rutgers University Press, 1997); and Anne Phillips, ed., *Feminism and Politics* (Oxford: Oxford University Press, 1998).

9. I have written with M. Jaqui Alexander about some of the effects of hegemonic postmodernism on feminist studies, in the introduction to *Feminist Genealogies, Colonial Legacies, Democratic Futures,* by M. Jaqui Alexander and Chandra Talpade Mohanty (New York: Routledge, 1997).

10. See, for instance, Michel Foucault, *Power Knowledge: Selected Interviews and Other Writings, 1972–1977,* ed. and trans. Colin Gordon (New York: Pantheon, 1980); Anour Abdel Malek, *Social Dialectics: Nation and Revolution* (Albany: State University of New York Press, 1981); and Mies, *The Lace Makers of Narsapur.*

11. For further discussion of these categories, see the unedited version of this essay in *Signs* 28, no. 2 (2002): 499–535. See also Arif Dirlik, *The Postcolonial Aura: Third World Criticism in the Age of Global Capitalism* (Boulder: Westview, 1997).

12. See Gustavo Esteva and Madhu Suri Prakash, *Grassroots Post-modernism: Remaking the Soil of Cultures* (London: Zed Press, 1998), 16–17.

13. Mohanram, *Black Body.*

14. See Zillah Eisenstein, *Global Obscenities: Patriarchy, Capitalism, and the Lure of Cyberfantasy* (New York: New York University Press, 1998), 1.

15. See, for instance, Ella Shohat, *Talking Visions: Multicultural Feminism in a Transnational Age* (New York: New Museum of Contemporary Art, 1998); Ella Shohat, "Area Studies, Transnationalism, and the Feminist Production of Knowledge," *Signs* 26, no. 4 (2001): 1269–1274; Ella Shohat and Robert Stam, *Unthinking Eurocentrism: Multiculturalism and the Media* (New York: Routledge, 1994); Inderpal Grewal and Caren Kaplan, eds., *Scattered Hegemonies: Postmodernity and Transnational Feminist Practices* (Minneapolis: University of Minnesota Press, 1994); Avtar Brah, *Cartographies of Diaspora: Contesting Identities* (London: Routledge, 1996); Lisa Lowe, *Immigrant Acts: On Asian American Cultural Politics* (Durham: Duke University Press, 1996); Lisa Lowe and David Lloyd, eds., *The Politics of Culture in the Shadow of Capital* (Durham: Duke University Press, 1997); Uma Narayan, *Dislocating Cultures: Identities, Traditions, and Third-World Feminisms* (New York: Routledge, 1997); Lila Abu-Lughod, *Remaking Women: Feminism and Modernity in the Middle East* (Princeton: Princeton University Press, 1998); Kamala Kempadoo, "Introduction: Globalizing Sex Workers' Rights," in *Global Sex Workers: Rights, Resistance, and Redefinition,* ed. Kamala Kempadoo and Jo Doezema (New York: Routledge, 1998), 1–28; Chela Sandoval, *Methodology of the Oppressed* (Minneapolis: University of Minnesota Press, 2000); and M. Jacqui Alexander, *Pedagogies of Crossing* (Durham: Duke University Press, forthcoming).

16. See Zillah Eisenstein, *Against Empire: Feminisms, Racism, and the West* (London: Zed

Press, 2004); Maria Mies, *Patriarchy and Accumulation on a World Scale: Women in the International Division of Labor* (London: Zed Press, 1986); Dorothy E. Smith, *The Everyday World as Problematic: A Feminist Sociology* (Boston: Northeastern University Press, 1987); Cynthia Enloe, *The Morning After: Sexual Politics at the End of the Cold War* (Berkeley: University of California Press, 1993); Saskia Sassen, *Globalization and Its Discontents: Essays on the New Mobility of People and Money* (New York: New Press, 1998). An early pioneering example of this can be found in Combahee River Collective's "A Black Feminist Statement," reprinted in *All the Women Are White, All the Blacks Are Men, But Some of Us Are Brave,* ed. Gloria T. Hull, Patricia Bell Scott, and Barbara Smith (Old Westbury, N.Y.: Feminist Press, 1982).

17. See discussions of epistemic privilege in Paula Moya, "Postmodernism, 'Realism,' and the Politics of Identity: Cherríe Moraga and Chicana Feminism," in *Reclaiming Identity: Realist Theory and the Predicament of Postmodernism,* ed. Paula Moya and Michael Roy Hames-Garcia (Berkeley: University of California Press, 2000), 67–101; Satya P. Mohanty, "The Epistemic Status of Cultural Identity: On *Beloved* and the Postcolonial Condition," in *Reclaiming Identity,* ed. Moya and Hames-Garcia, 29–66; Amie A. Macdonald, "Racial Authenticity and White Separatism: The Future of Racial Program Housing on College Campuses," in *Reclaiming Identity,* ed. Moya and Hames-Garcia, 205–228, see especially 52–68, 80–87, and 211–212.

18. Examples of women of color in the fight against environmental racism can be found in Mary Pardo, "Mexican-American Women, Grassroots Community Activists: 'Mothers of East Lost Angeles'" in *Women's Lives: Multicultural Perspectives,* ed. Gwyn Kirk and Margo Okazawa-Rey (Mountain View, Calif.: Mayfield, 2001), 504–511 in the magazine *ColorLines: Race, Color, Action,* and in *Voces Unidas,* the newsletter of the South West Organizing Project, Albuquerque, New Mexico.

19. Vandana Shiva, Asfar H. Jafri, Gitanjali Bedi, and Radha Holla-Bhar, *The Enclosure and Recovery of the Commons: Biodiversity, Indigenous Knowledge, and Intellectual Property Rights* (New Delhi, India: Research Foundation for Science and Technology, 1997). For a provocative argument about indigenous knowledges, see George J. Sefa Dei, "Rethinking the Role of Indigenous Knowledges in the Academy," *International Journal of Inclusive Education* 4, no. 2 (2000): 111–132.

20. Vandana Shiva, Rebecca Gordon, and Bob Wing, "Global Brahmanism, the Meaning of the WTO Protests: An Interview with Vandana Shiva," *ColorLines: Race, Color, Action* 3, no. 2 (2000): 30–32.

21. Eisenstein, *Global Obscenities,* especially chapter 5.

22. Arlif Drilik, "Place-Based Imagination: Globalism and the Politics of Place," *Review: A Journal of the Ferdinand Braudel Center for the Study of Economics, Historical Systems, and Civilizations* 22, no. 2 (1999): 151–187; and Grace Lee Boggs, "School Violence: A Question of Place," *Monthly Review* 52, no. 2 (2000): 18–20.

23. Boggs, "School Violence," 19.

24. In what follows, I use the terms "global capitalism," "global restructuring," and "globalization" interchangeably to refer to a process of corporate global economic, ideological, and cultural reorganization across the borders of nation-states.

25. Ella Shohat refers to this as the "sponge/additive" approach that extends U.S.-centered paradigms to "others" and produces a "homogeneous feminist master narrative"; see her comments in "Area Studies."

26. For an incisive critique of cultural relativism and its epistemological underpinnings, see Satya P. Mohanty, *Literary Theory and the Claims of History: Postmodernism, Objectivity, Multicultural Politics* (Ithaca, N.Y.: Cornell University Press, 1997).

27. Shohat, "Area Studies," 1271.

28. A new anthology contains some good examples of what I am referring to as a feminist solidarity or comparative feminist studies model. See Mary M. Lay, Janice J. Monk, and Deborah Silverton Rosenfelt, eds., *Encompassing Gender: Integrating International Studies and Women's Studies* (New York: Feminist Press of CUNY, 2002).

29. Arif Dirlik, *After the Revolution: Waking to Global Capitalism* (Hanover, N.H.: Wesleyan University Press, 1994).

30. While I know no other work that conceptualizes this pedagogical strategy in the ways I am doing here, my work is very similar to that of scholars like Ella Shohat, *Talking Visions* and "Area Studies"; Susan Sanchez-Casal and Amie Macdonald, (Introduction to *Twenty-First-Century Feminist Classrooms: Pedagogies of Difference and Identity,* ed. Susan Sánchez-Casal and Amie Macdonald (London: Palgrave, 2002); and Alexander, *Pedagogies of Crossing.*

31. The literature on gender and globalization is vast and I do not pretend to review it in any comprehensive way. I draw on three particular texts to critically summarize what I consider to be the most useful and provocative analyses of this area: Zillah Eisenstein's *Global Obscenities;* Marianne Marchand and Anne Runyan's edited volume, *Gender and Global Restructuring: Sightings, Sites, and Resistances* (New York: Routledge, 2000); and the *Signs* special issue, "Globalization and Gender," 26, no. 4 (2001).

32. Rhacel Salazar Parreñas, "Transgressing the Nation-State: The Partial Citizenship and 'Imagined Global Community' of Migrant Filipina Domestic Workers," *Signs* 26, no. 4 (2001): 1129–1154; see also essays in Kempadoo and Doezema, *Global Sex Workers*; and Jasbir Puar, "Global Circuits: Transnational Sexualities and Trinidad," *Signs* 26, no. 4 (2001): 1039–1067.

33. See Angela Davis and Gina Dent, "Prison as a Border: A Conversation on Gender, Globalization, and Punishment," *Signs* 26, no. 4 (2001): 1235–1241.

34. Patricia Fernandez-Kelly and Diane Wolf, "A Dialogue on Globalization," *Signs* 26, no. 4 (2001): 1243–1249, especially 1248.

35. Marchand and Runyan, *Gender and Global Restructuring*, 13.

36. Charlotte Hooper, "Masculinities in Transition: The Case of Globalization," in *Gender and Global Restructuring*, ed. Marchand and Runyan, 59–73. For similar arguments, see also Suzanne Bergeron, "Political Economy Discourses of Globalization and Feminist Politics," *Signs* 26, no. 4 (2001): 983–1006; and Carla Freeman, "Is Local:Global as Feminine:Masculine? Rethinking the Gender of Globalization," *Signs* 26, no. 4 (2001): 1007–1039.

37. There is also an emerging feminist scholarship that complicates these monolithic "globalized" representations of women. See Amy Lind, "Negotiating Boundaries: Women's Organizations and the Politics of Restructuring in Ecuador," in *Gender and Global Restructuring*, ed. Marchand and Runyan, 161–175; Aili Marie Tripp, "Combining Intercontinental Parenting and Research: Dilemmas and Strategies for Women," *Signs* 27, no. 3 (2002): 793–811; and Aihwa Ong, *Spirits of Resistance and Capitalist Discipline: Factory Women in Malaysia* (Albany: SUNY Press, 1987).

38. This description is drawn from Jeremy Brecher, Tim Costello, and Brendan Smith, *Globalization from Below: The Power of Solidarity* (Cambridge: South End Press, 2000); and from magazines like *ColorLines, Z Magazine, Monthly Review,* and *SWOP Newsletter.*

39. Boggs, "School Violence," 19.

40. See Marchand and Runyon, *Gender and Global Restructuring,* especially Hooper, "Masculinities in Transition," 59–73.

What Does Queer Studies Offer Women's Studies?

THE PROBLEM AND PROMISE OF INSTABILITY

NAN ALAMILLA BOYD

Last semester, I noticed that students in my Introduction to Queer Studies course (Queer Theory/Queer Lives) were just as interested in the *b*-word (bisexuality) as the *q*-word (queer). They perked up when I made references to the history of bisexual movements, and by the end of the semester they began to draw interesting connections between "bi" and "queer." Was bisexuality an identity, they asked, or a conceptual tool that functioned more like "queer"? Eager to embrace the promises of queer theory, they wondered if "bi," a term that many of them claimed as a seamless "sleeps-with-both-sexes" identity at the beginning of the semester, could also function to disrupt identity. Could they use bisexual along with queer as a social and political signifier that refused the history of exclusions associated with lesbian and gay identities? And could bisexual, as an identity-that-deconstructs-itself, function differently than queer? In other words, how different are the identities that comprise the rainbow of queer signifiers? Do lesbian, gay, bisexual, transgender, and queer (LGBTQ) do the same kind of cultural work? Does each of these terms have the same power to forge community and resist oppression?

Not surprisingly, Queer Theory/Queer Lives was developed and funded, as many queer studies courses are, through women's studies—in this case, the Women's and Gender Studies Department at Sonoma State University.[1] The queer studies/women's studies overlap provides an important frame for thinking through my students' theoretical jump from queer theory to bisexuality. I believe the slippage between bi and queer was facilitated by an uneasiness with the category "woman," in that the bi/queer analogy, in its postmodern application, unsettles the knowability of the body and the body's desires. The bi/queer analogy assumes that gender may not clearly follow so-called biological sex in the determination of so-called sexual orientation, and sexual-object choice may, in fact, take a back seat to gender-object choice or multi-gender desire, regardless of bodies and genitals. Over the course of the semester, bisexuality had shifted, in the minds of my students, from a body-based identity to a tool for the interrogation of modern sexual identities. But I wonder why this group of students was so willing to part with the body and the determinacy of the biologically sexed truth of one's self.[2] Interestingly, none of my students were women's and gender studies majors, though several of them later enrolled, and a larger than usual proportion were students of color. I'm wondering if it matters that the word "queer" drew them to women's studies rather than the subject "woman." If so, what does this mean for the future of women's studies? What does queer studies offer women's studies beyond the marketplace value of counting majors and minors (a vital practice at state-funded institutions)? I think the answer lies in the relationship between "gender" and "queer."

Leora Auslander wonders whether "gender" is to women's studies as "queer" is to lesbian and gay studies.[3] In other words, if gender stands for the deconstruction of gendered identities (i.e., male and female), do gender studies challenge the framing paradigm of women's studies in the same way that queer studies challenge the framing paradigm of lesbian and gay studies? What are the features of women's studies and lesbian and gay studies? And what is the political/cultural work of gender studies and queer studies? In this essay, I discuss the relationship between gender studies and queer studies, as emergent academic disciplines, by focusing on the question of origins and the possibilities (and hazards) each brings to its assumed predecessor. Also of interest are questions of institutionalization. Does lesbian and gay studies function similarly to women's studies in the minds of administrators and allies?[4] If so, how do the links between these two fields enable or prohibit questions of globalization as well as linkages to yet another interdisciplinary field, race/ethnic studies? In this essay, I trace the history of how gender studies grew alongside and out of women's studies, and then I compare these developments to the history of how queer studies grew out of and alongside lesbian and gay studies. In comparing these overlapping programmatic developments, I argue that queer studies, like gender studies, has challenged women's studies to move beyond the identity politics implicit in its origins. Queer studies offers women's studies newly fashioned interrogations of the sexed body, and, in doing so, it facilitates a productive tension or ongoing crisis between identity-based studies of oppression and the postmodern or post-humanist deconstruction of identity.

First, let me trace a brief and admittedly incomplete history of the development of these fields. Women's studies is an academic field that grew out of the social and political movements of the 1960s and 1970s. Many early women's studies programs were peopled by instructors housed within traditional disciplines who, because of their participation in women's liberation movements, began to bring the concepts of feminism to campus. As Mari Jo Buhle notes in her introduction to *The Politics of Women's Studies; Testimony from Thirty Founding Mothers,* "For many of the first teachers and students, women's studies and women's liberation were one and the same."[5] Scholars involved in feminist movements noticed the lack of scholarship on women—indeed, the lack of women faculty—on campus, and as they began to incorporate feminist theory and methods into their work, a new field emerged. The inception of women's studies curriculum overlapped with a surge in the number of women seeking higher education—by 1976 women comprised a record 45 percent of undergraduate students on U.S. college campuses—and women's studies courses became an important part of many women's college experience.[6] Inspired by feminist politics and emboldened by the increased raw numbers of women on campus, faculty and students worked hard to have women's studies courses (and programs) recognized and funded by campus administrators. The visibility of women on campus and integration of feminist perspectives within mainstream disciplines thus became two of the earliest goals of women's studies.[7] This was identity politics in action: the recuperation and addition of women to heretofore male institutions.

While women's studies curriculum has always addressed the social construction of gender and the political context of repressive sex/gender systems, what I am calling gender studies is a later phenomenon, the product of the 1980s postmodern or deconstructive turn in the humanities and social sciences. Emerging from within but often positioned at odds with women's studies, gender studies sought to denaturalize gendered bodies and displace the humanist project of early women's studies. Gender studies worked to pull the social construction of gender away from the sexed body and, thus, challenge the relevance of "women" as a coherent subject of study.[8] Gender studies also considers gender to be an intersectional phenomena, codetermined by race, class, sexuality, and nation (among other social and political structures).[9] In addition, gender studies is, purportedly, as interested in men and the social construction of masculinity as it is interested in women and the social construction of femininity.

Post-humanist and deconstructive analysis was not the only theoretical challenge to the identity-based response to oppression that early women's studies programs asserted. In the late 1970s and 1980s, the writings by women of color and lesbians problematized the primacy of gender as a category of analysis and asserted, instead, the interlocking influences of race, class, and sexuality in the lives of women. In the oft-quoted "Combahee River Collective Statement" of 1977, a coalition of black women activists called for a more complex analysis of gender so to account for the ways that race and class mediated gendered power and privilege. Following Combahee, the writings by women-of-color scholars, activists, and poets such as Gloria Anzaldúa, Cherríe Moraga, Angela Davis, Barbara Smith, and Audre Lorde also asserted the material influences of race, class, and sexuality on women's experiences of subjection and disenfranchisement.[10] The social construction of gender, these and many more writers argued, could not be isolated from other vectors of oppression, and the combined impact of multiple identities and social realities rendered "women" a vastly differentiated category, so much so that any assumption about women's commonalities could and should be called into question. The identity basis of women's studies was thus challenged by two traditions: the postmodern challenge to humanist concepts of subjectivity and the materialist challenge by "queer" women of color to the idea that women share the same political interests across race, class, and sexuality.

Lesbian and gay studies never achieved the programmatic status that women's studies has achieved, but it has a similar institutional history, arriving on the scene in the early 1970s. Like women's studies, lesbian and gay studies emerged directly out of the social and political movements of the 1970s, particularly the gay and lesbian liberation movements.[11] The Gay Academic Union, as historian John D'Emilio describes it, was an offshoot from the Gay Activists Alliance (a gay liberation organization), and it functioned to bring together gay and lesbian activists who had academic interests.[12] Like women's studies, early scholarship in lesbian and gay studies focused on recuperating gay and lesbian writers, thinkers, and historical actors, and the act of recuperation took on a politics of its own. Interestingly, many early lesbian and gay studies courses were housed within fledgling women's studies programs, marking an early cooperation between these two political/academic projects. But, by and large, much of the early work in lesbian and gay studies occurred outside of academia, by grassroots scholars, and their work has been incorporated into academia in fits and starts.[13] Lesbian and gay studies, as a result, has a somewhat different institutional history than women's studies: unable to secure support and funding within academic institutions, its attachment to and dependence on social and political movements has remained somewhat stronger.

Queer studies has a different history. It is institutionally similar to gender studies, as Auslander argues, but it has settled in academia much faster, particularly in the humanities. If job lines, publications, and conference presentations are indicators of institutional support, queer studies has, in many ways, superceded its grassroots predecessor, lesbian and gay studies.[14] Like gender studies, deconstructive analysis and challenges to the identity politics of early lesbian and gay movements frame the emergence of queer studies as a field.[15] Crucial to these developments are the writings of Michel Foucault, whose series of books on the history of sexuality provides a rich resource and vital foundation for what has come to be called "queer theory." Foucault argues that the social construction of sexuality is a fairly recent phenomenon in Western cultures, and it is this modern variety of sexual subjectivities that frames the emergence of contemporary homosexual and heterosexual identities. Basically, his theory argues that same-sex sexual behaviors have not always generated the kinds of identities we are familiar with in contemporary Western cultures, and it is important to understand that these modern identities are political tools, useful for the creation and reiteration of modern institutional structures. Sex is power, Foucault argues, and sexual identities make power available (and, conversely, unavailable) to different classes of people at different points in time.[16]

Foucault's theories about the relationship between sex and power resonate with the writings of a host of theorists, activists, and filmmakers who stress the limits of gay, lesbian, bisexual, and transgender identities in that these identities have failed to consistently account for the impact of racialization, globalization, class position, social geography, and embodiment (among other things) on the production of sex, gender, and sexual identities. The coherency of gay, lesbian, bisexual, and transgender identities has become increasingly unstable as questions of AIDS activism, global tourism, transgender politics, and new forms of embodiment have pushed their way from the margins to the center of academic and political discourse.

The development of queer studies (out of lesbian and gay studies) has not followed a single trajectory, and many of the queer studies scholars who teach queer theory work hard to balance the pull between identity politics, campus visibility, student mentoring, and queer theory. Most pertinent to this essay are the tensions that arise as gender studies and queer studies seem to move in on the academic territory of women's studies and lesbian and gay studies, respectively. But these relationships are not so respective because, as I mentioned above, lesbian and gay studies and queer studies are often institutionally situated within or alongside women's and/or gender studies programs, so the overlapping relationships flex and vex in unpredictable ways. What I want to comment on is the so-called generational conflict that emerges when postmodern or intersectional studies stand on the shoulders of identity-based political movements and their attendant academic formations.[17] How can scholars who de-center or de-emphasize the study of (U.S. white, heterosexual, middle-class) women within women's studies co-exist alongside the "foremothers" who built women's studies out of an effective politics of identity? Are the relationships that emerge truly generational? Ideological? Political? Can they be friendly and mutually supportive in an institutional context?

I recognize that there are programs that have handled the disciplinary growth of gender and queer studies much more effectively than the situation I am about to describe, but in my experience—having worked within several women's studies programs, one for almost a decade—the conflicts that emerge can be painfully serious, sometimes to the point of institutional crisis. At the University of Colorado, Boulder, for instance, struggles over the retention of junior faculty—all women of color—occurred at the same time as an implicit resistance to the development of both gender studies and queer studies. These disagreements culminated in an exodus of faculty at all levels (with the significant loss of all five junior women-of-color faculty) and the reduction of a thriving program from eight full-time employees in 2000 to a meager one and a half full-time employees in 2004.[18] At stake, I would argue, were differing definitions of feminism and different visions of women's studies.

As with many programs, the women's studies program at Boulder grew out of the early 1970s feminist/activist interests of students and faculty. As longtime chair Marcia Westkott reports in an institutional history, the program at Boulder began in 1974 with a few cross-listed courses, and it hired its first full-time faculty member in 1983. The program grew very quickly between 1983 and 1994, when it gained several new tenure-track lines and began to push for departmental status and a separate BA degree.[19] In her essay, Westkott describes the difficulties of institutionalization in the context of Colorado's conservative politics—and no doubt this had much to do with what transpired in the early 2000s—but when I arrived as a tenure-track hire in 1993, the program's curriculum was firmly attached to the recuperative scholarship that I associate with early women's studies. Furthermore, while the faculty and students enthusiastically embraced multiculturalism and disavowed heterosexism, they registered general agreement that gender studies and, to a lesser extent, queer studies were either regressive, apolitical, or outside the scope of women's studies.

In 1993, the core curriculum of the women's studies program at Boulder was based on an analysis of white women's oppression, particularly violence against women in the United States, though there were a few adjunct-taught electives that addressed the experiences of U.S. women of color and/or lesbians. In a genuine attempt to address the curriculum's cultural bias, faculty lines were developed to integrate or add information about racial, sexual, and global difference to the core curriculum. For instance, I was hired as a specialist in lesbian and gay history; but, as a Latina with a background in ethnic studies, I also taught courses on Latina social activism. A second person, a specialist on Native American women's religious traditions, was hired to teach courses on Native American women; and yet another, a specialist in the global sex trade, was hired to teach about African American women and develop Gender, Race, and Class, a new introductory course that would function as a companion to the long-standing and U.S.-based Introduction to Feminist Studies. The program also hired a specialist in American studies (originally from Asia) who would help develop and teach a core course on globalization and, finally, an Asian American who would develop courses on Asian American women. These examples illustrate the additive strategy of faculty development that was central to the growth of the women's studies program at Boulder, where lesbians and women-of-color faculty were valued for their contributions to a multicultural vision of women's studies. Even though the rapid expansion of the program felt like an institutional success in that a sizeable cohort of women-of-color scholars found themselves working together, the women's studies program could not grow beyond its initial programmatic investments. In this case, a politics of identity based on visibility and the integration of difference into mainstream disciplines eclipsed a "gender studies" analysis of the social structures that produce racial, gendered, and sexual meanings. For instance, when the cohort of junior faculty resisted, to varying degrees, their position as visible bearers of women's difference and asserted, instead, an intersectional analysis that decentered the primacy of women, highlighted racial politics, and critiqued the additive goals of multiculturalism, the women's studies community fell apart. In other words, while these dynamics played out differently over time and there were many instances of mutual support and genuine collegiality, in the end, it became difficult for the senior faculty to support the development of its junior faculty. Between 2000 and 2004, all five of the junior faculty hired between 1993 and 1999 decided to leave Boulder.

I believe that the problems at Boulder stemmed from competing definitions of feminism and different views of women's studies. At Boulder, the philosophy of recuperation and its dependence on identity politics cohered into an institutional and bureaucratic form, and the practice of women's studies became a study of mainstream feminist movements at its center with a panoply of racial and sexual differences swirling at the margins. Despite the urgings of junior faculty, the curriculum was not able to move beyond its original conceptual frame, and the study of women's oppression remained at the center of the women's studies program's curriculum. In this case, the politics of feminism depended on a reading of women's bodies as the natural site for emancipation. In other words, the identity "woman" was married to the female-sexed body, and the female-sexed body was the central subject of study within women's studies. The intersectional or post-humanist politics of what I am calling gender studies, particularly its emphasis on racial and global injustice, seemed to undo the hard work of early feminist recuperation by not naming women in its title, by not paying exclusive attention to women, indeed, by eschewing the politics of, in this case, multicultural recuperation. Herein lies the so-called generational conflict. If women's studies programs were built on identity-based recuperative politics and gender studies scholars challenge the foundational politics of academic institutionalization, how can gender studies scholars find a comfortable home in women's studies? How can women's studies scholars encourage (and tenure) the next generation of scholars when they all but bite the hands that feed them? I address this seeming conundrum not only to give voice to my experience (I don't intend to speak for my former colleagues at Boulder), but to address another question: What does queer studies have to offer women's studies and, conversely, what does queer studies gain from its linkage to women's studies? First let me briefly outline the institutional relationship between lesbian and gay studies and queer studies.

Lesbian and gay studies also treats bodies like readable maps to discern a politics of social change. In other words, lesbian and gay studies has historically shared with women's studies a certain body-based dependence on identity politics. Same-sex sexual behavior, in the past and present, marks a potentially revolutionary cohort, a liberationist struggle whereby certain kinds of people (homosexuals) articulate certain modern identities (lesbian and gay) so to increase their visibility to the state and expand their civil rights. Thus the AIDS activist slogan "silence equals death," moves from "visibility equals survival" to "scholarly attention equals civil rights." I argue that like women's studies, lesbian and gay studies (in its earlier institutional forms) became dependant on a politics of recuperation that reiterates and cements through repetition and sedimentation (in Judith Butler's terms) knowable subjects, namely "lesbians" and "gay men."[20]

Queer studies, on the other hand, purportedly resists the subject-building impulses of lesbian and gay studies, rendering bodies less than intelligible, identifying the state-generated impulses behind the articulation of coherent "sexual identities," and, more recently, grappling with the signifying practices of the body in such a way that both sexed (biological) bodies and gender seem to lose their attachment to each other. In this world, it is difficult to extract sexuality from the body's morphology because as bodies lose their attachment to "true sex"—the so-called truth of sex and gender revealed in the body's genitals, chromosomes, and/or hormones—the foundation for lesbian and gay studies becomes increasingly uncertain. As sex and gender unhinge, so does sexuality. For instance, a person with female genitalia who identifies as a man and desires feminine women might understand himself (or be understood by others) as butch, heterosexual, lesbian, transgendered, transsexual, bisexual, or queer (not a complete list). The variety of possible "sexualities" flags the increased instability of the body as a knowable signifier for sexual identity, and the variability of identity formation enables a closer look at the influences of race, class, nation, ethnicity, and social geography (rural,

urban, industrializing, postcolonial, etc.) on the production of sexual desires, practices, and/or identities. In other words, in its postmodern construction there is no
way to read sexual identity from the body's shape, desires, or sexual acts. When
read in the context of queer theory, body-based forms of knowledge seem to reiterate the terms of oppression, and the path to social (and sexual) freedom seems
to insist on the disavowal of identity politics and its policing practices. As a result, the academic distinction between lesbian and gay studies and queer studies
results in some thick classroom politics as students grapple with their evolving
identities, the politics of visibility, and the possibilities of cultural resistance.

The comparison between women's studies/gender studies and lesbian and gay
studies/queer studies is useful in that it identifies some of the tensions that emerge
as these academic fields grow and develop alongside each other. Assertions of identity have enabled the emergence of both women's studies and lesbian and gay studies, and challenges to identity via postmodern theories of subjectivity and
intersectionality have propelled these disciplines in new directions. Clearly, the
challenge to identity could not exist without the hard work of identity-based institutionalization, but the challenge is often taken personally, decried as apolitical,
and responded to unprofessionally. These vexed relationships frame the current
status of the field. However, because queer studies has institutionalized through
women's studies rather than lesbian and gay studies (there are simply too few academically funded lesbian and gay studies programs), there are other implications.
Queer studies scholars often find themselves in the seemingly paradoxical situation of performing "lesbian" or "gay" at the departmental or institutional level but
eschewing identity politics in the classroom. The deconstructive work of queer studies spills into other women's studies classrooms and, as with gender studies, the
challenge to a seemingly generational academic project of feminist recuperation
is replayed—but with a difference. Here, the difference is sexual and the result is
often homophobic. At Boulder, for instance, the women's studies program was frequently singled out by unfriendly administrators and, at a particularly crucial time,
state legislators for its so-called lesbian content. Queer studies sometimes seemed
to be the largest stumbling block to women's studies' institutional security, and
senior faculty and administrative allies sometimes took up a closeting strategy,
downplaying the relevance of lesbian and gay studies and queer studies to women's
studies curriculum.

The conflict between queer studies and women's studies gets more complex
as women's studies programs increasingly seek to hire queers of color to teach
globalization/postcolonial studies and/or race theory in addition to queer studies
and to function as an academic "two for" who literally stand in for difference, fulfilling the liberal integrationist desires of the academy while serving as a role model
for subaltern students and representing the program to the larger campus community as a model of multicultural possibilities. As a result, the intelligible performance of multiple and overlapping identities become a crucial—and emotionally
exhausting—prerequisite for employment.

These tensions frame the problem and promise that queer studies scholars
bring to women's studies programs as they further institutionalize. Queer studies

curriculum pushes women's studies away from identity-based interrogations of oppression and offers up new models for the analysis of sexed and gendered bodies—models that contain within them an intersectional (rather than additive) analysis of race, class, and nation. Rather than eclipsing identity-based studies of oppression and resistance, queer studies as a discipline offers an alternative perspective: a tension and a challenge. In my mind, women's studies must retain this tension in order to grow in new directions. Given that systems of oppression still exist (and are often a matter of life and death), identity-based analysis of lived experience must remain an important part of women's studies curriculum. We cannot live outside the dominant social order, and visibility is still often the most effective means of resistance in a rights-based society and capitalistic economy. But it is easy for an identity-based approach to maintain control of the curriculum or divisively reemerge in moments of economic or institutional crisis. What queer scholarship brings to women's studies is a constant provocation. The tension between recuperation and deconstruction maintains a constant critique or internal audit within the curriculum. Queer studies scholarship encourages explorations of the incoherent body, unsettling the naturalization or reification of body-based notions of femininity and masculinity, which, as we know, are difficult to sustain in a truly intersectional and global analysis. As such, queer studies promises new possibilities for exploring transnational systems of power and building links with programs dedicated to the study of race, ethnicity, and globalization.

Queer studies courses also invite a new cohort of students into the women's studies community, students who inhabit queer bodies and/or live the experience of multiple and overlapping gender, racial, national, and sexual identities. The tightrope of identity/anti-identity that queer studies students and faculty walk provides a rich and fertile ground for abstract analysis in the classroom but also a practical solution to the gulf between identity-based and deconstructive analysis. Because many queer studies students and faculty continue to perform identity on an everyday basis (and, as a bonus, can effectively align themselves with LGBTQ staff and administrators), they function as a signifier of social and political change, a human sign of politicized institutional engagement (as do women faculty and faculty of color), even as they challenge the limits of identity in the classroom. Furthermore, there are many ethnic studies students and faculty who walk the same tightrope between identity politics, role-modeling, and the classroom critique of coherent or essentialized identities. For this reason, queer studies scholarship can function as an intellectual bridge between women's studies and ethnic studies programs.

By way of conclusion, I want to offer two examples of recent scholarship in queer studies that do the intersectional work I have outlined above. The first example is Judith Halberstam's essay on the racialization of masculinity in drag king performances, and the second is Karin Aguilar–San Juan's essay on the problems of authenticity in queer Asian America.[21] Halberstam's essay takes as its starting point a comparison of drag king contests and performances. She observes that the drag kings that performed cabaret-style in ongoing shows tended to be white while a larger number of black, Asian, and Latina women participated in the less formal drag king contests. Halberstam draws on the history of both male impersonation within African American culture and racial segregation within lesbian public spaces in order to argue that the masculinities produced in contemporary lesbian night-clubs are always (already) racialized, whether or not they are performed by women of color. Halberstam links "nonperformative" masculinity to class and racial privi-lege, noting that "the theatricality, or lack thereof, in the drag king performance depends on whether the performer is attempting to reproduce dominant or minor-ity masculinities."[22] She argues, at the end, that there may be a rich and under-studied tradition of African American female masculinity that explains the pleasures associated with African American or Latina/o drag king performance and the rela-tive lack of theatricality associated with white hegemonic masculinity. In the tra-dition of gender studies, queer theory, and critical race theory, Halberstam examines the way racialization frames the production of new sexual and gendered cultures. Queer studies provides a lens to look at the vital interdependence of race and gender as they are produced in contemporary queer social spaces.

Aguilar–San Juan's essay makes a similar gesture but from the perspective of grassroots community organizing. In "Going Home: Enacting Justice in Queer Asian America," she confronts the trap of authenticity that arises when communi-ties unite around truth claims about identity rather than claims for justice. Most simply, Aguilar–San Juan explains that even though metaphors of home flag safety and authenticity in many Asian American communities, home can involve com-plex negotiations for queer Asian Americans. Aguilar–San Juan further warns that visibility is not always the best strategy for social change because by making our-selves visible, or speaking up, we participate in a process that naturalizes and au-thenticates some voices at the expense of others. In other words, the identity-based and multicultural approach to expanding women's studies cannot achieve the equal-ity and justice it anticipates without queer theory's interrogation of why certain identities or perspectives or subject positions are marginalized to begin with. In-stead of building or mobilizing communities, Aguilar–San Juan argues that iden-tity-based truth claims may actually create stumbling blocks to future organizing because there is no way to voice every nuance of identity. Moreover, the body— as a measure of authenticity—may not be the best "site of home."[23] In an appeal for justice, Aguilar–San Juan articulates a utopian vision for Asian American com-munity building, a vision that loosens the boundaries of inclusion and exclusion and guards against universalizing gestures. I want to apply this vision to the fu-ture of women's studies. I hope that as well-established women's studies programs continue to invite queer theory and critical race theory scholars onto their faculty, they will allow the most basic metaphors of home (the home many women find in their bodies) to be deconstructed and rebuilt on, perhaps, a less stable foundation.

Notes

I want to thank Liz Kennedy for encouraging me to write this essay. Her insight and editorial guidance, as well as the generous comments of several anonymous readers, helped bring this essay to life. I also thank Cindy Stearns and Charlene Tung, my colleagues at Sonoma State University, for modeling the best of women's and gender studies.

1. Sonoma State University is located about forty-five miles north of San Francisco. It is part of the California State University system and has approximately 7,500 students. In spring 2004, the Women's and Gender Studies Department counted almost fifty majors.

2. Michel Foucault explains the concept of "true sex" in his introduction to *Herculine Barbin* (New York: Pantheon Books, 1980).

3. Leora Auslander, "Do Women's + Feminist + Men's + Lesbian and Gay + Queer Studies = Gender Studies?" *differences: A Journal of Feminist Cultural Studies* 9, no. 3 (1997): 1–30.

4. Miranda Joseph discusses the analogy between lesbian and gay studies and women's studies in "Analogy and Complicity: Women's Studies, Lesbian/Gay Studies, and Capitalism," in *Women's Studies on Its Own,* ed. Robyn Wiegman (Durham: Duke University Press, 2002), 267–292.

5. Mari Jo Buhle, introduction to *The Politics of Women's Studies: Testimony from Thirty Founding Mothers,* ed. Florence Howe (New York: Feminist Press, 2000), xx.

6. By the mid-1970s, Florence Howe reports, "between 10 and 33 percent of all women undergraduates were enrolling in women's studies courses" (*The Politics of Women's Studies,* ed. Florence Howe, xxii).

7. See testimonies from Florence Howe, Nancy Hoffman, Sheila Tobias, and Jean Walton in "Naming the Problem: The Absence of Women from the Curriculum and Scholarship," in *The Politics of Women's Studies,* ed. Florence Howe, 3–54.

8. See, for instance, the various essays in *Coming to Terms: Feminism, Theory, Politics,* ed. Elizabeth Weed (New York: Routledge, 1989), particularly Joan Scott, "Gender: A Useful Category of Historical Analysis," 81–99.

9. Kimberle Crenshaw, "Mapping the Margins: Intersectionality, Identity Politics, and Violence against Women of Color," *Stanford Law Review* 43 (July 1991): 1241.

10. Combahee River Collective, "The Combahee River Collective Statement," in *Home Girls: A Black Feminist Anthology,* ed. Barbara Smith (New York: Kitchen Table/Women of Color Press, 1983), 272–282. See Cherríe Moraga and Gloria Anzaldúa, eds., *This Bridge Called My Back: Writings by Radical Women of Color* (New York: Kitchen Table, 1983); Barbara Smith, ed., *Home Girls: A Black Feminist Anthology* (New York: Kitchen Table/Women of Color Press, 1983); Angela Davis, *Women, Race, and Class* (New York: Vintage Books, 1983, c. 1981); Audre Lorde, *Sister Outsider: Essays and Speeches* (Freedom, Calif.: Crossing Press, 1984); Gloria Anzaldúa, *Borderlands/La Frontera: The New Mestiza* (San Francisco: Spinsters/Aunt Lute, 1987).

11. For a look at the link between lesbian and gay studies and community activism, see Jeffrey Escoffier, "Inside the Ivory Closet," *OUT/LOOK* 10 (fall 1990): 40–48.

12. John D'Emilio, "The Universities and Gay Experience," in *Making Trouble,* ed. John D'Emilio (New York: Routledge, 1992), 117–127.

13. For a more nuanced description of the history of the institutionalization of lesbian and gay studies, see Martin Duberman, introduction to *Hidden from History: Reclaiming the Gay and Lesbian Past* (New York: New American Library, 1989); Lisa Duggan, "History's Gay Ghetto: The Contradictions of Growth in Lesbian and Gay History," in *Sex Wars: Sexual Dissent and Political Culture,* ed. Lisa Duggan and Nan D. Hunter (New York: Routledge, 1995), 144–154; George Chauncey, "The Queer History and Politics of Lesbian and Gay Studies," in *Queer Frontiers,* ed. Joseph Boone et al. (Madison: University of Wisconsin Press, 2000), 298–315.

14. See Lisa Duggan, "The Discipline Problem: Queer Theory Meets Lesbian and Gay History," in *Sex Wars,* ed. Duggan and Hunter, 194–206.

15. Annamaria Jagose, *Queer Theory: An Introduction* (New York: New York University Press, 1996).

16. Michel Foucault, *The History of Sexuality,* vol. 1 (New York: Vintage, 1980). For further analysis of the impact of Foucault's writings on queer studies, see Robert J. Corber and Steven Valucchi, introduction to *Queer Studies: An Interdisciplinary Reader,* ed. Corber and Valucchi (New York: Blackwell, 2003), 1–17.

17. Like Linda Garber, I am uneasy with the phrase "generational conflict" because it falsely aligns (academic) age with ideological or political affiliation. See Linda Garber, *Identity Politics* (New York: Columbia University Press, 2001), 182–195.

18. With the budgetary crisis of early 2000s, these job lines returned to the College of Arts and Sciences with little hope that the program would secure replacement lines. In fact, in 2002 and 2003, the dean of Arts and Sciences at the University of Colorado, Boulder, considered dismantling the women's studies program altogether.

19. In fact, in 1994 women's studies was ranked seventh by a panel that evaluated the campus's sixty-one academic programs, establishing women's studies as a vital part of the campus community. Marcia Westkott, "Institutional Success and Political Vulnerability: A Lesson in the Importance of Allies," in *Women's Studies on Its Own,* ed. Wiegman, 293–311.

20. Judith Butler, *Bodies That Matter: On the Discursive Limits of "Sex"* (New York: Routledge, 1993). See also Corber and Valocchi, introduction to *Queer Studies,* 1–17.

21. Judith Halberstam, "Mackdaddy, Superfly, Rapper: Gender, Race, and Masculinity in the Drag King Scene," *Social Text* 52/53, vol. 15, nos. 3 and 4 (1997): 106–131. Karin Aguilar–San Juan, "Going Home: Enacting Justice in Queer Asian America," in *Q and A: Queer in Asian America,* ed. David L. Eng and Alice Y. Hom (Philadelphia: Temple University Press, 1998), 25–40.

22. Halberstam, "Mackdaddy," 115.

23. Aguilar–San Juan, "Going Home," 36.

PART II

How Does Women's Studies Negotiate the Politics of Alliance and the Politics of Difference?

Where in the Transnational World Are U.S. Women of Color?

SANDRA K. SOTO

The dominant culture dismisses minority studies as provincial, as the creation of "special interests," as an affront to the traditional intellectual's quest for universals. If there is a danger of multiculturalism's being recuperated in the interest of maintaining the concept and practices of nationalism, then there is also a danger of confirming the dominant view of minority studies by setting up postcolonialism as the "global" knowledge sanctioning the otherwise too "narrow" study of U.S. minorities.
Lora Romero, "Nationalism and Internationalism: Domestic Differences in a Postcolonial World."

Across the disciplines, a number of influential scholars are exploring paradigm shifts to better account for the restructuring of the state in the global economy, with its new and more closely interwoven multi-scaled networks and attendant transformations in ways of knowing, being, belonging and communicating, producing and consuming culture, and envisioning and practicing resistance.[1] While most of these scholars are careful to note that the nation-state is still hegemonic, the impulse has been to note its weakening power in relation to several axes: the increasing power of multinational corporations; technological advances in communication and transportation; the international division of labor; and new migration patterns which appear less unidirectional and more a process of multidirectional flows, less a marked rupture with countries of origin, and more enabling of multiple forms of belonging. One of the key demands said to be generated by these changes, therefore, is a *transnational* approach to contemporary objects of study. In this usage, "transnational" designates not only literal flows of people, commodities, and capital across national borders, but the specific and uneven ways that global capital constitutes social relations everywhere.

For all of the above reasons, transnational approaches are also seen as an effective way to launch a strong (and long overdue) departure from U.S.-centric scholarship in its many forms—most obviously, American exceptionalism and imperialist chauvinism. A less obvious and—I will be arguing—more perplexing elaboration of this departure is in the charge that fields such as ethnic studies and women's studies (both of which are often problematically named through the shorthand of "multiculturalism") only exacerbate U.S. centrism. This essay takes up that critique as it plays out in the emergent area of transnational feminist studies. More exploratory and preliminary than polemical or argumentative, the discussion to follow takes the query *Women's Studies for the Future* as an apt occasion for reflecting on some of the challenges that arise when transnationalism is positioned in contradistinction to feminist scholarship on women of color in the United States. The question of how the study of U.S. racial formations converges with transnational studies is perhaps nowhere more salient and pressing at the moment than in the politicized and rapidly transforming arena of women's studies, and it is here that I situate this essay. As the epigraph above by Lora Romero suggests, however, these issues have a longer history and have circulated through a number of academic fields. In order to contextualize this essay in a broader framework (both disciplinarily and temporally), therefore, I first turn to Romero's incisive response to an earlier critique of "multiculturalism."

In her brief but forceful essay "Nationalism and Internationalism: Domestic Differences in a Postcolonial World" (1995), Romero considers the possibility of coordinating postcolonial studies and U.S. ethnic studies and suggests that although these two fields might immediately appear congruent, even complementary and overlapping, there are a number of critical factors that can make their conjunction difficult.[2] What prompts this consideration is Amy Kaplan's essay "Left Alone with America: The Absence of Empire in the Study of American Culture," the introduction to her coedited anthology, *Cultures of United States Imperialism* (1993), which calls for a postcolonial departure from two paradigms underwriting the study of American culture: American exceptionalism and American multiculturalism.[3] Much of Kaplan's essay is devoted to tracing the denials and measured omissions that have created and sustained the paradigm of "exceptionalism" in relation to imperialism and colonialism. The national myth that the U.S. is exceptional because it is not an imperialist force occludes, as she argues, "the multiple histories of continental and overseas expansion, conquest, conflict, and resistance which have shaped the cultures of the United States and the cultures of those it has dominated within and beyond its geopolitical boundaries."[4]

Importantly, the shift in focus to the scale of foreign relations enabled by the internationalization of American studies would not, according to Kaplan, supplant attention to what Romero calls "domestic differences." Instead, the shift would make possible a more nuanced and a less provincial analysis of racial, ethnic, and gender categories within the United States by relating them to "the global dynamics of empire-building,"[5] a transnational analysis that is apparently unavailable so long as multiculturalism holds sway in the field:

The current paradigm of American studies today . . . emphasizes multicultural diversity and scholarly "dissensus" and analyzes American society and culture in terms of internal difference and conflicts, structured around the relations of race, gender, ethnicity, and class. . . . The new pluralistic model of diversity runs the risk of being bound by the old paradigm of unity if it concentrates its gaze only narrowly on the internal lineaments of American culture and leaves national borders intact instead of interrogating their formation. That is, American nationality can still be taken for granted as a monolithic and self-contained whole, no matter how diverse and conflicted, if it remains implicitly defined by its internal social relations, and not in political struggles for power with other cultures and nations, struggles which make America's conceptual and geographic borders fluid, contested, and historically changing.[6]

Although multiculturalism might seem to challenge the mythos of exceptionalism by, for instance, exposing the racial fault-lines that figuratively and literally structure the U.S. map, Kaplan suggests that it can actually *supplement* that exceptionalism, thereby helping to recirculate the denial of empire, solidify a binary relationship between domestic and foreign relations, and reify nationalism (albeit now in a pluralized form). Of course, by the 1993 appearance of Kaplan's essay, many scholars had already begun to express concern about multiculturalism for, among other reasons, focusing on culture while diverting attention from political economy and institutionalized processes of racialization, making it a lucrative discourse in corporate culture and diversity management. What Kaplan adds to that critique is a charge of parochialism, a criticism that has become more prominent since the appearance of *Cultures of United States Imperialism.*[7]

As Romero persuasively notes, however, a transnational approach would not necessarily be better positioned than a multicultural one to avoid recuperation, and, further, the critique of multiculturalism can actually resonate with the dominant (read nationalist) critique of multiculturalism. She also explains that the proposal that a postcolonial—rather than multicultural—approach is better suited to internationalizing American studies needs to better account for the power differentials between U.S. ethnic groups and postcolonial populations, between ethnic studies and postcolonial studies. These differentials, Romero argues, manifest themselves in a number of ways and arenas, including, precisely, in the contemporary academy. She explains:

Any number of phenomena characteristic of contemporary higher education reenact power differentials attendant upon the regionally specific nature of Anglo-European interaction with geographically disparate peoples of color, including the disinterest of [postcolonial] Latin Americanists in Chicano history and culture; the greater visibility (at least until recently) of postcolonial scholarship in U.S. universities; and the practice, on certain campuses, of representing faculty of color raised and educated outside the U.S. as affirmative action hires. This institutional history does not merely represent a failure on the part of postcolonial Latin American Studies to recognize that the border cuts both ways. Rather, it revisits the heterogeneous history of colonialism and renders it politically meaningful in the present.[8]

Where Kaplan commends Chicano studies for avoiding an insular, nationalist approach by adopting the tools of postcolonial studies, Romero shows that Chicano studies actually has not used—and perhaps cannot use—those tools as they are circumscribed by the historical existence of a colonial apparatus dependent on the elite education of a native population (geographically distant from the colonial power) and by anticolonial struggles for independence.

"Gender in a Transnational World"

The problems elaborated in both the innovative *Cultures of United States Imperialism* and Romero's critical response to its introduction are no more resolved today than they were a decade ago and, indeed, have become even more urgent as a growing number of influential scholars persuasively argue for methodologies and projects reflective of the internationalization of capital. In women's studies, these arguments are generated under the rubric of transnational feminist studies by such scholars as Inderpal Grewal, Ella Shohat, and Caren Kaplan (not to be confused with Amy Kaplan), all of whom are clearly influenced by Gayatri Spivak's nuanced critical attention to the international division of labor through a robust and eclectic blend of poststructuralist, Marxist, and feminist theories. Although the Romero/ A. Kaplan discussion is framed by the specific question of using *postcolonial* studies as an aperture for contesting U.S. exceptionalism, the arguments for reorienting women's studies toward the study of "gender in a transnational world" (to borrow from the title of a 2002 anthology coedited by Grewal and C. Kaplan) are deeply resonant—and no doubt overlap—with A. Kaplan's proposal.[9] If transnational feminist studies is obviously less engaged with the United States than is American studies, its point of departure is nonetheless elaborated as a U.S. focus in women's studies, for, according to C. Kaplan and Grewal, "despite a rise in the stated discourse in 'international' and 'global' Women's Studies, U.S. agendas of nation and imperialism still pervade the curriculum and research."[10]

Like the essays comprising *Cultures of United States Imperialism,* a good part of transnational feminist scholarship critically focuses on the production and institutionalization of knowledge, including "the role of national boundaries in the creation of interdisciplinary programs in the United States."[11] Transnational feminist studies, therefore, offers not just a rich archive of specific treatments on the uneven effects of global capitalism in the lives of women around the world, but also a much-needed, self-reflexive interrogation of the epistemological traditions in women's studies and related areas of study. My concern rests not with those two valuable projects themselves (from which I have learned a lot) but, again, with the suggestion (often in sweeping terms) that existing approaches to difference are incommensurate with transnational approaches because they naively operate according to outmoded national boundaries, or, in Shohat's terms, "inert, static maps": "The inert, static maps charted by ethnic studies, area studies, women's studies and gay/lesbian studies need to be mobilized to capture today's morphing, criss-crossing movements across regional and national borders."[12]

This incommensurability is drawn most sharply in C. Kaplan and Grewal's 2002 essay, "Transnational Practices and Interdisciplinary Feminist Scholarship: Refiguring Women's and Gender Studies." To bring into sharper relief the promise and necessity of transnational feminist studies, C. Kaplan and Grewal offer an array of critiques on various areas of study, including internationalism, multiculturalism, and ethnic studies. Where these areas see themselves as oppositional to hegemonic and national(ist) knowledge practices, C. Kaplan and Grewal aim to show that they are deeply complicit with those practices. They write, for instance, that internationalism "is based on existing configurations of nation-states as discrete and sovereign entities," "relies on humanist notions of diversity," and "is globalizing, hegemonic, and deeply unequal in its effects."[13] U.S. multiculturalism, on the other hand, is underwritten by "the legacy of cultural nationalism" and "creates a diversity of cultures that are ethnically and racially distinct," which, in turn, "reifies culture, replacing one set of stereotypes with another."[14] *Critical* multiculturalism, they add, "often relies on celebrations of hybridity in which cultures and nations remain discrete forms articulated as cultural rather than as also governmental or economic."[15]

As suggested by the contours of these critiques (only a small sampling of the many enumerated in their essay), C. Kaplan and Grewal, like A. Kaplan, are most concerned with the pluralization of difference and the reification of nationalisms. In contradistinction to—but also as a corrective for—these unwitting complicities, the authors call for transnational feminist practices which "involve forms of alliance, subversion, and complicity within which asymmetries and inequalities can be critiqued."[16] Unlike any other area of study, they argue, transnational feminist practices at once contest and deconstruct boundaries of all sorts (from national boundaries to the boundaries demarcating high from low culture) as they are self-critically aware of and thus on guard against complicity and are resolutely anti-essentialist.[17] In short, "the nationalisms and regionalism of area studies, the exceptionalism of American studies, the cultural nationalism of ethnic studies, and the domestic focus of mainstream Women's Studies are reworked by transnational feminist cultural practices of research and teaching."[18]

Of the many areas of study critiqued by C. Kaplan and Grewal, I want to pause over their critical genealogy of "women of color" as a politicized identity category and object of study:

> The development—and global-feminism models give rise to a highly mystified figure and object of study: the "Third World woman." This figure has been critiqued and unpacked by many feminists, but it persists in yet another form, which needs to be examined (Alarcón 1990; Mohanty 1991). We want to make a link between the "Third World woman" as an object of study and the rise of the concept of "woman of color" in U.S. ethnic

studies and women's studies. Both "Third World women" and "women of color" as political projects have had great salience in struggles for civil rights, decolonization, anti-racism, and progressive coalition politics in many contexts (hooks 1984a; Hurtado 1996; Sandoval 1991; Wong 1991). However, at a certain point, both of these concepts have come to represent the homogenized figure of racialized and sexual difference. Thus, the term "global" has come to mean a "common difference," and despite racial and national differences, woman remains a reified category. This position argues that all patriarchies are essentially alike; that female bodies are transhistorical and cross-cultural; and that resistance has to be mounted against this common patriarchy (Daly 1978; Morgan 1984; Rich 1979). In gender studies, which does not include patriarchy as a primary analytical category, the reified "woman" reemerges in the argument that gender categories and sexual identities are universal (Morris 1994).[19]

This description of the wide-reaching problems created when "women of color" and "Third World women" are used as tropes for difference in feminist scholarship and practices is a helpful reminder of the ease with which oppositional politics and knowledge practices can be recuperated by dominant logics. And, just as I am drawn to the *aims* of transnational feminist practices as elaborated by the authors, I share their concerns about the mystification and homogenization of difference, particularly when racialized subjects automatically carry the burden of its embodiment.

However, I want to suggest that the authors' own description of this mystification can actually further mystify it. In fairness to the authors, I hasten to add, their point is not to recuperate or de-homogenize women of color, but to enumerate a particular set of problems that is generated when racialized and gendered differences are not approached from a position that seeks to understand how those differences are constituted by transnational political and economic relations and leaned upon in certain strands of feminism. Nonetheless—and precisely because the problems identified by the authors are as prevalent and vexing as they suggest they are—the description of how these problems have come to be bears some unpacking. I especially want to call attention to the passage's evidentiary citations, which fill in the process of homogenization with so many actors and, at the same time, not nearly enough. While the trajectory names various areas of study and types of feminist projects and includes several parenthetical gestures toward many scholars, it assumes a sense of natural inevitably: "both of these concepts have come to represent the homogenized figure of racialized and sexual difference" (by whom? for whom? how?); "'global' has come to mean a 'common difference'" (for and by whom? how?). Moreover, what we might learn from the feminists who actually choose to organize under the signs of "Third World feminism" or "women of color"—for whom difference is anything but universal and for whom patriarchies are far from alike—is foreclosed as the agentive force of the passage rests with problematic discourses that embrace development narratives. The most curious feature of the trajectory, however, is its temporal slippage as it is punctuated by the 1970s and early 1980s ethos of Mary Daly, Robin Morgan, and Adrienne Rich—which is to say that the work cited to show the implications of these areas of study actually predates them.

In attempting to slow down this narrative of mystification in order to better understand it, I do not mean to doubt the problems identified by the authors. On the contrary, if transnational feminist studies is going to avoid the pitfalls that the authors associate with the study of women of color, it is crucial that we understand how those problems came to be. And, if "multicultural studies" in the United States has to be ever mindful of its proximity to corporate co-optation, so too does transnational feminist studies have to be wary of its proximity to globalization, as Bill Readings's *The University in Ruins* would suggest. For Readings, the dissolution of national culture under global capitalism (what he also calls "Americanization") has generated a large-scale shift in the function of the now "posthistorical" university, namely, a substantially different way of training citizen-subjects now that students no longer need the canonical training in national culture that they did when capitalism was intimately tied to the nation. In his words, "the University is becoming a different kind of institution, one that is no longer linked to the destiny of the nation-state by virtue of its role as producer, protector, and inculcator of an idea of national culture. The process of economic globalization brings with it the relative decline of the nation-state as the prime instance of the reproduction of capital around the world. For its part, the University is becoming a transnational bureaucratic corporation."[20] Although Readings's analysis merits further consideration in another forum (particularly in terms of his [over]emphasis on the waning of the nation-state), it offers an important reminder that any knowledge project, no matter how optimistically framed, is always already implicated in hegemonic power relations.

Demystifying Women of Color

In this section, I argue that it is *at best* premature to position women of color (as an area of study and/or political collective) in contradistinction to transnational feminist studies and practices. My claim depends on distinguishing the critical work produced under the sign of "women of color" from the ways that women's studies has responded to and utilized that work. That is, insofar as women's studies' frequent answer to the critique of its elision of race is to deploy various forms of tokenization and essentialist pedagogical practices, it becomes ever more imperative *not* to render those problematic answers synonymous with women of color themselves. Far from calling upon women's studies to more equitably or "multiculturally" parcel out its resources (such as they are), the expansive *and diverse* body of critical work by women of color offers a substantive critique of the field's foundational premises, particularly in relation to gender standpoint epistemology and bourgeois subjectivity, or, in Norma Alarcón's words, "the highly self-conscious ruling class white Western female subject locked in a struggle to the death with 'Man.'"[21] Indeed, I would argue that some of the problems identified by C. Kaplan and Grewal can be untangled at this location, by assessing women's studies' response (or lack thereof) to this challenge, a response that Alarcón calls "cosmetic,"[22] and that Chela Sandoval describes as "confusing straws and tools."[23]

One of the most revealing testaments of women's studies' inability to substantively address these critiques, and one worth reviewing here, is Sandoval's "Feminism and Racism: A Report on the 1981 National Women's Studies Association Conference." Writing in her capacity as secretary to the National Third World Women's Alliance, Sandoval explains how it is that the 1981 NWSA conference—whose theme "Women Respond to Racism" promised to finally address the issue head on—could produce yet more racism. "But we have seen how," she writes, "hidden within the very structure of the conference, the supports were already in place for such an accusation," from the organizational structure of the conference, which "became a maze in which participants played hide-and-seek games of knowledge," to the uneven quality of scholarship resulting from "the strategy of accepting every proposal submitted," to the tokenization of women of color on panels, through the refusal on the part of the organizers to waive the registration fee for working-class women of color.[24] But the most problematic feature of the conference as Sandoval describes it was the organization of the consciousness-raising groups which met every morning of the five-day conference. Magnifying the tokenization at work in the larger conference, the list of consciousness-raising groups included "one single title designated 'women of color,' while 'white' women were offered a series of lists signifying their diversity and emphasizing their choices: 'white/immigrant,' 'white/upper-class,' white/working-class,' 'middle-class,' 'educated,' 'Jewish,' 'experienced in CR groups,' and so on," and, thus, "in spite of good intentions the lists became another reminder of the multidimensionality of white women, while three hundred women of color found themselves seemingly without choice, classified and sorted into one room . . . eyeing one another in anger."[25] Such scenes of homogenizing tokenization and critiques thereof have become so familiar that I almost hesitate to recount this one. However, because the category "women of color" persists as a site of anxiety (in the form, for instance, of NWSA's consciousness-raising groups) and critique (as is evidenced in the very different concerns of C. Kaplan and Grewal, on the one hand, and Wendy Brown, on the other), Sandoval's dated account continues to be meaningful in the present.

Even in her insightful essay, "The Impossibility of Women's Studies," which takes us a long way toward understanding the historical reasons for, and effects of, women's studies' ongoing tokenization of women of color, Brown fails to unglue that tokenization from actual scholarship on and by women of color.[26] On one hand, that is, Brown cogently argues that women's studies' purported commitment to incorporating curriculum on women of color is actually guilt-driven: "faculty, curriculum, and students in women's studies programs are in a relentless, compensatory cycle of guilt and blame about race, a cycle structured by women's studies original, nominalist, and conceptual subordination of race (and all other forms of social stratification) to gender."[27] On the other hand, she allows the guilt of white women to be determining in the last instance, which is to say that she suggests that curriculum on women of color and the pedagogy used in those classrooms can *only* ever be circumscribed by guilt. Women of Color in the United States, the now-infamous University of California, Santa Cruz class she uses to build her argument, becomes the shorthand for the impossibility of women's studies to avoid its own self-flagellation. As she describes it, that class provides a space "in which students gained some exposure to the histories, literatures, and cultures of Asian American, African American, Latina, and Native American women, and in which white students in the course learned to 'decenter themselves' while women of color spoke."[28] Because Brown has that class stand in as exemplary of the always already guilt-driven approach to women of color, there is little, if any, room for disassociating the topic of the class from either its blasé brand of multiculturalism or its unspoken identitarian rules about who could and could not speak.

The suggestion that the study of women of color helps prove the impossibility of women's studies is especially surprising given Brown's highly persuasive juxtaposition of critical race theory and critical legal theory to reveal "the conundrum that distinctive models of power are required for grasping various kinds of subject production, yet subject construction itself does not transpire in accordance with any of these models."[29] Less than proving the impossibility of women's studies, this astute and crucial insight only convinces me more of the ongoing usefulness of the study of women of color, not instead of, or in opposition to, transnational feminist practices, but with them. The critical study of women of color helps us to understand the varied and unequivalent processes that generate racial difference, that gender subjects, and that encourage self-identification as women of color in a transnational world. But it can do so only when it does not depend (as it need not) on an additive, pluralist, guilt-inspiring, unmediated, or homogenizing critical apparatus.

With Brown's and C. Kaplan and Grewal's critiques in mind, I want to return to Sandoval's essay and briefly underline what is perhaps its richest and most promising, but least-cited, contribution. If Sandoval goes to great lengths to situate the conference scene that led to charges of racism, she also painstakingly describes the political differences and contestation among members of the Women of Color caucus. Most importantly, she calls attention to the caucus's acute self-awareness about the ease with which it could reify its own tokenization and homogenization: "Though empowered as a unity of women of color, the cost is that we find it easy to objectify the occupants of every other category. The dangers in creating a new heroine, a political 'unity' of third world women who together take the power to create new kinds of 'others,' is that our unity becomes forged at the cost of nurturing a world of 'enemies.' And in the enthusiasm of our empowered sisterhood, perhaps a greater cost lies in the erasure of our many differences. However, if one attribute of power is its mobile nature, there can be no simple way of identifying our enemies or our friends . . . and no simple unity for feminists of color."[30] Remarkably resonant with both C. Kaplan and Grewal's and Brown's concerns, Sandoval's (and the caucus's) early anti-identitarian critique illustrates that women of color are not synonymous with the unthinking, undifferentiated mass of difference that they are often expected to represent.

While Sandoval's account begins as a specific response to NWSA's interpellation of women of color, it is not myopically contained by the parameters of one conference. Instead, it opens onto a broader analysis of power relations and gender standpoint epistemology as they are enacted within and outside of feminist theory and women's studies and as they come up against national differences.[31] Moreover, because Sandoval's is only one of many such critical projects, we have access to a rich body of pedagogical material by women of color that decisively works against the homogenization, mystification, and sheer celebration of difference. Rather than exemplifying the source of the problem, that is, this body of work untangles it. Undergraduate courses in this area, therefore, have much more to offer than Brown would suggest, but only when not forced into "the progress narrative Women's Studies wishes to create for itself," to cite Rachel Lee.[32]

One of the most salient sites for contesting that progress narrative is in the very courses on which the narrative depends. This is also, of course, one of the most challenging sites from which to do this work, and, as one of the faculty members who regularly teaches these courses at the University of Arizona, I want to add to the list of frustrations enumerated by C. Kaplan and Grewal the tendency of these classes to draw students who are primarily interested in reading and discussing exotic *experiences* about and *stories* by women unlike themselves. I now make a practice of immediately opening my class U.S. Third World Feminisms: Theory, History, and Practice with a frank discussion about the linkages between the current seductiveness of "the subaltern" and colonial anthropology, and by having students read as an introduction to the course Joan W. Scott's "The Evidence of Experience."[33] Scott's brilliant critique of our attraction to the notion of unmediated experience, particularly in accounts of difference, helps me prepare the class to consider the particular workings of ideological systems that have generated and marginalized accounts of difference in the first place. In addition, I structure my course through a number of critical heuristics that challenge students to not simply absorb the syllabus as truth: What is "Third World" about this feminism? How and where does this feminism engage with national liberation movements in the Third World? Why and when are "women of color," "U.S. Third World Feminists," and "Third World Feminists" used as interchangeable signifiers? Who can self-identify as such and why? What are the similarities and differences between the politics underwriting this body of work and the transnational feminist practices called for by C. Kaplan and Grewal?

This is a crucial introduction to a syllabus that necessarily contains many readings explicitly inviting the experience-as-evidence approach, most significantly the 1981 watershed text *This Bridge Called My Back: Writings by Radical Women of Color,* which is decisively framed by its coeditors, Cherríe L. Moraga and Gloria E. Anzaldúa, as a collection of experiences: "As editors we sought out and believe we found, non-rhetorical, highly personal chronicles that present political analysis in everyday terms."[34] Moraga underlines the experiential force of *This Bridge* again in her introduction to the anthology's section entitled "Entering the Lives of Others: Theory in the Flesh" when she writes, "We are the colored in a white feminist movement. We are the feminists among the people of our culture. We are often the lesbians among the straight. We do this bridging by naming ourselves and by telling our stories in our own words."[35] When we can help our students resist the temptation—thickened now by Moraga's strong encouragement—to accept a politics circumscribed by unmediated experience, this model of "theory in the flesh" turns out to provide an exceptionally useful teaching tool. It exemplifies the close association between experiential writing (telling our stories in our own words) and an unending litany of identity politics, an association that is brought into sharper relief by reading carefully Toni Cade Bambara's much-less-cited foreword to *This Bridge,* which aptly notes that "it takes more than the self-disclosure and the bold glimpse of each others' life documents to make the grand resolve to fearlessly work toward potent meshings."[36] Our ability to create these teaching opportunities, however, depends on our taking the *differentiated* writings and politics of women of color seriously enough to seriously critique them.

I share this teaching anecdote to suggest that there is nothing inherent in the practices, writings, study, and politics of women of color that precludes us as teachers, scholars, students (and, indeed, as people who might ourselves identify with those practices and politics) from exploring (and challenging) the ways that women of color have become so thoroughly associated (and burdened) with experience, have come to be cited (both positively and negatively) as an undifferentiated monolithic category, and, ironically, have now come to be placed in contradistinction to transnational practices. While tracking and challenging these associations and citations includes such critical practices as pausing over the experiential thrust found in much of the key writing by women of color, it also includes tracing women's studies' own interpellation of women of color as the homogenized other.

Conclusion

It is probably not premature to say that women's studies now finds itself at a curious crossroads along the same lines that A. Kaplan identified as facing American studies ten years ago. To put it rather schematically, the very critical forces (call them "multicultural studies" in the American studies context and "women-of-color feminism" or "U.S. Third World feminism" in the women's studies context) which for the past twenty-five years have interrogated the fields' self-conceptions as bounded by a stable, unifying object of analysis, and have illuminated the fields' lack of self-critique regarding their politics of location, are themselves now being called into question for reifying the homogenizing categories they had initially sought to critique. That is, just as it became clear that women's studies finally needed to attend in a meaningful way to the critiques by feminists of color, a new body of scholarship suggests that a heightened engagement with the racialized dimensions of gender in the United States is fundamentally incommensurate—in fact, at odds—with the exigencies of understanding "gender in a transnational world." However, if, as I have been suggesting, what matters most is *how* we teach and write about domestic differences (which, again, is to say that there is nothing inherent about teaching a class on women of color that requires, for instance, the silencing of certain students, the celebration of others, or an insular, domestic focus), then there is likewise nothing inherent about transnational feminist studies that alleviates the problems identified in, for instance, Brown's essay.

Because transnational feminist studies promises to fundamentally transform women's studies curricula, scholarship, hiring practices, and program building, as indicated by recent job advertisements, conferences, publications, and course offerings, the question of how to pursue its aims while proactively addressing the "domestic differences" which Romero in her different but related context enumerates is that much more important. This question should be continuously explored *as* these relationships unfold both because it is too soon to tell what forms they might take, but also because, as the Romero/A. Kaplan discussion suggests, we already know that there are a number of potential stumbling blocks that could trouble those relations if left unattended. As C. Kaplan and Grewal themselves point out, if only in passing, they "hear from some of [their] colleagues that any strong curricular effort to work toward the international will undermine U.S. women of color and the gains they have made in Women's Studies curricula."[37] However, as I see it—indeed, as C. Kaplan and Grewal have helped me see it—the potentially vexed relationship between what here is configured as global versus local approaches in feminist studies is no superficial competition over women's studies' resources. Much more substantively, the answer to the question that titles this essay—Where in the transnational world are U.S. women of color?—threatens to be "nowhere" so long as women of color are conflated with the very problems that transnational feminists seek to redress.

Notes

For their generous and incisive critical feedback, I owe a debt of gratitude to Miranda Joseph, Elizabeth L. Kennedy, Agatha Beins, the anonymous editorial readers, as well as the audience participants (in particular Sonia Saldívar-Hull) at the 2003 meeting of *Mujeres Activas en Letras y Cambio Social,* where I presented an earlier version of this essay.

1. See especially Bill Readings, *The University in Ruins* (Cambridge: Harvard University Press, 1996); and George Yúdice, "Rethinking Area and Ethnic Studies in the Context of Economic and Political Restructuring," in *Critical Latin American and Latino Studies,* ed. Juan Poblete (Minneapolis: University of Minnesota Press, 2003), 76–102. See also Lisa Lowe, *Immigrant Acts: On Asian American Cultural Politics* (Durham: Duke University Press, 1996).

2. Romero, "Nationalism and Internationalism: Domestic Differences in a Postcolonial World," *American Literature* 67, no. 4 (1995): 795–800.

3. Amy Kaplan, "Left Alone with America: The Absence of Empire in the Study of American Culture," in *Culture of United States Imperialism,* ed. Amy Kaplan and Donald E. Pease (Durham: Duke University Press, 1993), 3–21.

4. A. Kaplan, "Left Alone with America," 4.

5. Ibid., 16.

6. Ibid., 14–15. Interestingly, and as Romero points out, Kaplan goes on to cite Chicano studies and borderlands studies as exemplary exceptions to the otherwise provincial approaches in multiculturalism. Kaplan understands those fields as bringing "an in-

ternational perspective to American studies in part by reconceiving the concept of ethnicity (traditionally treated as a self-enclosed entity) through the theory and politics of post-coloniality" (Kaplan quoted in Romero, "Nationalism and Internationalism," 796–797). But, as Romero astutely argues, Chicano studies has not actually utilized a postcolonial framework in any sustained way, even if some early Chicano historians experimented with the internal colonialism model (only to later discount it). See also Yúdice, "Rethinking Area and Ethnic Studies," for a slightly different account of the relations between Chicano/Latino studies and Latin American studies. For Yúdice, cultural studies in the United States has taken little notice of Latin American studies, largely because it erroneously seeks to understand Latin America through U.S. Latino studies.

7. See especially Avery F. Gordon and Christopher Newfield, eds., *Mapping Multiculturalism* (Minneapolis: University of Minnesota Press, 1996); Minoo Moallem and Iain A. Boal, "Multicultural Nationalism and the Poetics of Inauguration," in *Between Woman and Nation: Nationalisms, Transnational Feminisms, and the State,* ed. Caren Kaplan, Norma Alarcón, and Minoo Moallem (Durham: Duke University Press, 1999), 243–263; and Angie Chabram-Dernersesian, "'Chicana! Rican? No, Chicana Riqueña!' Refashioning the Transnational Connection," in *Between Woman and Nation,* ed. Caren Kaplan, Norma Alarcón, and Minoo Moallem, 264–295. See also Lowe, *Immigrant Acts,* in which she argues that "'multiculturalism' supplements abstract political citizenship where the unrealizability of the political claims to equality become apparent: it is the national cultural form that seeks to unify the diversity of the United States through the integration of differences as *cultural* equivalents abstracted from the histories of racial inequality unresolved in the economic and political domains" (30). For a counterargument, see John Beverley, "Multiculturalism and Hegemony," in *Critical Latin American and Latino Studies,* ed. Poblete, 224–238. Beverly argues that a multicultural identity politics—when it is conceived not as "essentially a demand for equality of opportunity," but "for *actual* epistemological, cultural, economic, and civic-political equality" (227)—can stand in as a "potentially *radical* force in the world today" (231).

8. Romero, "Nationalism and Internationalism," 798. A similar point is made by Ella Shohat, introduction to *Talking Visions: Multicultural Feminism in a Transnational Age,* ed. Shohat (New York: New Museum of Contemporary Art, 1998), 1–63. Shohat notes the irony that "the institutional embrace of a few third-world 'postcolonials,' largely by English and Comparative Literature Departments [in the United States], is partially a response to U.S. civil rights and affirmative action struggles, yet the enthusiastic consumption of the theoretical aura of the 'postcolonial' threatens to eclipse the less prestigious 'ethnic studies' field" (41). See also M. Jacqui Alexander and Chandra Talpade Mohanty, "Introduction: Genealogies, Legacies, Movements," in *Feminist Genealogies, Colonial Legacies, Democratic Futures,* ed. Alexander and Mohanty (New York: Routledge, 1997), xiii–xlii. They write, "the specificities of our national and cultural genealogies—being Black and Brown women—and our status as immigrants were constantly being used to position us as foreign, thus muting the legitimacy of our claims to the experiences of different racisms. . . . We remained (differently) less threatening than African American women to white women, who often preferred to deal with our 'foreignness' rather that our racialization in the U.S." (xiv–xv).

9. Caren Kaplan and Inderpal Grewal, eds., *An Introduction to Women's Studies: Gender in a Transnational World* (Boston: McGraw Hill, 2002).

10. Caren Kaplan and Inderpal Grewal, "Transnational Practices and Interdisciplinary

Feminist Scholarship: Refiguring Women's and Gender Studies," in *Women's Studies on Its Own,* ed. Robyn Wiegman (Durham: Duke University Press, 2002), 71.

11. Ibid., 69.
12. Shohat, *Talking Visions,* 46.
13. Ibid., 73–74.
14. Ibid., 74.
15. Ibid., 75.
16. Ibid., 73.
17. Ibid., 79–80.
18. Ibid., 76.
19. Ibid., 71–72.
20. Readings, *The University in Ruins*, 3.
21. Norma Alarcón, "The Theoretical Subject(s) of *This Bridge Called My Back* and Anglo-American Feminism," in *Making Face, Making Soul/Haciendo Caras: Creative and Critical Perspectives by Women of Color,* ed. Gloria Anzaldúa (San Francisco: Aunt Lute, 1990), 360.
22. Ibid., 357.
23. Chela Sandoval, "Feminism and Racism: A Report on the 1981 National Women's Studies Association Conference," in *Making Face, Making Soul/Haciendo Caras*, ed. Anzaldúa, 55.
24. Ibid., 58–59.
25. Ibid., ellipses in original.
26. Wendy Brown, "The Impossibility of Women's Studies," *differences* 9, no. 3 (1997): 79–101.
27. Ibid., 93.
28. Ibid., 80–81.
29. Ibid, 88.
30. Sandoval, "Feminism and Racism," 65.
31. This conference/caucus experience likely provided much of the raw material for Sandoval's emerging Foucaldian theory of "oppositional consciousness," which she would go on to develop in her widely cited essay, "U.S. Third World Feminism: The Theory and Method of Oppositional Consciousness in the Postmodern World," *Genders* 10 (spring 1991): 1–24.
32. Rachel Lee, "Notes from the (Non)Field: Teaching and Theorizing Women of Color," in *Women's Studies on Its Own*, ed. Wiegman, 89.
33. Joan W. Scott, "The Evidence of Experience," in *The Lesbian and Gay Studies Reader,* ed. Henry Abelove et al. (New York: Routledge, 1993), 397–415.
34. Cherríe L. Moraga and Gloria E. Anzaldúa, eds., *This Bridge Called My Back: Writings by Radical Women of Color,* expanded and revised 3rd ed. (Berkeley: Third Woman Press, 2002). liv.
35. Ibid., 21.
36. Ibid., xli.
37. C. Kaplan and Grewal, "Transnational Practices and Interdisciplinary Feminist Scholarship," 78.

Different Differences

Theory and the Practice of Women's Studies

Janet R. Jakobsen

Women's studies programs and depart-
ments have seen major successes since their inception in the early 1970s. Yet, surprisingly, we cannot count among these victories some of the issues that have been
major foci of feminist theorizing over much of that time.[1] While feminist theorizing has given much attention to both "the politics of difference" and the formation of "alliance politics," we have only rarely been able to build women's studies
programs on the basis of alliance or to produce programs that incorporate differences among women into their faculties, student bodies, or curricula.

Women's studies has by now produced a number of trenchant analyses of
the ways in which social differences are all too often the basis for social dominations, but we have not been able to overcome these problems in our institutional
practice. I will suggest, however, that this is not simply a problem of the split between theory and practice. Rather, I think we have a theoretical problem, as well
as a practical one. Our basic concepts—difference and alliance politics—have
reached the limits of their usefulness. As long as we think of our project in these
terms we will be caught in a cycle where each success produces a new form of
failure.

When we think about these problems we often tend to focus on women's
studies in isolation without taking into account the institutional setting which forms
the context for our practice. After all, the university is, to use Louis Althusser's
term, an "ideological state apparatus."[2] There are only three types of institutions
of higher education in the United States: (1) public institutions run by the state,
(2) private institutions run by churches and other religious institutions, and (3) other
private colleges and universities run as nonprofit corporations. Like many nonprofit undertakings (most notably hospitals), colleges and universities are facing
increasing pressure to corporatize, to move toward profit-making and to undo traditions of faculty governance and democratic process in the name of efficiency.[3]
If the state's prisons, not to mention K–12 education, can be run by for-profit corporations, why not its institutions of higher education? Perhaps most importantly
for our purposes, none of these institutional settings—corporation, state, or

church—is particularly feminist. In fact, most of them have long histories that depend on the subordination of entire classes of people, including women.

This institutional setting, then, creates certain contradictions for the project of women's studies, contradictions which mean that the narrative we tell ourselves about how women's studies should be can never be fulfilled, at least not in the current ways in which we tell this narrative. "But, women's studies should be different," the students often say: different from traditional disciplines and majors, different in its affiliation with social movement, different in its feminist pedagogy, democratic processes, and inclusiveness. And so it should. Yet, this statement is often part of an imagination of women's studies, shared by both students and faculty, as a perfectible island of difference profoundly separated from the rest of the university. This imagination is disabling in two ways: it does not allow us to examine the limits created by the institution, and it prevents us from exploring the ways in which women's studies needs connections to some other parts of the university to accomplish its goals, especially its goals relating to "difference." Rather, we have tended to imagine that all differences can be contained on the island that is women's studies.

The idea that women's studies can be different plays into one of the central methods used by the university to manage the type of social change that women's studies hopes to represent. As Chandra Mohanty has pointed out, the university is adept at managing both diversity and change.[4] Mohanty argues that within the structure of the university difference is seen as "benign variation (diversity), for instance, rather than as conflict, struggle, or the threat of disruption," and this approach to difference "bypasses power as well as history to suggest a harmonious empty pluralism." As Mohanty points out, this reductive pluralism facilitates an institutional approach to differences as "diversity management," where historical and political struggles are transformed into matters of individual prejudice and misunderstanding to be managed within institutions ranging from the "multicultural" university to the "multi-national" corporation.[5] The university's acknowledgment of differences contributes to this empty pluralism as long as differences are contained within separated—and manageable—units. From the perspective of the university, women's studies is simply one of these units.

The fact that the university works to manage, rather than simply halt, change explains both why we have witnessed massive change for women's studies over the last quarter century *and* why many of us feel that things haven't changed enough. It is neither that the institutionalization of women's studies does not represent change, nor that this change is insignificant. One wouldn't become a feminist educator if one didn't think that education was a good thing, not just for individuals but for the social collectivity. One of the purposes of radical research and pedagogical projects like women's studies is to resist the hegemonic implications of the academy as a whole. Rather, even as we have worked to subvert and change the institution, the university has worked to manage those changes to its own ends. Change itself is managed by channeling the motion—the social movement—that makes transformation possible along lines that maintain overarching hierarchies. In this sense the university allows for constant motion, but this mobility is geared toward the maintenance of static hierarchies. Social change that is recuperated back into hegemonic hierarchies could be termed "mobility for stasis."

The way in which mobility can work to reinforce hegemony is familiar to us from the narrative of individual class mobility of which the university is a part. While mobility through education can be incredibly important to individual students, this mobility can also be used to reinforce the system of class stratification as a whole because changes in individuals' lives stand in for social change. When some individuals can significantly change their lives, the injustice of the system becomes invisible, as does continuing class stratification. Despite the fact that there is constant mobility for individuals through education, the system as a whole remains static.

Mobility for stasis works because we can be constantly moving toward some goal and become invested in the feeling of progress. But, this progress narrative is a linear narrative that induces change along a single trajectory, thus denying contradictions, denying, for example, that even as there is class mobility (for individuals), economic classes (as a whole) remain in place.[6] As I will argue below, the concepts that we have used in attempting to change women's studies, concepts like alliance politics and the politics of difference, have not been able to sustain an analysis of contradiction and have, thus, pushed our efforts toward change along a single trajectory. But, as we have moved along this trajectory, because of the contradictions of the university, we have also reproduced our problems in new forms. While feminist theory has been focused on acknowledging "difference" or "differences," for many years, we have all too often treated these differences as the separable units that the university (along with other hegemonic institutions) manages so well.[7]

Even our major theoretical move toward overcoming these differences—alliance politics—begins from the assumption of bringing together already separated units. The basic problem is that alliances tend to depend on the very problem that they hope to overcome. Our normal way of undertaking alliances is to begin with units that are already separated from each other. Then we attempt to bring these units together without internally changing the units themselves. Judith Butler provides a good example of this point, arguing that insofar as queer studies scholars make feminist studies out to be always anti-sex, we undo the genealogy of specifically feminist sex radicalism that is a potential basis for holding together the study of gender and sexuality and for creating a politics that can respond to both the pleasures and the dangers of women's sexuality.[8] Despite the repeated calls for alliances in feminist theory, if we begin with a concept of women's studies that is already separated from ethnic studies or area studies, then we will fail to realize alliances in practice.

Moreover, once we are invested in progress, criticizing efforts toward change becomes particularly contentious because it seems as though such criticism discounts how hard we have worked and are working to make women's studies, the university, and even the world different. Through the course of this essay, I will suggest that such critique need not discount the important outcomes of our struggles. Regardless of how hard we have worked, of whether our will is strong or weak, our faith is good or bad, or we put our current theory into practice, we will not succeed until we reconceptualize the project at hand. In fact, we must give up on the idea that we can fully answer these problems and look to different types of strategies that are both alive to the contradictions inherent in the university and also support the feminist project of women's studies. We must give up on the progress narrative in which women's studies is always proceeding toward a future in which all will come right in the end.[9]

These are the conclusions I have reached after a decade of teaching and institution building in women's studies and a decade of study advocating both the politics of difference and alliance politics. In short, I come to these criticisms as a full participant in the paradigms that I seek to critique. I write this in a provocative manner, taking on models that have enabled much of our work and, yes, much of our progress over the last twenty-five years, not to undo this progress, but to create openings toward a different kind of future.

Hegemony and the Politics of Difference

We have been unable to realize our hopes in practice in part because we have been unable to conceptualize the obstacles that we face given that the academy is a central institution in the contemporary hegemony. Conceptualizing the specific issues of women's studies at this high level of abstraction may at first seem daunting, but it can also help to explain precisely why women's studies has been unable to fulfill its best intentions. Gramsci developed the concept of hegemony to explain the contradictory nature of power.[10] How is the status quo maintained in a complex system with multiple conflicting interests?

Hegemony allows for the management of these conflicts in part through the management of contradictions and disjunctions, thus turning incoherence into a strength rather than a weakness. For example, as both Eve Sedgwick and David M. Halperin have argued, heterosexism has proven so sustainable *because,* not in spite of, its incoherence.[11] Sedgwick famously recounts a court case in which a teacher who appealed his firing for being gay was turned down on appeal, not because he was gay, but because he had failed to disclose his homosexuality at the time when he was hired. The teacher faces an incoherent situation in which he has no good options. If he discloses his sexual identity initially he will never be hired, but if he fails to disclose his identity his firing is justified. In both cases the loss of his job turns on his identity, and yet the courts have effectively denied the role of identity in the case, thus closing off any avenue for protection under antidiscrimination law. This type of contradiction abounds in a hegemonic social formation.

Importantly, while such contradictions work to the benefit of hegemonic power, they can stifle possibilities for social change. *A Dictionary of Marxist Thought* describes contradiction as "a double-bind or self-constraint . . . where a course of action . . . generates a countervailing, inhibitory, undermining or otherwise opposed course of action."[12] As long as social movements focus on only one side of the contradiction, institutions, like the university, that support the status quo can counter movement efforts by shifting the forces of constraint to the other side. Thus, the very successes of social movements can set up countervailing problems. When it comes to the politics of difference, the fundamental contradiction of the contemporary hegemony is that differences are simultaneously sites of separation *and* sites of mutual constitution and interconnection.

Contemporary feminist practices often focus on the ways in which axes of difference—gender, race, class, nation—are intertwined such that their effects are mutually constitutive. Kimberlé Crenshaw's concept of "intersectionality" has come to be the predominant means of describing this intertwining.[13] The complication is that these "differences" have also been historically constituted as autonomous entities with different and sometimes contradictory effects.[14] Cornel West has made a trenchant argument, for example, that race has a "relative autonomy" from class.[15] This context has produced a historical trajectory in which the practice of social movement (and of those aspects of the academy tied to social movement) tends to swing back and forth like a pendulum between a focus on unities that deny differences and a focus on differences that denies interconnection. The trick is to be able to hold the two sides of this contradiction together.

Audre Lorde taught us long ago that difference is an issue of relation.[16] The issue for Lorde is not to do away with social differences but to change the social relations that produce difference as something to be hated and subordinated or repressed. The hegemonic social relations in which we find ourselves, particularly insofar as those relations are marked by capitalism, produce difference as "units"— fundamentally separate from each other—so that they can be commodified and packaged. This packaging obscures the mutual constitution of different "differences" and produces a politics organized by separate differences, rather than by their mutual constitution. In our rush to resist the problem of definitively separated units and to unearth the mutual constitution of differences, however, we have sometimes failed to hold onto the ongoing effects of the production of separable units of difference.

Part of what makes it so difficult to hold the two sides together is that the effects of relative autonomy can grow out of mutual constitution, so it seems that if we were to address mutual constitution we could also deal with the effects of relative autonomy. But, this perception fails to grasp the contradiction in full. In order to explore this complexity, I turn to an example taken from Marianne Torgovnick's 1990 book, *Gone Primitive.* I refer to this example because it is typical of much 1990s theorizing about differences and because Torgovnick connects several axes of difference in terms of their mutual constitution. In describing the formation of the idea of the "primitive" that was so central to racism in Western colonialism, Torgovnick writes as follows:

> [G]ender issues always inhabit Western versions of the primitive. . . .
> Freud's theories about sexuality, Malinowski's observations of male and
> female roles, have assured that how we conceive of the primitive helps
> form our conception of ourselves as sexual, gendered beings. . . . [W]hen
> the conventional substitution of females for primitives is avoided, other,

often class, substitutions may occur instead. Frequently, the working class or other subordinated segments of a population become associated or identified with primitives—the Irish, for example, or Jews . . . or U.S. blacks. These Others are processed, like primitives, through a variety of tropes which see them as a threatening horde, a faceless mass, promiscuous, breeding inferior.[17]

This rendering of mutual constitution points to the relations among gender, sexuality, colonialism, racism, and class hierarchy, but such a description also raises a number of questions: Are substitutions among differences merely "conventional"? Can any form of "othering" substitute for any other? At any time? In any place? In any way? What are the conventions and how are they formed? What are the specific effects of such substitutions? And, what are the specific effects of how we understand the relations among the terms?

We do need to look at how gender and colonialism are mutually formed, as Torgovnick does, but we also need to look at how they are distinct dominations. Instead, Torgovnick moves from mutual constitution, where the Western conceptualization of gender and sexuality is part of the process that forms Western conceptions of the "primitive," to substitution, where the "females" are substituted for "primitives." Mutual constitution and substitutability are not precisely the same thing, however.

The application of tropes across axes of domination works and has intellectual resonance because these tropes are conceptually connected in the formation of the subjects to which they are applied. It makes sense to substitute "females" for "primitives" because sexism helps to produce the racism of colonialism. And yet, this substitution in the context of domination tends to split axes of oppression, intensifying the effects of relative autonomy. Although substitution comes out of mutual constitution, it actively elides the constitutive connections between different forms of domination.

For example, feminists have raised concerns about the ways in which critics of colonialism, such as Frantz Fanon, present a portrait of the "colonized" as also "feminized."[18] In this sense, gender subordination substitutes for colonial subordination. But, the claim that the "colonized" are also "feminized" erases women among colonized peoples, making the colonized person implicitly male. Moreover, the close identification of gender and colonial domination in this scenario actually provides inducements for colonized men to distance themselves from rather than ally with women, claiming the privileges of masculinity at the expense of solidarity. And, this feminist criticism of colonized men can itself become implicated in the same divisive, dominative mechanism. Feminist criticisms of the patriarchal actions of men in colonized countries have often worked in the service of empire to reinforce the idea that colonized societies were primitive because of their different norms of gender and sexuality. Once again, gender domination substitutes for colonial domination in a way that intensifies the operation of racism and colonialism as separate from gender domination.

Mutual constitution of gender and colonial dominations or gender and racial dominations or colonial and racial dominations is often taken as a basis for alliance formation, but this is not necessarily the case. Whatever incentives that may be found to form alliances among those who share oppressions can be undercut, and they can be undercut precisely because these dominations are connected and yet can operate relatively autonomously from that connection. Mutual constitution can make for a substitutability that gives men from colonized countries and women from colonizing countries incentives to deny alliances based on mutual oppression, and, conversely, Third World women may be rightly leery of alliances with both First World women and Third World men.

The danger this contradictory social field presents is either that we will lose sight of the simultaneity and interlocking nature of oppressions by focusing on relative autonomy, or that we will be unable to analyze the distinct operations of different "differences" because of a focus on simultaneity. Until we deal with both sides at once, attempts at alliance formation will be subverted by the contradictory operations of differences within our hegemonic system. It is important to emphasize that difference itself is not the problem. Rather, the problem lies in the system that turns differences into dominations and then maintains those dominations through various contradictions. The question we face is whether we can address those contradictions.

Working in a Contradictory World

As it currently stands, the pendulum swings back and forth between sides of the contradiction have also tended to produce a cycle of guilt and recrimination about the politics of difference. As Wendy Brown has so clearly narrated, we set up the expectation in our students that women's studies can address any and all differences, and we have few good answers when our students ask why we have failed to incorporate any given difference within our programs.[19] We have so few answers, in part, because we face a contradictory social field, which means that we can never fully resolve the problem of difference. The relative autonomy of differences means that attempts to integrate differences into women's studies will be faced with the remainder of that which cannot be integrated, while the intersecting nature of differences means that the project of women's studies, insofar as it begins with the study of women or gender, will always be inadequate to the intersections.

This does not mean, however, that there is no way that we can change the practice of women's studies to address differences. If we change how we think about women's studies we might exchange guilt for action. We can give up the notion that women's studies will, sometime in the future, be perfectly antiracist, anti-heterosexist, anti-nationalist in exchange for a clear view of what we can do in the here and now. Recognizing our limits would allow us to discuss which of these changes we might make and how we might go about doing so. We can make strategic choices to change how our programs are structured. If we give up the notion that women's studies can resolve the problem of difference within itself, we might also strategize about how to make connections across the university, thus contributing to broader changes. Such a shift in conceptualization could also allow us to answer our students' expectations by delineating the reasons for the particular strategic choices we have made and articulating the limits that we, and they, face.

Women's studies programs (along with other programs in the U.S. academy) have tended to use two strategies to address social differences, strategies which also predominate in U.S. social movements: one is *multiplying* sites of study (or movement), most often by multiplying programs of study, and the second is *integrating* social differences into programs (or movements). Multiplying sites of study tends to address their relative autonomy, while integrating differences into women's studies has been an attempt to recognize that gender is mutually constituted with race, sexuality, nation, and class.

Women's studies was itself the result of the multiplying strategy, whereby the inability to address issues related to gender in the mainstream curriculum prompted the creation of a new site where this particular difference could be addressed. Similarly, other programs, particularly ethnic studies and area studies, were developed in response to problems in the dominant structure of the university. And this history is not simple. Sometimes women's studies developed in conjunction with ethnic studies. For example, Sonia Sanchez reported at a forum remembering the life of June Jordan that she and Jordan taught both black studies and women's studies at Berkeley, and only later did the two areas of study separate.[20] The simultaneous recognition and intertwining of difference that joint women's and black studies represented was not sustained, however, as the university exerted pressure to create "units" of study.

And, as we all know, the founding of women's studies did not solve the problem of women's "difference." Rather, once established as a separate field, women's studies faced its own problems of difference. As various critiques (many written very early in relation to the establishment of women's studies) have shown, racism, heterosexism, and nationalism among women were all issues that women's studies needed to address. In order to address its problems with difference, women's studies has also pursued both integrationist and multiplying strategies.

The move toward integration has been particularly evident in the profile of women's studies hiring practices. Shifts in women's studies hiring represent a necessary undertaking in response to struggles by women of color and lesbians for equal employment opportunities, but this particular approach has also had serious problems. Scholars who were often hired not just to pursue a field of study but to represent their difference within women's studies have found themselves tokenized and isolated. Simply hiring a woman of color in a women's studies department does not provide that scholar with sites across the university—for example, ethnic studies or cultural studies—that might support her work. When such sites do exist, but are not articulated with women's studies, the scholar may find herself pulled between two sites, which are not divided in her work, but which are fundamentally divided in the university. Moreover, programs assumed that these hires would produce curricular change, and those hired found themselves individually responsible for changes that actually need to run through the curriculum as a whole.

The limits of the strategy of integrating women's studies through hiring often prompted a return to the multiplying strategy. In ways both laudatory and discriminatory, women's studies has supported the formation of additional programs. In particular, lesbian and gay, queer, or sexuality studies programs have often grown out of women's studies programs, while women's studies has less frequently given its resources to the development of ethnic studies programs. This differential distribution of resources tends to reinforce connections between gender and sexuality while distancing connections between gender and race, once again instituting the study of gender and sexuality as implicitly "white." Although women's studies support for these new programs has often been extremely generous, this same move toward creating a new site could also be discriminatory as those who are "different" within women's studies are pushed outside of its bounds, implying that sexuality is somehow different from and outside of the concerns of "women."

There are a number of reasons for the difficulties associated with each of these strategies—integrating and multiplying—but the most fundamental problem is that each strategy addresses one side of the contradiction of social differences and, in so doing, establishes the other side of the contradiction as its new problem. Once women's studies is established as an autonomous field, it runs into the problem of not containing within itself "other" issues of race and class, sexuality and nationality. And so begins the second project of trying to integrate women of color, issues of class, and the relation of gender and sexuality or gender and (trans)nationality into women's studies. And yet, integration, too, is inadequate.

Perhaps the answer is to redouble our efforts, but doing so would not address the contradictory nature of social differences. Rather, we would remain in the cycle that this contradiction establishes. This is not to say that we should abandon our efforts to hire faculty members of color, for example, but that our focus on this method—and often on this method alone—has led us away from the types of actions that might actually allow women of color to thrive in a women's studies environment.

Alternatively, I would suggest that we need to change both the structure of our programs and the nature of our actions. We need to shift strategies.

To end the cycle in which we simply shift from one side of the contradiction to the other—from multiplying to integration and back—we need to take up both sides of the contradiction at once. This does not mean going back to the beginning and starting over so that women's studies is not set up as an autonomous unit in the first place. Rather, the fact that women's studies and ethnic studies or areas studies are separate units can be an advantage if these units are inter-related or inter-structured with each other.

The issue that we face is how to creatively combine units so as to slip the double bind of the contradiction that allows for the university's management of diversity. We need to turn both our theoretical and our practical attention to *how* best to make these connections. It is not enough simply to merge programs, nor can we simply skip over the particular differences that separate our programs in the hopes of moving on to a more general category or in the hopes of avoiding categorization altogether. We can construct connections that allow us to recognize differences without becoming trapped in them, and we can do so by building upon our already existing programs.

There will remain powerful forces, however, that will work to push attempts at building connections toward problematic unifications, and so this work must be undertaken strategically. In fact, the second half of the 1990s saw some universities suggesting that programs should combine into some vague notion of "other" studies. These suggestions appeared to be relatively thinly veiled cost-saving gestures on the presumption that combining programs would allow the university to reduce the currently available resources, resources that were won through difficult struggles.

There is a deeper reason to be skeptical of the fully integrated "other studies" option beyond the vicissitudes of the histories that have made us separate units and the need to protect resources that are already all too scarce. The move to the all-in-one approach merely reiterates the problem of difference at another level. Such all-in-one approaches address the interconnections among issues, but are less able to address their relative autonomy, a problem often borne out in practice. Michelle Taylor, in a 1999 masters thesis that she wrote at the University of Arizona, found that when it comes to social movements, large umbrella groups are less likely to support diversity and alliances than are smaller, more specified groups when they make connections among groups.[21] In a study of social movements in southern Arizona, Taylor investigated what type of environmentalist movements seemed to allow for the inclusion of or connections with feminist, antiracist, or economic issues. She found that those movements that dedicated themselves to including all issues under the large umbrella of environmentalism or even the connected umbrella of eco-feminism were the least successful at meeting this goal. Such umbrella movements tended to offer analyses that related all issues to a single center of movement. Rather than bringing groups together, establishing this center made it dominant, eventually marginalizing other concerns. Movements that set out to connect specific issues, like racial and economic justice with environmentalism (and these movements were often led by women), tended to be able to balance multiple concerns by making connections among them, rather than integrating them into a single whole.

Similarly, movements that have started as attempts to be open to all differences have not necessarily been able to embody that openness completely. In the 1990s the move toward queer politics and queer studies was, at its most utopian, not just a move to provide an umbrella for politics around proliferating sexual identities—gay, lesbian, bisexual, transgender—but was also an attempt to be open to any difference from dominant, normative life in the contemporary world. While queer politics has offered an important critique of both heteronormativity and the operation of normativity more broadly, there have now been a number of critiques of its ability to be fully open to the ways in which, for example, queer politics has not always been able to maintain progressive positions on issues of race or class. The white, urban, and often relatively affluent roots of queer politics have often been the unstated norm of queer activism.

These erasures of differences should not surprise us. Given the production of differences in our world, we have learned over and over again that a space which is unmarked by difference allows the dominant production of differences to operate without critique. This was, in fact, precisely the problem with new left politics, a problem that spurred much feminist activism. A movement that supposedly encompassed all forms of critique was actually driven by a white male and middle-class leadership and a set of white, male, and middle-class concerns. And then we saw the cycle repeat itself as the branch of the "women's movement" that developed out of new left politics supposedly encompassed the concerns of all women, but was dominated by those who bore an unmarked status with regard to race, sexuality, class, and nation. This problem of the overarching and unmarked group is what prompted the focus on the politics of difference that became central to women's studies and much feminist politics at least as early as the 1980s.

Just as these results are not surprising, they are not simply the historical accident of these particular movements. The fantasy that we can begin from a point of unmarked differences—that we can simply start from some kind of "people's liberation"—depends on the idea that "we"—whether that "we" names our social movements, our programs of study, or ourselves as individuals—have not already been produced in economies of difference. The women's bookstore in New York City recently changed owners and was transformed into an activist bookstore geared toward "people's activism," but with this shift the bookstore has not necessarily become more diverse. Now, instead of predominantly white, middle-class feminists, a new group of predominantly white, middle-class women and men who identify with a different set of progressive struggles tend to populate the space. Moving from a specific identification like "women's" to "people's" will not in and of itself undo either racism or classism and may institute new issues like sexism or heterosexism. We cannot forget that we have been marked simply by making one all-encompassing movement. Pat Parker named this problem succinctly when she wrote in her poem, "For the White Person Who Wants to Know How to Be My Friend," "The first thing you do is to forget that i'm Black. / Second, you must never forget that i'm Black."[22]

This analysis suggests that the fact that we already have autonomous units of difference may not be the problem in and of itself. Instead, if we reconceptualize how we understand the relationship between and among differences so as to avoid flipping back and forth between separable units and undifferentiated wholes, we can build on those programs.

Simply making connections across various already existing units is insufficient. As with alliance politics, if we move to connect units using what Elizabeth Spelman has termed an "additive" method, we begin with potential sites of interconnection already separated out.[23] For example, we are attempting to ally women's studies, where gender comes before race and ethnicity, with ethnic studies that are assumed to be masculinist. Women's studies can only effectively participate in connections *among* already existing programs if simultaneous changes are accomplished *within* women's studies. The question is, Can we move from these individual units of difference to a dual focus, one that addresses both the intersection and the relative autonomy of social differences?

Changing the Way We Work

In order to explain what this might look like, I will focus on one area of institutional change: the curriculum. It is important to note that curricular change does not in and of itself constitute institutional change. It can, however, be a step in building other types of relationships that can sustain broader institutional change.

I have suggested that the changes that we have made thus far under the rubrics of the "politics of difference" and "alliance politics" have been largely unsuccessful. Many women's studies programs are now shifting to a focus on "intersectionality" in the curriculum. Intersectionality provides a better means of addressing the contradictory constitution of differences than does the integrationist aspect of the politics of difference. It does not begin from the study of gender and then attempt to integrate the study of race and class into women's studies, but rather insists that the study of race and class *constitutes* the study of gender.

A curriculum organized around intersectionality would ensure that each course in the women's studies curriculum would consider throughout the syllabus the intersecting operations of gender, race, class, nation, and sexuality. This approach stands in contrast to most current curricula in which single courses focus on race or sexuality or nation (very few focus on class), while the rest of the women's studies curriculum remains focused on "women." Similarly, drawing intersections through an entire course requires changes in courses that now begin with a presumptively white, heterosexual subject—women—and then develop sections on women of color or lesbians. Neither the challenge nor the importance of this strategy should be underplayed. To develop a fully intersectional curriculum would be to change the way we most frequently narrate feminist history, challenge the analytical focus on gender and sexuality, and revamp the relation of courses to each other.

There are, however, limits to the effectiveness of this approach. Courses organized by intersectionality will never be "different enough." There will always be yet another difference that should be considered—disability or religion, for example. In fact, the relative import of these differences will shift over time as one or another social difference becomes salient. Ranu Samantrai, for example, has shown that as race and ethnicity were effectively challenged as markers enforcing social domination in Britain, the discourse shifted toward religion as a primary marker of community differences that could justify both restricted immigration and social segregation.[24] Racist ends were accomplished, but the language that accomplished these ends was that of religious difference. As long as the social conditions for the production of differences do not change fundamentally, differences will be produced in a never-ending list. Under such conditions, we will never be able to be fully intersectional.

There have, however, been some recent moves to shift women's studies toward more intersectional approaches, and these moves are worth considering. Most prominent has been the shift many programs and departments have made from women's studies to gender and sexuality studies. At their best these moves recognize that gender and sexuality are mutually constituted but should not be conflated.

Carolyn Dinshaw has argued that a notion of gender that has been repoliticized through transgender activism can be a crucial building block for a progressive program organized around gender and sexuality studies.[25] In this instance the shift to gender and sexuality studies implies an expansion of our notions of gender in addition to a focus on the mutual constitution of gender and sexuality. This expanded and repoliticized notion of gender may offer new ways of thinking through gender in relation to other axes of difference, but to do so would require more work than simply shifting to gender and sexuality studies. And, the institutionalization of gender and sexuality studies also immediately raises the question, why this particular intersection? And why not others? Why not race or class or nation?

Projects like the Center for Race and Gender at the University of California, Berkeley, and the Consortium for Gender, Race, and Ethnicity at the University of Maryland, College Park, represent a turn toward an equally important, but much less commonly institutionalized intersectional approach. The fact that gender and sexuality studies is now a relatively common way to organize academic programs, while gender and race are, if institutionalized at all, located in centers and projects, tells us that we need to attend to the differential operations of racism and heterosexism in relation to gender.

Another possibility in intersectional study, one that has been taken up quite effectively by the Women's Studies Department at the San Francisco State University, is to make transnational study the intersectional framework.[26] Rather than integrating transnational study into a curriculum organized around gender, by hiring yet another person who is tokenistically responsible for representing transnational study, this move involves a change in the curriculum as a whole. Developing a transnational curriculum can bring different differences together at the scale at which they are produced—that of global capitalism. It can allow us to track and integrate into the curriculum the type of shifts among different differences that Samantrai analyzes, so that our focus on one difference doesn't obscure discursive shifts toward others.

But, as with any such move, there are attendant dangers, and so shifting the entire curriculum to transnational study may not be the answer for all programs. The issue of scale alone—whether transnational or local—does not resolve the problem of difference. Further, not all transnational feminisms adequately addresses issues of difference, nor is transnational study or politics necessarily progressive; some transnational feminisms reassert imperialisms, some are extremely conservative sexually, some entail assertions of commonalities that run roughshod over the local issues that can be crucial in women's lives and in feminist politics. Thus, when we think of moving our curricula toward the transnational we must take care that such moves do not once again shunt aside local differences that are, in fact, the relevant issues for our particular context. In other words, if not undertaken with care, intersectionality grounded in transnationalism can cover over the specific differences it was meant to bring together.[27]

Another fundamental question that an intersectional curriculum faces is that it still tries to integrate all differences within the rubric of women's studies. Even as it includes the intersection of race and gender, for example, integrating the study of women of color into all women's studies classes, the curriculum still cannot contain all of the intellectual and historical currents that have constituted "women of color" as a subject. Such a project would require integrating the entire curricula of the various movement-based and area studies programs, a project which returns us to the problems of the super program. Rather, to address all of these currents we would need both an intersectional curriculum within women's studies and connections across programs of study.

It is important to address the fact that women's studies cannot contain all differences within itself if it is to have an effective answer to the question so frequently posed by students: But, why didn't you include [x] difference? The answer here is not to stonewall the students, but to acknowledge that the fantasy by which all differences can be included within women's studies is precisely that, a fantasy. Programs then face the project of making considered choices about how differences are included. There may, for example, be good reasons—reasons of geographical location or student demographics or the historical development of a particular program—to make certain issues primary. This is not to say that any issue should be ignored in an overall curriculum, but rather than asking, Why didn't we include [x]? we should ask other questions. What issues are most relevant given the context of this college or university? How do the courses relate to each other? If not all courses include a focus on disability, which do, and how do they relate to our other courses? If we use an intersectional approach, should we also have specific courses that are focused on gender and race or gender and religion?

The final and related limit faced by an intersectional curriculum is the ways in which even an intersectional curriculum, if undertaken under the rubric of women's studies, will tend to make gender a primary category of analysis. As much as we make the intersecting action of gender, race, and class, among others, the center of our project, the students still walk into a classroom marked by the rubric of women's studies. And as Elizabeth Spelman showed us in *Inessential Woman,* it makes a difference if you first walk through a door marked gender and then talk about race or if you first walk through a door marked race and then talk about gender.[28]

This question is in some ways about the status of women's studies itself. Why have a program based on walking through the door marked "women" first? The most obvious answer here is that there are literal as well as metaphoric doors in the world marked "women," and so it remains a salient category for analysis. These doors mark the operation of gender as a relatively autonomous category. It is extremely important that we can present the students with a clear rationale for the ongoing importance of women's studies as a relatively autonomous undertaking.

Thus, we must ask not only, Should we still have courses focused on one or two axes of difference—on gender and race, for example—but, Should we still have programs that are focused in terms of gender studies or ethnic studies or queer studies? Does intersectionality provide a means of producing a combined program that the idea of an overarching umbrella or single unit does not? Such a program would be an improvement on the idea of an overarching program in that the shift in focus to intersections among differences allows for the continuing analysis of differences as they are produced. Intersectionality does not resolve the problem of differences, however, because differences are produced through a contradictory process. We do not have a simple geometry in which relatively autonomous differences meet up periodically at various intersections. Rather, intersections are *internal* to relatively autonomous differences and intersecting differences are *simultaneously* autonomous. How best can we address this reality?

Given that any single approach can threaten to return us to one side or the other of the contradiction, my suggestion is that we take up multiple strategies. A simultaneously intersectional and autonomous approach would call for programs to become *interstructured.* Our task is both larger than we usually imagine and also smaller. It is larger in that our problems cannot be addressed only by changing women's studies: we must participate in, and sometimes initiate, changes that are greater than our individual programs. But, our task is smaller in that it can start at where we are. The fact that we have programs separated by gender, race, and sexuality is not the unspeakable secret that means we can never reach the goal of our progress narrative. The fact that we have different programs is partially an advantage. It creates a drag on the imperializing imperative of full integration, and it allows us to mark and address differences as they are embodied. Nonetheless, for this advantage not to be a reinforcement of segregationist problems, we cannot stop at this point. We must work to dynamically interrelate these programs.

There are a number of potential strategies for such a project, some quite ambitious, others very basic. How any one of these strategies develops will depend on the particular institution. All require building relationships among faculty and students in various departments and programs, work that can be slow and painstaking, but that has important rewards. One ambitious undertaking is to build cross-curricular projects that could provide a basis and a site for different programs to work together. It is also possible, however, to start small: joint speaker series, colloquia, or seminars may be important starting points. Something as simple as inviting program directors to get together once a month for an informal lunch to talk about university politics or student and curricular issues can be a means of beginning to form connections. From such relational work, new strategies for developing curricular and institutional change can develop.

Should we be able to build these relationships, there are various ways that we might shift the curriculum—both within women's studies and among programs. If, as Spelman suggests, it makes a difference whether we first go through a door marked gender or one marked race or one marked class, we not only must build intersectional courses, but must also shift kaleidoscopically among those axes or differences which we make primary. In other words, one would need to make the study of gender primary and then make the study of race primary and then return to gender and then to race and then to class, etc. There are various creative ways to build structures among programs to produce this effect. Women's studies at the University of Arizona has pursued the strategy of building a Chicana studies concentration into the major that would include courses taught outside of the Women's Studies Department. In other words, this concentration does not try to contain all differences within the context of women's studies, but builds on both the Chicana studies offerings *within* women's studies and those offered *among* various other programs, including Mexican American studies, Spanish and Portuguese and English. Thus, not only is the women's studies curriculum more diverse, but the students participate in making connections across the university.

Such concentrations do not have to be made out of whole cloth, however. Conversations between women's studies and other interdisciplinary programs can be started by asking our colleagues in other fields about the feasibility of requiring women's studies students to take a single course (not necessarily cross-listed with women's studies) in another field. Starting with a single requirement can begin to build curricular connections across programs and lay the basis for future collaborations. An even more preliminary step might be to request course lists from other programs each semester and post them as of potential interest to women's studies students.

Another possibility is presented by bringing together faculty from different units to team-teach courses. For example, what if we were to develop a course, team-taught across two programs, that was part of the required curriculum for both programs? Such a course would establish the intersectionality of fields without dismantling their relative autonomy. More ambitious still would be to produce the introduction to women's studies course found in many women's studies programs as a joint, and jointly taught, introduction to women's studies and another field like ethnic studies. The advantage of teaching the introduction in this way is that it would bring together questions of gender and ethnicity from the beginning of the students' education in both programs. It would encourage students to continue to think that race and ethnicity are part of women's studies and gender is part of ethnic studies throughout their subsequent education.

Team teaching and joint courses provide the opportunity to undertake a doable change, which could still have profound implications for both programs. Most importantly, the programs become connected and yet are also maintained as separate units. One of the blocks to such an approach is the way that most universities often refuse to count or otherwise establish roadblocks to team teaching. We can now understand this refusal on the part of the university in a new light. It is not just a cost-saving measure, ensuring one instructor for one course, but it is also a means of keeping the units of the university separate and distinct, part of its management of difference.

The fundamental challenge of teaching joint courses that are part of multiple programs is that one would have to take on directly the contradiction of mutual constitution and relative autonomy. To take on this challenge would establish a different set of expectations for our students. They would be able to explore the contradictions faced by the politics of difference from the beginning of their education. In the end, they might be better prepared to negotiate differences and to make connections across those differences.

It is true that the things that I have suggested would require major changes in how we do women's studies. Even if a department or program commits itself to small changes as starting points, the implications for how we think and do women's studies are profound. To begin any of these projects, we must at least have a clear understanding of the problems that we face and why our problems are so often recurrent. With such an analysis we can assess how best to make changes in the particular context in which we work.

As we enter the next quarter century of women's studies, let us celebrate our successes thus far. And, let us do things differently in the future.

Notes

I would like to thank my colleagues at both the University of Arizona and Barnard College for their many insights over the years. I would also like to thank the earlier readers of this essay for both their criticisms and insights, including members of the Women's Studies Program at Wesleyan University, Christina Crosby, Mary Pat Brady, and Kate McCollough.

1. For a discussion of successes and failures, see Robyn Wiegman, ed., *Women's Studies on Its Own* (Durham: Duke University Press, 2002); and Ellen Messer-Davidow, *Disciplining Feminism: From Social Activism to Academic Discourse* (Durham: Duke University Press, 2002). See also the introduction to this volume.

2. Louis Althusser, "Ideology and Ideological State Apparatuses (Notes toward an Investigation)," in *Lenin and Philosophy and Other Essays,* trans. B. Brewster (New York: Monthly Review Press, 1971), 127–186.

3. Richard Ohmann, *Politics of Knowledge: The Commercialization of the University, the Professions, and Print Culture* (Middletown, Conn.: Wesleyan University Press, 2003).

4. Chandra Talpade Mohanty, "On Race and Voice: Challenges for Liberal Education in the 1990s," in *Between Borders: Pedagogy and the Politics of Cultural Studies,* ed. Henry Giroux and Peter McLaren (New York: Routledge, 1994), 145–166.

5. Mohanty, "On Race and Voice," 146.

6. For a more extensive critique of the progress narrative, see Janet R. Jakobsen with Ann Pellegrini, "Introduction: World Secularisms at the Millennium," *Social Text* 64 (fall 2000): 1–27.

7. See Christina Crosby, "Dealing with Differences," in *Feminists Theorize the Political,* ed. Judith Butler and Joan W. Scott (New York: Routledge, 1992), 130–143.

8. Judith Butler, "Against Proper Objects," *differences* 6, no. 2–3 (summer–fall 1994): 1–26.

9. For further analysis of how our attempts to perfect women's studies may lead us further away from achieving racial or ethnic justice, see Rachel Lee, "Notes from the (Non)Field: Teaching and Theorizing Women of Color," *Meridians: Feminist, Race, Transnationalism* 1, no. 1 (autumn 2000): 85–109, see especially 91–92.

10. Antonio Gramsci, "Hegemony, Relations of Force, Historical Bloc," in *The Gramsci Reader: Selected Writings, 1916–1935,* ed., David Forgacse (New York: New York University Press, 2000), 189–221.

11. Eve Kosofsky Sedgwick, *Epistemology of the Closet* (Berkeley: University of California Press, 1990); David Halperin, *Saint Foucault: Toward a Gay Hagiography* (New York: Oxford University Press, 1995).

12. Tom Bottomore et al., eds., *A Dictionary of Marxist Thought* (Cambridge: Harvard University Press, 1983), 91.

13. Kimberlé Crenshaw, "Demarginalizing the Intersection of Race and Sex: A Black Feminist Critique of Antidiscrimination Doctrine, Feminist Theory, and Antiracist Politics," *University of Chicago Legal Forum* 4 (1989): 139–167.

14. Wendy Brown, "The Impossibility of Women's Studies," *differences* 9, no. 3 (fall 1997): 79–101.

15. Cornel West, "Marxist Theory and the Specificity of African-American Oppression," in *Marxism and the Interpretation of Culture,* ed. Cary Nelson and Lawrence Grossberg (Chicago: University of Chicago Press, 1988), 17–33.

16. Audre Lorde, *Sister Outsider* (Trumansburg, N.Y.: Crossing Press, 1984).

17. Marianna Torgovnick, *Gone Primitive: Savage Intellects, Modern Lives* (Chicago: University of Chicago Press, 1990), 17–18. I would like to thank Tracy Fessenden for bringing this passage to my attention.

18. Diana Fuss provides a complex reading of the passages in Fanon's *Black Skin, White Masks,* that are most frequently cited by feminists. See Diana Fuss, *Identification Papers* (New York: Routledge, 1995), 141–165.

19. Brown, "The Impossibility of Women's Studies," 93.

20. "Celebrating the Life and Work of June Jordan," City University of New York, April 12, 2003.

21. Michelle Taylor, "Ecofeminism in Theory and Practice" (master's thesis, University of Arizona, 1999).

22. Pat Parker, *Movement in Black (An Expanded Edition)* (Ithaca: Firebrand Books, 1999).

23. Elizabeth Spelman, *Inessential Woman: Problems of Exclusion in Feminist Thought* (Boston: Beacon Press, 1988).

24. Ranu Samantrai, *AlterNatives: Black Feminism in the Postimperial Nation* (Stanford: Stanford University Press, 2002).

25. Carolyn Dinshaw, "Women's Studies in the Twenty-First Century," panel discussion, City University of New York, 2001.

26. For a complex articulation of the possibilities and limits of transnational feminism in relation to women's studies, see Caren Kaplan and Inderpal Grewal, "Transnational Feminist Practices and Interdisciplinary Feminist Scholarship: Refiguring Women's and Gender Studies," in *Women's Studies on Its Own: A Next Wave Reader in Institutional Change,* ed. Robyn Wiegman (Durham: Duke University Press, 2002).

27. For in depth analysis of these issues see Sandra K. Soto, "Where in the Transnational World Are U.S. Women of Color?" in this volume.

28. Spelman, *Inessential Woman*, 144–145.

Women's Studies and Chicana Studies

LEARNING FROM THE PAST, LOOKING TO THE FUTURE

MONICA BROWN AND MIROSLAVA CHÁVEZ-GARCÍA

Chicana feminists' and Chicana studies' relationship to Euro-American feminists and women's studies has been (and continues to be) largely ambivalent since the women's movement and inception of the fields in the 1960s and 1970s. The nature of the relationship has to do largely with the fact that Chicana feminism and Chicana studies, though they emerged out of a common historical context with the (white) women's movement, dealt with specific political, economic, and social issues, leading to somewhat different agendas, approaches, and goals.[1]

The academy—be it conferences, classrooms, or hallways—has often been the tenuous meeting place for Chicana and Euro-American women scholars. These ambivalent relations have been exacerbated by what Mitsuye Yamada has called the "loyalty oath"—"a demand for exclusive allegiance either to Women's Studies or Ethnic Studies but not both." "U.S. multicultural feminists," Yamada argues, "have had to walk a tightrope because of the institutional quarantine on their overlapping areas of activism and inquiry."[2] Chicana feminists, academics, and activists have documented the difficulties in forging alliances with Euro-American feminists and women's studies in the 1970s, 1980s, and 1990s.[3] It is this continued state of conflict and struggle that motivated us to take on this subject even at the risk of being accused of "divisiveness" or, more worrisome, of putting white feminists (once again) at the center of critical inquiry.

Chicanas and Latinas are not the first or only women to critique Euro-American feminists' sometimes limited commitment to eradicating racism and classism as well as sexism within their ranks. Frustrated with Euro-American feminists attempt to "include" race, class, and sexuality, Chicanas and Latinas, like other women of color, left (and continue to leave) women's studies in search of more productive spaces in which to nurture their own intellectual and personal pursuits. As this essay will demonstrate, Chicanas and Latinas have had to carve their own spaces on what Gloria Anzaldúa has termed the "borderlands" (*las fronteras*) of

women's, Chicano, Lesbian, and Third World women's studies.[4] Chicanas' decision to do so has, unfortunately, led to a divide between Chicana and Euro-
American feminists and between Chicana studies and women's studies. Some
scholars and activists have tried to bridge this divide, though with mixed results,
while others have abandoned those attempts all together.[5] More recently, some have
wondered at the political efficacy of always being at the margins, the academic
borderlands—being neither here nor there—refusing totalization. In doing so, they
have argued, we risk being excluded from resources and opportunities allotted to
those "housed" in a specific academic locale.

In this essay, our goal is to offer some suggestions for the ways in which
Chicana, Latina, and Euro-American feminists, scholars, and activists can work
together to bridge feminist theory and practice, suggestions that take into account
what Chela Sandoval has termed "the strengths of our diversities."[6] As many Third
World and women-of-color scholars and activists have argued, we need to educate
ourselves about each other and our histories in order for us to dialogue effectively
across our differences.[7] We must also recognize our strengths and weaknesses and
come together willing to collaborate on feminist-womanist-*mujerista* projects. In
doing so, we hope to move away from a history of ignorance and antagonism and
toward theoretical and pedagogical transformation of women's studies. We recognize the limits of this essay, for it does not begin to address adequately the complexities, shared histories, and differences of women of color, transnational
feminists, and Euro-American women in the academy. Nor does it speak fully to
the rich and varied experiences of other Latina scholar-activists in the United States:
Puertorriqueñas, Salvadoreñas, Chilenas, Cubanas and other Latinoamericanas—
mujeres in the struggle against racial and sexual oppression. Nevertheless, our aim
here is to provide an understanding of the complex relationship of a teacher-scholar
located or affiliated with Chicana studies and women's studies. To do so, we begin with an overview of the history of Chicana feminism and scholarship and its
points of confluence and conflict with the development of Euro-American feminist theory and women's studies. By necessity, this is not a sweeping history, but
rather an examination of critical moments in the history of Chicana and women's
studies. Next, we discuss current Chicana feminist views about Euro-American
feminism and women's studies, exploring the social, political, economic, and racial issues that both unite(d) and divide(d) feminists. Finally, we conclude by offering some insights and constructive goals drawn from personal experiences with
both successful and unsuccessful collaborative projects and proposing areas for
future alliances and the implications of such partnerships.

Chicana feminism and Chicana studies developed within the Chicano movement of the late 1960s and 1970s and were shaped by the broader context of black
civil rights and women's, gay and lesbian, and Third World liberation movements.
The Chicano movement originated as a set of diverse local and regional struggles
for justice, civil rights, and political representation. Activists, men and women,
demanded equal rights under the law, access to education, immigration reform,
adequate housing and health care, and an end to police brutality and the Vietnam
War. Students and teachers, on high school and college campuses, in particular,

placed significant emphasis on the need to have Chicana and Chicano (or Chicana/o) interests represented at all levels of education. Chicanas/os articulated those demands within the context of cultural nationalism, with its emphasis on indigenous roots, communalism, political insurgency, and Mexican culture, particularly the patriarchal family.[8]

Activists' demands and pressure resulted in Chicano studies programs, centers, and departments across college, university, and high school campuses. The purpose of those new institutions was to study the interlocking social, political, and economic issues having the greatest impact on Chicana/o families and communities. At the same time, many activists believed these institutions would bridge the divide between research in the academy and activism in the community. The handful of Chicano (most of them male) scholars who entered the universities and took positions in Chicano studies in the late 1960s and 1970s drew from Marxist theory and anticolonial studies and developed their own theoretical models and frameworks. The result of their activity was an outpouring of research on Chicano families, the barrio, labor and political struggles, ethnic and cultural identity, and, eventually, immigration.[9] Visibly absent in the production of Chicano studies was attention to women, women's history, and the use of gender as a category of analysis.[10]

Chicana activists and scholars, many of whom had previous experience in community activism, labor unions, politics, and the women's movement, had identified a similar omission within the Chicano movement. Chicanas realized that the ideology of cultural nationalism, with its emphasis on *la familia*—a patriarchal institution that had been oppressive to women—relegated them to subservient roles within the movement, a condition that reflected their status in the larger community. Chicanas questioned the ideology and practices of Chicanos who preached power to *la raza* (the Mexican people) yet relegated many Chicanas to "female" duties such as answering the phone, making coffee, and servicing the men.[11]

The contemporary Euro-American women's movement, with its attention to women's inequality, sexism, and, eventually, homophobia, appealed to Chicanas, if only in a limited way. Early on, in the 1960s and 1970s, many Chicanas—lesbian and heterosexual—participated in the radical, lesbian, and mainstream organizations that comprised the women's movement. Like activism in the community and in the Chicano movement, women-identified spaces became an important "training ground" for shaping and giving meaning to Chicana feminist and *lesbiana* "consciousness." Gloria Anzaldúa's brief work with the Feminist Writers Guild shaped her writing, while Elizabeth "Betita" Martínez, activist, founder, and editor of *El Grito del Norte,* found a space with New York Radical Women.[12] Likewise, in the 1970s, as a graduate student, Emma Pérez, a Chicana lesbian writer and historian, turned to women's studies and the Women's Center at the University of California, Los Angeles (UCLA). There, she said in a recent interview, she found a "safe space."[13]

Nevertheless, Chicanas noted a lack of self-reflexivity in the women's movement in terms of racial, sexual, and class oppression. Chicanas argued that they suffered from race, class, and gender oppression, or what they called "triple oppression," and homophobia in the larger society. Thus, to Chicanas the idea of a universal "sisterhood"—as espoused by Euro-American feminists—erased the specificities of their experiences as well as the power differentials among women. Many Chicana activists also saw the women's movement as largely a middle- and upper-class phenomenon that focused on individualistic women's goals—goals that often depended on the domestic labor of black, brown, and working-class women. Furthermore, they envisioned themselves rooted in the collective Chicano/a community struggle and with issues such as poverty, welfare, child and elderly care, race discrimination, health care, the farmworkers' struggle, and prison reform, most of which the Euro-American women's movement often overlooked.[14]

Chicanas increasingly turned their attention to the Chicano movement and organized meetings and held conferences on the role of *la chicana* in *el moviemento,* with some arguing that Chicano liberation was not possible without Chicana liberation. Not all Chicanas agreed, however. In an effort to distance themselves from what they critiqued as *gringa* feminist agendas, a group of Chicana "loyalists" argued that they did not want to be "liberated" but, rather, supported *"la causa"* (the Chicano cause) and cultural nationalism. Chicana feminists argued that they did not want to separate themselves from el movimiento but wanted to focus on issues of *la mujer* in order to strengthen the movement's overall goals. Their interrogation of the nationalist and gender ideology and practices within the movement led them to issue scathing critiques of the movement and, eventually, to form their own organizations, publish their own newsletters and journals, and develop their own theoretical models and paradigms for analyzing and examining the historical and contemporary experiences of Chicanas.[15]

Not surprisingly, Chicanos and some Chicanas labeled the women who criticized the movement as counter-revolutionary *vendidas* (sellouts), *agringadas* (assimilated to the Euro-American mainstream), *malinchistas* (as "La Malinche," traitors to their race), *feministas* (like Euro-American feminists), and (with the intent to critique) *marimachas* (lesbians). The accusations, in turn, heated up debates among Chicana feminists, some of whom attempted to distance themselves from those whom they saw as "white-identified feminists" and from Chicana lesbians. Chicana lesbians, on the other hand, sought to make sexuality, as well as race, class, and gender, the source(s) of their identity politics. Rampant homophobia in the Chicano community was difficult to contain, however, and infected even the most "progressive" Chicana feminists, who sometimes isolated and marginalized Chicana lesbians.

Initially, in the late 1960s and early 1970s, many Chicana lesbians had gravitated not to the Chicano movement but to the women's movement, particularly to the vibrant and vocal lesbian movement, which professed to embrace Third World lesbian women. There, in women's writing groups, national women's organizations, and women's studies programs, Chicana lesbians sharpened and focused their critique of homophobia and sexism.[16] But, in time, many too became disillusioned with the women's movement and the dominance of white middle- and upper-class women in leadership positions who marginalized and silenced them, despite the rhetoric of inclusion. Black lesbian women, like Chicanas, experienced racism and classism in the lesbian movement and, in response, organized collectives and published their writings.[17] African American women's organizing and publishing as well as the exclusionary practices of the lesbian movement became the catalysts for Chicana lesbian writers, such as Gloria Anzaldúa and Cherríe Moraga, to undertake literary projects in which they articulated their own subjectivity and relation to Euro-American feminists, lesbians, and heterosexuals.

In the late 1970s, with the encouragement of Merlin Stone, a progressive Euro-American feminist-lesbian, Anzaldúa set out to document and compile the experiences of radical women of color, lesbians, and heterosexuals in "white" feminist circles and in the larger society. When the project proved too much for her alone, Anzaldúa recruited Cherríe Moraga, Chicana activist and author, to collaborate on editing the anthology. Published in 1981, *This Bridge Called My Back: Writings by Radical Women of Color,* was a seminal moment in the history of Chicana/o studies and Third World feminism more generally. The collection was an opportunity for women of color to come together to respond to white feminists' racism and ignorance and also an opportunity for women of color to talk to each other across the strengths of their diversities.[18] As Anzaldúa stated in an interview, she wanted her book to teach white women to listen to women of color. By the number of book sales (it sold more than forty thousand copies, went into a second and, most recently, third edition, and was translated in Spanish) it became evident to Anzaldúa that Euro-American women "were listening to the voices of women of color . . . and that women of color were listening to each other."[19]

Despite this optimism, two years later, in 1983, in the second edition of *This Bridge Called My Back,* Anzaldúa and Moraga pessimistically observed that "things [in women's studies and "white" feminist circles] have gotten worse. In academic and cultural circles, Third World women have become the subject matter of many literary and artistic endeavors by white women, and yet we are refused access to the pen, the publishing house, the galleries, and the classroom."[20] Three years later, in 1986, Maxine Baca Zinn and a distinguished cohort of U.S. Third World women scholars explored the institutionalization of white privilege and the ways in which it was manifested in the exclusionary practices at two of the leading women's studies journals, *Signs* and *Feminist Studies.*[21]

Since the publication of the first edition of *This Bridge Called My Back,* Chicana and Latina feminists have entered academia (albeit in scarce numbers) in Chicana/o studies, women's studies, and other mainstream programs and departments. From the borderlands of their respective fields, they have taken on the task of understanding the different ways in which the intersections of race, class, gender, and sexuality shaped their and their community's material reality, consciousness, and identity. Chicana writers, editors, and publishers have produced a prolific amount of work—theoretical, philosophical, activist, and feminist writing. Unfortunately, much of it went ignored and overlooked in early feminist writings.[22]

When Anzaldúa edited and published *Making Face/Making Soul: Creative and Critical Perspectives by Women of Color* in 1990, her work demonstrated how little things had actually changed in the previous decade, despite the attention Chicana lesbian texts, such as Cherríe Moraga's *Loving in the War Years* and

Anzaldúa's own *Borderlands/La Frontera,* had received in mainstream women's studies curriculum and classrooms. Similar critiques were echoed several years later, in 1992, when Tey Diana Rebolledo, one of the first Chicanas to direct a women's studies program, asked the question, "Chicana Studies: Is There a Future for Us in Women's Studies?"[23] Her analysis, while constructive and insightful, was less than optimistic. One of the problems she explored was the very same one Chicana feminists in the 1970s and 1980s articulated—the difficulty of integrating Chicana and Latina work into "mainstream books, journals, and collections."[24] She found that when women's studies scholars asked Chicanas and Latinas to submit their work for an anthology or other collection, too often they did it as an afterthought or as a form of tokenism. The result of such practices was (and is) to deny Chicanas voice and power in the decision-making process in women's studies and in academia in general. Another equally pernicious consequence of tokenization is appropriation of Chicana work with little acknowledgment of authorship or the recognition of the existence of a larger cohort of Chicana scholars, activists, and writers.[25]

A 1992 survey, conducted by Beatríz Pesquera and Denise Segura, of highly educated Chicana feminists, activists, and scholars found that such exclusionary practices made Chicanas reluctant to work with Euro-American women. Pesquera and Segura's survey of the members of MALCS (*Mujeres Activas en Letras y Cambio Social*)—"founded in 1983 by Chicana faculty and graduate students as a support and advocacy group and a forum for sharing research interests"—also demonstrated that the majority of Chicanas continued to criticize the racial and class biases and the lack of attention to their needs within the Euro-American women's movement.[26] Contemporary Chicanas and Latinas, Pesquera and Segura concluded in another essay which dealt with the same theme, were less concerned with finding ways to incorporate women in the male-dominated society than with finding ways to alter systems of inequality and exploitation engendered by capitalism.[27] Pesquera and Segura did note, however, Chicanas' and Latinas' consciousness of women's studies scholars' attempts to include working women as well as women of color in conferences, organizations, and, to some extent, agendas.

Indeed, we must acknowledge that writings of Chicanas and Latinas, as well as those of other women-of-color scholar-activists, which have been at the forefront of emerging feminist scholarship, have slowly made their way into women's studies circles. As Tey Diana Rebolledo observed, new courses dealing with race, ethnicity, class, and sexuality have been developed in women's studies programs, centers, and departments. The literary-activist production of Chicana, African American, and Third World women, in turn, has led some Euro-American scholars to interrogate feminist theory and praxis and to rethink their conceptual, pedagogical, and curricular frameworks. As such, mainstream feminists and women's studies scholars have paid increasing attention to the "isms" as well as privileges inherent in whiteness, middle-class status, and heterosexuality.

Notwithstanding the strides in women's studies, Margaret Villanueva and Rachel Lee have argued, in separate and recent works, 1999 and 2000, respectively, that women of color and their scholarship continue to be tokenized and marginalized.[28] In working with young Chicanas and Latinas at Northern Illinois University, Villanueva has observed the ambivalence of Latinas to work with Euro-American feminists, a reluctance largely stemming from their invisibility in the research, teaching, and workshops in the Women's Studies Program. These and other experiences led Villanueva to conclude that women's studies "ha[d] yet to be transformed."[29] For the transformation to take place, Villanueva suggested the inclusion of Chicana and Latina works in women's studies in general, the recruitment and retention of Latina scholars and students, and the "transformation of the underlying premises, assumptions, and canonical texts in the field."[30]

Lee, on the other hand, in her experience in teaching the only women-of-color class in the Women's Studies Program at UCLA—Women's Studies 130, which forms part of the core of the program—came to a similar conclusion. While she observed an investment in "colored women's bodies"—that is, in having a woman of color teach the course—she noted a "disinvestment" in integrating and teaching the scholarship of women of color in general. As such, the scholarship (and bodies) of women of color were (and are) primarily confined to one course, Women's Studies 130. Lee concluded by stating that, while Chela Sandoval's conception of an oppositional ideology allows us to be highly mobile and to enter and exit feminist circles at will, it also relegates us to the margins, at best, and renders us invisible, at worst, with no real space in which to cultivate our research and writing. Lee concluded by urging women of color to claim a territory, to move from the borderlands to the center of scholarly inquiry—whether it is in or outside of women's studies. Or else, Lee warned, we face the possibility of disintegration.[31]

Whether women-of-color scholars, including Chicanas, will respond to or engage in dialogue with Lee's call has yet to be seen. What is known is that the recent attempts by women of color to dialogue with women's studies scholars have, in many ways, backfired and, instead, led to increasing antagonisms. Since the late 1980s, women's studies feminists have identified a "crisis" in the field, with some implicitly arguing that the critiques of racism by women of color have led to the questioning of the basic premises and future of the field. In Villanueva's own experiences, when Euro-American feminist scholars are confronted with racist practices, the latter often react with "denial, explanations of improvements already made, or entrenched defensiveness."[32] In her essay, Lee also noted the defensive posturing from several women's studies scholars who have lashed out against the "guilt" and "anger" assailed by women of color. These women's studies scholars, Lee stated, have displayed "outright hostility" and attacked not only women-of-color scholarship but also their pedagogy in feminist journals.[33] Ultimately, Lee believes, "the question of race and women of color in women's studies has deepened the uncertainty of women's studies and feminism," a proposition that has many women's studies and Third World women scholars concerned.[34]

As a Chicana feminist (Chávez-García) and a Latina feminist (Brown) engaged in studying and teaching the lives, literature, and history of Chicanas and Latinas in the United States in and outside of women's studies, we are compelled to build upon the work of critics such as Gloria Anzaldúa, Cherríe Moraga, Denise

Segura, Beatríz Pesquera, and Margaret Villanueva, among many others who have come before us. We do so striving to keep the dialogue open—the tentative bridges and structures in place—to build strong and revolutionary foundations. We, like each feminist teacher-scholar discussed thus far, have been shaped by our individual experiences, and writing this essay has given us the space for personal reflection. *Chávez-García:* Though dedicated to the study of the lives and history of Mexican women as a graduate student, I never considered women's studies as an "option" until later in my professional life. In graduate school, my perception was that women's studies was a place for white women's history and that the only institutional home available to me outside my discipline (Chicana/o history) was Chicano/a studies. Perhaps it was my own false perception that excluded me from women's studies, but there was little in the women's studies curriculum or campus activities to suggest otherwise. *Brown:* As a newly graduated PhD, I had gone back to my doctoral institution for a visit. The mother of a two-year-old, and pregnant with my second child, I ran into my former professor, a past director of women's studies, active member of National Women's Studies Association (NWSA), and a strong feminist presence on campus. She took one look at me and exclaimed, "Monica! Haven't you ever heard of birth control?!" It was as though my visibly pregnant body had given her permission to make a value judgment on my choice and, going even further, to suggest that it was my own ignorance that led me to what, apparently, was unthinkable: two babies pre-tenure. I was a woman of color whose body was out of reproductive control—a familiar narrative outside of academia as well, though with far more serious consequences.

Brown and Chávez-García: Lastly, we'd like to share another unfortunate and yet familiar experience that occurred at the start of our collaboration on the issues addressed in this essay. A couple of years ago, we submitted a proposal, "Chicana/Latina Studies and Women's Studies: Problems and Possibilities," to the Future of Women's Studies: Foundations, Interrogations, Politics conference, held at the University of Arizona, celebrating the twenty-fifth anniversary of the Department of Women's Studies. To our knowledge, and at the conference itself, we comprised the *only* panel dealing *exclusively* with Chicana/Latina issues. Soon, the conference organizers contacted us, asking if we would be willing to "combine" our workshop/presentation with one focusing on Jewish American women. Later, we also discovered that the organizers had asked two separate panel proposals focusing on Native American women to combine. We declined the offer, and, to the credit of the organizers, we had a productive conversation about why we felt so strongly about needing a full session to present our ideas and engage in a dialogue and why we objected to the request itself. In the end, the organizers complied with our appeal.

What does all of this have to do with Chicana feminists' relationship to Euro-American feminism(s) and women's studies? How do these tensions impact the possibility of creating bridges across our difference? We argue that they have a direct bearing on how we create alliances and how we manage to (or not to) work with one another. As we have noted, coalition building both within and without the academy has been difficult to forge due to racial, ethnic, class, and cultural differences as well as distrust. One way in which we can build alliances is to work on projects that draw from each other's strengths and that incorporate mutual collaboration and effort. We can do this by planning and holding conferences, building interdisciplinary programs and departments, publishing books and articles, and developing feminist theory and praxis. But before we can successfully work together, we—Chicanas, Latinas, Euro-American women, and Third World women—need to interrogate our own privileges as scholars and academicians vis-à-vis the communities we seek to represent. Even though many Chicana and Third World women come from working-class families and poor neighborhoods that suffer from neglect, we/they are no longer in those underprivileged positions. As feminists, scholars, and activists—lesbian and heterosexual—we often have access to resources, support, and status that are generally denied to members of our communities of origin. We need to come to the table with Euro-American feminists with an understanding of the power and powerlessness we possess in order to come to an honest discussion of the kinds of relationships and feminist community we can forge. Anything less is built on false pretenses.[35]

It is evident that Chicana studies and women's studies programs have come a long way and that their paths have, at times, continued along their own trajectory, while at other times, intersected, and clashed. As Chicana and Latina feminists, we have a lot of work to do in evaluating our current positions and where we want to be in ten, twenty, or thirty years. We see several goals in our struggle for change. We need to begin with self-critique—by interrogating our own feminist theories and praxis and noting whether they are inclusive of all Chicanas and Latinas, whether lesbian, heterosexual, working class, or professional, if we seek to represent those voices. We need to be mindful of our global sisters in struggle and avoid a U.S.-centric critical and social agenda. We also need to recognize and build upon successful collaborations with Euro-American feminists and within women's studies departments and not homogenize and reduce the lives of Euro-American women, who represent a variety of ethnic and class backgrounds, religions, sexual preferences, and lived experiences. We also need to consider Rachel Lee's call to claim territoriality, to locate a space from which to carry out our work.

Euro-American feminists and women's studies scholars, on the other hand, need to continue their work, acknowledging their own race and class privilege, and explore the ways they contribute to the oppression and continued colonization of women of color. They need to work, along side women of color, to change women's studies curricula that erase or tokenize the lives of and scholarship by women of color.

In conclusion, we would like to discuss what we see as the necessary twin efforts, both the need to forge connections across classes, ethnicities, religions, nationalities, and sexualities in women's studies programs as well as what we see as the continuing need for women of color in the academy to set their own agendas, envision their own spaces for creativity and collaboration on issues related to race, gender, and sexuality, and to continue to challenge the racism embedded in the academy. For many, this is a matter of survival—and until women's studies programs are a more supportive space for Chicanas and Latinas, some will continue to turn elsewhere for community and, when given the opportunity, leave. We would like to end with two examples of what these efforts might look like.

At the University of California, Davis, feminist scholars from departments and programs across the campus collaborate in the Center for Gender and Global Issues (GGI), housed in the Women and Gender Studies Program. A research and teaching center, it also focuses on making links between national and international (Third World) feminists. In the last few years, GGI has been looking for new relationships to build with other women's and feminist organizations on campus, including the Chicana/Latina Research Center (CLRC). As a member of both centers, Chávez-García views this as an opportunity for GGI and CLRC to forge alliances through working groups and research clusters, which the latter center has recently initiated. Through such alliances, Chávez-García sees possibilities for the development of new agendas that bridge feminist-scholar-activists' diverse ethnic, racial, class, political, and economic circumstances and that have the potential for constructive and instructive collaboration. Conferences, workshops, and colloquia addressing how we can forge cross-racial, cross-ethnic, and cross-class collaborations are only some of the ways in which we can create linkages across our differences.

In Arizona, women of color from Arizona State University, the University of Arizona, and Northern Arizona University recently attempted to do just that: They collaborated on a tri-university conference, Gathering at the River: Women of Color in the Arizona Academy, organized by and for women of color and their allies. The goal of the conference was to gather faculty, staff, and students from across the state in order to share their experiences, research, and activism on behalf of women of color and further coalition building across the state. The conference made possible the long overdue need to dialogue and debate and certainly reaffirmed the fact that no single women-of-color perspective or even one Chicana or Latina voice exists. Additionally, participants had the chance to discuss in depth the differences between ethnic minority women in the United States and our international sisters. Several white feminist allies also came and participated in what were, at times, very painful discussions, particularly when discussing race and racial identities and the way they intersect with gender, sexuality, and white privilege.

The conference demonstrated that it is a challenge for all of us to listen to one another across the divide of our differences—some of our conversations led to defensiveness, conflict, and even anger. And, yet, these conversations clearly needed to take place. Why, we wondered, were these conversations and conflicts not a central part of women's studies conferences? With such a large group of Arizona students and teachers whose research focused on women of color, why weren't (and aren't) our Arizona women's studies programs more diverse? Why are we seemingly unable to move beyond conflict and how can we make conflict productive? The conference was only a beginning exploration of these questions. Unfortunately, many of us went back to our respective programs and departments with unsatisfactory answers.

Finally, it is our hope and goal that we can revisit these questions and create more spaces for such collaborations—within and outside women's studies programs as well as ethnic and mainstream programs and departments. We call on Euro-

American feminists to listen to the continued critiques and conversations on race, but not with defensiveness and anger or the compulsion to rank or compare oppressions—rather, as attempts by Chicanas and other feminists of color to bridge the gap between our lives and their own, attempts to live and work in an antiracist, antisexist, and antihomophobic environment and society.

Notes

We would like to thank the editorial board, an anonymous reviewer, Theresa Delgadillo, and Joe Boles for their incisive written comments and critiques. We would also like to acknowledge and thank those colleagues who shared their thoughts on this project: Jeff Berglund, Angie Chabram-Dernersesian, Victoria Enders, RosaLinda Fregoso, Sheryl Lutjens, Kimberly D. Nettles, and Beatríz Pesquera.

1. Though this paper is written from a Chicana and Latina (Peruvian American) feminist perspective, the focus is limited to the field of Chicana studies and the writings of Chicana feminists. We use the term "Chicana" to refer to women of Mexican and Mexican American descent, "Latina" to refer to women of Central and South American and Caribbean descent, and "Euro-American" to identify women of European descent living in the United States. We employ the phrase "the women's movement" to refer to the broad coalition (and often disparate groups) of women's organizations and groups that developed in the 1960s and 1970s. For some of the most recent studies examining Chicana and Euro-American women's relationship within and without academia, see, for example, Margaret Villanueva, "Ambivalent Sisterhood: Latina Feminism and Women's Studies," *Discourse* 21 (fall 1999): 49–76; Rachel Lee, "Notes from the (Non)Field, Teaching and Theorizing Women of Color" *Meridians* 1 (2000): 85–109; and Patricia Zavella, "The Problematic Relationship of Feminism and Chicana Studies," *Women Studies* 27 (1989): 25–36.

2. Yamada quoted in Ella Shohat, introduction to *Talking Visions: Multicultural Feminism in a Transnational Age,* ed. Ella Shohat (Cambridge: MIT Press, 1998), 41.

3. For Chicanas' early writings that critiqued Euro-American feminists and women's studies, see, for example, Sylvia González, "The White Feminist Movement: The Chicana Perspective," *Social Science Journal* 14 (1977): 68–76; and Tey Diana Rebolledo, "Chicana Studies: Is There a Future for Us in Women's Studies?" in *Chicano Studies: Critical Connection between Research and Community,* ed. Teresa Córdova (Albuquerque, N.M.: National Association of Chicano Studies, 1992), 32–37. For a more recent critique, see, for instance, Beatríz M. Pesquera and Denise Segura, "With Quill and Torch: A Chicana Perspective on the American Women's Movement and Feminist Theories," in *Chicanas/Chicanos at the Crossroads: Social, Economic, and Political Change,* ed. David R. Maciel and Isidro D. Ortíz (Tucson: University of Arizona Press, 1996), 231–147. For similar critiques by women of color, lesbians, and Third World women, see, for example, Gloria Hull, Patricia Bell Scott, and Barbara Smith, *All Men Are Black, All Women Are White, but Some of Us Are Brave* (Old Westbury, N.Y.: Feminist Press, 1982); and Chela Sandoval, "Women Respond to Racism: A Report on the National Women's Studies Association Conference, Storrs, Connecticut," in *Making Face, Making Soul: Creative and Critical Perspectives by Women of Color,* ed. Gloria Anzaldúa (San Francisco: Aunt Lute, 1990), 55–74.

4. Gloria Anzaldúa, *Borderlands/La Frontera: The New Mestiza* (San Francisco: Spinsters/Aunte Lute, 1987).

5. Some women of color think it is "hopeless" to work with white women. See, for

instance, Eva Young, Tracy McDonald, and Karen Kahn, "Whatever Happened to Women's Liberation?" *Sojourner: The Women's Forum* 16 (September 30, 1990): 5. Others, however, see possibilities; see Chandra Talpade Mohanty, "Crafting Feminist Genealogies: On the Geography and Politics of Home, Nation, and Community," in *Talking Visions,* ed. Shohat, 488.

6. Sandoval, "Women Respond to Racism," 65–67.

7. Young, McDonald, and Kahn, "Whatever Happened to Women's Liberation?" 5; and Mohanty, "Crafting Feminist Genealogies," 488.

8. Beatríz M. Pesquera and Denise Segura, "Beyond Indifference and Antipathy: The Chicana Movement and Chicana Feminist Discourse," *Aztlán* 19 (1992): 72. For general studies on the Chicano movement, see, for instance, Ernesto Chávez, *"Mi Raza Primero/My People First": Nationalism, Identity, and Insurgency in the Chicano Movement in Los Angeles, 1966–1978* (Berkeley: University of California Press, 2002); and Carlos Muñoz Jr., *Youth, Identity, and Power: The Chicano Movement* (New York: Verso Press, 1989).

9. See, for example, Mario Barrera, *Race and Class in the Southwest: A Theory of Racial Inequality* (Notre Dame: University of Notre Dame Press, 1979); and Rudy Acuña, *Occupied America: The Chicano's Struggle toward Liberation* (San Francisco: Canfield Press, 1972).

10. For a few of the early works that did deal with Chicana history, see, for instance, Rosaura Sánchez and Rosa Martínez Cruz, eds., *Essays on La Mujer* (Los Angeles: Chicano Studies Research Center Publications, 1977); Marta P. Cotera, *Diosa y Hembra: The History and Heritage of Chicanas in the United States* (Austin: Information Systems Development, 1976); and Adelaida del Castillo, ed., *Between Borders: Essays on Mexicana/Chicana History* (Encino: Floricanto Press, 1990).

11. For Chicanas' early writings that critiqued the Chicano movement, see, for example, Cynthia Orozco, "Sexism in the Chicano Studies and the Community," in *Chicana Voices: Intersections of Class, Race, and Gender,* ed. Teresa Córdova (Austin: Center for Mexican American Studies, University of Texas, Austin, 1986; reprint, Albuquerque, N.M.: University of New Mexico Press, 1993), 11–18; and Adaljiza Sosa-Riddel, "Chicanas and El Movimiento," *Aztlán* 5 (spring/fall 1974): 155–165.

12. AnnLouise Keating, "Writing, Politics, and las Lesberadas: Platicando con Gloria Anzaldúa," *Frontiers* 14 (fall 1993): 105–131; and Elizabeth Martínez, "In Pursuit of Latina Liberation," *Signs* 20 (summer 1995): 1019–1028.

13. Mia Anderson, "Faculty: Challenge Everything! Says Emma Pérez," *Hispanic Outlook in Higher Education* 10 (February 25, 2000): 13.

14. For Chicanas' issues with the white women's movement, see, for instance, Alma García, ed., *Chicana Feminist Thought: The Basic Historical Writings* (New York: Routledge, 1997), 192–264.

15. Pesquera and Segura, "Beyond Indifference," 74–75.

16. Keating, "Writing, Politics, and las Lesberadas," 105–131; María C. González, "This Bridge Called NWSA," *NWSA Journal* 14 (2002): 71–81; and Anderson, "Faculty: Challenge Everything!"

17. For their writings, see, for example, Smith, *All Men Are Black, All Women Are White.*

18. Cherríe Moraga and Gloria Anzaldúa, eds., *This Bridge Called My Back: Writings by Radical Women of Color* (Watertown, Mass: Persephone Press, 1981; 2nd ed., New York: Kitchen Table Press, 1983).

19. Anzaldúa quoted in Keating, "Writing, Politics, and las Lesberadas," 108. For the third edition, see Moraga and Anzaldúa, *This Bridge Called My Back,* expanded and rev.

3rd ed. (Berkeley, Calif.: Third Woman Press, 2002); for the Spanish edition, see Cherríe Moraga and Ana Castillo, eds., *Este Puente, Mi Espalda: Voces de mujeres tercermundistas en los Estados Unidos* (San Francisco: ISM Press, 1988).

20. Anzaldúa and Moraga, *This Bridge Called My Back,* 2nd ed., 61.
21. Maxine Baca Zinn et al., "The Costs of Exclusionary Practices in Women's Studies," in *Making Face, Making Soul,* ed. Anzaldúa, 29–41.
22. See, for example, one of the first Chicana feminist journals, *Encuentro Feminil,* published in 1973; for collections of early Chicana feminist writings, see García, *Chicana Feminist Thought,* 8.
23. Rebolledo, "Chicana Studies," 32.
24. Ibid., 34.
25. Terri de la Peña, "On the Borderlands with Gloria Anzaldúa," *Off Our Backs* 21 (July 31, 1991): 1–4.
26. Pesquera and Segura, "Beyond Indifference," 76.
27. Pequera and Segura, "With Quill and Torch," 237.
28. Villanueva, "Ambivalent Sisterhood," 49–76; and Lee, "Notes from the (Non)Field," 85–109.
29. Villanueva, "Ambivalent Sisterhood," 51–55.
30. Ibid., 66–68.
31. Lee, "Notes from the (Non)Field," 96; and Chela Sandoval, "U.S. Third World Feminism: The Theory and Method of Oppositional Consciousness in the Postmodern World," *Genders* 4 (spring 1991): 2–24.
32. Villanueva, "Ambivalent Sisterhood," 55.
33. Lee, "Notes from the (Non)Field," 90–96.
34. Ibid., 96–97.
35. Lee's discussion of the "blind spots" we often possess as women of color stimulated our interest on this issue. For another recent study on the differences among Chicanas, see Patricia Zavella, "Reflections on Diversity among Chicanas," *Frontiers* 12 (1991): 73–85.

Feminism, Anti-Semitism, Politics

Does Jewish Women's Studies Have a Future?

Esther Fuchs

This chapter argues for a serious engagement with the status of Jewish studies in the women's studies curriculum. I suggest that the ambivalent relationship between these academic communities stems in part from a latent, unacknowledged element of anti-Semitism in the women's studies academy, as, indeed, has been argued before. However, I suggest as well that Jewish studies for its part differs structurally and paradigmatically from women's studies in its relative lack of interest in race and class issues. The ambivalent relationship between these academic fields then stems from epistemological and scholarly paradigms—the fields are structurally different, and, therefore, there is very little dialogue between them. Moreover, both fields are polarized, because neither focuses on the Israeli-Palestinian conflict, a supposedly nonacademic issue whose implications for the current state of mutual estrangement cannot be ignored. The political explosiveness of the Israeli-Palestinian conflict and the perception of Jews in general as a privileged class have been claimed as justifications for dismissing anti-Semitism as a feminist category of analysis. Jewish women's studies has not considered these arguments,[1] nor have we—scholars and students of this field—attended to issues of religion, culture, class, race, and ethnicity as divisions between and among Jewish women today, divisions that could enrich and revitalize rather than undercut the Jewish feminist curriculum. Though I argue that the insularity of Jewish women's studies ought to be challenged, that we ought to translate Jewish concepts and terms into the language of all women's struggles, I would argue that women's studies only contributes to this insularity by excluding Jewish feminist scholarship and thought from the curriculum. This chapter cuts both ways, then. It both validates and challenges the thesis that anti-Semitism keeps Jewish scholarship out of the women's studies curriculum. By revisiting this theoretical debate I hope to outline a methodology that keeps past debates open for revision and review. The methodology of working out a future by recovering past debates provides us with a historical perspective on our present concerns and prevents repetition.

Current scholarly critiques of the women's studies academy do not engage with politics. More specifically, current critiques of academic anti-Semitism focus on scholarship at the expense of politics. For the most part they do not address the question of Jewish class structure in the West or the Israeli-Palestinian conflict. In the first section I present current Jewish feminist critical articulations regarding the ambivalent relationship between politics and scholarship, between Jewish studies and women's studies, as constituted in the American academy. In the second section I revisit the debate about anti-Semitism in the women's movement, highlighting the political dimensions that ought to be brought back into Jewish women's studies. Though they disagree about the issue of class and the Israeli-Palestinian conflict, Bulkin and Bourne do not engage each other's positions, a problem that continues to haunt the burgeoning field of Jewish women's studies.[2] In the third section I revisit Evelyn Torton Beck's essay on anti-Semitism in the women's studies curriculum. Though aware of Bulkin and Bourne's arguments, Beck shifts the focus from politics to scholarship. In the last section I suggest how we may be able to combine politics and scholarship by focusing on an activist agenda attentive to questions of class, race, and Middle Eastern politics.

Feminism in Jewish Studies

Feminism as a critique of male-dominated institutions and discourses began to penetrate the academic halls of Jewish studies in the United States in the late 1980s. The pioneering anthologies dealt mainly with Jewish religious practice and belief.[3] In the late 1980s monographs and critical essays began to appear on the Bible, rabbinics, history, and theology.[4] In the 1990s several interdisciplinary collections of essays appeared.[5] Anthologies of Jewish women's writing have appeared as well in various literary traditions.[6] Women began to emerge as objects of specialized historical reconstruction and literary inquiry, even in Holocaust studies, creating much controversy and resistance.[7] Recently, essays have been published on the need to use gender as a theoretical tool for transforming the entire field of Jewish studies.[8] The passionate embrace of feminism by women in the Jewish studies academy has not been matched by an equal embrace of Jewish studies in women's studies. Despite the growing awareness of ethnic, religious, and national minority discourses in women's studies, and despite the insistence on multicultural, multiethnic, and international "feminisms," the new inclusiveness has not reached Jews.[9]

Although it is difficult to point to clear and stable boundaries between Jewish studies and women's studies, neither of which is a monistic or monolithic entity, and while the very existence of Jewish feminist scholarship and courses on Jewish women defy such boundaries, it is nevertheless the case that few women's studies graduate programs offer specializations in Jewish studies, few major women's studies conferences include Jewish studies sections, few leading journals in

women's studies include articles or review essays on Jewish studies, few anthologies on the history or evolution of women's studies include references to Jewish
women's studies, few of the leading Jewish feminist scholars are known or mentioned outside of their limited areas of specialization, and few Jewish studies scholars direct women's studies programs in the United States. Leading Jewish feminist
scholars have given some expression to their disappointment and frustration, though
in a rather subdued manner.

In the introduction to their book, *Feminist Perspectives on Jewish Studies,*
Lynn Davidman and Shelly Tenenbaum note the ongoing indifference toward Jewish
feminist scholarship.[10] They reject the perception of Jewish women as part of the
white middle class, drawing parallels between the exclusion of Jews and of women
of color: "Proponents of multiculturalism, in their attempts to clarify the singular
experiences of excluded racial and ethnic minorities, too often ignore the experiences of Jews. In this schema, Jewish women are doubly marginal: as women they
have been invisible in the disciplines of Jewish studies, and as Jews they have increasingly been seen as part of the dominant white majority."[11] Davidman and
Tenenbaum are right in their condemnation of the exclusion of Jews from the
multicultural curriculum, and I agree with their representation of Jewish women
as double outsiders. They clearly and correctly dismiss the argument regarding Jewish class privilege, but do they dismiss it because privileged women can and should
fight class prejudice and discrimination, or because Jewish women are not privileged or not white? My point is that Davidman and Tenenbaum's brief dismissal
of the exclusionary practices of academic feminism is insufficient. They do not
consider the political association of Jewish studies with political support for Israeli policies of occupation and with American class privilege. Nor do they consider the fact that Afro-American women may challenge the facile analogy they
draw between Jewish women's struggle for recognition and the economic struggles
of women of color.[12]

In one of the most striking meditations on the double marginality of the Jewish woman in the United States, Laura Levitt uses the metaphor of the ambivalent
embrace to characterize her place as a Jewish feminist within the women's studies
community.[13] Levitt's insightful autobiography charts the slippery trajectory that
refuses her a home in the women's studies community, a community that does not
acknowledge her difference. Levitt's autobiography outlines the emotional and psychological wounds she suffers as a result of her political homelessness in the Jewish reform context and in the American liberal context. But like Davidman and
Tenenbaum, she remains fixed on anti-Semitism (and antifeminism) as primary
factors, without introducing the complicating factors of her color and class privilege. Levitt offers a sensitive reading of Nancy K. Miller's personal narrative about
the latter's isolation as a Jew in the feminist academy.[14] She does not, however,
come to terms with what Miller describes as sources for ambiguity and discomfort with her own Jewish identity, namely, "the agonies of Middle-East politics,
the status of Jews as a privileged class in the U.S., and the structure of competing
oppressions."[15] Levitt's focus on the Jewish woman as victim of double isolation

prevents her from dealing with political and social complications that are confronted by the texts she explores so sensitively.

The fact is that I share the anguish and frustrations described by Lynn Davidman and Shelly Tenenbaum, and by Laura Levitt. As a professor in a large state university, teaching courses like Women in Judaism, Feminist Approaches to the Bible, and Israeli Women, I feel that I am still on the periphery of the real thing. There is a certain suspicion on the part of Jewish students of the relevance of feminism to Jewish culture and literature, and a certain anxiety that feminism as such will undermine their search for roots and a stable identity. On the other hand, there are prejudices and a staggering lack of knowledge among non-Jewish students about Jewish texts, religion, and history. But most problematic is the distance from women's studies projects and committees on campus. The separation between women's studies as an entity apart from my work on Jewish feminism is on some level fictional because my courses are cross-listed with the women's studies program at the University of Arizona, where I have taught since 1985. Yet a certain line divides us. The boundaries are fluid and porous, and yet, there is an invisible demarcation, a distinction that most feminist Jewish studies scholars recognize. So though I am a tenured professor, I continue to feel somewhat insecure. I know my isolation is a problem that has been described by peers and colleagues, but I am never too sure whether it is an objective reality or the product of my own inadequacies as a scholar and a teacher.

Much as I agree with my friends and colleagues in Jewish women's studies about the need to confront anti-Semitism in the women's studies academy, I insist that we do so only after we recognize our difficulties within a historical perspective and within a context of a debate that has already been going on for at least two decades. Forgetting the arguments of those who preceded us, both those who addressed the problem of anti-Semitism in the women's movement and those who addressed it in the realm of the feminist academy, will only condemn us to repetition and deprive us of the insights that may complicate our research and revitalize our field.

Anti-Semitism in the Women's Movement

Elly Bulkin's "Hard Ground: Jewish Identity, Racism, and Anti-Semitism" (1984) articulates a Jewish feminist identity politics and an analysis of anti-Semitism in the women's movement.[16] Her position regarding the legitimacy of Jewish feminist identity politics and the urgent need for a serious recognition of anti-Semitism as a feminist issue are repudiated by Jenny Bourne's "Homelands of the Mind: Jewish Feminism and Identity Politics" (1987).[17] While Bulkin argues for a recognition of anti-Semitism as a category of oppression equal in significance to racism and anti-Arabism, Bourne discounts it as Zionist propaganda, a memory rather than a political reality. While Bulkin argues that anti-Semitism must be included in the feminist agenda for change, Bourne argues that anti-Semitism does not and cannot compare to the colonial and racial oppression inflicted by Israeli policies on Palestinians in South Lebanon, the West Bank, and Gaza. For Bourne, the Israeli policies of invasion, occupation, and collective punishment engender not anti-Semitism but anti-Zionist criticism that is fully justified.

Though they disagree about the Israeli-Palestinian issue and anti-Semitism, both Bulkin and Bourne agree about the centrality of these issues and share a conviction about Jewish feminist activist commitment. I suggest that these essays can work as entries into a re-configured activist Jewish women's studies intent on cultural assertiveness and critical self-awareness. Because their arguments are so crucial, they justify detailed summary.

Having established the subtle and not so subtle manifestations of anti-Semitism in American society, Bulkin sets out to distinguish between various kinds of anti-Semitic ideologies. She clarifies that the religious anti-Semitism of the Spanish Inquisition ought to be distinguished from the economic and racial anti-Semitism of the Third Reich, and from the ideological manifestations of anti-Semitism in the United States. All three must be distinguished from the political persecution of Jews in Arab lands in the 1940s and 1950s and the onslaughts on Falasha Jews in Ethiopia in the 1980s. In addition to geography and history, class as well must be reckoned as a category of distinction, as poor Jews have always been more vulnerable to institutional anti-Semitism than well-off Jews.

Bulkin notes that a central tenet of American anti-Semitism is the totalizing perception of Jews as a privileged and overly influential class. The idea of Jewish influence ignores a large segment of the Jewish population in the United States, Canada, and Latin America, and almost half the Jewish population in Israel, known as Sephardim or Mizrahim.[18] Mizrahi, or Eastern (non-European) Jews, mostly from Muslim countries, have been disadvantaged economically and politically. Even Ashkenazi (European) Jews in the United States have hardly acceded to the powerful positions that are frequently attributed to them, including executive positions in large banks, the auto and oil industries, public utilities, and other conglomerates where American interests are defined and economic policies shaped.[19]

Nevertheless, Bulkin claims that white skin privilege may have helped American Jews leave the working class within one or two generations. She distinguishes between the effects of internalized anti-Semitism and the pressure of cultural assimilation suffered by American Jews as a group and economic oppression with which Americans of color had to contend.[20] Bulkin emphasizes that parallels between racism and anti-Semitism must not blind Jews to the important asymmetries between them.[21] In the United States, where skin color has determined categories of social difference, Afro-Americans rather than Jews have been the victims of physical persecution and economic pressures.

Regarding the Israeli-Palestinian conflict, Bulkin positions herself as supportive of both the Palestinian and the Jewish national movements. She draws a distinction between a valid criticism of Israeli policies and an anti-Semitic tendency on the left to single out Israel for special treatment. On the other hand, Bulkin condemns what she considers anti-Arab racism that presents Palestinian women as mere pawns of Arab men and ungrateful recipients of Israeli progress. She insists that Jewish feminists in particular and Western feminists in general recognize the interlocking nature of oppression and realize that Palestinian women cannot realistically divide "women's" issues from "Palestinian" issues. At the same time she focuses on the solidarity and alliance work accomplished by Israeli feminist groups. While she denounces in the strongest terms Israel's use of cluster bombs in Lebanon in 1982, she reminds us that any attempt to single out Israel for especially harsh criticism is anti-Semitic.

Bulkin argues that the extremism, inflammatory rhetoric, and combative posturing that characterize leftist discourses about the Middle East undermine understanding and communication and run counter to the interests of feminists on both sides of the political divide. She concludes that genuine dialogue does not entail abandoning basic principles and that solidarity and alliances between Jewish and Palestinian feminists should not be confused with the abandonment of differences in position and interpretation. She refuses the oppositional, dichotomizing approach that blames either the Israelis or the Palestinians.[22]

In "Homelands of the Mind: Jewish Feminism and Identity Politics" Jenny Bourne criticizes the new Jewish feminist identity politics as articulated in Bulkin's essay. Her theoretical point is that Bulkin has abandoned the charge of progressive politics to fight on behalf of the "truly oppressed" (namely, the economically deprived classes) and joined a personalized form of self-indulgent cultural politics. She claims that the category of "oppression" has replaced "exploitation" in the context of Jewish feminist identity politics and that the relatively unimportant question, Who am I? has replaced the question, What is to be done?[23]

Bourne maintains that class is the most important category for a cogent feminist analysis. Even though I accept her insistence on materialist criticism, I wish she responded to Bulkin's class analysis of Jews as a group and of anti-Semitism as an ideology of hatred. She ignores Bulkin's references to Jews of color and of disadvantaged classes and avoids the connection of anti-Semitism and the exaggerated perception of Jews as an advantaged class. Rather than develop, challenge, or analyze, Bourne simply repeats the arguments that Bulkin already refuted. She argues that Jews at present do not suffer from the same conditions of exploitation confronted by most women of color.

Bourne argues that anti-Semitism is a memory rather than a reality. She does not mention the growing vulnerability of Jews to attacks by Muslim fundamentalists, a fact as troubling in Europe of the 1980s as it is today. Nor does she mention the growing popularity of neo-Nazism in Germany, nor does she mention anti-Jewish hate crimes on American campuses, nor does she discuss the rise of the "revisionist" movement of Holocaust denial especially in Europe in the 1980s and to a lesser extent in the United States. She argues that Jews face no serious physical threat at present, though there is much anxiety about cultural survival. These anxieties make no sense within the framework of a materialist, socialist, and feminist analysis. She chides both Jews and feminists for focusing on cultural identity. Both "feminists and Jews have become petrified in the particularity of their experience."[24]

Finally, Bourne argues that the new Jewish feminism is the result of an "attempt to come to terms with Israel."[25] In this context Bourne indulges in precisely the kind of inflammatory rhetoric that Bulkin condemns. Her matter-of-fact conflation of Zionism, a national ideology, and Israel and her repudiation of Israeli policies without differentiating between right- and left-wing parties shut off the dialogical and open-ended discourse recommended by Bulkin. Bulkin devotes a substantive part of her essay to discussing the Palestinian problem, and yet Bourne argues that Bulkin and all Jewish feminists have avoided the issue. Furthermore, implying that "Jews" and "feminists" are homogeneous groups, Bourne all but ignores Bulkin's remarkably detailed explanation of the connection between her Jewish roots and her radical politics.

Nevertheless, Bourne's critique of the new Jewish feminist identity politics can serve as a good point of departure for an alternative trend within Jewish women's studies. Her warning against solipsism and cultural self-indulgence are especially relevant today. Despite her misrepresentations of Bulkin, there is much in her essay that is valuable to an articulation of a Jewish feminist academic program that combines both an interest in the past and a concern for the future, a commitment to political activism and an interest in social change. Her points about materialist criticism, politics, class, and race are of vital importance to Jewish academic feminism today as it struggles to clarify its theories and methods. "The question that needs to be asked is not what constitutes our identity, but what is identity for? Identity for what?"[26] Bourne's insistence on creating "the correct alliances and [on] fighting the right fights" articulates an activist agenda for Jewish women's studies.[27] Bourne's essay ends thus: "We can only learn and confirm our identity, in other words, through our actions. What we do is who we are."[28] Bulkin's essay ends with a very similar statement: "But I do believe in the absolute necessity of fighting anti-Semitism and racism and in the possibility of political change. And I do know that there is much work to be done."[29] Despite their disagreements, both Bulkin and Bourne share a commitment to social change, and both offer a much-needed practical map for an activist Jewish feminist future within the academe.

The 1990s: Anti-Semitism in the Feminist Academy

Evelyn T. Beck's article on anti-Semitism in the feminist academy is the first critical assessment of the relationship between the women's studies curriculum and Jewish studies.[30] Beck shifts the focus of the debate from politics to scholarship. She dismisses Bourne's critique as a virulent attack on Jewish women's search for identity. Though she elaborates and develops some of Bulkin's insights, she avoids the latter's self-critical comments regarding Jewish attitudes to race and class. To her, anti-Semitism is the only explanation for the ambivalent relationship between the women's studies and Jewish studies academies.[31]

In "Jewish Invisibility in Women's Studies" Beck argues that the silencing of Jewish issues in women's studies is as much a result of anti-Semitic pressure as the result of Jewish self-censorship: fear of being perceived as too pushy or aggressive, fear of being attacked as politically incorrect, fear of being excluded. Another cause of self-silencing is the confusion of Jewish feminists about two separate and apparently opposing identities: Judaism and feminism. While the contribution of second wave Jewish feminists to the women's movement has been acknowledged, it is in their capacity as feminists rather than as Jews that they have been recognized. Beck traces the current academic manifestations of anti-Semitism to the 1920s and 1930s, noting that the American women's movement failed to condemn fascist persecutions of Jews in Europe in the late 1930s and early 1940s.

Beck notes that, when it is mentioned at all, Judaism is portrayed as more misogynous and retrograde than other religions.[32] Work published more recently by leading Jewish feminist scholars bears her out. Thus, for example, Susannah Heschel has documented anti-Semitic representations of Judaism, often serving as an undisguised apologetics for Nazi misogyny in work by German feminist theologians.[33] Judith Plaskow has documented anti-Semitic bias in historical representations of Jewish women in the Second Temple period.[34] Plaskow demonstrates how New Testament historians often fail to acknowledge that the early followers of Jesus were Jewish women who were apparently free to move about, unshackled by the restrictive rules attributed to rabbinic Judaism. Misogyny is often identified as an early Jewish flaw from which early Christianity is often exempt. Amy Newman has documented anti-Semitic misrepresentations of Jewish origins in feminist theory, notably in work by Julia Kristeva.[35]

Beck also directs her attention to the cultural wounding entailed in the proliferation of contemporary stereotypes of the "JAP" (Jewish American princess) in American literature, media, and popular culture. She perceives the hateful representations of the privileged Jewish woman as the product of misogyny as well as anti-Semitism. The loud, pushy, lazy, self-indulgent, frigid, and greedy Jewess is the butt of both Jewish and anti-Semitic humor.

Beck condemns the failure of women's studies to frame anti-Semitism as a specific category of feminist analysis, a failure that is often obscured by the repeated emphasis on class and race. She perceives this emphasis as a sort of rigid orthodoxy, an inability to think freely beyond prescribed epistemological categories. For Beck the "Jew" cannot and should not accommodate such rigid prerequisites: "Clearly, then, if the concept 'Jew' does not fit the categories we have created, then I suggest we need to rethink our categories."[36] In a more recent article on the exclusion of Jews from the multicultural curriculum, Beck argues that the Jew presents a different kind of difference, one that most academic formulations cannot recognize just because the Jew defies the conventional categories of ethnicity, race, and religion combining and transcending all three categories. She rejects the new demand that Jews prove how and why they should fit into categories of multicultural studies. Rather than objective criteria, she identifies the academic demands of the new multicultural curriculum as the manifestations of a political agenda, the playing out of power relations within the multicultural academy.[37]

Beck recommends that women's studies anthologies consider including such historical documents as *The Memoirs of Glückel of Hameln,* published originally in Yiddish in the seventeenth century.[38] An awareness of this extraordinary autobiography would challenge the impression that pre-modern Jewish women have nothing to contribute to modern feminist consciousness and undermine stereotypes of Jewish female historical passivity, dependence, and illiteracy.

Beck's questions, critiques, and recommendations continue to be valid and relevant today. Though she herself did not emphasize race and class in her pioneering essay, we can develop and refine the project of building a Jewish feminist curriculum by adding to *The Memoirs of Glückel of Hameln* a text about a Sephardic or Mizrahi woman, perhaps the biography of Doña Gracia Nasi. An awareness of ethnicity will help those who are concerned not only about the past of Jewish women, but about the political and activist futures of Jewish women's studies.

Over a decade after the publication of Beck's important essay, questions of criteria, pedagogic objectives, and texts have yet to be raised as part of a coherent discussion about the future of Jewish women's studies. I would suggest that these questions are important in light of the availability of anthologies and monographs on women in almost every period from the Bible to modernity. What kinds of texts do we wish to recommend for inclusion in the Jewish women's studies curriculum? What kind of students do we wish to create? What do these texts teach about gender, race, class, the Israel-Palestine conflict, or anti-Semitism for that matter? Can these texts inspire social change in addition to shoring up cultural empowerment? In discussions of Israeli feminism, do we include Israeli-Arab women, Russian and Ethiopian immigrants, "foreign" workers, "older" women, lesbians? Beck's essay ought to challenge us not only to expose and analyze anti-Semitic bias in feminist scholarship but to identify lacunae in current scholarship on Jewish women. It ought to inspire us to think about pedagogic goals, priorities, and methods that will enable a greater integration and inclusion of Jews and Judaism in the women's studies curriculum.

The Future of Jewish Feminist Studies

Women's studies must confront the serious charge of anti-Semitism as articulated by Bulkin and Beck. An effort must be undertaken to consult with Jewish feminist scholars and check for relevant texts and cases before printing textbooks and introductions that appear to be inclusive. Women's studies ought to enter into a serious dialogue with Jewish feminist scholars, become acquainted with the principles that inform our field. Jewish feminist scholars, for their part, ought to reflect on the goals of a Jewish feminist curriculum, its pedagogic principles, and the future of the field as a whole.

Current anthologies in Jewish women's studies do not show sufficient awareness of the political implications of academic research and of class and racial divisions between and among Jewish women. Theoretical discussions about activist commitment and ethical vision are missing from the current explosion of publications on the history of Jewish women. The current wealth of publications reveals increasing specialization and a further remove from theoretical and pedagogic questions regarding Jewish women's studies as a field. Above all, the discussion of academic priorities has not been consistent. Criteria for the selection of seminal texts for our basic introductory collections have not been discussed.

Within the field of Jewish history, for example, how do we decide what women are important? Do we want to teach about women who achieved great fame and influence, women of power and social status, women of skill and talent, women whose success and recognition may have been achieved because of their class privilege?[39] Should we study Jewish women because they were Jewish, because they refused to convert to Christianity, because they remained loyal to Judaism, or because the texts they wrote and the lives they lived can inspire future generations to rethink the world as we know it? Do we want to prove that Jewish women were just as devoted to Judaism as the men? In that case we ought to continue teaching *The Memoirs of Glückel* as well as the writings of Pauline Wengeroff, in addition to the legacy of women's religious expression and women's devotional prayers.[40] Or do we want to teach about women who may have been ambivalent about their Judaism, the likes of Rahel Varnhagen, Sarah Bernhardt, Rosa Luxemburg, Emma Goldman, Gertrude Stein, Simone Weil, Hannah Arendt—women who are rarely mentioned in most current Jewish feminist historical or literary anthologies? If we are to embrace the full spectrum of Jewish women's creativity, we must consider the work of controversial Jewesses, whose lives and work may, in fact, have more relevance and meaning to most women's studies students, Jewish and non-Jewish. If, in addition to Bertha Pappenheim, who founded the first Jewish German feminist movement in 1904, if, in addition to Manya Shohat, Ada Maimon, and Henrietta Szold, we consider teaching about the revolutionary women I mentioned, women who can be conceptualized as "proto-feminists," then we can proudly proclaim a legacy of a hundred years of Jewish feminism, a legacy we can legitimately offer as worthy of inclusion in any women's studies curriculum. If we do not restrict our discussion to the "kosher" Jewish women who have been recognized by previous Jewish studies scholars as historical figures, but venture outside the usual categories established by normative Jewish studies histories and literary anthologies to include less conventional women, and if, in addition, we consider including in the feminist canon the Jewish women who contributed to the second wave of feminism in the United States, then we will have changed the face of Jewish studies as well as women's studies.

If Bulkin and Beck are right and numerous feminists in the women's movement downplayed their Jewishness because of latent anti-Semitism, it ought to be up to us to read this suppression and denial in their writings and thus reclaim for them an identity they may have been reluctant to admit. These texts have been read as women's texts, not as Jewish women's texts, and, while they do not necessarily discuss Jews and Judaism, there is much in their revolutionary fervor and sense of solidarity with all women that reflects their unique cultural tradition.

Though teaching courses by and about Jewish feminist thinkers is already an act of social transformation and change, I would stress the need for an activist project specific to Jewish women's studies teachers and students. In addition to celebrating the proliferation of writings by Israeli (mostly Ashkenazi) women since the 1980s and the abundance of feminist midrashim (biblical interpretations), ceremonies, liturgies, and rituals conceived by American women, we must ask ourselves, *Cui bono*? Who benefits from this abundance, and who are its intended consumers? To what extent do recent anthologies of Israeli women's fiction and poetry reflect underprivileged Israeli women, notably Mizrahi and Palestinian women?[41] Do the new stories reveal a political re-vision of the Israeli-Palestinian conflict? To what extent do these stories grapple with the circumstances of women living under occupation in the West Bank and the Gaza Strip?

Though psychoanalytic and aesthetic questions are pertinent to Hebrew literary research, I believe, it is time to become aware of the political implications of women's writing beyond the issues of sexual egalitarianism in Israeli-Jewish society and history.

I would like to suggest that as a first step toward clarifying academic and pedagogic goals for Jewish women's studies we consider starting from an activist rather than a theoretical point of departure. In "Toward a Multicultural Politics: A Jewish Feminist Perspective" Martha Ackelsberg appropriately raises the question of political activism as part of a Jewish multicultural definition of priorities.[42] In a way she echoes both Bulkin's and Bourne's call for action as the best way to construct identity and theory. Activism for Ackelsberg is the most effective way toward consolidating alliances between and among women of diverse economic and ethnic backgrounds. "The activities of diverse groups of women at the grassroots level to [sic] address housing cost and quality, food costs, battery, welfare reform, school desegregation, toxic wastes, or a variety of other issues remain to be effectively tapped as resources for theory."[43] Ackelsberg proposes the free play of anarchic pluralisms as a model for Jewish feminist activism.[44] This model, I would suggest, ought to be considered by teachers and students of Jewish women's studies as part of a future activist reorientation of the field. I would only add to this a commitment to support Mizrahi activists in their struggle for change and the sort of pacifist international activism that is vital for the continued success of Israeli and Palestinian pacifist activists.

As Bulkin made clear, there is neither contradiction nor competition between a commitment to ending anti-Semitism and a commitment to ending racism or class prejudice among Jewish women and between them and others. Nor is there a contradiction in supporting both Israel and Palestine to find a just resolution of the conflict. On the one hand, without a commitment to materialist analysis Jewish feminism may indeed degenerate into the kind of narcissistic solipsism and idealist identity politics Bourne warned against. On the other hand, as Beck suggested, too restrictive or rigid an emphasis on class and race at the expense of anti-Semitism may shut off rather than encourage research and creativity. Playfulness and responsibility, creativity and planning, difference and alliance, a culturally empowering vision and an activist agenda, and, above all, the ability to listen to each other, to respond to each other's positions, to engage our differences—all these are needed as scholars of Jewish women's studies claim their long-denied and rightful place in the multicultural and transnational curriculum of women's studies.

Notes

I would like to thank Elizabeth Kennedy, Agatha Beins, and the anonymous readers for their thoughtful comments. The current version of the chapter owes much to their helpful responses. The remaining imperfections of the chapter are not related in any way, shape, or form to their meticulous editorial work.

1. Jewish women's studies comprises the undergraduate and graduate courses currently offered in academic institutions usually as part of the Jewish studies curricula in disciplines ranging from Bible to history, from rabbinic literature to sociology, from theology to Holocaust studies. I am drawing a distinction here between Jewish women's studies and Israeli women's studies, an area vitally interested in race, ethnicity, and class issues, as well as the politics of the Israeli-Palestinian conflict. See my book, *Israeli Women's Studies: A Reader* (New Brunswick, N.J.: Rutgers University Press, 2005).

2. See my chapter "Jewish Feminist Scholarship: A Critical Perspective," in *Studies in Jewish Civilization,* ed. Leonard Greenspoon and Ronald Simkin (Omaha: Creigton University Press, 2003), 225–246. See also my "Critique and Reconstruction," in *Women in Jewish Life and Culture,* ed. Esther Fuchs, a special issue of *Shofar* 17, no. 2 (winter 1999): 1–11.

3. See, for instance, Elizabeth Koltun, ed., *The Jewish Woman: New Perspectives* (New York: Schocken Books, 1976); Susannah Heschel, ed., *On Being a Jewish Feminist* (New York: Schocken Books, 1983); Rachel Biale, *Women and Jewish Law* (New York: Schocken Books, 1984).

4. See, for instance, Esther Fuchs, *Israeli Mythogynies: Women in Contemporary Hebrew Fiction* (Albany: State University of New York Press, 1987); Esther Fuchs, *Sexual Politics in the Biblical Narrative: Reading the Hebrew Bible as a Woman* (Sheffield: Sheffield Academic Press, 2000); Judith Romney Wegner, *Chattel or Person: The Status of Women in the Mishnah* (New York: Oxford University Press, 1988). In theology, the first monograph was published in 1990. See Judith Plaskow, *Standing Again in Sinai: Judaism from a Feminist Perspective* (San Francisco: Harper and Row, 1990).

5. See, for instance, Judith R. Baskin, ed., *Jewish Women in Historical Perspective* (Detroit: Wayne State University Press, 1991); Maurie Sacks, ed., *Active Voices: Women in Jewish Culture* (Urbana and Chicago: University of Illinois Press, 1995).

6. See, for instance, Naomi B. Sokoloff, Anne Lapidus Lerner, and Anita Norich, eds., *Gender and Text in Modern Hebrew and Yiddish Literature* (New York: Jewish Theological Seminary of America, 1992); Sylvia Barack Fishman, ed., *Follow My Footprints: Changing Images of Women in American Jewish Fiction* (Hanover and London: Brandeis University Press, 1992).

7. See, Carol Rittner and John K. Roth, eds., *Different Voices: Women and the Holocaust* (New York: Paragon House, 1993); Dalia Ofer and Lenore J. Weitzman, eds., *Women and the Holocaust* (New Haven and London: Yale University Press, 1998); Esther Fuchs, ed., *Women and the Holocaust: Narrative and Representation* (Oxford and Lanham: University Press of America, 1999); S. Lillian Kremer, *Women's Holocaust Writing: Memory and Imagination* (Lincoln and London: University of Nebraska Press, 1999).

8. See Miriam Peskowitz and Laura Levitt, eds., *Judaism since Gender* (New York and London: Routledge, 1997).

9. See, for instance, Robyn R. Warhol and Diane Price Herndl, eds., *Feminisms: An Anthology of Literary Theory and Criticism* (New Brunswick, N.J.: Rutgers University Press, 1997); Marilyn Jacoby Boxer, ed., *When Women Ask the Questions: Creating Women's Studies in America* (Baltimore and London: The Johns Hopkins University Press, 1998).

10. Lynn Davidman and Shelly Tenenbaum, eds., *Feminist Perspectives on Jewish Studies* (New Haven and London: Yale University Press, 1994).

11. Ibid., 13.

12. See, for instance, Barbara Smith, "Between a Rock and a Hard Place: Relationships between Black and Jewish Women," in *Yours in Struggle: Three Feminist Perspectives on Anti-Semitism and Racism,* ed. Elly Bulkin, Minnie Bruce Pratt, and Barbara Smith (New York: Firebrand, 1984), 75.

13. Laura Levitt, *Jews and Feminism: The Ambivalent Search for Home* (New York and London: Routledge, 1997).

14. See Nancy K. Miller, "Dreaming, Dancing, and the Changing Locations of Feminist Criticism, 1988," in *Getting Personal: Feminist Occasions and Other Autobiographical Acts,* ed. Nancy Miller (New York and London: Routledge, 1991), 72–100.

15. Ibid., 96–97.

16. Elly Bulkin, "Hard Ground: Jewish Identity, Racism, and Anti-Semitism," in *Yours in Struggle: Three Feminist Perspectives on Anti-Semitism and Racism,* ed. Elly Bulkin, Minnie Bruce Pratt, and Barbara Smith (Ithaca, N.Y.: Firebrand Books, 1984), 89–193.

17. Jenny Bourne, "Homelands of the Mind: Jewish Feminism and Identity Politics," *Race and Class* 29 (1987): 1–24.

18. For excellent analyses of this ethnic and social divide in Israel, see Ella Shohat, *Israeli Cinema: East/West and the Politics of Representation* (Austin: University of Texas Press, 1989); Shlomo Swirsky, *Israel: The Oriental Minority* (London: Zed Books, 1989).

19. Bulkin, "Hard Ground," 114.

20. On internalized anti-Semitism, see Adrienne Rich, "Split at the Root," in *Nice Jewish Girls,* ed. Evelyn T. Beck (Watertown, Mass.: Persephone Press, 1982), 67–84. See also Irena Klepfisz, *Dreams of an Insomniac: Jewish Feminist Essays, Speeches, and Diatribes* (Portland, Oreg.: Eighth Mountain Press, 1990).

21. See also Barbara Smith's "Between a Rock and a Hard Place," in *Yours in Struggle,* ed. Bulkin, Pratt, and Smith, 75.

22. In this sense her approach is post-Zionist. For a survey of the major developments, see Laurence J. Silberstein, *The Postzionism Debates: Knowledge and Power in Israeli Culture* (New York: Routledge, 1999); Virginia Dominguez, *People as Subject, People as Object: Selfhood and Peoplehood in Contemporary Israel* (Madison: University of Madison Press, 1989).

23. Bourne, "Homelands of the Mind," 1.

24. Ibid., 20.

25. Ibid., 4.

26. Ibid., 21–22.

27. Ibid., 22

28. Ibid., 22.

29. Bulkin, "Hard Ground," 193.

30. Evelyn Torton Beck, "Jewish Invisibility in Women's Studies," in *Transforming the Curriculum: Ethnic Studies and Women's Studies,* ed. Johnnella E. Butler and John C. Walter (Albany: State University of New York Press, 1991), 187–197. This chapter was originally published as "The Politics of Jewish Invisibility," *National Women's Studies Association Journal* 1, no. 1 (1988): 93–102.

31. Beck, "Jewish Invisibility in Women's Studies," 190.

32. Ibid., 167.

33. Susannah Heschel, "Configurations of Patriarchy, Judaism, and Nazism in German Feminist Thought," in *Gender and Judaism: The Transformation of Tradition,* ed. T. M. Rudavsky (New York: New York University Press, 1995), 135–156.

34. Judith Plaskow, "Anti-Judaism in Feminist Christian Interpretation," in *Searching the Scriptures: A Feminist Introduction,* ed. Elizabeth S. Fiorenza (New York: Crossroad, 1993), 117–129. See also Amy-Jill Levine, "Discharging Responsibility: Matthean Jesus, Biblical Law, and the Hemorrhaging Woman," in *A Feminist Companion to Matthew,* ed. Amy-Jill Levine (Sheffield: Sheffield Academic Press, 2001), 70–87.

35. Amy Newman, "The Idea of Judaism in Feminism and Afrocentrism," in *Insider/Outsider: American Jews and Multiculturalism,* ed. David Biale, Michael Galchinsky, and Susannah Heschel (Berkeley and Los Angeles: University of California Press, 1998), 150–181.

36. Beck, "Jewish Invisibility in Women's Studies," 193.

37. Evelyn Torton Beck, "Jews and the Multicultural University Curriculum," in *The Narrow Bridge: Jewish Views on Multiculturalism,* ed. Marla Brettschneider (New Brunswick, N.J.: Rutgers University Press, 1996), 163–177.

38. *The Memoirs of Glückel of Hameln,* trans. Marvin Lowenthal (1932; reprinted, New York: Schocken Books, 1960, 1977).

39. See Paula Hyman and Deborah Dash Moore, eds., *Jewish Women in America: An Historical Encyclopedia* (New York: Routledge, 1997).

40. See, for instance, Ellen M. Umansky and Dianne Ashton, eds., *Four Centuries of Jewish Women's Spirituality* (Boston: Beacon Press, 1992); Chava Weissler, *Voices of the Matriarchs: Listening to the Prayers of Early Modern Jewish Women* (Boston: Beacon Press, 1998).

41. See, for example, Risa Domb, ed., *New Women's Writing from Israel* (London: Vallentine Mitchell, 1996); Yael S. Feldman, *No Room of Their Own: Gender and Nation in Israeli Women's Fiction* (New York: Columbia University Press, 1999).

42. Martha Ackelsberg, "Toward a Multicultural Politics: A Jewish Feminist Perspective," in *The Narrow Bridge*, ed. Brettschneider, 89–14.

43. Ibid., 100.

44. Ibid., 99.

Beyond Pocahontas, Princess, and Squaw

INVESTIGATING TRADITIONAL FEMINISM

MARY JO TIPPECONNIC FOX AND SHEILAH E. NICHOLAS

In this essay we address the absence of American Indian women's voices in Western thought and in the interpretations of their lives, thereby rendering them "powerless" in the literature and scholarship on tribal people and societies. As American Indian women and as indigenous women scholars, we seek inclusion and offer our voices and perspectives based in our lived experiences. We articulate the roles established by tribal customs and traditions that continue to be practiced in most contemporary tribal societies. Also, we begin to explore the concept of "Indian feminism."

The persistent and pervasive stereotypes of Pocahontas, princess, and squaw implore us to begin our essay with a look at the evolving images of American Indian women perpetuated by popular culture and media. We find these stereotypes continue to influence the intellectual discourse on American Indian women in institutions of higher education, especially among students. It becomes essential that we begin by eliminating the void brought about by the absent voices of American Indian women in the scholarship that defines them. We recognize that this requires us to seek new avenues and methods of research and, more importantly, collaboration across disciplines and with non-Indian scholars. As such, we present the findings of Virginia Bergman Peters's study on the activities and responsibilities of Mandan, Hidatsa, and Arikara tribal women of the Upper Missouri River Valley as a research model that directs attention to women's activities as a potential site for understanding the significance and status of American Indian women in tribal societies.[1] We intend this framework to open pathways for new and exciting dialogue. Foremost, we seek to ensure that the perspectives of American Indian women are represented in the discussions of tribal communities.

Evolving Images and Stereotypes

The first pictorial representations of the New World featured Indian women as symbols of an exotic land filled with riches, as depicted in Jan Van der Stact's

1580 and Philipp Galle's 1592 portraits of America.[2] The long-held European image of women as "queen of the land" was bestowed uncontested upon American Indian women as well. For approximately two hundred years (since 1575), the Indian woman, as queen and princess, symbolized the New World.

The American Indian woman was portrayed first as Amazonian with Roman features, draped in leaves, feathers, and animal skins, often sitting on an armadillo. She was a full-bodied, nurturing, powerful, but somewhat ominous Mother Goddess figure. As the colonies moved toward independence, she became less formidable and less Roman in physical features.[3] In the nineteenth century, the statue of Lady Liberty, who stands atop the dome of the U.S. Capitol building, was modeled on this image.[4] Later, the Indian maiden as princess became a popular image on patent medicines and tobacco products.[5]

The most captivating and persistent Indian princess image is that of Pocahontas, daughter of Powhatan, chief of the Algonquians in the Tidewater region of Virginia. According to legend, when Powhatan ordered the death of Captain John Smith, leader of Jamestown, Pocahontas threw her body over him to spare his life. Her act was perceived as a willingness to sacrifice her own life for the love of a white man and endeared her in European eyes.[6] This version of the story was reintroduced with the 1995 release of the film *Pocahontas* by the Disney Corporation. Biased perspectives of the European and later the Euro-American male not only created the image of the princess but also the squaw. ("Squaw" is an Algonquian word for a married or mature woman, which over time became a derogatory and demeaning term.)

The stereotypes about the powerlessness of American Indian women, particularly as squaws, have had exceptional longevity: "The women, . . . besides the onerous role of rearing the children, also transport the game from the place where it has fallen; they are the hewers of wood and drawers of water; they make and repair the household utensils; they prepare food; they skin the game and prepare the hides like fullers; they sew garments; they catch fish and gather shellfish for food; often they even hunt; they make the canoes; they set up tents wherever they stop for the night—in short, the men . . . concern themselves with nothing but the more laborious hunting and waging of war."[7] This quote from a Time-Life coffee-table book, probably more so than scholarly literature with similar descriptions, has greatly influenced the general public's perception of American Indian women as squaws, beasts of burden, and powerless. Whereas such activities, in fact, illustrate the ability of American Indian women to traverse with skill and ease both the female and seemingly male domains of what is understood as the division of labor in Western thought.

Since early contact and the subsequent colonization of indigenous people in North America, American Indian women have occupied a highly visible yet voiceless position in existing literature and the media. In the last twenty five years, even while research and literature on American Indian women has utilized the more sensitive non-Indian female voice, the voices of tribal women remain largely absent. Without their voices, interpretations of their lives will continue to be incorrect, incomplete, or underdeveloped.[8] Consequently, the historical images imposed by non-Indians upon American Indian women continue to be an issue in contemporary times.

Articulating a Tribal Perspective

Putting forth a tribal perspective evolved from our experience in teaching a university course, American Indian Women, offered through American Indian studies (AIS) and cross-listed with women's studies. We utilize the works of various authors but specifically the works of Laura Klein and Lillian Ackerman, *Women of Power in Native North America,* Virginia Bergman Peters, *Women of the Earth Lodges: Tribal Life on the Plains,* and Nancy Shoemaker, *Negotiators of Change: Historical Perspectives on Native American Women,* for this essay.[9]

From these works, we find that central to Western curiosity about American Indian women are the concepts of power, status, and personal autonomy and how these were and are manifested in their tribal culture and contemporary lives. Did American Indian women have power and status equal to that of men? What is the source of their power or authority? How was the gender balance affected by colonization? These questions posed by Nancy Shoemaker are those that compel much of the scholarly research on American Indian women in women's studies, American Indian studies, and related areas.[10] These questions also serve as the catalyst for the discussion we present in this essay.

Shoemaker and Klein and Ackerman, who provide historical and ethnographic information on the lives of American Indian women, focus on the diversity that existed and continues to exist among tribal societies. This diversity stems from the particular linguistic and cultural responses of tribal cultures to the environment of their geographic regions that made them uniquely different from each other. We also point out that traditional and contemporary tribal societies share common characteristics and historical experiences, particularly those occurring at the hands of Europeans and Euro-Americans.

Shoemaker points out that previous and current scholarship on American Indian women has provided substantial evidence that points to gender, age, and kin as the essential organizing principles determining one's identity and role within Indian societies. According to Shoemaker, *independence* arose primarily from an inherent respect for individual autonomy and from the structure of different kinship systems, *authority* was determined either by woman's productive or reproductive role, while *lineage* appeared to be more important than marriage in determining significant relationships, corresponding responsibilities, and consent. She further posits that gender differences, while essential for organizing behavior, were also flexible and variable and subject to cultural guidelines, but the freedom to choose and improvise was allowed. Her findings support the notion that gender is a socially constructed category and not biologically determined.[11]

Peters, in her study of women's activities among the Mandan, Arikara, and Hidatsa tribes, proposes that to understand the significance of American Indian women in their tribal societies, current research must look at the domestic activities of tribal women with a new perspective. In this context it becomes self-evident that women have economic significance stemming from control over their labor and the means of production. Women's activities are well documented in anthropological and ethnographic studies and we concur that re-examination of this material offers the potential for valuable new insight about the status of American Indian women in their societies, both past and present.

Klein and Ackerman venture to address the "silence" that has confined Indian women to the images described. They suggest that perhaps the silence is, in fact, a lack of dispute regarding their roles within their societies and refer to this lack of dispute as a silence of familiarity."[12] According to the authors, in societies where no dispute regarding gender roles exists, silence would be expected. For those who are not members of such societies and therefore not privy to the societal rules regarding gender roles, the attempt is to fill in the silence. The result has been that the silence was filled with the notion of powerlessness of American Indian women—the Western bias.[13] From our cultural backgrounds we know that domesticity does not equal powerlessness. To the contrary, in Indian societies and particularly "in a matrilineal society like Hopi, the woman in her domain is head of the family which affects all of the affairs in the pursuit of life—economic and religious—and is acknowledged by the husband and all males in the extended family and community itself."[14]

In the ensuing discussion, we endeavor to articulate a perspective which we coin "tribal" because it is grounded in membership in our tribal communities (Comanche and Hopi) and from our experiences as American Indian women beginning with our early socialization into and continued connection to the culture and traditions of our respective tribal societies. In itself, a tribal perspective is different from an "Indian" perspective, one often referred to in contemporary terms as "pan-Indianism." We define "pan-Indianism" as all encompassing, a move toward a generic perspective that may ignore, misinterpret, and generalize lived experiences. We recognize that our personal life experiences are greatly influenced by our tribal cultures but provide the impetus for offering a unique perspective. We hope that our efforts might solicit the interest and voices of other American Indian women and thereby contribute to the fields of American Indian studies and women's studies. It is also important that we state that our personal experiences and reflections are unique to ourselves and do not necessarily (re)present the perspectives of all American Indian women.

Virginia Bergman Peters: New Avenues for Research on American Indian Women

Peters's 1995 study on the activities and responsibilities of Mandan, Hidatsa, and Arikara tribal women of the Upper Missouri River Valley offers strong potential as a research model in recovering American Indian women from an invisible and silent past.[15] In particular, we identify those aspects of her research methodology we feel provide new avenues for further research to be undertaken by both Indian and non-Indian women scholars alike.

Peters's interest in American Indian women was generated in a class on the

Mandan, Hidatsa, and Arikara. She describes these tribal women as independent people with personal, economic, and political goals of their own while living in balance with men. Her study involved an extensive examination of the research material that included descriptions of the Mandan, Hidatsa, and Arikara tribal cultures during the first half of the nineteenth century, eyewitness sources from 1738, and the works of historians and anthropologists up to the time of the study. Of these accounts, Peters states, "The written works and paintings of these men are rich in details of the way of life in the upper Missouri. However, all of these chronicles were narratives by men about men."[16]

Consequently, the paradox created in the portrayal of the women of these cultures as beasts of burden and slaves to their male masters in the accounts of Euro-American men who documented their visits among these tribes intrigued her. Whereas, Peters learned these tribal women were admired for their agricultural feats and renowned for their ability as traders with linguistic aptitude that facilitated their exchanges with other Indians and with Europeans and Americans as well as for their self-reliance and competency as entrepreneurs. Peters states, "It was only by recording what women did and how they acted in given situations that I could bring them to the center of the picture." In doing so, Peters found that women worked in every aspect of village life, including seemingly male-dominated ceremonial rituals, completely female-centered activities, and religious, economic, and social affairs in which they were partners with men. All three societies were organized around women's labor, and life for the Mandan, Hidatsa, and Arikara took place within the framework of matrilineal kinship and matrilocal residence. Her findings also revealed that the single most important factor in village society was the surplus of corn that the women produced. "It was the basis of the Plains network and the source of the village wealth. It was the foundation on which their society was built and around which it was structured. Women owned the fields and worked them with sisters and daughters. Because they worked together, it made sense for them to live together. . . . Men and women each had their defined roles in village society, but there was an element of reciprocity between sexes and generations that permeated every aspect of village life."[17]

As practiced, reciprocity between sexes and generations and through matrilineal clans, the extended families, and age-grade societies established a strong, well-balanced system. According to Peters, by paying attention to the activities of women, "much light has been shed on the relationship between the sexes and on the status of women in the village tribes"[18]

The Significance of Women's Work and Position of Authority
Women's activities and responsibilities were absolutely crucial, for they provided the practical support for all aspects of village life.

> Women prepared the supplies . . . for the hunting parties; . . . [p]rocessed slain buffalo into usable products and food; conducted their own ceremonies, aided the men in the performance of their rituals, and provided the necessary assistance for the men's advancement in society, . . . gave birth

to the next generation and tended to the last when it died; . . . controlled all of the tribe's land and material goods, and made the attainment of those goods possible through their paramount activity, the growing of corn. The corn not only fed the tribes, but, as recognized in the myth of Mother Corn, was essentially the source of all bounty, for it was the surplus of corn and the trade which it generated that made the village Indians' way of life possible.[19]

Positions of authority were earned; the most important qualification was having the reputation for showing concern for the old and for those in need. Peters adds, "*responsibility* for—rather than authority over—others, . . . *linkage,* not dominance, seems to be the system by which the village agricultural tribes . . . lived, and that . . . has helped them survive to this day."[20]

Re-examination of ethno-historical accounts, specifically focusing on the activities of women, as Peters has demonstrated, illuminates new avenues of research for explaining gender ideology in tribal societies.[21] More importantly, the significance of women's work is revealed and better understood. Although Peters's study affirms that the activities of the women of these cultures remain primarily in the domestic spheres, these activities are presented as "absolutely crucial" responsibilities that ensured the survival of the people in all aspects. Additionally, the social organization of these societies emanates from the significance of women's domestic activities. Women's activities, their biological ability to generate life, and responsibility for the livelihood of the total community then are revealed as the sources of power, status, and authority sought in Western thought.

Socialization of Females
From earliest childhood, girls and boys were taught their respective roles and duties. Peters states, "Very early in life, the activities of boys and girls diverged."[22] The training of women, which began in the household, indicates that they were educated to assume their roles and become equally responsible for the livelihood of the total community.

The significance of a young Arikara girl's transition to womanhood was conveyed through a special public ceremony for the young woman upon reaching puberty. According to Peters, a highly respected old man or woman officiated by speaking to the young girl about her new status as a woman. New clothing was prepared, symbolizing her new life, her new relationships to the tribe, and her new adult responsibilities. Prayer marking this event was said so that she was kept in the right way of life and so that she would become an honored mother of the tribe. A grandmother would privately instruct the granddaughter in the principles of the tribe: to care for the home, ensuring that all in it would be comfortable and happy; to be hospitable, helpful, and kind to strangers and neighbors; to be dutiful to her husband, careful of his honor, proud of his achievements—for this, he, in turn, would cherish her, ensuring a happy life together.[23]

Essentially, the principle of "reciprocity between the sexes and generations," the intricate system of relatedness, obligation, and respect that governed their world, was made known to the young woman. Hers was to assume a role of responsibility and obligation to her people and aspire to become an honored woman in the community.

Oral Traditions and Ceremonies

Oral traditions of the people also become a new avenue of research for explaining gender ideology in tribal societies. Peters states, "Since theirs was an oral culture, . . . their beliefs and experiences . . . had passed . . . on from generation to generation through the ceremonies which were a part of every activity in the village and through the stories told by one generation to another."[24]

Peggy Reeves Sanday (cited in Peters) explains: "Oral traditions contain within them a conception of the natural or initial order of things. By articulating how things are in the Beginning, people . . . make a basic statement about their relationship with nature and about their perception of the source of power in the universe. This relationship and its projection into the sacred and secular realms hold the key for understanding sexual identities and corresponding roles."[25] This is evidenced by the oral traditions of all three tribes, where "the acts of creation are not performed by one omnipotent God . . . [but by] a god who finds a fellow deity and shares the responsibility with him. Together they wander until they come upon the source of their existence: the female (mouse), the source from which the creators came, and the female (toad), the ground itself, the ground of being."[26] In these cultures, the controlling deity of the annual growth of plants was female; the female presence was found to be a strong and vital aspect in the supernatural world of all three tribes.

According to Peters, the actions of the people in their daily life reflecting their reverence for earth and all its gifts are better understood within the context of oral tradition. In turn, their social organization also reflected their recognition of women as responsible for turning nature's gifts, animals, plants, the earth producing the corn, into the necessities of life: food, clothing, lodging, tools—all necessities of life as well as life itself. There was a great dependence on women and their regenerative powers.

Today, the works of poet scholars such as Paula Gunn Allen (Laguna Pueblo/ Sioux), Luci Tapahonso (Navajo), and Laura Tohe (Navajo) draw strongly on the oral traditions of their respective tribal societies and their personal experiences to provide a more accurate portrayal of American Indian women, one that serves to combat stereotypes of them. Oral traditions—tribal histories, stories, songs, rituals, social institutions, and customs—encompass all those aspects of tribal societies that perpetuate the culture into the future and ensure the survival of the people.

As American Indian women scholars become active participants in the reinterpretations of women's activities, female socialization patterns, female presence in oral tradition and ceremonies, their perspectives move us toward developing the concept of Indian feminism.

Power, Authority, Status, and Personal Autonomy—A Tribal Perspective

The research agenda on American Indian women has been driven by the concepts of power, authority, status, personal autonomy, influence, and equality. These terms become problematic for our discussion because we must consider that these Western concepts may not have an equivalent in native languages or thought because "institutional" forms of power did not exist in tribal societies. Instead, we view them as politically defined perspectives emanating from a manmade political system. This is a system which does not allow for any movement away from a male-oriented society, pronouncing man as the dominating figure, declaring males as owners of property and heads of households, and establishing legal definitions and laws based on man's authority, which the "woman" follows.[27]

Furthermore, tribes are based on kin relationships whereas the nation-state is a legal construction. Kinship, which includes women as well as men, established in a remote past by custom becomes "the right way of doing something" and has the effect of law for its members, although not codified law. Citizenship in a nation-state, however, may exclude women, people of color, or any other group in the society. "Tribe," therefore, moves us away from a history that is often exclusionary to one that is inclusive. In addition, kinship makes reciprocity a moral and social obligation not a legal obligation. Even though tribes are now nation-states working under formal constitutions, this does not undermine the kinship system in place or the tradition of customary practices, which impose obligation on tribal members—women, men, and children. The formal rules and policies of modern tribal governments acknowledge these traditional systems as they stand.[28] Therefore, caution must be taken in using such concepts and terminology as power and equality in interpreting the lives of American Indian women.

Gender Ideology, Gender Identity, and Indian Feminism

Gender ideology in many tribal societies is embedded in community life and maintained through a strong, well-balanced system among the sexes and generations. The roles of societal members and the connecting network of relationships through clan, kinship, and religious systems of most tribal societies stem from long-established practices in survival of the group within a particular environment. They were based on a cultural orientation that recognized biology while constructing a gender ideology through oral traditions and social institutions. Thus, the capacity for survival of both women and men emanated from biology and culture, appearing as natural, i.e., the Great Law of the Iroquois, and was undisputed.[29] This biology of humanity in the natural sense also acknowledged the "miracle of biology"—generating life—thereby giving special status to women and to the union of man and woman.[30] Women felt their place and position through clan, kinship, and religious systems without threat or intervention by men or political systems. Influence over others came through example—living in a culturally sanctioned way—which the documentary record, usually focusing on exceptionalism, does not often incorporate.

Therefore, the issues of equality, power, and status in the relation of women to men, as raised by the women's movement, may be viewed with skepticism because, essentially, these ideas are alien to the Indian experience. Bea Medicine, a Sioux anthropologist, has often stated that Indian women do not need liberation because they have always been liberated within their tribal structures.[31] In the larger sense, American Indian women have held significant influence in directing or helping direct decisions in secular or even religious affairs in their tribal societies. Even under new or coexisting (traditional and non-Indian) systems of selecting tribal leaders, American Indian women are full participants.

This turns our focus back to the social systems from which the concepts of equality, power, and status emanate. We describe mainstream America as a society in which competition is a fundamental governing principle. In a competitive society, an individual's rights, defined and codified into law, are applied and played out in economic and political arenas. Equality, power, and status, then, are achieved through economic and political accomplishments of individuals and lead to a situation of sociopolitical confrontation between the sexes. The resultant power struggle is manifested in the myriad of disparities which have "held" women down and have been the catalyst for feminists and the women's movement.

In tribal societies, individual rights are not the issue; instead, the notion of "rights" is expressed as "just" treatment for every individual. For example, the long history of men's and women's roles, or the "law," particularly in Hopi society, is defined in the context of ritualism—if one takes her/his rightful place as woman/man, the community is in harmony—where the emphasis is on getting the other to do her/his rightful duty so that the community enjoys the balance. Therefore, in a communal society such as Hopi, the importance is on each individual, each man and woman, working for the total benefit of the community. In contemporary Hopi society, while women and men continue to be defined in terms of traditional roles, these roles have expanded to include new opportunities coming from outside. "Hopi feminism," then, continues to exist in the latent power women are afforded through the matrilineal clan system.[32] We are arguing that in tribal societies there was a profound understanding of the power of women; femaleness was highly valued and both respected and feared. This understanding was reflected in the beliefs, attitudes, and laws of tribal people, yet, as Paula Gunn Allen states, "feminists too often believe that no one has ever experienced the kind of society that empowered women and made that empowerment the basis of its rules of civilization."[33] This perspective contributes to the continued invisibility of American Indian women. The "disputes" over these issues in American culture, deriving from Christian ideals of womanhood and competitive society, become potentially harmful to the Indian community as a whole. Already, such disputes have seeped into Indian communities in various ways (media, literature, education, wage economy) and have had a powerful influence on the community's youth and, consequently, a detrimental impact on the community as a whole.

The institutions of Indian cultures embody "togetherness" with all activities directed toward the care of the family. Therefore, American Indian women did not and may not find the idea of separate spheres for men and women confusing. The traditional roles of women (as defined by specific tribes), the care of family, and the intricate system of relatedness and obligation continue to have meaning for American Indian women and provide the foundation that assists in incorporating and accommodating change.

Colonization

As Shoemaker has noted, the introduction of a new, European gender ideology may have introduced confusion for American Indians and/or American Indian women in their native beliefs about gender.[34] Colonization did impact and influence tribal societies, and they were in varying degrees permanently changed. Gender roles changed and tribal men and women adapted to new circumstances (Indian education, wage economy), new environments (reservations, urban life), and confronted new challenges (dislocation, stereotyping, poverty, domestic violence) to ensure the survival of their people. This new gender ideology, aligned to fit Euro-American expectations within the American economy, required American Indian women to merge traditional beliefs with cultural innovation. Many face and confront this struggle with an innate sense of self-empowerment based in cultural values, attitudes, and beliefs. The following narrative of one of the authors offers an example of how the influence of cultural beliefs and values continues to figure significantly in the contemporary lives of Indian women.

> After some years of marriage, three children, and a teaching profession, I struggled with the demands made on me as a wife, mother, and educator. My greatest struggle was with the demands of running a household, specifically, the daily cooking of meals, especially because I did not particularly enjoy this "female" activity. The evidence of my struggle was more than the average number of overcooked and/or boring meals that made mealtimes strained. I finally turned to my mother about this struggle. In our native language, she emphatically stated, "You are a mother, and you are a wife. It is your responsibility to nourish your family by preparing the meals. If you prepare the meals with anger or resentment, essentially, you are feeding your children, your family, the anger and resentment within you.

Her admonishment was profound and left a vivid impression in my mind of my responsibilities, foremost as mother and wife. It brought to light that the division of labor between woman and man shaped both personal and tribal identity.

Many of the traditional responsibilities and obligations of the American Indian woman as mother, clan mother, trader, agriculturalist, educator, and preserver of culture and traditions continue and are, in fact, gaining renewed respect and attention. There appears to be a new consciousness about the need for tribal communities to look to their traditions and customary practices to seek answers to contemporary issues and problems. In many tribal communities, women are leading the efforts to preserve, maintain, and regain the language, customs, and traditions of their respective tribes. American Indian women are recognized as Keepers of the Heart (the Indian spirit), Mothers of Nations, Clan Mothers, and Beloved Women. They continue to be grandmothers, mothers, daughters, medicine women, and warriors. In leadership roles, American Indian women are driven by their sense of responsibility and obligation as tribal women.

For the most part, American Indian women's place within their tribal communities remains undiminished and they continue to participate fully in all tribal affairs and have applied this experience as participants in the larger society as well. This is demonstrated by American Indian women such as Eileen Luna Firebaugh (Choctaw/Cherokee), whose work addresses the contemporary issue of violence against women in tribal communities; Vivian Juan Saunders, chairwoman of the Tohono O'odham Nation; Kathy Wesley-Kitchyan, chairwoman of the San Carlos Apache Tribe; and Joni Ramos, president of the Salt River Pima-Maricopa Indian Community, who are visibly asserting their voices in political and social arenas as they nurture and sustain their tribal communities and people.[35]

American Indian Women: The Challenge for Research

"Pocahontas," "princess," and "squaw" are trenchant images deeply rooted in our society. We must insist upon and expect accurate images of American Indian women in future research and scholarship. American Indian studies and women's studies are two interdisciplinary areas where the source of this potential exists. The challenge, according to Devon Abbott Mihesuah, Oklahoma Choctaw scholar, is to understand the complexity of American Indian women and tribal society and to have a genuine respect for another way of dialogue so that the voices of American Indian women become a part of the feminist discourse.[36]

As suggested by Peters, a re-examination of the anthropological and ethnohistorical literature as a means of illuminating new avenues of research is essential and offers much potential for generating new directions of research on American Indian women. We must document "what was" and "what remains" following the impact of colonization. The ancestral languages of tribal societies must be included in this research agenda.

Today, more American Indian women scholars like Devon Mihesuah, Delphine Red Shirt, Wendy Rose, and others are articulating, defining, and asserting themselves in tribally specific terms. Moreover, the works of non-Indian scholars, such as Nancy Shoemaker, Virginia Peters, Laura Klein, and Lillian Ackerman, among others, are contributing significantly to the scholarship on American Indian women in a manner that allows us to see Indian women from new points of view and attitudes of mind. Such works complement each other and challenge the research and scholarship on American Indian women toward broadening the field of debate and discourse. The responsibility rests with scholars and, more specifically, American Indian women scholars to seek the opportunity for American Indian women to, at long last, tell their own stories.

Notes

1. Virginia Bergman Peters, *Women of the Earth Lodges: Tribal Life on the Plains* (Norman: University of Oklahoma Press, 1995).
2. Betty Bell, "Gender in Native America," in A *Companion to American Indian History,* ed. Philip Deloria and Neal Salisbury (Malden: Blackwell Publishers, 2002), 312.
3. Rayna Green, "The Pocahontas Perplex: The Image of Indian Women in American Culture," in *Unequal Sisters,* ed. Ellen Carol DuBois and Vicki L. Ruiz (New York: Routledge, 1990), 15–21.
4. Bell, "Gender in Native America," 312
5. Green, "The Pocahontas Perplex," 19.
6. Rayna Green, *Women in American Indian Society* (New York: Chelsea House Publishers, 1992).
7. Time-Life Books, ed., *The Woman's Way* (Alexandria: Time-Life Books, 1995), 21.
8. Devon Abbott Mihesuah, *Indigenous American Indian Women, Decolonization, Empowerment, Activism* (Lincoln: University of Nebraska Press, 2003), 3–8.
9. Laura E. Klein and Lillian A. Ackerman, eds., *Women and Power in Native North America* (Norman: University of Oklahoma Press, 1995); Peters, *Women of the Earth Lodges;* and Nancy N. Shoemaker, ed., *Negotiators of Change: Historical Perspectives on Native American Women* (New York: Routledge, 1995).
10. Shoemaker, *Negotiators of Change.*
11. Ibid.
12. Klein and Ackerman, *Women and Power,* 4.
13. Ibid.
14. Emory Sekaquaptewa, personal communication with the author, 2004.
15. Peters, *Women of the Earth Lodges.*
16. Ibid., xii.
17. Ibid., 5.
18. Ibid., xiv.
19. Ibid., 64.
20. Ibid., 167.
21. Ibid., 23.
22. Ibid.
23. Ibid., 74–75.
24. Ibid., 24.
25. Ibid., 23.
26. Ibid., 26.
27. Emory Sekaquaptewa, personal communication with the author, 2000.
28. Ibid., 2004.
29. Paula Gunn Allen, *The Sacred Hoop: Recovering the Feminine in American Indian Traditions* (Boston: Beacon Press Books, 1986).
30. Sekaquaptewa, personal communication, 2004.
31. Gretchen M. Bataille and Kathleen Mullen Sands, *American Indian Women Telling Their Lives* (Nebraska: The University of Nebraska, 1984).
32. Emory Sekaquaptewa, personal communication with the author, 2003.
33. Allen, *The Sacred Hoop.*
34. Shoemaker, *Negotiators of Change.*
35. Eileen Luna, "Protecting Indian Women from Domestic Violence," *National Institute of Justice Journal* 246 (2001): 28–30.
36. Mihesuah, *Indigenous American Indian Women,* 3–8.

PART III

How Can Women's Studies Fulfill the Promise of Interdisciplinarity?

Disciplining Feminist Futures?

"Undisciplined" Reflections about the Women's Studies PhD

Vivian M. May

Introduction: Contemplating the (Perceived) Problem of "Excess" in Women's Studies

While revising this chapter, I started to think about my recent experience in collaboratively organizing and coordinating a national conference about the women's studies PhD.[1] Although this was the conference's focus, in the end many of us noted how difficult it seemed to actually *discuss* the women's studies PhD. Why? How could so many women's studies doctoral students and graduates have run up to me with their unarticulated or unheard longings for the field, seemingly unable or, perhaps, unwilling to voice their ideas in the more formalized spaces for dialogue that we, the conference committee, had devised? Similarly, why, in hallways and bathrooms, did I hear similar comments of frustration and disbelief from women's studies department chairs and faculty members teaching in doctoral programs? How could the women's studies PhD—its parameters, methods, implications, and goals—still somehow be an absent presence *at its own conference?*

This persistent state of unimaginability concerning the purpose, method, or role of the women's studies PhD is revealing and merits closer analysis. Partly, it connects to the field's ongoing debates around excess—the alleged impossibility of "doing everything," of being accountable to multiple methods, constituencies, identities, geographies, and activisms. Thus the women's studies PhD continues to seem unthinkable partly because, in the larger context, so many in the field think it impossible or undesirable for women's studies to be accountable to plural yet contesting visions, methods, theories, bodies, and spatialities. However, this so-called problem of excess could, in fact, be understood as no problem at all. The very "messiness," indeterminacy, and lack of sameness that signify problems to others are, to me, part of the promise of both the women's studies PhD and the field. In fact, nostalgic efforts to adhere to some form of coherence, or to retrieve an originary women's studies that allegedly thrived and existed before things became so "contested," stifle women's studies' potential.

At the fall 2001 conference about the women's studies PhD, Beverly Guy-Sheftall asserted the need to further, rather than undermine, women's studies' "inclusive intersectional analytics": Frances Smith Foster borrowed from Toni Cade Bambara's 1980 novel, *The Salt Eaters,* and queried, in regard to racial politics in women's studies, "Are you sure . . . that you want to be well?" Inez Martinez asked members of the field to (re)educate our imaginations; Layli Phillips urged women's studies to be more accountable to poverty and to women outside the academy; and Rosemarie Garland Thomson spoke of the fruitfulness of a feminist disability studies framework of "universal usability." All of these scholars articulated hope for the field at the same time that they questioned old habits of mind, interaction, and institutionalization. These old habits, which reinforce much-critiqued practices of omission, exclusion, and forgetting, can be seen as grounded in a fear of the unknown, a means of avoiding the discomfort and risks that come with creating change and yet, paradoxically, also a means by which we replicate the very structures and dynamics we *claim* as a field we most want to transform.

From my point of view, the women's studies PhD is a key site for fostering such hopes while also asking difficult questions of ourselves and others. That these visionary and critical projects must be twinned rather than separate is crucial for conceptualizing the field's future. Indeterminacy and discomfort can be understood as places of possibility rather than signs of women's studies' dissolution. Rather than implausible, the women's studies PhD should be imagined as part of a larger effort in the field to enact pedagogies and methodologies of risk in the face of fear and to ignite our imaginations in the face of oppression. I am not denying that, in many institutions, "Women's Studies is embattled, ridiculed, dismissed, and marginalized."[2] However, in response to this situation, women's studies must not be a space of constraint in which we replicate, without question, what we already know but have chosen to ignore or forget.

The Impossible, the Implausible, and the Irrational, or, "You Have a PhD in Women's Studies, But What's Your Field?"

Despite the growing number, nationwide, of women's studies departments, tenure-lines, graduate programs, and undergraduate majors, having a women's studies PhD can still provoke curiosity, in both a positive and negative sense: those inside and outside the academy can perceive it as both valuable and implausible simultaneously. This conundrum illuminates some key methodological issues facing the field. To better understand women's studies' continued "impossibility" and the implications of this for the field's future, I examine some epistemological assumptions foundational to deficit-model assertions that the women's studies PhD is inherently lacking. In this essay, my particular focus is upon the debates and paradoxes within women's studies and among feminist scholars. This is not to deny that the field is resisted, even thwarted, by others in the academy. In addition, I use the terms "feminist" and "women's studies scholar" interchangeably, but by no means do I intend to collapse the many distinctions that could be drawn among scholars who self-identify or who are identified as feminist/women's studies scholars.

Rather than prove women's studies to be adequately disciplined and assert that it sufficiently matches normative epistemological and methodological measures, my goal parallels Robyn Wiegman's: to "define the impossibility of coherence as the central problematic and most important animating feature of feminism as a knowledge formation."[3] I am therefore working from an understanding of women's studies as an area of inquiry and knowledge production that resists closure, invites conversation, and promotes a reflexive capacity for "ongoing reinterpretation" and accountability.[4] By delineating some of the field's current challenges and paradoxes, I am not simply highlighting women's studies' failures. As Caren Kaplan and Inderpal Grewal argue, women's studies must take up "an interdisciplinarity that destabilizes, critiques, and challenges rigid methodological practices."[5] With this goal in mind, I analyze gaps between feminist theories about the value of multiplicity and intersectionality and women's studies' tendencies toward monological practices and structures within higher education.

Because of its scope, the women's studies PhD has sometimes been perceived as a jumbled hodgepodge of methodologies and therefore characterized as *especially* lacking a tidy, unified subjectivity and an epistemology of mastery that, in other contexts, feminist scholars have sought to transform. These perceptions signify that the field has not gone far enough in drawing from its own theoretical and political insights—an analysis also raised by Miranda Joseph, who finds evidence of women's studies scholars "forgetting our own scholarship" when it comes to institutionalization.[6] However, by focusing on this paradox, I do not want to simply begin another round of ritualized disclaimers about the field:[7] rather, I want to contribute to the ongoing interpretation and re-examination that are key to the field's vibrancy and future.

Contrary to Mary Romero's assertions about the dangers of further institutionalizing women's studies,[8] boundary defense does not have to become our operative paradigm over boundary crossing, theory does not have to depose practice, nor does institutionalization necessarily entail multidisciplinary stasis rather than interdisciplinary synergy. Thus, working from a range of feminist theories, we could ensure that "both/and" epistemologies inform our institutional configurations and practices: we need to continue to thoughtfully resist institutionalizing hierarchy and binary oppositions without de facto resisting institutionalization. By further engaging feminist theory as a key resource for our institutional and political practices, women's studies will not only strengthen possibilities for social and educational change, but also communicate the extent to which it takes itself seriously as an area of academic and political engagement.

Feminist theoretical insights about subjectivity as multiple, the dangers of oppositional thought, the pitfalls of rationalist epistemes, or about the intersectional politics of racism, sexism, heterosexism, and ableism, prompt us to reflect upon how women's studies can better enact what Paulo Freire calls conscientization. Freire defines "conscientization" as a state of becoming that entails linking consciousness to action for change—rather than sustaining "mechanistic" models of education and self that reinforce status quo hierarchies and inequalities.[9] Moreover, by using feminist theory as a primary resource for structural decisions and policy building in the field, we would be more able to conceptualize women's studies as a "compounded space," rather than a static, bounded territory.[10]

By imagining structural models grounded in a range of feminist theories and by formalizing a spatial/intellectual paradigm of "compounded" space, further institutionalizing of women's studies does not de facto require an "equivalence between the disciplines and the nation-state," a model which Chabram-Dernersesian critiques in her essay about the institutionalization of Chicana/o studies.[11] She contends that structural and metaphorical analogies between the interdiscipline of Chicana/o studies and the Chicano/a nation problematically reinforce "an imaginary notion of the nation as a unified cultural community, by marginalizing, dispossessing, displacing, and forgetting other ethnicities."[12] Similarly, suppression, homogenization, and containment via national borders are the very dynamics women's studies should also continue to work against, not only theoretically, but also institutionally and politically. In other words, because women's studies is *conceptually* grounded in articulation, intersectionality, and cross-fertilization, our *institutional practices* need to more closely match a model of ecological thinking. Lorraine Code defines "ecological thinking" as "respectful of boundaries, yet committed to boundary-crossing in the interests of understanding the links, acknowledging ruptures, translating responsibly across local differences to preserve and extend meanings at the same time."[13] Code offers a methodological challenge to remain open and reflexive, but also to cross over and rupture the comforts and "self-certainties" of our "epistemic imaginations."[14]

In best practice, the women's studies PhD can offer both the time and space for disrupting our own assumptions in order to stretch and enhance our imaginations. Women's studies' increased institutionalization offers an occasion for thinking about the dangers of marginalization, dispossession, and forgetting what discipline building can entail while also recognizing and valuing the potential of new ways of knowing that can be fostered by securing women's studies' future in the academy. The challenge for the field lies in forging institutional models that sustain coalition politics and ecological knowing without replicating modes of colonialist nation building.

What Is the Value of a Women's Studies PhD?

Sneja Gunew describes how "feminist work within disciplinary areas is intrinsically embedded in a larger framework of accreditation and professionalization associated with specific disciplinary training"; frequently, rather than an "integrated," systematically theorized interdisciplinarity, "the reality is a smorgasbord ... structured along ... disciplinary lines."[15] Gunew pushes for more adequate theorizing about what we mean by interdisciplinarity. Moreover, she suggests that the field's categories of analysis have become over-sedimented such that "class, gender, and race ... function in increasingly universalized and unnuanced ways to prevent the very notion of porous cross-cultural, internationally sensitive collaborations that . . . are the exciting future of Women's Studies."[16] Gunew's desire for women's studies to remain "ready at all times to question its own terminology and methodology—its own basis for authority"—is particularly relevant to discussions of the women's studies PhD.[17] Doctoral programs, students, and graduates may be best equipped to begin answering questions about methodological differences and epistemic and political authority. What intellectual, social, and political value does an interdisciplinary women's studies PhD hold for engaging in these debates? Does a women's studies PhD have a different epistemological starting point? Is there value in this difference?

In her 1892 book, *A Voice from the South,* in the chapter entitled "What Are We Worth?" black feminist educator Anna Julia Cooper asserts, "The world is often called cold and hard. I don't know much about that; but of one thing I am sure, it is intensely practical. . . . It may not be unprofitable then for us to address ourselves to the task of casting up our account and carefully overhauling our books. . . . But what do we represent to the world? What is our market value?"[18] Embroiled in debates about the "right" kind of education for black Americans, Cooper was deeply critical of capitalism's influence and the primacy of *its* needs rather than the needs of the people when structuring an adequate education. Manipulating rhetorics of the market commodities, Cooper astutely documented the "worth" of a liberal arts education for all persons and refused the idea that only white people were deserving of and capable of an education for intellectual, moral, and political leadership.

The world continues to be "intensely practical": maybe we should examine what kind of "return" women's studies is earning (after only a short period of investment in the doctoral degree) and identify how the field could generate greater "value" for itself and others. At this juncture, as the number of freestanding women's studies PhD's increases, perhaps women's studies needs to overhaul its own books—to rethink its practices, past and present. For instance, as Kaplan and Grewal argue, the "Cold War roots of Women's Studies have not been fully examined."[19] What aspects of the field deeply connect to global capitalism's expansion? How might the field's stymied ability to engage with multiplicity and difference be connected to this past? Minoo Moallem points out that "the modern institution of knowledge based on the abstraction of mind and the exclusion of bodies" (the model Cooper fought against a century ago) continues to mean that, in women's studies, "the presence of difference is by definition a form of displacement of the normative"—difference, in other words, continues to signify deviance.[20]

I therefore contend that women's studies' potential for greater returns continues to be thwarted by lingering attachments to epistemologies of mastery, institutional formations romanticizing marginality, and persistent desires for unity within the field. That the field doubts its own rationale and rationality can be seen in ways both small and large, from women's studies job advertisements to surprising metaphors and analogies about women's studies, to structural decisions and desires in the academy. For example, over the past five years there have been more women's studies position openings than ever before, but if you analyze the job descriptions as texts, what surfaces? Many advertisements reveal an internal tension: they ask for interdisciplinary *teaching* experience, but implicitly favor disciplinary *scholarship* or *degrees;* or they ask for women's studies training, but preferably within a particular area, immediately disciplining interdisciplinary applicants.[21]

Because women's studies is often unable to articulate its own rationale, it is important to testify to what is learned by earning this degree and by offering it. Despite stereotypes of incoherence or of a "soft" or impractical education, having a women's studies PhD can be enormously pragmatic: for example, it provides "hands-on" experience negotiating academic policy and institutional politics, both frequently based in nineteenth-century notions of disciplinarity. As graduate students matriculate from women's studies, they will have to find ways to communicate their value to the academy, to private foundations and corporations, to public institutions and agencies, to community organizations, and to themselves. As faculty members teaching in programs/departments offering graduate degrees, we must also engage in this work—it is essential, epistemologically and politically, to assert the field's "worth" on our own terms and not be passive in the face of increasingly popular *rhetorics* (but not necessarily critical practices) of "excellence," "globalization," and (cost-effective) "interdisciplinarity" in the contemporary university.

Feminist interdisciplinary training translates into an ability to cross boundaries, to forge alliances, to ask important but often "unthinkable" questions, and, sometimes, to accomplish critical projects others think implausible. Women's studies' focus on the intimate connections between knowledge and power offers a heightened capacity to contend with institutional structures, policies, and procedures. That women's studies offers excellent preparation in this regard was highlighted in the *Chronicle of Higher Education,* which examined how many of the most successful women deans, provosts, and presidents have had some relation with women's studies in their careers.[22] And yet, we must be cautious when celebrating "women's" advances in higher education without acknowledging that the majority of women in upper administrative posts remain white,[23] while women of color continue to occupy positions of what Rachel Lee calls "fetishized marginality."[24] Thus, in addition to in-depth experience with cognitive flexibility and a collaborative outlook, earning a women's studies PhD requires engaging in internal and external critiques of the field—its own gaps, errors, politics—and seeking to change it for the better.

Because feminist theory offers multiple contexts for understanding the "discipline-or-punish" dynamic of institutions, women's studies graduates know that every interaction with state legislators, administrators and deans, hostile and allied colleagues, and students presents pedagogical opportunities for communicating not only the abstract academic value of women's studies, but also the concrete outcomes in terms of university mission and community relations. Women's studies should not wholeheartedly embrace the "new university." Rather, like Jeanette McVicker, I believe that "Women's Studies can open up spaces of resistance even within the corporate 'University of Excellence.'"[25]

Understanding how knowledge and power influence one another, both historically and presently, means taking the institutionalization of women's studies seriously while remaining ever thoughtful about how we shape and re-shape institutional affiliations and structures. And although women's studies has become more institutionalized in the university than some thought possible, its presence is still, in many respects, tentative. Biddy Martin argues that women's studies has "arrived" and is "institutionalized on equal footing with other academic and administrative units."[26] But, where has it arrived and on what terms?

Simply asserting that women's studies has "arrived" can emphasize troubling imperial concepts of universal and homogenous space-time. This rhetorical move suppresses unevenness, differences, and gaps in the field in terms of race-ethnicity, class, and geographic region. Shirley J. Yee contends that mostly white, Anglophone, and/or middle-class females pursue women's studies degrees and enter women's studies leadership due to a variety of factors, from racism within women's studies and in society at large to economic necessity.[27] Lee demonstrates that once such exclusions are addressed by seemingly "inclusive" curricular changes and hiring practices, "'women of color' are perceived as too much 'inside' the field," rather than outside it, and deep anxieties over women's studies' institutional role and scope emerge.[28] Beverly Guy-Sheftall suggests that this anxiety signifies a continuing "inability to deal with difference" at predominantly white universities while, at the same time, women's studies remains peripheral at many historically black colleges and universities and within many black studies and African American studies programs.[29]

Women's studies also has little presence in community colleges and an often tenuous presence in comprehensive public institutions, where the majority of students spend some portion of their college education. Moreover, few graduate degrees in women's studies are offered at Ivy League institutions—and certainly no PhD's.[30] Of course, women's studies has not entered the K–12 curriculum, nor is it a requirement, much less an offering, in most colleges of education, where future educators, administrators, and school curricula are being shaped. In addition, very few states recognize a women's studies BA for teacher certification in our public schools.

Claiming "equal" institutional viability with other academic units also overlooks how grants, fellowships, and post-doctorates are almost exclusively tethered to disciplinarity and, when interdisciplinary, rarely name women's studies as a fundable area of expertise. Declaring equality obscures the large number of women's studies programs just starting, or those that exist at a subsistence level. Many programs have no coordinator or must hire junior faculty to direct and build a program. Others have no curricular or faculty guidelines, or have no resources with which to develop and regularly offer a core of courses, to grant degrees, or to secure independent faculty lines.

To acknowledge these disparities is not to downplay women's studies' successes. However, such geographic, racial, and economic realities must inform any discussion of the field's future. Of course, this unevenness takes place within larger contexts of opposition toward women's studies, be it open hostility or quiet indifference. Women's studies, therefore, continues to enter the academy furtively by hiding controversial course content under prosaic titles to pass curriculum committees, or by piecing together joint appointments and sometimes random course offerings from other departments to create programs and degrees.[31] In times of economic constraint, such strategies can put women's studies in various undesirable roles, such as that of the object of charity, or of the thief pilfering course fees, lines, and stipends from more established programs. Moreover, jointly appointed faculty often find themselves apologizing for or closeting the nature of their work in order to appease their home departments.

This is well illustrated in Leora Auslander's discussion about creating the University of Chicago's Center for Gender Studies. Her essay reveals deep tensions between allegiance to disciplines and to women's studies, tensions that are not unique to her institution: the paradoxes emerging from her essay are more common than not. Auslander describes how the faculty at her institution chose to be a center and not a department because they "wanted to assure that the formalization of [their] work would not inhibit the conceptual and methodological openness . . . and intellectual and pedagogical innovativeness and energy that [their] informal network had allowed."[32] However, she later writes, "All of our faculty owe primary allegiance and time to their home departments, and we have limited power to influence renewals, tenure decisions, and promotions. Most of the work done for the center is invisible and, when noticed, sometimes (*understandably*) resented by departmental colleagues."[33] Auslander accepts her faculty's need to authorize themselves within their disciplines not only for recognition but for survival: implicitly, she finds it understandable, that is, reasonable, that they apologize for, hide, and even accept resentment for their work in gender studies. This tension suggests that despite assertions to the contrary, choosing *not* to departmentalize places the faculty at risk as surreptitious border crossers and retains women's and gender studies as a space marginal to the core of scholars' endeavors.

In combination, all of these factors suggest a situation of uneven development for women's studies, a circumstance that some state is inevitable given women's studies' continued attachment to disciplinarity.[34] More importantly, the question of whether "equality" to the disciplines is our epistemological and political goal remains unasked and unanswered. Does women's studies have latent attachments to a cultural feminist or assimilationist model of simply aiming for "equal rights" within the academic status quo? As a site of affiliation, of cross-listed and borrowed labor, women's studies' institutionally tentative existence ironically reifies the epistemologies, methods, and structural elements that many feminists seek to change in the university. The continued preference within women's studies for loose structures and the concomitant resistance to securing institutional viability via departmental status, control over tenure and faculty lines, and authority over curricular content and offerings suggests the degree to which women's studies hasn't taken institutionalization seriously.[35]

In response to the query borrowed from Cooper, "What are we worth?" I have emphasized the institutional know-how, collaborative vision, reflexivity, boundary-crossing abilities, and intersectional research skills that are the value-added results of women's studies doctoral training.[36] Nonetheless, nebulous institutional structures and implicit (or sometimes outright) opposition to women's studies doctoral degrees lead one to wonder if the field's own practices foster a state of diminished returns, such that the field's potential worth is always underestimated.

Women's Studies: Transformative at the Undergraduate Level, but Incoherent and Irrational beyond the BA?

Having discipline and being disciplined continue to be valued in the academy to such an extent that even though the women's studies PhD exists, its being is still described as improbable and illogical. In other words, a women's studies PhD (both the degree and the person) becomes an ontological and epistemological impossibility. For example, Wendy Brown writes, "If uncertainty about what constitutes a women's studies education is a persistent whisper in all undergraduate program development, it positively howls as a problem at the level of graduate training. . . . We have struggled repeatedly to conjure the intellectual basis for a Ph.D. program in Women's Studies."[37]

Arguments such as Brown's unevenly ascribe only to women's studies the messiness and border crossing that also occur within more established disciplines. Of course, some forms of border crossings are sanctioned and more valued; others are framed as illogical or less desirable. Although the academy has become increasingly interdisciplinary, there is still a higher value placed on traveling across boundaries from an established disciplinary home such that a graduate certificate or concentration in women's studies with a disciplinary PhD becomes more desirable, for example. Moreover, repeated assertions of impossibility are not simply misinterpretations: they signify an active, open resistance, a frame of unthinkability.[38]

Such bewilderment about the purpose of a freestanding interdisciplinary women's studies PhD seems particularly ironic in that the field has spent the last thirty years arguing the *merits* of interdisciplinarity, asserting the necessity of a socially conscious education, and advocating the ideals of education as a libratory practice. Women's studies claims to be central to the contemporary university, but then chooses marginality therein, signifying a sense of ambivalence, embarrassment, or apology about its own purpose and methods. Where does such embarrassment come from? Why apologize now, at this time? Placing the field's epistemological debates in larger political and educational contexts is instructive. Once women's studies' internal deliberations about knowledge and power are positioned in a wider context, an array of questions emerges.

What does it mean, for example, that the women's studies doctorate seems unviable at the same time as constructivist approaches to learning are being pushed aside in the K–12 classroom? Nationwide, school districts are being forced to return to "skill-and-drill" learning models with concomitant universal testing paradigms that value uniformity over variety, quantifiable or "hard" assessment measures over qualitative or "soft" approaches, and authoritative learning models over dialogic ones. How do the politics and methods of a "leave-no-child-behind" mandate, and its ripple effects for K–12 educational policy and research, intimately relate to issues facing interdisciplinary, identity-based fields in higher education? Moreover, what impact are the numerous reversals of bilingual education or of affirmative action having upon higher education and upon women's studies itself? What implications might this educational climate hold for interdisciplinary, qualitative, and narrative methodologies focusing on identities and knowledges as located, political constructs meant to be contested and transformed?

This conservative turn to more "neutral" educational models helps clarify *external* critiques of women's studies. However, why does women's studies question its own rationale just when the women's studies PhD becomes a reality? There must be a reason why feminism in the academy is "owned by the disciplines,"[39] or why women's studies' "interdisciplinary intellectual aspirations remain substantially unfulfilled."[40] I think the answer lies, in part, in how we have conceived of women's studies as a site of transformative potential but have defused that potential by attempting to *assimilate* women's studies to conventional academic parameters.

Even though women's studies has its roots in constructivist, libratory educational models, it is embedded in the academy, which functions according to disciplinary divisions and institutional structures shaped by rationalist epistemologies. Rationalism defines knowledge as "out there" to be discovered—knowledge isn't variable according to context or culture, but absolute. Through rigorous observation, or "spectator epistemologies," knowledge can be rendered visible and replicated by other knowers anywhere at any time. This narrow model of knowing has been constructed as if it were universal: it values objectivity or "the view from nowhere." Knowledge supposedly transcends particularity and is unmarked by class, race, region, time, sex, or sexuality. Neither context nor embodiment has an impact on or any import to knowledge production: they are epistemologically irrelevant, even problematic.

This model has had many negative repercussions. Historically, only certain subjects and contexts were presupposed and pre-selected as paradigmatic, to the exclusion of, for example, women, racial and ethnic minorities, slaves, the poor, sexual minorities, and the disabled: all of these groups have, in different ways, been thought to lack the autonomy, independence, control, regimen, and reasoning capacity necessary to be a "universal" knowing subject.[41] Disciplinarity is intimately connected to these knowledge models, for it entails dividing knowledge into discrete categories demarcated by canons to be mastered. Canonizing is about ordering, ranking, and controlling certain intellectual paradigms to the exclusion of others, in ways that suppress knowledge's inherent messiness and multiplicity. Ward Churchill, in analyzing whiteness's role in U.S. higher education, asserts that disciplinarity "readily lends itself to—perhaps demands—the sort of hierarchical ordering of things, both intellectually and physically, which is most clearly manifested in racism, militarism, and colonial domination, class and gender oppression, and the systematic ravaging of the natural world."[42] Importantly, Churchill's analysis suggests that disciplinarity, whiteness, and masculinity are characterized by intertwining but not analogous epistemologies of mastery.

Feminist theorists have, obviously, critiqued these narrow models of knowing and the knowing subject because of their exclusion and hierarchy, their reliance on the Cartesian mind-body split, and their limited understanding of where knowledge lies, who can be a knower, and what elements should be considered when talking about the act of knowing. For example, María Lugones's definition of "playfulness" challenges attitudes of agonistic dominance and arrogant perception embedded in "ruly" ways of knowing and interacting. She writes, "The playfulness that gives meaning to our activity includes uncertainty, but in this case the uncertainty is an *openness to surprise.* This is a particular metaphysical attitude that does not expect the world to be neatly packaged, ruly."[43]

Yet despite the wide range of feminist theorists who affirm difference, discontinuity, and unruly multiplicity, women's studies' sense of self and origin narrative continue to be framed in ways that reinvoke ruly ways of thinking and being. For example, in response to an article by feminist critic Susan Gubar, Robyn Wiegman questions Gubar's implication that differences and contentiousness in feminist criticism function as annoying interruptions of an otherwise harmonious situation. Weigman challenges how "the epistemological and disciplinary, not to mention political, differences among the scholarly archives of postcolonial, U.S. ethnic, and poststructuralist feminisms are diminished [by Gubar] as 'debilitating rhetorics . . . that made us cranky with one another.'"[44]

Melancholy among "us" over the differences that supposedly interrupt otherwise good-humored feminist scholarship/community is intimately related to fears about disciplinary coherence that is threatened to be spoiled by the breadth of interdisciplinary, multicultural, and transnational educational models: difference is supported on the one hand and taken away on the other.[45] Once again, Anna Julia Cooper's words are illustrative. In her essay "Woman versus the Indian," she describes "Wimodaughsis (a woman's culture club whose name is made up of the first few letters of the four words wives, mothers, daughters, and sisters)."[46] Yet when a "colored lady, a teacher in one of our schools, applies for admission," it soon becomes clear that Anna Shaw, the club's leader, had "not calculated that there were any wives, mothers, daughters, and sisters, except white ones" such that "*Whimodaughsis* would sound just as well, and then it need mean just *white mothers, daughters, and sisters.*"[47]

Cooper's century-old (yet still relevant) analysis underscores Wiegman's point: the origin story of an Edenic, whole women's studies or feminist movement torn asunder by "new" knowledge of embodiment (race, sexuality, nation, disability) is flawed. Feminist scholarship and activism have *always* had multiple configurations and locations. Moreover, as Wiegman contends, "to hunker ourselves down in the disciplines, to cast a nostalgic gaze at a past that now finds comfort in the sanctity of discipline-as-home, to reject the compelling possibilities of new knowledges and knowledge formations: these critical positions abandon academic feminism to an institutional framework that is already out of step with the kinds of issues that such a political project must confront."[48]

Given the extensive feminist scholarship focusing on the centrality of difference to thinking about and among women, it is ironic that much resistance to women's studies seems to stem from intertwined attachments to rationalism, disciplinarity, and unity. At the same time that feminist scholars seek to transform education and, by extension, social relations, we also seek (often unknowingly) to protect and even retain the familiar. Shaped by sanctioned and recalcitrant ways of thinking and being, we replicate the very paradigms and practices we aim to undo. I do not mean that "we" are all the same or are influenced by the *same* kinds of circumstances or contexts but that we are, differently, across time and space, caught within the very structures and circumstances we seek to transform.

Of course, this paradox is not new: in fact, examining "caughtness" has been key to much feminist theorizing. Audre Lorde, for example, reminds us that "we have, built into all of us, old blueprints of expectation and response," which means that "the true focus of revolutionary change is never merely the oppressive situations which we seek to escape, but that piece of the oppressor which is planted deep within each of us."[49] Because such attachments to familiar blueprints are not always conscious, antiracist educator Joyce E. King outlines the importance of addressing what she calls *dysconsciousness* if we are to work toward change. King defines "dysconsciousness" as "an uncritical habit of mind (including perceptions, attitudes, assumptions, and beliefs) that justifies inequity and exploitation by accepting the existing order of things as given."[50]

Signs of women's studies' dysconscious attachments to rationalism and unity, which reflect "an uncritical identification with the existing social order," can be found in the analogies and metaphors used to describe and delimit the field of women's studies in general and the women's studies PhD in particular. In her examination of the politics of location and travel writing, Caren Kaplan suggests that accountability is key to shifting our terms of inquiry and action from tolerance models that "make space" for difference within existing frameworks to transformation of the intellectual, political, and structural paradigms at work.[51] Thus, examining embedded assumptions about the appropriate role or location of women's studies is key to shifting the field's own terms of inquiry. So, in addition to the analogies discussed so far (of lack, bad moods, or of women's studies as an add-on or accessory), what other metaphors and values emerge in debates about the field? What do they naturalize or reinforce?

Women = Intellectual Inferiors:
Women's Studies = Intellectually Inferior?

Intellectually inferior, confused, "insane," unstable, irrational, lacking, mysterious, unclassifiable—nineteenth-century diagnosis of gendered and raced "otherness," or turn-of-the-twenty-first-century discussion of women's studies by feminist scholars? As Geraldine Pratt writes, "Metaphors are . . . representational strategies that help us to think and articulate ways of being . . . [and] they open up some avenues of thought and necessarily close down others."[52] What do our own metaphors about our field reveal? What gets closed off in feminist scholars' discussions about the women's studies doctorate? Women's studies has recently been described, by feminist scholars, as impoverished, intellectually fragmented, even superficial. Interdisciplinary feminist scholarship, particularly the PhD, supposedly suffers from "breadth without depth."

The recommended prophylactic against such dangers is disciplinary depth (or penetration) and an affair with women's studies on the side. Akin to the role of the other woman, women's studies is asked to remain peripheral to core issues in the disciplines. Discussions on the Women's Studies Listserv (WMST-L) about advising students against pursuing a women's studies doctorate are often pragmatic and could be considered examples of accountability toward students, given the current state of affairs in women's studies. In particular, suspicions emerge around the apparently random "intellectual bricolage" of the women's studies PhD,[53] also characterized as focusing on "a little of this, a little bit of that" without rhyme or reason.[54] Paradoxically, acting "responsibly" toward women's studies undergraduates or MA students seems to require a certain betrayal of women's studies as a field. For instance, many are troubled by women's studies' apparent methodological "rootlessness."[55] The women's studies PhD is perceived as insufficiently coherent and ordered and this apparent "lack of discipline" comes to signify diminished judgment in need of control, despite the value of being on the move or in movement articulated by such scholars as bell hooks and Barbara Christian.[56]

Without questioning their implicit drive to oneness, expectations such as Freidman's for unity of method, shared questions and goals, cumulative scholarship, and depth or penetration prevail as the characteristics of knowledge that can be mastered, thereby worthy of a PhD and also faculty status.[57] Has women's studies retained attachments to imperial models of dominion, such that putting interdisciplinary feminist theory and scholarship at the center of inquiry seems incomprehensible? Friedman and others, including Wendy Brown, cannot conceive of the women's studies PhD as having much rationality at all. Friedman declares that it "is an impossible and not even desirable dream. Echoes from *Moby Dick* haunt me: 'That way *madness* lies.'"[58]

Rather than echoes from *Moby Dick,* feminist disability studies scholars might hear echoes of ableism in fears about the disorder known as the women's studies PhD. Often, interdisciplinarity is linked, metaphorically, to stereotypes of disabled bodies as undesirable, deviant, and insane—as bodies that instill fear and fitful hauntings in normate populations. As Rosemarie Garland Thomson explains, "Constructed as the embodiment of corporeal insufficiency and deviance, the physically disabled body becomes a repository for social anxieties about . . . vulnerability, control, and identity. . . . The disabled figure operates as the vividly embodied, stigmatized other whose social role is to symbolically free the privileged, idealized figure of the American self."[59] Thomson's insights suggest that the field of women's studies remains attached to not only rationalist epistemologies, but also concomitant individualist ontologies. Has women's studies become the figuratively fixed ground against which to measure the freedom of other subjects?

Not all anxieties about interdisciplinarity are as openly enamored with intellectual and corporeal control as Friedman's charges of madness or Gubar's accusations of the "*debilitating*" nature of being accountable to differences among women.[60] Nonetheless, attachments to coherence via discipline are common. In an interview with Joan Scott, Brown University student Kathryn Cook asks of the women's studies PhD, "Where's the rigor, the coherence?" She states that the purpose of a PhD is to "push and further question traditional disciplinary logic."[61] Postings on WMST-L are analogous: "since these disciplines are what we're here to critique, augment, correct, and transform, we'd better know what we're working with. . . . I fear we'll lose our footholds in the curriculum and become peripheral generalists, claiming knowledge of all fields but accepted by none."[62]

Ironically, such arguments frame women's studies as primarily a *reactionary* project that aims to correct, augment, or rework traditional disciplinary paradigms from within the disciplines. The preference for women's studies to remain relational in its scholarly identity, thereby granting the field the illustrious role of acting as knowledge's helpmate, seems contrary to feminist critiques of relational definitions of women, definitions that ascribe both social role and social value according to the services they provide others. Moreover, the repeated characterizations of women's studies' interdisciplinarity as undisciplined, illogical, and ill-conceived signify a continued inability to imagine difference as productive of anything akin to knowledge, which thereby reinforces a problematic ideal of an original or future utopia of undifferentiated oneness. The failure to conceive of women's studies and the women's studies PhD as a constructive project that goes beyond the reactive is troubling, for without academic support in terms of funding opportunities, publishing forums, full faculty lines, and departments, it is difficult, if not impossible, for women's studies to develop "boundary-crossing, comparative, and interrogative problem-focused scholarship."[63]

In addition to metaphors of deficiency faulting women's studies for its ill or unstable body of knowledge, the field is also characterized as a muse, here to offer inspiration. Like ladies' auxiliaries, women's studies is apparently best served by volunteerism and doing "more with less" as all dutiful daughters or wives should. Women's studies is even applauded for its infinite capacity and even natural mandate to "serve" other units in the academy, bringing to mind stereotyped roles of maid and mammy that invoke both biological racism and gendered essentialism. Spatially, women's studies is often thought of as a "safe haven" for those located elsewhere in the university, even though many feminist scholars, including Megan Boler, bell hooks, and Lynet Uttal, question ideals of comfort and unity in women's studies classrooms.[64]

Thus, although pedagogical insights about comfort are relevant to discussions of women's studies' institutionalization, this connection has not yet been adequately made. Otherwise, women's studies would not be imagined as a site of reprieve, offering a diversion from the mundane, an "exotic" holiday. Friedman even asserts that women's studies provides stimulating places to *travel* to from a disciplinary home, but that it is not a place where viable academics would likely choose to *live*.[65] Similarly, women's studies is applauded for broadening horizons, a paradigm that sounds rather akin to nineteenth-century adventures to the colonies for educational travel.[66] Frank Davey argues that imperialist modernism is characterized by a willingness to "appropriate the local while being condescending toward its practice."[67] Is this double dynamic at work in women's studies? Is women's studies only to operate within what Trinh T. Minh-ha names "appropriated difference," within the "Master's sphere of having"?[68]

Feminist scholarship and scholars have been inherently shaped by paradox: our marginal positioning in the academy initially functioned as the condition of our possibility, but it also limits our future. Equating women's studies' fluidity, interdisciplinarity, and multiplicity with madness, lack, absence, escape, exotic travel, or with servile roles, is disturbing and insulting. Lorraine Code describes such sedimented ways of thinking as "a system of metaphorics," an "instituted social imaginary" that helps to construct and maintain "the limits of what the society defines as thinkable."[69]

I suggest that sedimented "social imaginaries," revealed in many of the metaphors and analogies in debates about women's studies as a field, reinforce limits of thinkability and suggest that a problem of *understanding* is also at work. Because understanding frequently operates according to a binary (either something fits ready-made frames of reference or it is incommensurable, outside of logic), the issue here is *not* a "matter of [women's studies] being ignored or even misunderstood"; rather, it is a matter of "being understood all too well in a way that disallows recognition that there is still something that needs to be understood."[70] In other words, women's studies is often "understood" too readily, in ways that assimilate the field to the familiar, erase its tensions, deny its multiplicity, and obscure its important differences. Again, women's studies continues to assess itself according to parameters of knowing and being that we have thoroughly critiqued in our theories.

Instead of retaining and reinforcing rationalism and disciplinarity as the normative assessment measures, or seeking to smooth over differences, why not consider interdisciplinarity and multiplicity as productive, open sites for action and creativity? As Wiegman argues, "differences do not render academic feminism mirthful and unconflicted, nor do they allow us to assemble a coherent, unified collectivity. What they do enable is an academic feminism unconstrained by the demand to be singular."[71]

Refusing Theory/Practice Binaries: Feminist Theory and Interdisciplinary Methods

The tension between feminist theories of multiplicity and women's studies monological practices requires further consideration but also suggests that feminist theory might be a source for rethinking our practices of and expectations for women's studies in the academy. Feminist theory's insights about the inherent value in, as Anzaldúa describes it, taking "Tu camino de conocimiento" across boundaries to do "the creative work of putting all the pieces together in a new form," can help the field to shift.[72] For example, Patti Lather describes the pedagogical need "to see ambivalence and differences not as obstacles, but as the very richness of meaning-making and the hope of whatever justice we might work toward."[73] Anzaldúa contends that "developing a tolerance for contradictions

[and] . . . ambiguity" is essential to moving "away from set patterns and goals."[74] And, Simone de Beauvoir argues that "ambiguity must not be confused with . . . absurdity. To declare that existence . . . is ambiguous is to assert that its meaning is never fixed, that it must constantly be won."[75] In other words, ambiguity is a site for feminist movement and for continuous action and engagement, not despair.

How can feminist theories further shape our practices and inform our institutional structures in ways that allow for heterogeneity without containment, for institutionalization of women's studies that is not exclusionary yet is strong enough so that women's studies will not disappear, as Marilyn Boxer worries it might?[76] How can we take interdisciplinarity and intersectionality seriously without adopting an "either/or" oppositional stance toward women's studies' disciplinary connections, foundations, and affiliations? What might "both/and" curricula, structures, and methods look like, in other words? Instead of seeking to assimilate women's studies to pre-existing paradigms, an approach Lugones and Uma Narayan argue is destructive of difference, why not put feminist theory to work?[77]

For example, how might a methodology that uses feminist theory as its starting point look? By using feminist theories from a range of sources, I have sketched an initial rubric to articulate the kind of "methodology" that a women's studies PhD offers. I offer this interpretation not as an authoritative statement about the definitional core of women's studies, but rather as an invitation, even a provocation, toward further discussion about methodological parameters, the role of feminist theory in women's studies practices and structures, and even whether seeking to define women's studies methods falls prey to the very kind of "disciplining" of knowledge I have argued against. Such qualifiers aside, I contend that interdisciplinary feminist methods could be characterized by the following definitional parameters:

> Women's studies seeks to transform ordinary/accepted modes of thinking *and* understands its own theories and practices to be open to critique, actively reflected upon: women's studies methods are not inherently good or virtuous just because they come out of women's studies or feminist theory.[78]

> Women's studies methods are therefore skeptical, deconstructive, and unruly while also constructive and committed to change. They entail a conscious rupture with tradition while always seeking to be mindful of the paradoxical ways that we reinvoke the systems we seek to transform.[79]

> Women's studies looks to multiple sources for knowledge, has multiple starting points for analysis, and also redefines the parameters of knowledge and its foundations. Its epistemological practices are intersectional and cut across disciplinary, identity, spatial, and bodily boundaries.[80]

> Because intersectionality requires a both/and way of knowing and a degree of open-mindedness toward ambiguity, women's studies methods do not necessarily seek to smooth over or eradicate paradoxes and differences, but find them to be spaces from within which to work. Intersectional prac-

tice therefore entails a shift in perception as well as openness toward discomfort as a site of learning and change.[81]

Women's studies methods are connected to inspiring a desire for change, entailing an understanding of the import of affect in knowledge production so that academic practices connect to social transformation.[82]

I offer this sketch of a women's studies methodology not only to counter assertions that an interdisciplinary women's studies research method is inconceivable, but also in the hope that future conversations about women's studies methodologies—which, broadly conceived, also connect to or even encompass institutional epistemologies and structures—will flourish. I am convinced that taking women's studies seriously requires recommitting ourselves to linking feminist theory and practice, both within and outside of higher education, so that we won't continue to punish and deride feminist theoretical paradigms when we come across them in the flesh and so that we can more effectively enact educational and social change.

As Homi Bhabha reminds us, "the effectivity of thinking through difference is to keep thinking through these nodal textiles and not to give any one of them . . . an a priori authority."[83] In other words, we need to reconfigure knowledge's parameters to favor multiplicity, not force consensus. Anzaldúa asserts the need to move toward "divergent" ways of thinking, to encourage "mental nepantilism" or border-crossing flexibility.[84] At the same time, Lee reminds us of the need to be wary of romanticizing the "decidedly seductive" but ultimately troubling idea of "roving activist practice" in which women of color, in particular, are *alluded* to but, in the end, become "all eye and no body."[85]

Perhaps we might pause next time we ask why women's studies methods and practices are charged with unintelligibility, particularly in our graduates, to remember Judith Butler's insight that coherence and continuity are socially instituted and maintained norms of intelligibility.[86] Moreover, remembering Chandra Mohanty's definition of colonization can better inform our notion of the subject of women's studies. Mohanty states that colonization is "the structural domination and suppression of the heterogeneity of the subject(s) in question," which is why critics like Carol Boyce Davies point out the need to maintain a "resistance to fixity," or why Eve Sedgwick underscores the need to "resist knowingness" and maintain multiplicity.[87] The next time a women's studies PhD is asked why her research or her pedagogy doesn't "fit" preconceived ways of thinking, perhaps she should remind her inquirer that Alice Walker's character Shug recommends getting the "man off your eyeball," that Anzaldúa underscores the importance of a conscious rupture with oppressive traditions to foster change, or that Code has illustrated the necessity of "loosening the hold" of dominant ways of knowing so that imaginative space, a space of not-knowing, can open up.[88]

By unintentionally embracing models of rationalism and disciplinarity that require women's studies to function as peripheral to the core of academic enterprise, we elide focusing on how to create policies, practices, and guidelines for structuring imaginative openness in the field toward its past and future practices. Trinh Minh-ha states that "transformation requires a certain freedom to modify, appropriate, and reappropriate without being trapped in imitation."[89] This freedom is what the women's studies PhD offered me, and it is the core of what I seek to pass on to my own students.

Notes

I would like to thank several people for providing me opportunities to further develop my ideas: Elizabeth Kennedy and Bonnie Zimmerman, for inviting me to be part of a plenary focusing on women's studies graduates at the National Women's Studies Association Conference in 1999; Frances Smith Foster and Emory University's Institute for Women's Studies, for inviting me to present an earlier version of this work for the 2000–2001 Women's Studies Colloquium series; all members of the planning committee for the fall 2001 conference on the women's studies PhD (Beverly Guy-Sheftall, Frances Smith Foster, Sally Kitch, Wendy Kolmar, Inez Martinez, Claire Moses, Jean O'Barr, Stephanie Shields, and Bonnie Zimmerman); and Linda Basch/National Council for Research on Women, for inviting me to moderate a panel about the women's studies PhD at their 2002 annual conference. I have been privileged to be included in these formative conversations. I would also like to thank Elizabeth Kennedy and Agatha Beins for their thoughtful feedback on this essay. Finally, I would like to thank the anonymous reviewers for their insightful commentary.

1. An earlier version of this essay, entitled "Disciplinary Desires and Undisciplined Daughters: Negotiating the Politics of a Women's Studies Doctoral Education," appeared in *NWSA Journal* 14, no. 1 (spring 2002): 134–159. The conference, "The PhD in Women's Studies: Implications and Articulations," occurred October 12–14, 2001. The website is http://www.depts.drew.edu/wmst/ws_Ph.D./MainPage.htm.
2. Caren Kaplan and Inderpal Grewal, "Transnational Practices and Interdisciplinary Feminist Scholarship: Refiguring Women's and Gender Studies," in *Women's Studies on Its Own*, ed. Robyn Wiegman (Durham, N.C.: Duke University Press, 2002), 67.
3. Robyn Wiegman, "The Progress of Gender: Whither 'Women'?" in *Women's Studies on Its Own*, ed. Wiegman, 107.
4. Lorraine Code, *Rhetorical Spaces: Essays on Gendered Locations* (New York: Routledge, 1995), 135.
5. Kaplan and Grewal, "Transnational Practices," 66.
6. Miranda Joseph, "Analogy and Complicity: Women's Studies, Lesbian/Gay Studies, and Capitalism," in *Women's Studies on Its Own*, ed. Wiegman, 268.
7. Lorriane Code, "How to Think Globally: Stretching the Limits of Imagination," *Hypatia* 13, no. 2 (1998): 76.
8. Mary Romero, "Disciplining the Feminist Bodies of Knowledge: Are We Creating or Reproducing Academic Structure?" *NWSA Journal* 12, no. 2 (2000): 148–162.
9. Paulo Freire, *Letters to Cristina: Reflections on My Life and Work* (New York: Routledge, 1996), 81–189.
10. Angie Chabram-Dernersesian, "'Chicana! Rican? No, Chicana Riqueña!' Refashioning the Transnational Connection," in *Between Woman and Nation: Nationalisms, Transnational Feminisms, and the State,* ed. Caren Kaplan, Norma Alarcón, and Minoo Moallem (Durham, N.C.: Duke University Press, 1999), 273.
11. Ibid., 288.

12. Ibid., 270.

13. Code, "How to Think Globally," 80.

14. Ibid., 74.

15. Sneja Gunew, "Feminist Cultural Literacy: Translating Differences, Cannibal Options," in *Women's Studies on Its Own*, ed. Wiegman, 50.

16. Ibid., 64.

17. Ibid.

18. Anna Julia Cooper, *A Voice from the South* (New York: Oxford University Press, 1988), 228–229, 233.

19. Kaplan and Grewal, "Transnational Practices," 70.

20. Minoo Moallem, "'Women of Color in the U.S.': Pedagogical Reflections on the Politics of 'the Name,'" in *Women's Studies on Its Own*, ed. Wiegman, 372.

21. For a more detailed textual analysis of these advertisements, please see my 2002 *NWSA Journal* article, "Disciplinary Desires and Undisciplined Daughters."

22. Kit Lively, "Women in Charge: More Elite Universities Hire Female Provosts, Creating a New Pool for Presidential Openings," *Chronicle of Higher Education*, June 16, 2000, A33–A35.

23. Beverly Guy-Sheftall, personal correspondence with author, 2002.

24. Rachel Lee, "Notes from the (Non)Field: Teaching and Theorizing Women of Color," in *Women's Studies on Its Own*, ed. Wiegman, 88.

25. Jeanette McVicker, "The Politics of 'Excellence,'" in *Women's Studies on Its Own*, ed. Wiegman, 241.

26. Biddy Martin, "Success and Its Failures," *differences* 9, no. 3 (1997): 102.

27. Shirley J. Yee, "The 'Women' in Women's Studies," *differences* 9, no. 3 (1997): 55.

28. Lee, "Notes from the (Non)Field," 80, 88.

29. Beverly Guy-Sheftall, "Whither Black Women's Studies, Interview with Evelynn M. Hammonds," *differences* 9, no. 3 (1997): 37, 39. Please note: this essay is reprinted in this collection—please refer to it for further details.

30. Discussed by Jean O'Barr during a planning committee dialogue for the fall 2001 conference about the women's studies PhD.

31. Judith A. Allen and Sally L. Kitch, "Disciplined by Disciplines? The Need for an *Interdisciplinary* Research Mission in Women's Studies," *Feminist Studies* 24, no. 2 (1998): 289.

32. Leora Auslander, "Do Women + Feminist + Men's + Lesbian and Gay + Queer Studies = Gender Studies?" *differences* 9, no. 3 (1997): 3.

33. Ibid., 18, emphasis added.

34. Allen and Kitch, "Disciplined by Disciplines?" 286.

35. Ibid., 287.

36. At a retreat for the University of Maryland Women's Studies Department and affiliate faculty (March 2–4, 2001), Sally Kitch, of Ohio State, introduced this concept of "value-added" in a panel about interdisciplinarity and women's studies.

37. Wendy Brown, "The Impossibility of Women's Studies," *differences* 9, no. 3 (1997): 84.

38. Judith Butler, "Imitation and Gender Insubordination," in *The Lesbian and Gay Studies Reader*, ed. Henry Abelove, Michele Aina Barale, and David M. Halperin (New York: Routledge, 1993), 307–320.

39. Robyn Wiegman, "What Ails Feminist Criticism? A Second Opinion," *Critical Inquiry* 25 (winter 1999): 375.

40. Allen and Kitch, "Disciplined by Disciplines?" 293.

41. For more about epistemic ignorance and conventions, see Code, *Rhetorical Spaces;* Charles W. Mills, *The Racial Contract* (Ithaca, N.Y.: Cornell University Press, 1997); and Naomi Scheman, "The Unavoidability of Gender," in *Women, Knowledge, Reality,* 2nd ed., ed. Ann Garry and Marilyn Pearsall (New York: Routledge, 1996), 26–33.

42. Ward Churchill, "White Studies: The Intellectual Imperialism of U.S. Higher Education," in *Theorizing Multiculturalism*, ed. Cynthia Willett (Malden, Mass.: Blackwell, 1998), 342.

43. María Lugones, "Playfulness, 'World'-Travelling, and Loving Perception," in *Making Face, Making Soul Haciendo Caras: Creative and Critical Perspectives by Feminists of Color*, ed. Gloria Anzaldúa (San Francisco: Aunt Lute Books, 1990), 400.

44. Wiegman, "What Ails Feminist Criticism?" 368.

45. Trinh T. Minh-ha, *Woman, Native, Other* (Bloomington: Indiana University Press, 1989).

46. Cooper, *A Voice from the South,* 80.

47. Ibid., 81.

48. Wiegman, "What Ails Feminist Criticism?" 377.

49. Audre Lorde, *Sister Outsider* (Freedom, Calif.: Crossing Press, 1984), 123.

50. Joyce E. King, "Dysconscious Racism: Ideology, Identity, and the Miseducation of Teachers," in *The Education Feminism Reader*, ed. Lynda Stone with G. Masuchika Boldt (New York: Routledge, 1994), 338.

51. Caren Kaplan, *Questions of Travel: Postmodern Discourses of Displacement* (Durham, N.C.: Duke University Press, 1996), 169, 189.

52. Geraldine Pratt, "Geographic Metaphors in Feminist Theory," in *Making Worlds: Gender, Metaphor, Materiality,* ed. Susan Hardy Aiken, Ann Brigham, Sallie A. Marston, and Penny Waterstone (Tuscon: University of Arizona Press, 1998), 13.

53. Susan Stanford Friedman, "(Inter)Disciplinarity and the Question of the Women's Studies Ph.D.," *Feminist Studies* 24, no. 2 (1998): 312.

54. Joan Scott with Kathryn Cook and Renea Henry, "The Edge: Interview," *differences* 9, no. 3 (1997): 145.

55. Friedman, "(Inter)Disciplinarity and the Question," 312

56. bell hooks, *Feminist Theory: From Margin to Center* (Boston: South End Press, 1984); Barbara Christian, "The Race for Theory," in *Making Face, Making Soul*, ed. Anzaldúa, 335–345.

57. Friedman, "(Inter)Disciplinarity and the Question," 309, 315–317.

58. Ibid., 318, emphasis added.

59. Rosemarie Garland Thomson, *Extraordinary Bodies: Figuring Physical Disability in American Culture and Literature* (New York: Columbia University Press, 1997): 6–7.

60. Susan Gubar, "What Ails Feminist Criticism?" *Critical Inquiry* 24 (summer 1998): 902, emphasis added.

61. Scott et al., "The Edge: Interview," 145.

62. Knight, March 2, 1999. http://www.listserv.umd.edu/archives/wmst-1.html.

63. Allen and Kitch, "Disciplined by Disciplines?" 281.

64. Megan Boler, *Feeling Power: Emotions and Education* (New York: Routledge, 1999), 175–203; bell hooks, *Teaching to Transgress: Education as the Practice of Freedom* (New York: Routledge, 1994), 36–44; Lynet Uttal, "Nods That Silence," in *Making Face, Making Soul*, ed. Anzaldúa, 317–320.

65. Friedman, "(Inter)Disciplinarity and the Question," 313.

66. John Willinsky, *Learning to Divide the World: Education at Empire's End* (Minneapolis: University of Minnesota Press, 1998), 23–55.

67. Frank Davey, *Reading Canadian Reading* (Winnipeg, Manitoba: Turnstone Press, 1988), 119.

68. Trinh T. Minh-ha, *When the Moon Waxes Red: Representation, Gender, and Cultural Politics* (New York: Routledge, 1991), 84

69. Lorraine Code, "Rational Imaginings, Responsible Knowings: How Far Can You See from Here?" in *Engendering Rationalities,* ed. Nancy Tuana and Sandra Morgen (Albany: SUNY Press, 2001), 272.

70. Susan Babbitt, "Objectivity and the Role of Bias," in *Engendering Rationalities,* ed. Tuana and Morgen, 303.

71. Wiegman, "What Ails Feminist Criticism?" 379.

72. Gloria E. Anzaldúa, "Now let us shift . . . the path of conocimiento . . . inner work, public acts," in *This Bridge We Call Home: Radical Visions for Transformation*, ed. Gloria E. Anzaldúa and Analouise Keating (New York: Routledge, 2002), 540, 546.

73. Patti Lather, *Getting Smart: Feminist Research and Pedagogy with/in the Postmodern* (New York: Routledge, 1991), 145.

74. Gloria Anzaldúa, *Borderlands/La Frontera* (San Francisco: Aunt Lute Books, 1987), 79.

75. Simone de Beauvoir, *The Ethics of Ambiguity* (New York: Citadel Press, 1948), 129.

76. Marilyn Boxer, "Remapping the University: The Promise of the Women's Studies Ph.D." *Feminist Studies* 24, no. 2 (1998): 387–402.

77. Lugones, "Playfulness"; Uma Narayan, "Through the Looking-Glass Darkly: Emissaries, Mirrors, and Authentic Insiders as Preoccupations," in her *Dislocating Cultures: Identities, Traditions, and Third World Feminism* (New York: Routledge, 1997): 121–157.

78. Anzaldúa, *Borderlands*; Code, *Rhetorical Spaces;* Kaplan, *Questions of Travel;* Elizabeth V. Spelman, *Fruits of Sorrow: Framing Our Attention to Suffering* (Boston: Beacon Press, 1997); Gayatri Spivak, *In Other Worlds: Essays in Cultural Politics* (New York: Methuen, 1987).

79. Anzaldúa, *Borderlands*; Gloria Anzaldúa, "En Rapport, In Opposition: Cobrando cuentas a las nuestras," in *Making Face, Making Soul,* ed. Anzaldúa (San Francisco: Aunt Lute Books, 1990), 142–148; Judith Butler, *Gender Trouble: Feminism and the Subversion of Identity* (New York: Routledge, 1990); Lorde, *Sister Outsider;* María Lugones, "Hablando cara a cara/Speaking Face to Face," in *Making Face, Making Soul,* ed. Anzaldúa, 46–54; Lugones, "Playfulness"; Minh-ha, *Woman, Native, Other;* Eve K. Sedgwick, *Epistemology of the Closet* (Berkeley: University of California Press, 1992).

80. Paula Gunn Allen, "Something Sacred Going on out There: Myth and Vision in American Indian Literature," in *The Woman That I Am: The Literature and Culture of Contemporary Women of Color*, ed. D. Soyini Madison (New York: St. Martin's Press, 1994), 547–559; Anzaldúa, *Borderlands*; Gloria Anzaldúa, "Haciendo Caras, una entrada," in *Making Face, Making Soul,* ed. Anzaldúa, 142–148; Christian, "The Race for Theory"; Code, "How to Think Globally"; Patricia Hill Collins, *Fighting Words: Black Women and the Search for Justice* (Minneapolis: Minnesota University Press, 1998) and *Black Feminist Thought: Knowledge, Consciousness, and the Politics of Empowerment* (London: HarperCollins, 1990); Kimberlé Williams Crenshaw, "Mapping the Margins: Intersectionality, Identity Politics, and Violence against Women of Color," *Stanford Law Review* 43, no. 6 (1991):1241–1299; Toni Morrison, "Rootedness: The Ancestor as Foundation," in *The Woman That I Am*, ed. Madison, 492–497; Chela Sandoval, *Methodology of the Oppressed* (Minneapolis: University of Minnesota Press, 2000); Leslie Marmon Silko, "Landscape, History, and the Pueblo Imagination," in

The Woman That I Am, ed. Madison, 498–510; Alice Walker, *In Search of Our Mothers' Gardens: Womanist Prose* (New York: Harcourt Brace, 1984).

81. Anzaldúa, "Haciendo Caras, una entrada," xv–xxviii; Beauvoir, *The Ethics of Ambiguity;* Butler, "Imitation and Gender Insubordination"; Chabram-Dernersesian, "'Chicana! Rican? No, Chicana Riqueña!'"; Code, *Rhetorical Spaces;* Collins, *Black Feminist Thought;* Freire, *Letters to Cristina;* hooks, *Teaching to Transgress;* Sandoval, *Methodology of the Oppressed;* Lynet Uttal, "Inclusion without Influence: The Continuing Tokenism of Women of Color," in *Making Face, Making Soul*, ed. Anzaldúa, 42–45; Uttal, "Nods That Silence."

82. Chabram-Dernersesian, "'Chicana! Rican? No, Chicana Riqueña!'"; Christian, "The Race for Theory"; Collins, *Black Feminist Thought;* bell hooks, *Talking Back: Thinking Feminist, Thinking Black* (Boston: South End Press, 1989); Alison Jaggar, "Love and Knowledge: Emotion in Feminist Epistemology," in *Women, Knowledge, Reality,* 2nd ed., ed. Ann Garry and Marilyn Pearsall (New York: Routledge, 1996), 166–190; Morrison, "Rootedness: The Ancestor as Foundation"; Sandoval, *Methodology of the Oppressed;* Spelman, *Fruits of Sorrow.*

83. Homi K. Bhabha, Gary A. Olson, and Lynn Worsham, "Staging the Politics of Difference: Homi Bhabha's Critical Literacy," in *Race, Rhetoric, and the Postcolonial*, ed. Olson and Worsham (Albany: State University of New York Press, 1999), 25.

84. Anzaldúa, *Borderlands*, 377–378.

85. Lee, "Notes from the (Non)Field," 99, 83, 99.

86. Butler, "Imitation and Gender Insubordination."

87. Chandra Talpade Mohanty, "Under Western Eyes: Feminist Scholarship and Colonial Discourses," in *Third World Women and the Politics of Feminism,* ed. Mohanty, Ann Russo, and Lourdes Torres (Bloomington: Indiana University Press, 1991), 52; Carole Boyce Davies, "Other Tongues: Gender, Language, Sexuality, and the Politics of Location," in *Women, Knowledge, Reality,* 2nd ed., ed. Ann Garry and Marilyn Pearsall (New York: Routledge, 1996), 344; Sedgwick, *Epistemology of the Closet*, 12, 44.

88. Alice Walker, *The Color Purple* (New York: Harcourt Brace, 1982), 197; Anzaldúa, *Borderlands*, 198, 381; Code, *Rhetorical Spaces*, 39.

89. Minh-ha, *When the Moon Waxes Red*, 161.

Toward a New Feminist Internationalism

Miranda Joseph, Priti Ramamurthy, and Alys Eve Weinbaum

Increasingly, globalization is the horizon of the feminist imaginary in the United States. Witness the popularity, post-Beijing, of the "women's rights are human rights" slogan, the proliferation of development projects (especially micro-credit schemes) that target women, and, in the academy, the scholarly focus on feminism and globalization in journals such as *Hypatia* (1998), *Women's Studies Quarterly* (1998), *Feminist Economics* (2000), and *Signs* (2001), as well as new faculty lines in "transnational," "international," and "global" feminism. The political and intellectual projects of so-called transnational, international, or global feminism at these diverse sites are heterogeneous in purpose, content, and practice. In this essay we examine and critique several of these projects, focusing on several of those that either universalize "women" and/or idealize "local" feminist efforts. We mark our joint contribution to the debates over the global expansion of feminist studies by the use of the term *feminist internationalism*.[1]

In a series of field-shaping essays, Inderpal Grewal and Caren Kaplan have advanced what they label "transnational feminist studies," a project that integrates feminism, poststructuralism, and Marxism while avoiding the shortcomings of any one of these approaches taken alone.[2] We largely concur with their agenda; our work would not be possible without theirs. We note, however, that they specifically reject the term *internationalism* because of its orthodox Marxist connotations and because, they argue, it risks emphasis on the nation-state and relations among nations whereas they prefer to emphasize global processes that transcend particular nations and produce supranational effects. While we recognize their critique and the risks involved, we embrace the term and concept of internationalism precisely because the national remains a crucial scale of analysis. Nation-states are powerful global forces that shape individual lives (notably, globalization has failed to eclipse nation-states as many predicted in the 1990s). As importantly, we elect *feminist internationalism* to signal a shared reliance on, and sense of the continued relevance of, the analytics of Marxism in rethinking women's studies and feminist knowledge production, and to invoke (so that we might draw upon) the historical relationship between women's movements and Marxist conceptualizations of politics. In short, with feminist internationalism we underscore the significance of global capitalism to gender formation and the necessity of prioritizing political economy when producing critical knowledge about sex and gender in contexts of intensified nationalism, globalization, and intranational inequities.

What unites the three individually authored sections of this essay—each of which is distinct in its approach and focus—is that each proposes that feminist scholarship make use of modes of analysis that take economic processes seriously so that we may explore the links between social/cultural formations and economic processes. Together, our three sections suggest that feminist scholars and women's studies practitioners examine the relationship between the conditions of women's lives worldwide—conditions that are grossly uneven due to differential imbrication within the global economy—and the feminist production of knowledge about globalization, particularly in our shared location, the U.S. academy.

In the first section, Priti Ramamurthy deploys a macrological empirical analysis to map the new economic ordering within an increasingly integrated world, revealing the global economy as gendered and generative of intensely uneven development. She suggests that recognizing the limits of a U.S.-centered women's studies project that focuses on cultural and domestic formations and ignores its connections with global economic inequities is necessary to clear the ground for a new feminist internationalism. In the second section, Alys Eve Weinbaum examines two of the dominant approaches to producing feminist knowledge about globalization in the U.S. academy, offering critiques of the liberal multicultural and global/local frameworks developed to study women in globalization from the vantage point of the United States. She illustrates how a notion of "America as the world" implicitly animates many feminist discussions and argues that a newly conceptualized feminist internationalism must involve becoming conscious of the place from which "we" speak. In section three, Miranda Joseph argues that mainstream and feminist discourses on economic globalization rely upon a highly problematic opposition of community and capitalism. Against this opposition she proposes a feminist poststructuralist Marxism that locates particular communities in a relation of supplementarity with global capitalist processes. She argues that such a theory can help to locate U.S. women's studies, even as it suggests a reconceptualization of the institutional formation of women's studies. The essay concludes by posing questions that open our collaboration to further elaboration, problematization, and refinement by others.

The Gendered Politics of Economic Globalization (by Priti Ramamurthy)

In the narrowest terms, globalization is understood as the greater integration of national economies through markets. Described thus, as the process through which goods, capital, people, and ideas flow across national boundaries in larger quantities and more rapidly, neoliberal economics predicts that all will gain a sense of well-being from globalization. According to neoliberal logic, economic globalization working through free markets will increase the availability of goods, capital, and technology in the South and reduce the price of commodities and services in the North, thereby leading to higher incomes and consumption, employment growth, and the reduction of poverty all around. In fact, this expectation is contradicted by increasing numbers of people in many parts of the world, especially women and children, who live in absolute poverty. Accompanying widespread poverty on a global scale is the growing inequality—the gap between the richest and poorest—of incomes. Despite the economic integration of national economies in the 1990s, the wealth and wage gap between the North and the South, between the richest and poorest nations, and within many countries is increasing. Most of the benefits of rapid economic growth in the most populist nations of China and India, for example, are going to the wealthiest 20 percent of the population. Inequality in consumption is obscene; in the crudest terms, 20 percent of the world's people in rich countries account for 86 percent of the world's consumption, while the poorest 20 percent consume 1.3 percent.[3]

Nor is poverty exclusive to the South (though it is certainly starker there). In the United States, despite nine years of record economic expansion from 1991 to 1999, an expansion linked in public discourse to the benefits of globalization, the number of poor families made up 11.8 percent of the population in 1999, higher than at any time since the 1970s. In 2002, due to the recession, poverty levels rose even higher to 12.1 percent and 33 million U.S. citizens went hungry. Income inequality has also increased in the United States over the past twenty years. Racial differences continue to be markers of poverty; the poverty rate for whites, at 8 percent, was significantly lower than the poverty rate for American Indians (25 percent), African Americans (24 percent), Hispanics (23 percent), and Asian and Pacific Islanders (13 percent).[4] As Stuart Hall has argued, in our current moment, "Race . . . is the modality in which class is 'lived,' the medium through which class relations are experienced, the form in which it is appropriated."[5]

From a macrological perspective, race is also always gendered and gender is also always raced. In the United States, gender differences in poverty levels have greatly intensified over the past forty years. More than 50 percent of all poor families were headed by single women in 2000, as compared to 21 percent in 1960.[6] Single-women-headed households are the largest and fastest growing segment of those in poverty. Although increasing numbers of women entered the workforce in the 1990s, for many the kind of employment available provided less than the minimal income that is the cutoff for the calculation of the poverty rate (less than seventeen thousand dollars annually for a family of four in 2000). The poverty rate in African American and Hispanic single-women-headed households is higher than that of whites. In 2001, 35 percent of black children and 29 percent of Hispanic children under six lived in poverty. This corresponds to the continued weightiness of race and gender in access to education and to high paying jobs.[7] The Institute of Women's Policy Research found that black, Hispanic, and other women of color all experience material hardship, defined as lack of access to stable housing, telephones, food, and medical and dental care, during periods of unemployment at substantially higher rates than whites do. While poor single-parent families of all races (no longer receiving welfare benefits) have slipped deeper into poverty, black women were found to fare worse than other groups.

These high poverty rates, I argue, point to the limits of a U.S.-centric feminism which does not analyze the relationship between such "cultural" rights as a woman's freedom to divorce or not marry (a right hard-won by feminism in the United States) and the economic inadequacy of wages for those outside of normative (white, middle-class, two-person, heterosexual) unions and the global economics of wages. They also point to the bankruptcy of an analysis that promotes U.S. multiculturalism, the equal acceptance of "cultural" differences, in the face of the continued everyday experiences of race and gender as economic relationships in the United States. This lack of analytical rigor is often exported by U.S. feminism (as Weinbaum illustrates in the section that follows) and fails to link the mutual but not similar or equivalent predicaments that globalization produces for women in the United States and in non-U.S. locations.

As a first step toward a *new feminist internationalism*, I begin by charting links or connections at three institutional scales: the international, the national, and the household.[8] At the international scale, the most significant difference in the material futures many women (and men) face is still linked to past histories of global integration—that is, the history of colonialism and white settlement. Broadly speaking, acknowledging the history of the South as the post-colonies and the North as the ex-imperial powers enables the recognition that the positive effects of global integration are still largely skewed in the favor of the North. In aggregate terms, 80 percent of world trade originates in the North and 75 percent of the investments that cross national borders are intra-Northern flows. As in the colonial past, for large swathes of the South, African countries in particular, exports are still in the form of primary commodities or raw materials. Not only is the *value-added* (the amount by which the value of an article is increased at each stage of its production) of primary commodities low, but over the past twenty years their real value has fallen so that the ability of some countries to buy even basics like food and medicines in hard currency markets has eroded.

A second trend in global political economy is that over the past twenty years labor intensive manufacturing has shifted from the North to the South. Just ten countries in the South, however, have received a disproportionate amount (over 75 percent) of all foreign direct investment and financial flows.[9] Any benefits from this shift—greater production, employment, and higher than average wages—have therefore flowed to very few countries. A third trend is that international aid flows from the North to the South have decreased by more than half since the mid-1980s. Lacking the capital for infrastructure investment (hospitals, schools, banks, roads, irrigation, and so on) Southern states have had to turn to private capital and loans to fill the gap left by diminishing foreign aid flows. Consequently, international debt owed by the South to multilateral institutions and Northern commercial banks has increased.[10] Often, this borrowing is under the rubric of structural adjustment programs (SAPs), programs designed to redirect national resources to producing commodities that are internationally tradeable, to attracting foreign capital, and to reducing government expenditures. SAPs come at a tremendously high social and economic cost and, through the 1990s, were coeval with large-scale migrations, the rise of vicious nationalisms and religious fundamentalisms, civil wars, and increasing domestic violence.

As a result of continuities with the colonial past and the transformations in the international organization of production of the past twenty years, the South itself has become much more differentiated. On the one hand are the East Asian "exemplars of growth," where poverty rates have fallen and average incomes have risen substantially. On the other hand are the sub-Saharan African economies, where real incomes and consumption levels have decreased through the 1980s and 1990s and poverty rates have risen both in absolute numbers and as a percentage of the population.[11]

Although the differential gender impacts of globalization trends are *not* generalizable, certain long-term trends are legible and noteworthy.[12] The most significant is the feminization of labor in two senses. First, there has been a rapid and dramatic increase in the number of women working in paid economic activity in all regions and nations of the world.[13] And, second, even as more women are now paid for the work they do, the conditions of labor have become increasingly flexible and informal. Consequently, highly exploitative work arrangements proliferate—irregular, part-time, out-sourced, self-employed, and home-based work. These conditions, which used to characterize "women's work," now characterize the conditions of all labor, thus leading to the common assessment that global labor processes and forces have become feminized.[14] In all countries women still earn less than do men. This is also true of the United States. If, however, the U.S. women's studies project is limited to producing subjects who fight on the narrow grounds of wage equality for themselves in the here and now, it will remain oblivious to the global political economy by which U.S. gender discrimination is partly produced and of which it is symptomatic. It is to these macrological processes that I now turn.

Within the global trend of the feminization of labor, in the North, since the early 1970s, there has been a shift in the sectoral distribution of production and labor from manufacturing industries to the service sector. In the United States, the process has been unequally raced, with black men losing many of the jobs in manufacturing.[15] Those manufacturing jobs that were recently deskilled or flexibilized have been filled by women at a faster rate than by men; many work in industries, like the garment industry, where conditions have worsened over time. In the United States and United Kingdom recent migrants from Asia often work in such industries and are pitted against women working in their countries of origin.[16] For women in the North, by far the largest growth in employment has been in care or service industries: health, education, and social services.[17] In global cities in both the North and South women work as cleaners, domestic workers, data processors, in food service, tourism, and the sex and leisure industry. In other words, women are the invisible workers whose work supports the global professional managerial class working in multinational corporations and the international financial services sector.[18] Often the "dirtiest" jobs are done by women of color; thus commodified social reproductive work is constitutively raced.[19]

In the South, women have been integrated into the global economy through the new international division of labor or the shift of labor-intensive manufacturing offshore from the North. This pattern of industrialization has been characterized as "female-led as much as export led."[20] First adopted by East Asian countries, where millions of women manufacture electronics, garments, footwear, and toys mainly for U.S., Japanese, and European markets, many Southern countries are now trying to follow this strategy. Yet, foreign direct investment in manufacturing accounts for *only* 2 percent of total wage employment in the South.[21] Over half of all Southern women continue to work in agriculture, where the conditions of work are low pay and insecurity. In South and West Asia, and in sub-Saharan Africa, there are indications of the feminization of agriculture as women attempt to eke out a livelihood from the land and the sale of their labor, while men migrate in search of nonagricultural work. Globalization has also precipitated a shift within the agricultural sector toward commercialization, export crops, and agribusiness contract farming. Often this has come at the expense of women's participation in subsistence farming, which provides a system of food provisioning outside of market exchange. In short, the globalization of agriculture has disproportionately impacted women because of male patterns of migration and exposed their employment and food provisioning to the vagaries of the metropolitan market.

The next scale of institutional analysis is the national; because the specific structure of national economies and the gender and cultural politics of national regimes diverge greatly, so does how women enter into and are affected by globalization. In countries like Taiwan and Singapore, for example, the gender wage gap has increased; however, the gender gap has decreased in countries like El Salvador and Sri Lanka. In the United States, three-quarters of the reduction in the gender wage gap is not from women's wages rising, but from falling male real wages or a downward harmonization between men and women.[22] At the level of national budgets, the repatriated earnings of migrant women workers have been a major source of foreign exchange for the Philippines, Indonesia, Sri Lanka, and Thailand, and these flows are routinely included in national economic development plans. A less blatantly state-coordinated strategy is the migration of women from Central and Eastern Europe as well as the Philippines, Thailand, and elsewhere to western Europe and the United States as sex workers and mail-order brides. Even a casual perusal of sex ads in U.S. newspapers and weeklies is sufficient to sketch the cultural constructions of race and nationality that mediate these economic relationships.

Across states that have "successfully" followed the export-led industrialization strategy, cultural politics also vary so that in some instances younger, unmarried women are naturalized as the best "phase" workers, while in others older, married women with in-laws who can care for children are constructed in this way. These multiple cultural constructions of which phase of a woman's life is best for world factory work cannot be understood outside of the contradictions between capital's need for the next generation of workers (that is, for social reproduction) and its need for efficient and cheap workers today. Thus, the ways in which states have opportunistically intensified or recomposed gender ideologies in some instances and decomposed them in others inflects the supposedly singular process of economic globalization with cultural specificity.[23]

Within nation-states, which women are provided for as "citizens" differs. In the past few decades, in all Western democracies, new patterns of immigration have called into question (once again) who can truly be citizens and what sorts of economic rights they have if they are not of the cultural national majority. In Southern states, where resources were severely limited in the first place and now are even more so due to the pressures of neoliberalization, the democratic state is forced to address the needs of its citizens piecemeal. The likelihood that this will be on the basis of particularistic and incommensurate group claims—of religion, race, ethnicity, or caste, for example—is now even stronger. In such circumstances, majoritarian groups often use the difference of gender to discriminate against minority groups. In India, for example, claims for a Muslim woman's rights to alimony were supported by the patriarchal and anti-Muslim Hindu religious right, which then demanded that a "uniform," that is, Hindu, code be imposed on all religious groups in India. These kinds of claims, often in the language of rights, complicate the making of feminist claims on the state solely on the grounds of gender inequity.

At the third scale of analysis, the household, globalization is changing the intrahousehold allocation of labor, land, and income. Transformations in the composition of households, in the degree of resource pooling, and in the organization of marriage, parenting, and kinship are also manifest. The relationship between paid and unpaid work, in particular, has been extensively researched in the context of feminist analyses of structural adjustment policies.[24] It is now accepted, even by the World Bank, that SAPs have a disproportionately negative effect on women.[25] As state-supplied subsidies for water and electricity and social services like education and medical care are either cut or privatized, social reproduction becomes more difficult especially for already vulnerable women situated in poor households. Research has shown how the shortening of hospital stays, for example, has increased women's care work; this is as true in the United States as in "distant" Southern countries. The costs and burdens of structural adjustment and economic restructuring are thus being passed on to women whose unpaid reproductive labor and under-compensated work within households bear the brunt of national policies of globalization.[26] Often, women have had to turn from formal to informal work or to kinship networks for family survival during times of SAP-induced crises.

By focusing on the gendered inequalities of economic globalization in this section, my purpose was to begin the work of developing a non-reductionist understanding of gender grounded in material conditions. My purpose is not to resurrect a coherent economic subject, "woman," or to herald utopian collectivist political action based on women's shared victimhood under globalization. On the contrary, I argue that we must recognize both the similar predicaments of women in disparate but non-equivalent social formations—Asia and Asian America, for example—and their mutual and connected but not similar exclusions. U.S. women's studies, then, will have to resist the temptation to simply add "globalization" or "nationality" to the race, class, sexuality, disability litany as the object of its study of gender difference. And at the same time it must accept the fact that only hiring faculty with country-specific expertise will not solve the problem either. Both of these moves would repeat the error of adding in (by assuming equivalence between the categories race, class, sexuality, nation) instead of changing the terms of the debate. As an alternative, we need to develop our expertise in—and hire experts on—the social and economic processes that differentially link localities to globalities.

The Global Politics of Feminist Knowledge Production (by Alys Eve Weinbaum)

As the previous section demonstrates, macroeconomic forces shape women's lives as globalization intersects with gendered and racialized ideologies at the international, national, and household scales. Here I draw out the implications of the empirical trends while negotiating two distinct, albeit intertwined, aims. First, I seek to examine the imbrication of U.S. feminist knowledge production within differentiated processes of globalization. Second, I hope to provoke thinking about an alternative heuristic with which we might articulate a more politically viable analysis of the current situation—one that does not reify globalization's impact on women but rather keeps pace with it. Much of what follows emerges from reflection on my teaching of a graduate course on the possibilities and pitfalls of making the move from a U.S.-centered feminist multicultural approach to globalization (one that has all too often been liberal and essentialist in conception and thus unable to develop what Stuart Hall has called a "politics of difference"[27]) to a new *feminist internationalism* that takes uneven economic power and grossly uneven distributions of wealth and resources seriously.[28]

As my students and I discerned, several of the most pronounced difficulties of undertaking a global reorientation within feminist knowledge production are common enough to lend themselves to schematization. First, efforts to globalize feminism often view U.S. feminism as a viable national export. One consequence of the global Americanization of feminism is that feminist complicities in globalization are obscured and the following series of pressing questions bypassed: What does globalization look like to women from elsewhere? Is liberal feminism an adequate response to globalization? Does feminism shore-up larger neoliberal agendas, including structural adjustment policies and projects? How does the globalization of U.S. feminism participate in the production of subjects for capitalism? How does it obscure unequal distributions of power and resources within the United States, rendering invisible the South in the North? Because these questions are rarely posed, what goes unnoticed is that the *globalization of feminism* can serve as an alibi for a form of *feminist globalization* with deep ties to older forms of colonialism and imperialism.

While the blind spot I am attempting to identify is neither entirely dominant, nor without its critics, it remains noteworthy because of its structuring presence within the style of feminism that has emerged as an enduring product of the U.N. conferences on women beginning in Mexico City in 1975 and gaining momentum in the lead up to and aftermath of the Beijing conference in 1995. The upshot is that in three decades feminism in the United States has become increasingly wed to the human rights agenda, the well-known mantra of which rings out "women's rights are human rights." Although I might have focused on any number of anthologies in outlining the pitfalls of this feminist style, I have chosen *Is Multiculturalism Bad for Women?* edited by Joshua Cohen, Matthew Howard, and Martha C. Nussbaum, because this volume has been marketed not only to academics but to a wider "cross-over" audience.[29] Instructively, the volume presents a spectrum of answers to its title query, even as it leads off with, showcases, and finally endorses an essay (originally published in the *Boston Review of Books*), by political scientist Susan Moller Okin, which resoundingly answers the title's query in the affirmative.[30] As Okin insists, multiculturalism is unequivocally bad for women because it sanctions claims made in the name of cultural rights, claims that erode the foundations of the universal human rights created to protect women and men alike. For this reason, feminists cannot afford to be solicitous of the singular perspectives of groups who condone polygamy, female genital cutting, purdah, and an array of other practices commonly cited by human rights advocates as oppressive to women. In selecting those practices that are seemingly "excessive," and in postulating a necessary antagonism between "feminism and multiculturalist concern for protecting cultural diversity," Okin ends up reproducing a slight of hand that pervades work that globalizes U.S. feminism.[31] She prioritizes gender difference over differences of race, religion, class, and ethnicity, while in so doing she implies that globalization of feminism necessarily entails universalization of a particular understanding of women's oppression, one that obscures the unevenness of women's economic exploitation on national and international scales, both within nations and within households.

Other contributors to the volume take issue with Okin's recommended export around the world of her particular version of feminist human rights, challenging her definitions of feminism, multiculturalism, and so-called special interest politics by calling attention to the problems with liberal arguments that rely, as do human rights arguments, upon universalization of the singular prerogatives of those advancing them (the contributions by Bonnie Honig, Homi Bhabha, Bhikhu Parekh, Sander Gilman, and Azizah al-Hibri all stand out in this regard). And yet the cumulative argumentative weight of the dissent is offset by those responses to Okin that unite to express broad, if qualified, agreement, often modifying her position toward firmer commitment to a dominant (read "universal") political morality. In the end, the volume voices three conceptual monoliths. First, "women" is an incontestable, universally recognizable political category and protection of human rights is the proper terrain of global feminism. Second, "special interest politics" and "multiculturalism" are one and the same, as acknowledgment of class, caste, cultural, racial, ethnic, and/or religious differences divisively fragments the unity of the world's women. And, somewhat predictably, liberalism is global feminism's natural political idiom. As the book's form (a polemic accompanied by positions for and against) attests, dissenting positions and unresolvable political differences can be effectively transcended within an overarching liberal consensus.

The second problem that pervades feminist work on globalization is that found in scholarship that culls and juxtaposes "local" women's movements that have emerged in response to globalization. Such scholarship locates and, to its credit, examines the various positions occupied by women within globalization, seeking to understand the gendering of "global culture" in a diverse array of local situations. And yet, although ostensibly focused on local struggles, globalization is here posited as a homogenizing force that brings women together by rendering women in a multiplicity of locales in possession of a common plight, resistance to which is then construed as expressive of a shared "global" political agenda. Even as the problems raised by what I shorthand as "global/local feminism" differ in emphasis from those raised by human rights feminism, both projects fail to produce a robust "politics of difference" in the context of globalization.

Although scholars and activists who produce volumes comprised of local feminisms rarely foreground the issue, the concept of *culture* that they deploy already embodies an instructive paradox. Culture is by definition particularistic; culture is the set of values or practices of some part smaller than some whole, and yet there can be no concept of culture without an appeal to universal criteria.[32] The perennial problem in the U.S. context is that study of local experiences does not attend fully to the incommensurability (and unevenness) of experiences of globalization—to the fact that every worldview, including that produced by seeking out and culling local struggles to create a global portrait, is highly particular.

Even when feminists work with materials from around the world in U.S. women's studies classrooms, treatment of texts remains U.S.-centric until the power dynamic that structures their circulation and reception is foregrounded and made into a central object of analysis. Questions that might enable such an analytic process include the following: What gets lost when "we" produce objects of local knowledge? What are the economic and ideological conditions under which "we" gain access to the archive of so-called global feminism? What does our ability to produce an archive for global feminism tell us about our own local experience? What (un)ethical relations enable access to other women's lives and experiences and to readings of the texts they produce? And finally, what is the backdrop against which "we" constitute ourselves as students and researchers (knowledge-producing subjects) with a shared sensibility of the "globe," not to mention the academic community and the larger Anglophone academy within which it is situated?[33]

No single culture (however multicultural or diverse) has unmediated access to another culture. Culture, to borrow a formulation from Fredric Jameson, is by definition relational. Culture "is the nimbus perceived by one group when it comes into contact with and observes another. . . . [It is] a vehicle or a medium whereby the relationship between groups is transacted."[34] To imagine that feminist scholars and students situated in the United States can apprehend the impact of globalization on the cultural formations and political movements of "women around the world" without intimate knowledge of the languages and social conditions in which such cultural formations and political movements are articulated is (to paraphrase Gayatri Chakravorty Spivak) to eliminate the potential insight that comes from becoming conscious of the place from which we speak. Put slightly differently, the idea of "global culture" is always an expression of what Stuart Hall has deftly labeled the "dominant particular."[35] It is an expression of our particularity as much as an expression of the locality of the other woman who is apprehended by us. Thus, for U.S. feminists a principal challenge is that of becoming attuned to the existence of the dialectic between universality and particularity in which all knowledge producers are ensnared.

On the eve of the new millennium, Amrita Basu's influential volume, *The Challenge of Local Feminisms: Women's Movements in Global Perspective,* was being widely used in women's studies courses as a means to introduce students to local feminist projects around the world. I focus on it here as it emerged as the only volume on global feminism that my graduate students had previously encountered and the principal one that they were electing to teach to their own undergraduates.[36] While Basu's collection is in equal measure noteworthy and ambitious in its attempt to represent the world's women and their political movements, the "global perspective" that it promises is not identified as an expression of a "dominant particular." Instructively, the volume is divided into four parts (Asia; Africa and the Middle East; Latin America; Russia, Europe, and the United States) that roughly carve up the world according to criteria used by the United Nations and development agencies. Individual articles on political contestations ranging from the Chipko movement in India to popular feminism in Mexico comprise each section and together provide the reader with the impression of representing the diversity of movements in the larger geographic regions that demarcate the book's four parts. As my colleague Tani Barlow has argued, the case studies collected reproduce "the national" as "the local" and erase the possibility of subnational feminisms, even as they assume that all feminisms are either pan-national or supranational.[37] I would add to this that the production of all national movements in which women are involved as feminists erases the possibility that "feminism" might itself be contested subnational terrain. And thus, the collection taken as a whole, although clearly created to clear space for Third World women's voices in the First World, runs the risk of creating for readers the illusion of familiarity with a variety of local feminisms. This is an aspiration boldly emblazoned on the volume's cover: a montage of sepia-tinted photographs of women from around the world, holding children, protest signs, and raised fists. It is *as if,* taken together, the individual causes could be viewed *as if* they were common, *as if* the juxtaposition of disparate images and the shared articulation of a political agenda are one and the same.

Unfortunately, the manner in which many global feminist anthologies promote the consumption of "local" feminisms by U.S. students, with access to the "global" as frame of reference, has precedent and longevity, stretching back to Robin Morgan's *Sisterhood Is Global: The International Women's Movement Anthology,* forward to Julie Peters and Andrea Wolper's *Women's Rights, Human Rights: International Feminist Perspectives,* and on to Rosalind Petchesky and Karen Judd's *Negotiating Reproductive Rights: Women's Perspectives across Countries and Cultures.* In such volumes (as in many others that might be included in this genealogy[38]) the conception of the globe is similar to that set forth by the

United Nations and its agencies, while the conception of coverage emerges as a form of regional tasting. Each women's movement is positioned as another in a potentially infinite series that can be represented as if all parts were equally representative, amenable to similar forms of analysis, and necessarily involved in shared political articulation.

While feminist work on globalization may first appear to enable basic "geopolitical literacy" in the language of difference, on closer inspection it proffers a meager vocabulary unable to complexly describe unequal distributions of resources, and a peculiar grammar that takes for granted the position of the subject of both enunciation and reception.[39] For these reasons it is unable to contend with the significant differences that become visible among women from an economic, materialist vantage point. Such global feminism is about making difference visible in a world theater whose stage has been designed to showcase international politics and policy rather than the structural inequalities and systemically uneven developments that *separate even as they connect* us.

Lest my argument be misconstrued, I close by emphasizing yet a third trend in feminist work on globalization—a scholarly formation, distinct from the human rights feminism, that is complicit with neoliberalism and the global/local feminism that invokes local knowledges and yet collapses differences. In a significant cluster of anthologies that develop the concept of "transnational feminism," an important alternative emerges. In volumes ranging from Inderpal Grewal and Caren Kaplan's *Scattered Hegemonies: Post Modernity and Transnational Feminist Practice* to Jacqui Alexander and Chandra Talpade Mohanty's *Feminist Genealogies, Colonial Legacies, Democratic Futures,* and on to Caren Kaplan, Norma Alarcón, and Minoo Moallem's *Between Women and Nation,* discussion of a range of feminist movements in non-U.S. contexts is presented alongside that of women-of-color movements within the United States and movements that cross or contest national borders. In these volumes the local is certainly produced as an object of study, and yet the reader is never required (or interpellated) by the anthology's form to conjure a global perspective out of these local particulars. Instead, the reader is offered "scattered" geopolitical locations, incomplete geopolitical coverage, and interrupted "genealogies." And thus, while the locales and local movements that are treated by transnational feminism certainly accept the risk of being read as local symptoms of homogenizing global forces, the emphasis rests on differences and dispersions, unlikely solidarities and coalitions.

At the same time that transnational feminism paves the way for the new feminist internationalism that this essay hopes to spark and begin to contour, it nonetheless shares a descriptive vocabulary with the very processes of which it is critical—the processes of transnational capital expansion. For this reason—as a way of addressing the necessary simultaneity of complicity and resistance—we offer *feminist internationalism.* This concept is at once indebted to and in deep dialogue with the efforts of transnational feminism and at the same time hopeful about contributing a heuristic that is differently useful. Internationalism is, after all, the language of Marxism. It is unapologetically beholden to the utopian promise of international solidarity (as opposed to unity or commonality), and it is resolutely aimed at exposure and redress of structural inequalities. Feminist internationalism thus holds out the possibility of knowing and transforming capitalism precisely by mobilizing the differences (often visible in the form of gendered and racialized essences) that transnationalism proliferates as it makes capitalism flexible and acquisitive and at the same time opens it to contestation.

As I hope is evident, I have argued neither against doing feminism in the context of globalization, nor against learning with and from the struggles fought by women situated in other locales. Rather, I am arguing for a carefully crafted feminist heuristic that will allow us to discern how and when feminist work on globalization becomes too complicit with neoliberal international agencies, policies, and politics to sustain a critical posture toward the transnational capitalist processes that such work seeks to identify, analyze, and contest.

Community and Capitalism: Women's Studies and Globalization (by Miranda Joseph)

I feel like a latecomer to internationalism; for a very long time I worked exclusively on the United States. I jumped scales just a few years ago, (re)situating my discussions of U.S. cases in a global frame. It might be worth asking if I jumped or if I was pushed by the very pervasiveness of globalization discourse in both popular media and academic literature. The pervasiveness of the discourse, as David Harvey and J. K. Gibson Graham have pointed out, makes globalization itself seem monolithic and inevitable. And while the expansion and intensification of capital accumulation is certainly a fact with which to reckon, if our engagement with it is going to be an intervention rather than merely a reproduction, as Weinbaum argues above, we must think carefully about the terms with which we engage it. And there is a lot of good work that, like Ramamurthy's discussion in the first section of this essay, reframes globalization as a process of uneven development,[40] as a process that engages in complex ways with local, regional, and national social formations, reterritorializing even as it deterritorializes,[41] situating globalization not as something new but rather as a new version of colonialism and development.[42] My own critique of what I call global/localization discourse explores the ways that the discourse of globalization reiterates but also revises a long-standing discourse of community to create and legitimate the particular social formations—and social hierarchies—necessary to but generally disavowed by capitalism, a discourse of abstraction and equivalence.[43]

I present this critique here because, like other progressive movements, feminism tends to idealize community as a site of equality and communion, as the basis for political collectivity, as the goal of political activism, as the pure space of us against them. Further, the problematic feminist strategy of celebrating the local even while making all locales equivalent, a strategy that Weinbaum has identified, participates quite precisely in the reiteration of the discourse of community within globalization discourse.

The long-standing discourse of community posits community as the "other" of capital.[44] Whether it is viewed as a problematic barrier to modernization or a long lost past for which we yearn nostalgically from our current fallen state of alienation, bureaucratization, and rationality, community is located as prior in time to "society." The discourse of community likewise distinguishes community from society spatially, as local, involving face-to-face relations, where capital is global and faceless; community is all about boundaries between us and them, boundaries that are naturalized through reference to place or race or culture or identity, while capital would seem to denature, crossing all borders and making everything and everyone equivalent. Further, this discourse contrasts community to modern capitalist society structurally: the foundation of community is supposed to be values, while capitalist society is based only on value (economic value). Community is posited as particular, where capitalism is abstract. Posed as its other, its opposite, community is often presented as a complement to capitalism, balancing and humanizing it.

Globalization discourse suggests that capitalism now attends ever more precisely to place and culture, addressing us, through niched production and marketing, in our diversity and particularity. Pro-capitalist promoters of globalization make explicit arguments about the crucial role that social formations play in the expansion of capital and about the dependence of capital on community, on culture, on subjectivity. For instance, in *Trust,* Francis Fukuyama argues that kinship is crucial to the success or failure of various nations and regions within globalizing capital: "If the [modern] institutions of democracy and capitalism are to work properly, they must coexist with certain premodern cultural habits that ensure their proper functioning. Law, contract, and economic rationality must . . . be leavened with reciprocity, moral obligation, duty toward community, and trust, which are based in habit[s, customs, and ethics] rather than calculation."[45] "Liberal political and economic institutions depend . . . on the family, the primary instrument by which people are socialized."[46]

This attention to the local and communal within globalization discourse might seem to resolve the community-capital binary. However, insofar as globalization discourse claims that globalization is new and is newly discovering community (which it does, thereby reiterating a kind of first-contact narrative), and insofar as it articulates the communities that participate in capitalism as analogous to each other (which it does, articulating an endless series of social formations as potential sites of production and consumption), it continues to position communities as both autonomous from (existing prior to) capital and from each other.

It is important to note that analogy compares relationships and not objects themselves; so, as Amy Robinson points out in her work on the analogy between race and sexuality, the Scholastic Aptitude Test's analogy section takes this form: A is to A's domain as X is to X's domain. Analogy serves as a particularly useful tool in the ongoing process of naturalizing the changing social formations necessary to capitalism both because it isolates each term in its own domain (making various communities equivalent but not equal) and because of its extraordinary power to articulate any social formation with capital.[47] For example, in *The End of the Nation State,* business consultant Kenichi Ohmae proposes that "regions," defined as units that are internally coherent and analogous with each other based on per capita GNP (gross national product), will follow "a fairly predictable trajectory along which priorities shift as economic areas move through successive phases of development."[48] "This notional GNP ladder . . . does apply across dividing lines defined by culture, to all developing economies. . . . The pull of the global economy . . . is universal—and universally attractive."[49]

The "GNP ladder" (a relation to which makes various regions/cultures analogous) applies across cultures, and yet culture does seem to correlate with the stage of a particular region on the ladder, becoming the organic source of inequality. Globalization appears merely to respond to these culturalized economic differences rather than being seen as a product of the history of colonialism or development. Like the long-standing discourse of community, then, global/localization discourse dehistoricizes and legitimates the differences in wealth among communities and the power hierarchies within communities.

Against this discourse of autonomous community, I argue that community is performatively constituted through production and consumption and that community supplements capital, that it fills a void in the circuit of capital by providing those (racially, sexually, nationally) differentiated subjects needed to fill diverse roles within capitalism (for instance, as manual laborers, as managers, as owners, as consumers with desires for differentiated commodities). In order to make this argument, I undertake poststructuralist readings of Marx's key arguments. While Marx's texts can be used—I use them—to stave off both economic and linguistic determinism, poststructuralism and Marxism have frequently arrayed themselves against each other to the detriment of each (not unlike poststructuralism and feminism). As many theorists have pointed out, orthodox Marxist social analysis has been plagued by a tendency toward economic determinism; in eschewing the play of signification, such a Marxism is simply unable to address the complexity of contemporary social formations. In its appreciation of signification, poststructualism is very good at accounting for the complexity of cultural processes but tends not to give capitalism its due as arguably the most powerful generator of signification and, thus, social organization. Against this opposition, I propose a reading of Marx that aims to elicit neither a political program nor a teleological narrative (in which the proletariat serves as protagonist), but rather, through attention to the openings in Marx's texts, a structural analysis of capitalism as itself an open process, open specifically to the social. The purpose of this poststructuralist return to Marx is to produce a comprehensive theory that can link the political economy of the sign with the international division of labor and that can situate particular social and cultural formations, particular communities, in relation to globalizing capital (in all of its historical forms) and, thus, in relation to each other.[50] In other words, the aim is to generate an analysis that can answer Ramamurthy's and Weinbaum's call to attend to the structural (material and discursive) processes that separate even as they simultaneously connect women (but not only women).

The most important insight enabled by such a return to Marx is recognition of the necessary imbrication of abstraction with particularity, of abstract value with particular use values (especially labor power). In his analysis of the commodity (the form in which wealth appears in capitalism), Marx makes it clear that *value* (a "form of appearance" of abstract, socially necessary labor) must be embodied (in particular use values) to circulate. However, he also shows that such embodiment presents capital with constant resistance. To keep capital moving, capitalists have to do a lot of work, inventing technologies of production, transportation, and communication to decrease "turnover" time, but also endlessly reshaping subjects and social formations. This insight makes it possible to see both the ongoing dynamic connections between communal formations and capitalist processes and the relationships among so-called communities, without flattening the social relations of capitalism into a simple proletariat-bourgeoisie binary.

This insight also makes it possible—and, I would suggest, along with my coauthors, crucial—to situate women studies itself in global capitalism. In order to understand the political and economic constraints on and implications of our work as scholars, teachers, and institutional servants, we need to understand how women's studies fits into the larger project of the academy as an "ideological state apparatus"—productive of both subjects and objects of knowledge, power, and capital—and how that project is shifting along with the shift to globalization, that is, shifting (at least in part) from the production of national subjects to the production of analogous, differentiated subjects of capital.[51] To a significant extent, the institutional growth and success of women's studies can be attributed to this shift, which makes difference less a threat than a profitable opportunity.[52]

Even as we recognize the complicity of our knowledge production, we also have to be aware of and work to contest the ways our production of knowledge about the conjunctions of economic processes and sexual, racial, and gendered social formations is constrained by an institutionalized distinction between culture and economy, between the humanities and social sciences, between postmodernism and empiricism, a distinction that reproduces—or is simply another iteration of— the community-capital binary. Even interdisciplinary programs such as women's studies and other units organized under the rubric of identities (such as, at the University of Arizona, Mexican American studies, Africana studies, American Indian studies) can, internally and/or in their isolation from and competition with each other, reiterate such distinctions. (Here at the University of Arizona, for instance, Mexican American studies has defined itself as focused on "applied social science," while ceding the study of Mexican American "culture" to the Chicana studies concentration within women's studies.) The constraints on our knowledge and politics produced by such institutional manifestations of dominant discursive oppositions between culture and economy and between community and capital lead me to think that making women studies a site of a critical feminist internationalism requires institutional transformation.

We must engage only with great caution institutional norms such as trajectories of growth from program to department or from offering undergraduate degrees to offering PhDs. And we must contest the divisions that we ourselves endlessly reiterate between theory and practice, between academic work and activist work. To simply idealize "activism" as a practice taking place in a real world out there (so often called "the community"), while discounting, as we so often do, the powerful real-world implications of our own practices, is both a failure of analysis and a denial of our own responsibilities. In order to situate women studies as a practice that produces subjects of capitalism (even as we undertake critical readings of the activisms with which we seek to engage), we must bring "theory" to bear—and especially, I would suggest, theories that can attend to the imbrication of economy with culture. At the same time, to avoid the self-centered universalizations and generalizations against which Ramamurthy and Weinbaum warn us, our theories must be informed by in-depth knowledge of specific differentiated social formations. Taken together, the imperative to a theoretical "analysis" that can account for the interplay of culture and economy and the imperative to deep particular knowledges require a rather different shape to women studies than what we often find in the programs that have developed into departments. We need to reimagine women studies as a generator of networks and relationships (among and between disciplines, identities, social movements) rather than an elaborator of canons, as a facilitator of innovative courses of study rather than a set of core courses, as a project that is flexible rather than permanent and stable. And, of course, as soon as I say *flexible,* I am back in the language of globalization itself—a good place to stop.

Questions for the Future

Discussion amongst ourselves, and with the audience when we presented an earlier version of this essay as a conference panel,[53] about the possibilities of a new feminist internationalism have led us not to a finite set of solutions for women's studies or feminist knowledge production about and within globalization, but rather to questions that will require greater elaboration by ourselves and, we hope, by others as well. It is clear, for instance, that the institutionalization of women's studies at various universities and colleges across the United States offers a case study in uneven development; the relationships of particular women's studies programs and departments to globalization—and to the constraints and opportunities it provides—are thus quite diverse and in need of greater specification. And the question of how women's studies is situated in relation to larger divisions of knowledge into discrete domains (humanities versus social sciences; international and area studies versus studies of U.S. ethnic groups) likewise requires (and receives in other essays in this volume) further exploration.

Our proposal that political economic analysis and Marxism, in particular, play a central role in feminist analyses opens a set of challenges for women's studies teaching and research: Do we teach Marx or Marxism within the women's studies curriculum? Do we use Marx in our research? For those who answer "yes" to these questions, there is still much debate to be had over how to bring in Marxism, especially how to present it to potentially resistant students. But also, at least for many in our original audience, the question of whether the forms of Marxism most readily available in the U.S. academy represent a re-imposition of "Western" and "patriarchal" frameworks, as well as a denigration and/or marginalization of other potentially more useful knowledge systems, remained pressing. And we also need to ask (keeping our prior question about institutionalization and divisions among domains of knowledge in mind), how does Marxist political economic analysis differ in different disciplinary locations (literature versus political science, for example), and how are these disciplinary approaches different from those that might be taken in women's studies? Can women's studies provide a context for generating strong (not uncritical) readings of Marxism as a powerful critique of capitalism and globalization? Can we provide ourselves with a version of Marxism that allows us to see our complicities, one that might not be available in other disciplinary locations?

Another crucial set of questions, raised but not answered by our collaboration, includes the following: How do we undertake the institutional and curricular changes necessary to move from a U.S.-centered women's studies to a feminist internationalism? And what are the implications of such a shift? What are the differences between looking at racial formations in the United States and thinking about how racial, ethnic, and national formations operate elsewhere? What happens to the identity politics that are a staple of U.S.-centered forms of women's studies in an international context?

Finally, while we clearly do not find the binary opposition of activism and theory to be a productive one, we hope our essay provokes renewed examination of the relationship between women's studies as a teaching and research project and politics outside the academy. Is the development of feminist internationalism within the academy an adequately conceptualized project if it does not include and/or engage feminists working in nonacademic institutional locations?[54] Can a turn to feminist internationalism in the women's studies curriculum help students to understand and intervene against capitalist globalization?

In closing with these questions, rather than with answers, we hope to contribute to a discussion that still needs to take place if women's studies classrooms, programs, and departments are to emerge as sites of critical feminist internationalism in the future.

Notes

1. "Internationalism," in the sense we use it, was first used in conjunction with a conference organized by Tani Barlow and Alys Eve Weinbaum, The New Feminist Internationalism, convened at the University of Washington in Seattle in February 2000. Miranda Joseph and Priti Ramamurthy participated in that event. "International," in a similar sense, also appears in the formulation of the 2002–2003 Duke seminar series, Feminism, Transnationalism, and the International, organized by Tina Campt, Ranjana Khanna, and Robyn Wiegman.

2. See the introduction to Inderpal Grewal and Caren Kaplan's coedited collection, *Scattered Hegemonies: Postmodernity and Transnational Feminist Practices* (Minneapolis: University of Minnesota Press, 1994), and their essays, including "Transnational Feminist Cultural Studies: Beyond the Marxism/Poststructuralism/Feminism Divides," in *Between Women and Nation: Nationalisms, Transnational Feminisms, and the State*, ed. Caren Kaplan, Norma Alarcón, and Minoo Moallem (Durham: Duke University

Press, 1999), 349–363; "Postcolonial Studies and Transnational Feminist Research Practices," *Jouvert* 5, no. 1 (2000) (http://social.chass.ncsu.edu/jouvert/vsil/grewal.htm); and "Transnational Practices and Interdisciplinary Feminist Scholarship: Refiguring Women's and Gender Studies," in *Women's Studies on Its Own*, ed. Robyn Wiegman (Durham: Duke University Press, 2002), 66–80.

3. United Nations Development Program, *Human Development Report, 1998* (New York: Oxford University Press, 1999).

4. U.S. Census Bureau, *Poverty in the United States, 1999* (Washington, D.C.: Government Printing Office, 2000).

5. Stuart Hall, "Race, Articulation, and Societies Structured in Dominance," in *Black Cultural Studies: A Reader,* ed. Houston Baker, Manthia Diawara, and Ruth Lindeborg (Chicago: University of Chicago Press, 1996), 55.

6. U.S. Census Bureau, *Poverty in the United States, 1999.*

7. Alongside the greater number of single-women-headed households is the disproportionate number of adult African American and Hispanic males who are incarcerated in the U.S. prison-industrial complex.

8. I base my analysis on United Nations Development Program, *Human Development Report, 1998*; United Nations, *1999 World Survey on the Role of Women in Development* (New York: United Nations, 1999); World Bank, *World Development Report 2000/2001* (New York: Oxford University Press, 2001); Ajit Singh and Ann Zammit, "International Capital Flows: Identifying the Gender Dimension," *World Development* 28, no. 7 (2000): 1249–1268.

9. United Nations, *1999 World Survey on the Role of Women in Development*, 9.

10. World Bank, *World Development Report 2000/2001*, 314.

11. Ibid., 25.

12. Candace Howes and Ajit Singh, "Long-Term Trends in the World Economy: The Gender Dimension," *World Development* 23, no. 11 (1995): 1895–1911; Singh and Zammit, "International Capital Flows."

13. United Nations, *1999 World Survey on the Role of Women in Development*.

14. Guy Standing, "Global Feminization through Flexible Labor," *World Development* 17, no. 7 (1989): 1077–1095; United Nations, *1999 World Survey on the Role of Women in Development.*

15. Randolph Persaud and Clarence Lusane, "The New Economy, Globalization, and the Impact on African Americans," *Race and Class* 42, no. 1 (2000): 21–34.

16. That the "Asia" of origin for workers in the "home-working" sector in Britain is more likely to be India or Pakistan, and in the United States, more likely Vietnam or China, speaks to differing histories of colonial engagement and migration and the incomplete project of "equal" citizenship for racial minorities in these countries.

17. United Nations, *1999 World Survey on the Role of Women in Development*, 10.

18. Saskia Sassen, *Globalization and Its Discontents* (New York: New Press, 1998).

19. Evelyn Nakano Glenn, "From Servitude to Service Work: Historical Continuities in the Racial Division of Paid Reproductive Labor," *Signs* 18, no. 1 (1992): 1–43.

20. Susan Joekes and Ann Weston, *Women and the New Trade Agenda* (New York: UNIFEM, 1994).

21. United Nations, *1999 World Survey on the Role of Women in Development*, 9.

22. Ibid., 16.

23. This is an extension of Ruth Pearson's discussion of the multiple ways in which women have been incorporated into Third World industrialization and her apt questioning of whether this always leads to greater equality. Ruth Pearson, "Nimble Fingers Revisited,"

in *Feminist Visions of Development: Gender Analysis and Policy*, ed. Cecile Jackson and Ruth Pearson (London and New York: Routledge, 1998), 171–188.

24. Lourdes Beneria and Shelley Feldman, eds., *Unequal Burden: Economic Crises, Persistent Poverty, and Women's Work* (Boulder: Westview Press, 1992); Pamela Sparr, ed., *Mortgaging Women's Lives: Feminist Critiques of Structural Adjustment* (Atlantic Highlands: Zed Books, 1994).

25. World Bank, *World Development Report 2000/2001*.

26. Diane Elson, "Gender Awareness in Modeling Structural Adjustment," *World Development* 23, no. 11 (1995): 1851–1868.

27. See Stuart Hall, "Minimal Selves," in *Black British Cultural Studies,* ed. Houston A. Baker Jr. et al. (Chicago and London: Chicago University Press, 1996), 117.

28. I refer to From Feminist Multiculturalism to Feminist Internationalism? a course offered at the University of Washington in 2000. These reflections are based also on my co-organization with Tani Barlow of the New Feminist Internationalism (February 2000 conference) and on my work with the Modern Girl around the World Project, a collaboration of six scholars seeking to do feminist internationalist scholarship across disciplines, national boundaries, and geographical areas of expertise. For further information see http://depts.washington.edu/its/moderngirl.htm.

29. Joshua Cohen, Matthew Howard, and Martha C. Nussbaum, eds., *Is Multiculturalism Bad for Women? Susan Moller Okin with Respondents* (Princeton: Princeton University Press, 1999).

30. I make similar observations in "Review of *Is Multiculturalism Bad for Women? Susan Moller Okin with Respondents; Mappings: Feminism and the Cultural Geographies of Encounter;* and *Critical Condition: Feminism at the Turn of the Century,*" *Signs* 27, no. 1 (2001): 294–300.

31. Cohen et al., *Is Multiculturalism Bad for Women?* 10.

32. This critique builds on collaborative work on the invocation of the idea of "global culture" in the context American Studies. See Alys Eve Weinbaum and Brent Hayes Edwards, "On Critical Globality," *Ariel: A Review of International English Literature* 31, nos. 1–2 (2000): 255–274.

33. Here the question of translation becomes inescapable. Contemporary U.S. feminism's relationship to the globalization of English is all too often overlooked. Although questions of translation are beyond the scope of this essay, suffice it to say that most international feminist exchanges are mediated in one of the five UN languages and that the majority of feminist anthologies are published in English. On the necessity of using practices of cultural translation to resist appropriation of subaltern texts by dominant knowledge projects, see Gayatri Chakravorty Spivak, *Death of a Discipline* (New York: Columbia University Press, 2003). On the politics of translating and receiving Third World women writers in the Euro-American context, see Amal Amireh and Lisa Suhair Majaj, eds., *Going Global: The Transnational Reception of Third World Women Writers* (New York and London: Garland Publishing, 2000).

34. Fredric Jameson, "On 'Cultural Studies,'" *Social Text* 34 (1993): 34.

35. Stuart Hall, "Old and New Identities," in *Culture, Globalization, and the World-System,* ed. Anthony King et al. (Minneapolis: University of Minnesota Press, 1997), 67.

36. See Amrita Basu, *The Challenge of Local Feminisms: Women's Movements in Global Perspective* (Boulder, Colo.: Westview Press, 1995). In collaboratively designing syllabi for a future course they might teach on "feminism in globalization," many students included Basu's volume, some positioning it as an authoritative text, others including it as an object to be critically assessed.

37. See Tani Barlow, "Teaching International Studies in a Globalized Frame," manuscript, 1999.

38. Other texts within this genealogy include Kathleen Barry, Charlotte Bunch, and Shirley Castley, eds., *International Feminism: Networking against Female Sexual Slavery: Report of the Global Feminist Workshop to Organize against Traffic in Women* (New York: International Women's Tribune Centre, 1984); Aruna Rao, ed., *Women's Studies International: Nairobi and Beyond* (New York: Feminist Press, 1991); and Joanna Kerr, ed., *Ours by Right: Women's Rights as Human Rights* (London: Zed Books, 1993). Indeed, any anthology that culls "local" feminisms *without* raising questions of access, translation, reception, or the possibility that failure of local feminisms to intersect is as significant as their overlap, might be included here. In response to the volumes listed above, see Amireh and Majaj's *Going Global,* especially the editors' introduction and Marnia Lazreg's "The Triumphant Discourse of Global Feminism: Should Other Women Be Known?" 29–38; and Gayatri Chakravorty Spivak's "Diasporas Old and New: Women in the Transnational World," *Textual Practice* 10, no. 2 (1996): 245–269.

39. The term "geopolitical literacy" is Susan Stanford Friedman's. See Susan Stanford Friedman, "Locational Feminism: Gender, Cultural Geographies, and Geopolitical Literary," in *Feminist Locations: Global and Local, Theory and Practice,* ed. Marianne DeKoven (New Brunswick, N.J.: Rutgers University Press, 2001), 13–36.

40. David Harvey, "Globalization in Question," *Rethinking Marxism* 8, no. 4 (1995): 1–17.

41. See Kevin Cox, ed., *Spaces of Globalization: Reasserting the Power of the Local* (London: Guilford Press, 1997); and Arif Dirlik, "The Global in the Local," in *Global/Local*, ed. Rob Wilson and Wimal Dissanayake (Durham: Duke University Press, 1996): 21–45.

42. Neil Smith, "The Satanic Geographies of Globalization," *Public Culture* 10, no. 1 (1997): 169–189.

43. Much of my section of this essay is scavenged from my book *Against the Romance of Community* (Minneapolis: University of Minnesota Press, 2002). The argument I offer very briefly here about global/localization discourse is elaborated in chapter 5: "Kinship and the Culturalization of Capitalism: The Discourse of Global/Localization" (146–169).

44. This discourse might be said to provide the structuring narrative of the discipline of sociology, and I would argue that this discourse also structures contemporary debates over multiculturalism and diversity, informs much progressive political organizing, and is institutionalized in the distinction between nonprofit and for-profit corporations. For a substantiation of these claims and an elaboration of the argument made in this paragraph, see my introduction, "Persistent Critique, Relentless Return" (1–29), and chapter 1, "The Supplementarity of Community with Capital; or, A Critique of the Romantic Discourse of Community" (30–68), in my *Against the Romance of Community.*

45. Francis Fukuyama, *Trust: The Social Virtues and the Creation of Prosperity* (New York: Free Press, 1995), 11, 5.

46. Ibid., 4–5.

47. Foucault says of the use of analogy in the sixteenth century, "Its power is immense, for the similitudes of which it treats are not the visible, substantial ones between things themselves; they need only be the more subtle resemblance of relations. Disencumbered thus, it can extend, from a single given point, to an endless number of relationships." Michel Foucault, *The Order of Things* (New York: Pantheon Books, 1970), 21.

48. Kenichi Ohmae, *The End of the Nation State: The Rise of Regional Economies* (New York: Free Press, 1995), 21.

49. Ibid., 24.

50. Gayatri Chakravorty Spivak calls for such a project in "Scattered Speculations on the Question of Value," in *In Other Worlds,* by Spivak (New York: Methuen, 1987), 154–175.

51. I discuss precisely this drama, taking my own department as a case study, in "Analogy and Complicity: Women's Studies, LGBT Studies, and Capitalism" in *Women Studies on Its Own*, ed. Wiegman, 267–292.

52. Lorenia Parada-Ampudia's essay in this volume offers a compelling example of the kind of self-reflexive scholarship that is needed. In it she describes the transformations of women studies in Mexico that have ensued in relation to the Mexican debt crisis, the emergence of neoliberalism, and the concomitant non-governmental organization of feminism.

53. We originally presented this work at the Future of Women's Studies: Foundations, Interrogations, Politics, a conference at the University of Arizona, Tucson, 2001.

54. This question was raised by Amber Hollibaugh (who self-identified as an activist, author, and independent filmmaker) at our original conference presentation.

Laboratories of Our Own

New Productions of Gender and Science

Banu Subramaniam

*How do you live and think together beneath a light that warms our
bodies and models our ideas, but which remains indifferent to their
existence? We contemporary philosophers cannot ask this question
while ignoring the sciences, which, in their very separation, converge
to ask it, even to exacerbate its terms. And when "the world" means
purely and simply the planet Earth, . . . when humanity is finally
solidary and global in its political existence and in the exercise of
science, it discovers that it inhabits a global Earth that is the concern
of our global science, global technology, and our global and local
behaviors. This is the reason for the necessary synthesis.*
—Michel Serres, *Conversations on Science, Culture, and Time*

Welcome to the twilight zone. Welcome
to the world of oppositional spaces, liminal zones, those borderlands, that nebulous fuzzy space between disciplines, continents, identities, nationalities—the space
that at one moment seems like nowhere, belonging to nothing, with no identity,
which at the same time is also about being everywhere, belonging to everything
with multiple identities. The fault lines that appear in this liminal interdisciplinary work shatter self-contained disciplines, binary thinking, unitary knowledge,
and oneness, the quest for a uniform whole. Fortunately, twilight zone always comes
with possibilities, solutions, and resolutions—and always with a twist. In this essay, I will trace my journey in one such fault line, the fissures between women's
studies and the sciences.

My interdisciplinary work began in women's studies. I was midway in my
graduate career in the biological sciences. Leaving India for the first time, I entered
a graduate program in the sciences with little understanding of what it entailed.
All I knew was that I was enraptured with evolutionary biology, and my dreams
and ambitions ever since I was a little girl were to spend a lifetime in science, in
particular, evolutionary biology. However, the naïve conceptions of science that
inhabited my imagination were severely tested in graduate school. Arriving in a

new continent and country, I found everything new and I had a difficult time fitting in. With time, I found myself growing increasingly uncertain and unsure about my abilities and talents. I wasn't sure I belonged in the sciences any more. When I entered the women's studies office as a graduate student in the biological sciences, I came to inquire how I might be able to leave the sciences for a different sort of future in women's studies. To be honest, other than being a feminist for as long as I could remember, I knew very little about what it was that women's studies did. With a "proper" British-style education system in India, I had specialized very early and my training had until then been exclusively in the sciences. Indeed, since tenth grade, other than English and a second language we were required to take, I had never taken a course in the social sciences or the humanities. With my naïve conceptions of women's studies, I drew strength from my passionate feminism and set out to see whether women's studies held a future for me!

The irony of the situation always amazes me. For, rather than leave the sciences, women's studies offered me the tools to stay in science.[1] It allowed me to understand the process that caused me to doubt my own abilities and dreams that I had spent my early life dreaming. It helped me develop a framework to recapture my earlier fascination for thinking and doing science. And I did, indeed stay on in the sciences and finish my doctoral degree and, in addition, a graduate certificate in women's studies. When I left graduate school, I left with what seemed like two rich sets of training, credentials, and tools—one in evolutionary biology and a second in women's studies.

The realities of inhabiting the two worlds of women's studies and the sciences are more than I can deal with most of the time. I feel I move between these two worlds, fighting to be recognized as the scientist in the sciences, yet constantly defending feminism and feminist scholarship. Conversely, I fight to be seen as a "real" feminist in women's studies, yet challenge the myths of science as a monolithic entity and scientists as bearded rationalists developing the latest bomb. My life is in them both, constantly precarious and tenuous, while I am criticizing, challenging, defending, and supporting all at once, one to the other.

Before turning to the future of women's studies, which is the theme of this anthology, I want to first offer an analysis of where I think we are with the project of feminism and science. I want to relate my journey, this life in the twilight zone, the fruits of my aspirations to be a scholar in women's studies and the sciences, because it is instructive of the historical disjunctions between the disciplines, ones that are not only epistemological and methodological but also institutional. The analysis uses anecdotes and experiential accounts of my days with scientists and feminists. One of the central challenges of working simultaneously on "feminism" and "science" is that while many of the practitioners in the field of feminist science studies are trained as both feminists and scientists, amply demonstrating that feminism and science are deeply and intimately connected, these worlds are, in practice not in conversation with each other. Despite my deep commitment to the project of feminism and science, in practice, I experience a deep sense of disjuncture—institutionally, administratively, culturally, and often even intellectually. While feminists/scientists have laid out a brilliant analysis of the nature and scope of the project of feminist science studies, we have yet to embrace the transformative power of this critique. In this essay I want to elaborate some of the challenges in working in the interstices of the (inter)disciplines of women's studies and the sciences. In the first section, I explain why I find the intersection of feminism and science such a fundamentally important and crucial connection for the sciences. As a scientist, I will explore a critique of the sciences to examine what the field of feminist studies of science and women's studies offers studies of the natural world. And yet, scientists refute and resist every challenge to the scientific enterprise and claims of objectivity. In the second section, I explain why I find the project of feminism and science an equally compelling connection for feminists. As a feminist scholar, I will explore a critique of women's studies and the feminist studies of science to explain why, as a scientist, I find this body of work wanting and inadequate for the project of feminism and science. In the last section, I offer some thoughts of why the project of feminism and science continues to be such a problematic and difficult one.

The Feminist Scholar in the Sciences

So what does feminism have to offer the sciences? I will begin with a story. A few years ago, I met a woman on a plane while traveling from Durham to New York. During the course of our conversation I told her about my work on women in science and engineering. She told me that she was once very interested in a future in the sciences and was thinking of majoring in chemistry. She explained that one experience changed it all. She recounted a field trip her class made to a desert region:

> You know, as we drove through this desert region, we stopped at a spot where there was absolutely no sign of life of any kind around. Miles of desolate, harsh ground with not a living plant or insect to be seen. As I walked around in the midst of this inhospitable region, I spotted a tiny plant. It was the tiniest of plants, barely an inch off the ground. It had four small leaves and at the top of the plant was a small blue flower, the bluest flower you ever did see. There was something so delicate, fragile, and beautiful about this little creature in the middle of nowhere that I felt compelled to catch it on film. So I set up my tripod and was figuring out the best angle and distance to catch this miracle of a life. While I did this, our biology professor walked by and spotted the plant. Without a word or a glance, he bent down and pulled out the plant. He tore out the leaves, few of the petals, and shook the seed pod. "Yup!" he said aloud, "A legume, just as I thought." And with that he flung the plant aside and walked on. Forget the fact that he disrupted my photograph. But the picture of him unnecessarily pulling out that plant, unmoved, unfeeling, unthinking, just to prove his hunch on plant classification is an image I can never

forget. That captures my experiences with scientists—they lack ethics, aesthetics, and humanity. It was so unethical, what he did. Why did he need to destroy that plant?

In my years of working with individuals in science and engineering, this is not an uncommon story. Not all women, of course, care about ethics and aesthetics or subscribe to essentialist notions of women as caring or ethical beings. But many women in science identify problems with the "context" of science, describing science as a world that is not welcoming. And the reasons and stories are as diverse as there are women. Some women describe science and scientists as hostile to their presence as women, where through comments and actions fellow scientists make it known that women are not welcome in the scientific world. This might involve jokes that mark women as sexual beings and not competent scientists; actions that question the credibility and ability of women scientists by belittling or trivializing their work, giving women a harder time in preliminary examinations, around the lab, or during promotion and tenure; and informal activities in bars and tennis courts, where women are not invited even though they might enjoy a good drink or game of tennis. These social realms eventually exclude women from informal chats on science and social networks that can be central to the scientific process.

A more sustained answer to the question on feminism and science lies in a growing body of scholarship that has emerged in women's studies. Early work on women in science documented the low numbers of women, and an even lower number among Nobel laureates or National Academy of Science members. About three decades ago, there was a shift from thinking about "women in science," to beginning to look at the relationship between gender and science.[2] This body of work in women's studies is referred to as the feminist studies of science or the literature on gender and science. I think it is a powerful, systematic, and well-developed critique that unfortunately has remained outside the sciences, as much work in the social studies of science has. Most of this work is not anti-science per se (although pockets of it are) but rather is a self-reflective exercise in how science falls short of its own goals of objective, value-free work. Indeed, several prominent scholars in this area were trained as scientists. Their work shifts the focus from "biological sex" and "human nature" to focusing on gender, and from men and women in science to talking about the culture of science.[3] If one looks at the history of science, science can be viewed as a social enterprise that reflects a history that has been dominated by Western, upper-class, heterosexual, men.[4] Scholars argue that there is something inherent in the "institution of science," in the "discourse and language of science," and in the "ideology" of science that reflects its history.[5] One must, therefore, examine not only numbers of women, but, indeed, the institution of science itself, its embeddedness in the social, cultural, and political fabric of cultures, societies, and nations.

The central theme of these studies of science is the social construction of scientific knowledge.[6] The popular conception of science as marching toward greater and greater truth purely by objectively following facts, they argue, is a myth.[7] An analysis of the history of science shows that science is far from being gender neutral or value free. These scholars document how social policies use "scientific knowledge" to reinscribe social stereotypes of masculine and feminine, justifying the continued subjugation of women.[8] Further, this scientific knowledge used to determine social policy is itself socially constructed—gender and racial stereotypes of the culture are encoded into scientific theories themselves.[9] For example, the history of eugenics and social Darwinism documents the mass stigmatization and eventual sterilization of groups of people deemed "unfit."[10] An analysis of early craniometry shows that scientists produced results purporting sexual and racial differences with little evidence or in spite of the evidence.[11] Similarly, the Tuskegee syphilis tests, IQ testing, and various biologically determinist arguments document the inherent racism and sexism in scientific practices with profound social consequences.[12] Sociobiology and its current incarnation of evolutionary psychology document the potent power of science and scientists to reify social categories and assumptions of gender, race, class, and sexuality.[13] There are the more subtle cases, for example, Emily Martin, who explores how gender norms in the larger culture get encoded into romance tales based on stereotypical gender imagery in narratives of the egg and the sperm.[14] Londa Schiebinger argues that the group to which we belong, Mammalia, was so named because of the social context of science—the group was named during a big campaign in England to promote breast-feeding. Therefore, even though mammals are defined by many characteristics, it is the feeding of the young that ultimately marked and named the group.[15] This is not surprising in a culture where we name nature as female, where a focus on breast-feeding would only add to our self-definition as a species where women are the caregivers.

The literature in the social studies of science documents precisely this tautology time and again: a dual process and circular reasoning—of science constructing gender and gender constructing science—that have together proved to be a potent tool in maintaining the status quo. Social privilege is thus scientifically encoded into biological privilege through the institution of science; and biological privilege is socially encoded into social privilege through the institutions of public policy and politics.

Critiques of biological determinism are central to the feminist critiques of science.[16] Scholars have challenged the inferiority of women's biology, the medicalization of women's bodies on the grounds of poor experimental design, inadequate data, incorrect assumptions, poor controls, overstated conclusions, or by extrapolating from studies of animals to humans.[17] While scientific theories may change, while the details of studies may change, the subordination of the same groups remains. And these theories are often inconsistent and remain Eurocentric, and class based. It is through a close, careful, historical documentation that feminist scholars have revealed that science has served the interest of the ruling class.

I knocked on the doors of women's studies wanting to leave science because I felt I didn't belong there anymore. Instead, I left with a rich set of critiques that helped me understand my own alienation within the culture of science. The critiques gave me the tools to understand science as a set of historically derived practices and cultures that mediate the study of nature. It taught me to examine the genealogy of primary concepts in my subdiscipline, discipline, and, indeed, science itself. It provided me with the understanding of how cultural practices and beliefs enter into scientific hypotheses, language, and theories despite the best intentions of individual scientists. It also taught me how inextricably interconnected nature, politics, and discourse are in our understanding of nature. It provided me with the methods to investigate the role of gender in scientific culture's conception of a scientist and what that meant for those of us who were women.

While my newfound frameworks were empowering and exciting, they were also marginalizing within the culture of science. While the feminist studies of science were immensely transformative to me individually, there was little I could do with that knowledge within my life in the sciences. Some progressive faculty and students acknowledged that scientific culture did alienate students who were women, minorities, Third World, working class, or gay. However, any challenge to scientific objectivity was consistently refuted. They argued that the social studies of science were useful to understand social dynamics within science, but not scientific methodology, epistemology, or process.

My own interest had grown bolder. I wanted to be a researcher who continued to work in both the biological sciences and in feminist science studies—to work both *on* science and *in* science. The project in which I was and am interested was and is a reconstructive project for science. I want to use the insights from feminist science studies in the practice of science. And so, armed with new dreams and visions of interdisciplinarity and the conviction that this was an important and exciting project, I entered the foray of interdisciplinary work. I spent the next few years located in a women's studies program but with a joint appointment in a biology program.

The Scientist in Women's Studies

I want to now turn to the other half of this binary—the scientist in women's studies. So what might the sciences have to do with women's studies? The feminist studies of science are again eloquent on the subject. Anne Fausto-Sterling, in her piece on building two-way streets between feminism and science, discusses the impact of the human genome project: "It has all happened so fast that we hardly know what's hit us. Biologists face a transformation of their workplace, while feminists must watch a scientific project unfold that promises the return of eugenics in a modern and grand scale and has implications for the role of women in reproduction and mothering that are just beginning to evidence themselves. Feminists (with few exceptions) have missed the entire event because they aren't well enough educated to pay proper attention to scientific change, while rank and file biologists stand bewildered because they have few skills enabling them to apply astute critical analyses to their own fields."[18]

Feminist studies of science emphasize the profound impact science and technology has and continues to have on the lives of women. Scholars such as Ruth Bleier, Anne Fausto-Sterling, Stephen Jay Gould, Sandra Harding, Ruth Hubbard,

Evelyn Fox Keller, Richard Lewontin, and Helen Longino have been critical in challenging bad, politically fraught, and dangerous brands of science. The liberatory power of such critique can be best seen in the work of scholars and activists working on women's health. Their work has resulted in the National Institute of Health requiring research protocols to include both females and males if the disease occurs in both sexes,[19] the creation of an Office of Research on Women's Health at the National Institute of Health, and writings such as *Our Bodies, Ourselves.*[20] In short, as feminist scholars of science warn us and as feminist health scholars and activists have demonstrated, in a world dominated and increasingly defined by science and technology, feminists just cannot afford to ignore science.[21]

While the feminist studies of science underscore the importance of science and technology, I want to argue in the rest of this section that in my experience this position has largely remained as rhetoric within the women's studies community. I want to begin by relating an anecdote. One morning, I was sitting in my office when a colleague came running in to ask me a burning question she had. How was it, she asked, that a wet nurse could produce milk for a baby she had not carried? What fascinated me about this question was not the question itself, but why she had chosen to come bursting into my office with this query. I am not a mother; I do not go around professing interest in mothering, nursing, or childcare. I work on plant biology and have never professed expertise in human reproductive biology. The answer she gave me was that she thought I was the best qualified as the resident scientist in the program.

In talking to other scientists who have begun to work in women's studies, this is not an uncommon experience. We have our own sets of jokes. A student related to me recently how, during the previous week at a major women's studies event, she was called on as the only scientist to solve the problem of the malfunctioning slide projector. And in that instance, she solved it by plugging the instrument into an electric socket. It isn't as though there aren't many instances when a scientist has forgotten to plug in an instrument, or even that there aren't scientists who are technophobes. But the instances I am talking about in women's studies are a repeated and willful refusal to be scientifically and technologically literate—not by idiosyncratic individuals but often by entire programs.

The distancing of science and technology does not remain merely a personal choice of individuals but is reproduced in the ways in which women's studies programs are run. In my experience, the core disciplines that define women's studies are squarely in the humanities and social sciences. This is apparent in the faculty we have, in the research questions we develop, in the courses we offer, and in the students we train. Too few women's studies programs teach about science or, indeed, require their students to be scientifically literate. Do any women's studies majors around the country have a science requirement? While many introductory women's studies courses do not engage with the sciences at all, even when they do, it is exclusively in the realm of critique. By only teaching critiques of science, we are in the danger of producing students who reject all forms of scientific investigation and knowledge. Instead, how do we encourage scientifically literate and intelligent feminist students who become the constructors of new forms of scientific knowledge—knowledge that engages feminist ideals of justice and equality for the betterment of all people?[22]

If women's studies programs do not encourage scientific literacy in their own students, do they work with feminist scientists? The answer again is no. In my experiences, most institutions work with women scientists and engineers through Women in Science and Engineering (WISE) programs that are peripherally related to women's studies programs, if at all. WISE programs are constructed around decreasing the alienation and isolation of women scientists by providing role models, mentors, and support networks. For the most part, they do not engage with the feminist studies of science. Therefore, unlike the earlier generation of feminist scholars in the social sciences and humanities who returned to their primary disciplines with feminist tools to transform their disciplines, feminist scientists do not return to their home departments with tools to challenge the intellectual foundations of their disciplines. As a scholar in both disciplines, I develop programs and projects that try to bridge the gap between women's studies and the sciences. Over the last few years, I have consistently found women and men scientists interested in participating in joint projects with women's studies, however resistant they may be to the ideas presented. It is the feminist scholars who inevitably claim to be "too busy," "not interested," or "not qualified."

The more time I spend in women's studies, the more I come to realize that the feminist studies of science situate the difficulty of the project of feminism and science as a problem with the sciences. Take two well-known collections both entitled *Feminism and Science,* one edited by Evelyn Fox Keller and Helen Longino and the other by Nancy Tuana.[23] Both volumes feature influential essays in feminist science studies, and every one of them is about a critique of the sciences—be it about scientific epistemology, methodology, language, sociology, or history. While the articles are important and profound, nowhere in these volumes is any acknowledgment that the difficulty of the project of feminism and science might also lie with a problem in the construction of feminism, in its own epistemology, methodology, language, sociology, or history.

What I want to argue here is that the difficulty of the project of feminism and science is as much a failure of women's studies as it is about the sciences. While women's studies, and the feminist critiques in particular, have created a rich body of literature in understanding the resistances and hostility of the sciences to issues of feminism, there has been little exploration of the resistances and hostility of women's studies to issues of science. Feminist scholars have remained content maintaining their epistemological purity in critiquing the sciences from the outside and not in engaging with the sciences as collaborators or practitioners. And thus, the project of feminism and science has ended up being in practice about transforming the sciences. Unless we transform both the sciences and women's studies, unless we are willing to take a good look inside, until we can chart pathways on how these transformations can be achieved by individuals in institutions and disciplines, the feminist critiques of science will remain critiques outside the sciences and will have little impact on science or working scientists.

Laboratories of Our Own

In her 1987 essay on the tensions between women scientists and feminist critics of science, Evelyn Fox Keller names what she sees as *the* question that feminist critics of science must address:

> So far, my discussion has been about the shift in mind-set from working scientist to feminist critic. A true rapprochement, however, requires that the shift be charted also in reverse. That is to say, feminist critics of science must at the very least reclaim access to the mind-set of the working scientist. . . . While beliefs, interests, and cultural norms surely can and do influence the definition of scientific goals as well as the criteria for success in meeting such goals, they cannot in themselves generate either epistemological or technological success. By themselves, without the co-operation of nature, beliefs cannot lead to the generation of useful knowledge. Our analysis began with the question of where and how the force of beliefs, interests, and cultural norms enters into the process by which effective knowledge is generated. The question that remains is: Where and how does nature enter into that process? How do nature and culture interact in the production of scientific knowledge? I suggest that this last question, however difficult, is *the* question that feminist critics of science, along with other social critics of science, must now address. Until we do, our account of science not only will not, but also cannot, be recognizable to working scientists.[24]

In constructing the essay in this form—a focus on the sciences and then on women's studies—I am reifying certain binaries (women's studies/science, humanities/sciences, culture/nature, etc.) and risk re-invoking C. P Snow's famous essay on the sciences and the humanities as "two cultures."[25] And yet, experientially, the dissonance seems very real. In every institution at which I have been, the sciences and women's studies are located in different buildings (often at opposite ends of campus) and are administratively in separate colleges, with entirely different histories, methodologies and epistemologies, and intellectual practices. These differences, I realize, are embedded in deep histories. And yet, as someone who was introduced to feminist science studies late in life, for me the project of feminist science studies has such deep resonance, such profound intellectual potential that it seems to be a project worth fighting for and working toward. I find myself extremely fortunate in arriving at a historical moment when there is a field like "feminist science studies" already defined. Much of this work has been developed by those who are feminists and scientists, who have already created a framework and an intellectual tradition of crossing these binaries. And yet, despite this body of work, the institutional chasms between the two fields are real and deep.

At first, my work in women's studies and my work in the sciences were entirely separate. In the sciences, I worked on my experiments, analyzed my results, and worked on writing my dissertation. In women's studies I took courses on history, feminist methods, and feminist theories. It was a schizophrenic experience with two lives that rarely communicated to each other. A glimpse into the possibility of interdisciplinary work began fortuitously enough. While in women's studies, trying to understand my experiences as a Third World graduate student in the sciences, I had a revelatory conversation. In a rather rare occurrence, a colleague in women's studies, in response to my telling her that I was working on my dissertation in biology, asked me for an explanation of my research in biology.[26] I explained to her that I worked on flower color variation in morning glories and was trying to understand whether natural selection worked to maintain flower color variation and, if so, what evolutionary mechanisms might be responsible for this maintenance. My colleague nodded and said, rather nonchalantly, "Oh, you work on diversity!" While this might seem obvious enough to many, it was for me a moment of revelation. Someone had just bridged the worlds of nature and cultures for me and it was a connection I had never imagined.

In thinking about this question, I decided to return to my doctoral dissertation on the maintenance of flower color variation in morning glories. The work in the original dissertation was framed within the confines and traditions of the discipline of evolutionary biology. And the question I wished to ask was, If informed by the insights of feminist and social studies of science, would this dissertation have been different? And if the answer is yes, as I believe, how so? Would it involve just a change in the language used, the framing of the questions, the scope of the problem, the gathering of data, or all of them? Or would it, indeed, lead to a different set of experiments than the ones I conducted? At what points can science studies offer alternate configurations of scientific practices and processes? What would these be? This was the project feminist science studies inspired—connecting the natural and cultural worlds by a simultaneous exploration of both.

What would it mean for women's studies to engage with the sciences as its own? Not at arms length, not with fear, not with paranoia, but owning it as ours to shape, to empower? What would it mean for us to have laboratories of our own? How would these transform the physical realities of universities as well as the intellectual spaces we occupy? And what would be the relationships of feminisms and the sciences in these new formulations? The failure of feminism and science has been marked by our ambivalences. On the one hand, we critique Western feminism for its Eurocentric, masculinist biases, and yet we want to embrace that very monster to save women's lives. We are suspicious of the manipulations of biotechnology, the master's tools that render women invisible, commodify women's bodies, and yet we look to "oncomouse" to cure breast cancer.[27]

At the heart of my problems with the project of feminism and science, I have come to realize, is my interest in being a researcher who continues to work in both the biological sciences and in feminist science studies—to work both *on* science and *in* science. The *on science/in science* project seems like a deceptively simple formulation, but I believe it is at the heart of the tensions between feminism and science that haunt me.

In attempting the bridge work, the more I tried to bring the worlds of women's studies and the sciences together, the further they seemed to drift apart. A feminist scholar and a scientist, little did I realize that I would soon be marked as "the scientist" in women's studies and "the feminist" in the sciences. Bruno Latour's formulation in his book *We Have Never Been Modern* seems very useful in this instance.[28] In this book, he marks the impulse to be modern as involving two sets of practices. First, the "work of purification," whereby we create two entirely distinct ontological zones: that of the nonhuman/natural world, on the one hand, and that of human/cultural world, on the other. And so I came to realize that although I had two sets of tools, training, and methods, one in evolutionary biology and a second in women's studies, they were each developed for the study of these two distinct worlds—of nature and culture. Alongside this work of purification, Latour also elaborates a second set of practices, namely, the "work of translation," which creates mixtures between the world of nature and culture or hybrids of nature and culture. Such is the paradox of the moderns—"the more we forbid ourselves to conceive hybrids, the more possible their interbreeding becomes." As he puts it, "In the eyes of our critics the ozone hole above our heads, the moral law in our hearts, the autonomous text, may each be of interest, but only separately. That a delicate shuttle should have woven together the heavens, industry, texts, souls and moral law—that remains uncanny, unthinkable, unseemly."[29]

In retrospect, my task was not simple at all. On the one hand, we carry on the work of purification in the academy by creating different sets of disciplines, tools, and methods and reify the separation of the worlds of human and nonhuman, nature and culture. However, this work of purification creates hybrids of all kinds between nature and culture, and this is precisely what the feminist and social studies of science have and continue to uncover and make visible. I want to argue that the tools and methods of the feminist studies of science are still squarely in the zone of the human/cultural world, and this is the source of my difficulty in bringing these worlds together. Women's studies provided me with the tools and methods to *de*construct science, not *re*construct it—to work *on* science not *in* science. The context of women's studies and the sciences as disciplines, practices, commitments, theories, tools, and methods makes my commitment to transform and work in both women's studies and the sciences impossible. For a reconstructive project for science, we must study both nature and culture together.

This to me is precisely the work of feminist science studies. While the accomplishments of feminist science studies are, indeed, considerable, much of the work focuses on critiques of science already done, often historical or philosophical. But, can we use the hindsight of history for foresight into the future? Can we move from critically evaluating work already done in the sciences (crucial though this critique is) to actually engaging and developing a research agenda in the sciences? The challenge, it seems, is to build a road map for collaborative work in the sciences and women's studies. I think our primary task is a rethinking of the approaches and questions of the feminist studies of science. While there are undoubtedly multiple alternate formulations, I want to suggest one.

One formulation is taking the project of reconstruction seriously. We need to learn to work with scientists, with science, and with the materiality of nature, to understand, in Keller's words, "how nature and culture interact in the production of scientific knowledge."[30] We need to grapple with the relationships between the daily lived reality of scientists, the social relations and histories that mark scientific culture, the construction of scientific practices and laboratories, and the process of scientific investigation, analysis, and conclusions. We need to figure out how and where nature and culture interact in all these modes of scientific practice. For this task, feminist scholarship offers us a rich array of frameworks, critiques, tools, methods, methodologies, and epistemologies. The field is fertile for our laboratories, for new kinds of experimentation, for multiple modes of knowing and knowledge construction. Rather than being defined by the object of study, i.e., a study of men/women or masculinity/femininity, women's studies is increasingly defined as a set of feminist approaches. These approaches are varied and numerous, studying questions across the disciplines. While they do not employ a single methodology, they are all committed to challenging dominant paradigms in disciplines and working to de-center traditional ways of knowing. What marks "feminist" work from other social critics who refuse analyses of gender, race, class, or sexuality is an analysis of difference and power. Feminist frameworks are marked by an attention to difference, power, and the politics of knowledge, recognizing that sex and gender are intricately intertwined with race, class, sexuality, and other social variables. However, by focusing on the approach of study and not the object of study, we open the possibilities of feminist work—one can employ feminist approaches to study cultures, bodies, diseases, plants, or rocks. What if we began to study science and nature with a similar multiplicity of approaches? What if we began to de-center traditional paradigms in the sciences, without necessarily foregrounding sex or gender? We could articulate intervention points in scientific practice. And we could explore how the feminist studies of science can offer us alternate configurations of scientific practice. The challenge in all this is in imagining new laboratories, in developing new tools and strategies to actualize our visions. And for this we must educate and reorient ourselves. What is in store for us is not merely a transformation of the sciences, but also a transformation of women's studies.

Binaries pervade our configurations of feminism and science. We do not have to and we must not buy into it. We must make room for the chemical composition of concrete that make our houses strong, the engineering of our electrical wiring, the insulation, the walls and windows that keep our bodies and souls warm, the construction of the roofs that keep the cold, sleet, and rain at bay. We must make room for the materiality of our bodies, of DNA, of cells, of anatomy and physiology in our understandings of our bodies and our minds. Nature and culture together construct our minds and thoughts, our bodies, our sciences, our genders, our sexes, our sexualities, our races, our diseases, and our medicines. If we give ourselves permission and time to engage with science and scientists, we can go someplace new.

Notes

An earlier version of this essay was presented at Duke University, January 23, 1998.
1. I am deeply indebted to Jean O'Barr, Nancy Rosebaugh, and Mary Wyer, whose kindness, commitment, patience, and intellectual openness and rigor were eye-opening.

2. Evelyn Fox Keller, *Secrets of Life, Secrets of Death: Essays on Language, Gender, and Science* (New York: Routledge, 1992).

3. Bill Moyers, "An Interview with Evelyn Fox Keller," in *A World of Ideas II: Public Opinions from Private Citizens,* ed. Bill Moyers (New York: Doubleday, 1990), 73–81.

4. Ruth Bleier, *Feminist Approaches to Science* (Elmsford, N.Y.: Pergamon, 1986).

5. See Ruth Hubbard, *The Politics of Women's Biology* (New Brunswick, N.J.: Rutgers University Press, 1992); and Evelyn Fox Keller and Helen Longino, *Feminism and Science* (Oxford: Oxford University Press, 1996).

6. Donna Haraway, *Primate Visions: Gender, Race, and Nature in the World of Modern Science* (New York: Routledge, 1989).

7. Londa Schiebinger, *Nature's Body: Gender in the Making of Modern Science* (Boston: Beacon Press, 1993).

8. Harding, Sandra, *Whose Science? Whose Knowledge? Thinking from Women's Lives* (Ithaca, N.Y.: Cornell University Press, 1991); Londa Schiebinger, *The Mind Has No Sex? Women in the Origins of Modern Science* (Cambridge: Harvard University Press, 1989).

9. See Keller and Longino, *Feminism and Science.*

10. Daniel Kevles, *In the Name of Eugenics* (New York: Knopf, 1985).

11. Stephen Jay Gould, *Mismeasure of Man* (New York: W. W. Norton & Company, 1984); Schiebinger, *The Mind Has No Sex?*

12. James Jones, "Tuskegee Syphilis Experiment: A Moral Astigmatism," in *The Racial Economy of Science: Toward a Democratic Future,* ed. Sandra Harding (Bloomington: Indiana University Press, 1993), 275–286.

13. For a detailed examination, see Sandra Harding, *The Racial Economy of Science.*

14. Emily Martin, "The Egg and the Sperm: How Science Has Constructed a Romance Based on Stereotypical Male-Female Roles." *Signs* 16, no. 3 (1991): 485–501.

15. Londa Schiebinger, "Why Mammals Are Called Mammals," in *Nature's Body*, by Schiebinger, 40–74.

16. Bleier, *Feminist Approaches to Science.*

17. Sue Rosser, *Biology and Feminism: A Dynamic Interaction* (New York: Twayne, 1992).

18. Anne Fausto-Sterling, "Building Two-Way Streets: The Case of Feminism and Science," *NWSA Journal* 4, no. 3 (1992): 341.

19. Rosser, *Biology and Feminism.*

20. Boston Women's Health Collective, *Our Bodies, Ourselves* (Boston: Boston Women's Health Collective, 1994).

21. See Ruth Perry and Lisa Gerber, "Women and Computers: An Introduction," *Signs* 16, no. 1 (1990): 74–101; Donna Haraway, "*Simians, Cyborgs, And Women: The Reinvention of Nature.*" (New York: Routledge, 1991).

22. Fausto-Sterling, "Building Two-Way Streets."

23. Keller and Longino, *Feminism and Science*; Nancy Tuana, *Feminism and Science* (Bloomington: Indiana University Press, 1989).

24. Evelyn Fox Keller, "Women Scientists and Feminist Critics of Science," *Daedalus: Journal of American Academy of Arts and Sciences* 116 (1987): 89–90.

25. C. P. Snow, *The Two Cultures* (London: Cambridge University Press, 1993).

26. I am deeply indebted to Mary Wyer, who has always asked the critical questions that have propelled me into areas I would never have imagined.

27. Donna Haraway, *Modest_Witness @ Second-Millennium. Femaleman_Meets Oncomouse^{tm}: Feminism and Technoscience* (New York: Routledge, 1996).

28. Bruno Latour, *We Have Never Been Modern* (Cambridge: Harvard University Press, 1993). Anne Fausto Sterling also draws on Latour's work in "Science Matters, Culture Matters," *Perspectives in Biology and Medicine* 46, no. 1 (2003): 109–124.
29. Latour, *We Have Never Been Modern,* 5.
30. Keller, "Women Scientists and Feminist Critics of Science," 90.

PART IV

What Is the Continuing Place of Activism in Women's Studies?

Women's Studies, Neoliberalism, and the Paradox of the "Political"

DAVID RUBIN

Women's studies is itself a site of regulation.
Rachel Lee, "Notes from the (non)Field: Teaching and Theorizing
Women of Color"

Throughout several recent essays, Robyn Wiegman calls into question the increasingly fashionable argument that academic institutionalization represents a dead end for feminist praxis.[1] According to Wiegman, the popularity of this view among some contemporary feminist scholars not only suggests a resurgent backlash against theoretical scholarship, but, more importantly, also suggests a backlash against one of the most successful projects twentieth-century feminism inaugurated, women's studies. This means, paradoxically, that academic feminism today has begun to turn, as Wiegman succinctly puts it, against itself. In the face of this problematic, Wiegman asks what couldn't be a more timely question: Why has the epistemological, pedagogical, *and* political intervention originally articulated by the "invention" of women's studies in the late 1960s and early 1970s come to be cast as that which now, in the new millennium, foils feminism writ large?

In meditating on this quandary, Wiegman implicitly raises but does not fully answer another essential question, a question I want to take up here: When contemporary women's studies is charged with being too "academic" and not "political" enough, what is the political *presumed* to signify? That is, what kind of work does the political do for women's studies and its critics, and is there a way to do that work differently, a way to move beyond the familiar reiterations and entrenched limitations of the theory/practice divide?

After a brief discussion of disciplinarity, neoliberalism, and what I call the paradox of the "political," this essay will offer a critical reading of one of the most extensive evaluations to date of the political status of contemporary women's studies, Ellen Messer-Davidow's 2002 *Disciplining Feminism: From Social Activism to Academic Discourse.*[2] My reading is intended as evidence that rethinking the presumed relation between women's studies and the political can prove valuable on at least three related counts. First, if we follow Rachel Lee in understanding women's studies as a site of regulation, it becomes possible to conceive the political as something other than a mere signifier of a particular social domain or camp affiliation. With an eye to the play of regulatory power within the institutional field, the category of the political comes into view as a profoundly powerful disciplinary device. Its deployment shapes knowledges and discourses. But it also shapes bodies and alliances, as well as the uneven grounds of thought and agency across domestic and international feminist scenes. Second, conceptualizing the political as a regulatory category brings into relief the shortcomings of binary and prescriptive approaches to feminist praxis. Though these shortcomings have been thoroughly critiqued in feminist discourse, feminists have also stalled on the question of alternatives. While I don't confront the reasons behind that limbo here, I do argue that more dynamic and subversive logics of praxis are available *within* feminism's vast critical archive. Third, rethinking the political as a regulatory category helps to resituate the enduring debate over the theory/practice binary in women's studies as not solely internal to the field but as deeply implicated in contemporary transnational economic processes, processes such as the globalization of neoliberalism. Placing this debate in global perspective raises important questions about the divergent political roles that women's studies can potentially play in relation to the forces of neoliberal hegemony today.

The Disciplinarity of the Political

Mari Jo Buhle has argued that women's studies, unlike other disciplines, emerged out of the political analyses fashioned by twentieth-century social movements.[3] According to Marilyn Jacoby Boxer, women's studies originated in the United States out of a simultaneous desire to transform the production of knowledge, the condition of women, and the sociopolitical landscape as a whole.[4] Both Buhle and Boxer hold that a unique or genuine proximity to the political is a pivotal ideal upon which women's studies was built. By centering the political, their goal is to preserve at the very heart of women's studies a strong link between the question of social justice and the practices of feminist teaching and scholarship.

From Wiegman's perspective, privileging the political in this way also has at least one crucial drawback. In "Academic Feminism Against Itself" Wiegman points out that the political can become a disciplinary mandate in women's studies, subjecting forms of feminist thought and praxis that stray from the normative definition of the "political" to regulatory consequences.[5] To counter the disciplinarity that results from institutionalizing the political as the field's raison d'être, Wiegman suggests that the relation between women's studies and the political ought to be supplemented by theoretical inquiry and critique. Though she does not deny that some forms of academic feminism may have more practical applications than others, Wiegman also emphasizes the need to question the disciplinary operations of the "practical" in women's studies. Why automatically privilege, she queries, the instrumentalization of practice and politics over their analytic theorization? Hasn't women's studies demonstrated the need to be critical of the emphasis on instrumentalization in other domains, such as body politics and labor, wherein instrumentalization means precisely women's sexual and economic exploitation? Wiegman thus defends the production of theory in women's studies precisely for its non-instrumental value, which she invests for its power to generate self-reflexive feminist epistemologies, unconventional historiographies of women's studies and feminism, and non-normative political imaginaries.

Though Wiegman's immediate goal is to forestall the backlash against theory in women's studies, I think her analysis also points toward other productive directions of study. When Wiegman asks in passing how the long-standing debate over the theory/practice divide in women's studies is being reshaped by the transnational corporatization of the university—wherein, as the late Bill Readings predicted, anti-intellectualism and market rationality have begun to supplant practices of intellectual inquiry and ethical accountability[6]—she highlights the need for fostering politically attentive *and* theoretically rigorous accounts of globalization's intersection with the institutional formation of the field. In this respect, Wiegman's analysis enables me to argue that the question of women's studies and the political also deserves to be situated in relation to the rise of what political economists and counter-globalization activists have begun to call neoliberalism.

The Politics of Neoliberalism

In contemporary political theory, neoliberalism is referenced as the set of dominant ideas and practices that supports global capitalism.[7] In general, leftist critics theorize neoliberalism as a powerful, refurbished liberal economic philosophy which, as Wendy Brown argues, eschews the "political" concerns of liberalism—"poverty, social deracination, cultural decimation, long term resource depletion and environmental destruction"—but privileges liberalism's economic component.[8] Dating back to fiscal developments that began to congeal unevenly around the world in the late 1960s and early 1970s, neoliberalism as economic doctrine rationalizes and promotes the expansion of the so-called free market. More precisely, neoliberalism takes an administrative role in a set of ongoing transformations in the structure of global capitalism. These transformations include the international integration of national financial markets, the expansion of transnational corporate power, the shift to post-Fordist strategies of flexible accumulation, the dismantling of international trade regulations, the intensive privatization of nearly every imaginable sector of market space, and the escalating proletarianization of the majority of the global workforce.[9]

According to Walter D. Mignolo, neoliberalism's contemporary globalization represents a hegemony unparalleled except perhaps by that of European empire during the period of colonial modernity.[10] Furthermore, Mignolo suggests that neoliberalism is, in fact, fundamentally based on a set of economic principles inextricable from the ideology of coloniality itself, an ideology which, he says, is today alive and well despite the "end" of territorial colonialism in the post–World

War II era. Like imperialism, neoliberalism is an economic and political system that is partly held in place by a complex ideological apparatus. While much neoliberal ideology codes free market expansionism *as if* it were a politically "neutral" process—as if neoliberalism transparently represented the unequivocal democratization of globalization—Mignolo contends that neoliberalism's success actually depends upon the discursive evacuation of questions of economic and social justice from the processes of its globalization. Neoliberalism's economic hegemony, Mignolo explains, is constituted by a conglomeration of interactions that empower mobile corporate entities by amplifying their ability to control flows of goods, information, labor, and capital. At the same time, the rise in corporate power is relative to the increasing disenfranchisement of flexible laboring bodies. As a pro-corporate, market-centered rationality, neoliberalism is an economic orthodoxy that strives to instrumentalize the interests of capital accumulation at all costs—indeed, often no matter what the human and planetary cost.

I turn to neoliberalism here to complicate the question of the relation between women's studies and the political with which I began. If neoliberal globalization constitutes the attempt to universalize the subjugation of politics under the rule of economics, then "being political" would have to in some way involve refusing that hierarchy. But what would it mean for women's studies to be political in this sense? In order to get at the challenges opened up by that question, let me explain what I call the paradox of the "political" before examining some of the reasons why it may become crucial for women's studies to theorize a radical critique of neoliberalism in the immediate future.

The Paradox of the "Political"

*Why would the problem of identification not be, in general, the essential problem
of the political?*
        Philippe Lacoue-Labarthe, "Transcendence Ends in Politics"

Carl Schmitt's famous maxim holds that the "political" formally emerges when one can distinguish friend from enemy.[11] In more abstract terms, Ernesto Laclau and Chantal Mouffe define antagonism as the constitutive element of politics.[12] This means, as Donna Haraway has shown, that "objective" political analysis is impossible insofar as political analysis always involves an act of situated judgment that is politically biased toward particular interests.[13] As Haraway is careful to stress, situatedness doesn't imply relativism. Rather, recognizing situatedness is a crucial step toward generating better knowledges. The problem is that situatedness also embeds politics into a logic of paradox. Since no political act can extricate itself from the realm of situated judgment, politics cannot transcend antagonism. Even if one's politics are a politics of "peace," those politics still seek to eradicate other forms of politics such as the politics of "violence." That desire for eradication, though intended to suppress violence, replicates the structure of antagonism that the politics of peace finds unjust in the politics of violence.

The quandary here is that, in seeking to be political, a field such as women's studies can potentially reproduce practices that much of its institutional energy has been dedicated to critiquing, practices that establish various hierarchies and perpetuate the inequalities which they generate. This dilemma is compounded by the fact that within politics, wherein utopian vision and empirical description often coalesce with ideological operations, the moment of political judgment remains irreducibly situated. That politics is ideologically saturated goes without saying. But if, following Paul de Man, we define "ideology" as the confusion of reference with phenomenalism, then politics is also about parading the performative as the constative, staging the prescriptive as the descriptive.[14] Put differently, supporting a politics implies not simply an antagonism toward alternative political programs, but an antagonism aimed at their suppression. In this sense, the political is always already constituted by a double movement, an opening and a closure: the political is at once a flight toward the possibilization of antagonism and a flight toward its impossibilization. This is, in short, its governing paradox.

I noted above that women's studies is now more frequently than ever derided for having become a politically impoverished institution. That is, women's studies is today accused by many of having become the "enemy" of feminist politics. Thus Ellen Messer-Davidow's *Disciplining Feminism* suggests that the goal of women's studies ought to be to reclaim the political by rejecting academic feminism's theoretical turn and by instead courting capital and the nation-state as political resources. As I hope to show, Messer-Davidow's argument at once exemplifies the paradox of the "political" and opens up the question of neoliberalism proper. Within the political context of neoliberal hegemony as I outlined it above, if women's studies was to court the nation-state and capital without radically opposing their exploitative configuration under transnational capitalist conditions, women's studies could itself feasibly become complicit with the extension of the vast inequalities produced by the globalization of neoliberalism.

The Politics of Institutionalization in Global Perspective

In *Disciplining Feminism: From Social Activism to Academic Discourse,* Messer-Davidow considers whether feminism's academic institutionalization has contributed to the dismantling of feminism as a political enterprise. As her subtitle indicates, Messer-Davidow argues that feminism's historical passage from the "streets" to the "university" was a process in which the move "from social activism to academic discourse" ultimately disciplined feminism's political promise. To make this argument, Messer-Davidow analyzes the problems feminists originally faced when institutionalizing women's studies and the problems they now face as a result of its institutionalization. Part 1 of the book, "Confronting the Institutional-Disciplinary Order," asks how the institutional structures of the university affected women during the rise of the second-wave movement. Here Messer-Davidow shows how and why second-wave feminism articulated a profound political challenge to the climate of sexist oppression in the 1960s, and she also delineates how the U.S. social order responded by attempting to reconsolidate its masculinist hegemony across social, legal, and university discourses. Feminism's full-fledged integration into the academy is the crux of part 2, "Institutionalizing and Intellectualizing Feminist Studies." Assessing the normalizing functions of institutionalization, Messer-Davidow claims that the expansion of feminist knowledges (in the forms sanctioned by the disciplines) also compromised the political potential of academic feminism. The third and final section of the book, "Crystallizing the Future," asserts that conservative organizations have been more successful than feminist organizations in constructing agencies for change. Recommending that feminists take lessons in political strategy from conservatives' victories, Messer-Davidow contends, "The solution today is not to abandon the national and local organizations [feminists] built but to retool them for greater political effectivity."[15]

While *Disciplining Feminism* is exemplary for the scope of its research and for its genuinely interdisciplinary methodology, its central thesis that academic institutionalization has circumvented feminism as a politics doesn't stand up to serious scrutiny. One could, for instance, cite any number of well-known studies that demonstrate the productive interplay between women's studies and contemporary U.S. feminist activist projects.[16] A stronger counter-argument, however, can be forged by expanding the analytic to include a comparative, global perspective. By doing so, I hope to suggest that had Messer-Davidow explored the history of women's studies and academic feminism in terms of the increasing development of international feminist activism, her study would have almost without a doubt reached different conclusions.

There are multiple sources on international feminism; Chandra Mohanty's 2003 article "'Under Western Eyes' Revisited" convincingly indicates the breadth and depth of this movement and the scholarship about it.[17] As essays from the collection *Transitions, Environments, Translations: Feminisms in International Politics,* edited by Joan W. Scott, Cora Kaplan, and Debra Keates, collectively suggest, international collaborations among women's studies scholars and feminist activists from East Asia, Europe, Africa, the Americas, and elsewhere have been central to the formation of feminism as an international phenomenon.[18] A quarter century ago, the United Nations Decade for Women was spotlighting the accomplishments of such joint efforts in the popular press.[19] More recent events, such as the "war" on Iraq, have been occasions for extensive collaborative organizing between feminist scholars and activists.[20] Though these collaborations have clearly encountered political stumbling blocks and sometimes fallen into distressing complicity with certain nationalist and capitalist initiatives, their existence is nevertheless a testimony to the lasting supplementarity between feminism as a knowledge project and feminism as a political project.[21]

While Messer-Davidow's analysis gives academic feminism short shrift in this respect, what remains useful in her account is the question of how feminisms become disciplined by various institutional forces. Following Messer-Davidow's analysis, students of women's studies and feminism are challenged to rethink not only how institutionalization disciplines feminism, but also how globalizing forces do—for instance, how the increasing privatization of the public sphere under the influences of neoliberalism, and the concurrent institutionalization of nonprofit-sector feminist activism, is regulating the shape of the contemporary political field.[22] Consider too that with the progressive withering of the welfare state across the globe, non-governmental organizations (NGOs) have increasingly begun to take charge of work that used to be allocated to the state.[23] Becoming institutionalized in assorted "civil society" formations, feminist NGOs, like other forms of institutionalized activism, have arguably acceded to many of the regulatory constraints of what we might call the institutional-disciplinary order of transnational capitalism.

From this angle, what Sabine Lang calls the "NGOization" of feminism can be understood in Messer-Davidow's terms as another kind of disciplinary technology at work in the disciplining of feminism.[24] As Lang explains it, the NGOization of feminism is the reduction of feminism's existence to the contained sites of non-governmental institutions. Lang argues that the NGOization of feminism is a process in line with, rather than a challenge to, neoliberal globalization. She suggests that feminist NGOs most often perform the role of crisis management, mediating between, for instance, transnational pharmaceutical companies and local reproductive health clinics, or between state judiciaries and domestic women's rights groups. In this context, wherein NGOs often work with transnational "development" agencies, which compete for rural subaltern women's participation in micro-credit programs, and bodies like the International Monetary Fund (IMF) and the World Bank enforce "structural adjustment" policies on impoverished states, it thus seems inaccurate to focus, as Messer-Davidow does, on the U.S. academy as feminism's primary political disciplinarian.[25]

The Straw (Wo)man Hidden in the Theory/Practice Divide

The privileging of practice is in fact no less dangerous than the vanguardism of theory.
            Gayatri Spivak, "Criticism, Feminism, and the Institution"

According to Messer-Davidow, academic institutionalization has generated for feminism a fundamentally irreconcilable gap between intellectual work and activist work, instituting what she calls an irreparable "cleavage between knowing change and doing change."[26] From this catalytic fracture, Messer-Davidow posits the resulting fracturing of actors from structures, individuals from communities, and academics from politics.[27] As the book description on *Disciplining Feminism*'s back jacket reads, "feminism in the academy . . . is now entrenched in its institutional structures and separated from national political struggle."

The argument that doing change and knowing change are made essentially incommensurable by academic institutionalization unfortunately continues to resonate with many people, including some feminists. To be sure, it is often difficult to see the direct applicability of theoretically dense scholarship to immediate political problems. However, my experience as an activist involved in mobilizing the fall 1999 counter-globalization demonstrations against the World Trade Organization (WTO) meetings in Seattle has given me a more complex perspective on theory's relation to the political.

By "theory," I mean analyses that set out to unpack, dissect, and rethink certain received assumptions, discourses, institutions, and power relations. For some of my comrades in the WTO protests, grappling with such analyses proved decisive for political praxis. Reading and discussing theory gave us the conceptual vocabulary and analytic tools to make sense of how transnational flows of capital and geopolitical relations between states partially structure people's life-worlds in contradictory but also sometimes systematic ways. Since neoliberal globalization is not a transparent process, its complexity demands that it be read with care. Recognizing this, the counter-globalization movement as I understand it uses theory to read the politics and the economics of global *political economy*. Its activism is constructed on the basis of its reading practices. And this is why the movement is increasingly becoming so dynamic. Counter-globalization is a struggle of cross-border organizing on multiple fronts, a mobilization against a whole host of forces: corporatism, U.S. imperialism, transnational exploitation, environmental depletion, feminization of poverty, war, racism, and numerous other irrevocably *political* problems that result from globalization neoliberal-style. Though theory alone cannot solve these problems, thinking theoretically about their underlying power dynamics remains an extremely useful resource for oppositional political movement.

As Liza Featherstone has demonstrated in her remarkable collection of writings with members of United Students Against Sweatshops (USAS), today counter-globalization activists continue to use theory for their diverse political projects.[28] These projects include international petitioning against the unregulated status of the IMF as well as more local actions like the spring 1999 sit-in by the Duke chapter of USAS in Duke president Nan Keohane's office. There, Duke USAS members protested Keohane's refusal to add a full disclosure clause to her 1997 university code that would list licensees' factory locations. After thirty-six hours of occupation, Keohane finally gave in. Similar protests, though not all as successful, have taken place at Georgetown, Wisconsin, Notre Dame, the University of Arizona, and elsewhere.

Coming from a perspective in solidarity with USAS, when I entered graduate school in 2001 I became suspicious of much of the theory-bashing talk I heard in classes and at conferences, especially from fellow graduate students. If part of our task as responsible graduate students isn't to learn the histories and languages of feminism and politics in multiple sites, then what should our task be? Having pursued graduate work in women's studies and cultural studies for several years now, it often seems to me that those in the academy complain more about the apoliticality of "theory" than most of the activists I have worked with. Perhaps this is just the idiosyncrasy of my own peculiar experience; I cannot say. Regardless, the argument that doing change and knowing change cannot constructively supplement one another feels too much like a ruse. Following Wiegman, I would contend that it is *this binary itself* that is disabling. When approached via a supplementary rather than binary logic, it becomes possible to see theory *and* practice as both relationally constitutive and relationally interrogatory—to see that they can and, indeed, do work together to enhance a variety of *praxes,* including the collective praxis of imagining and enacting political and economic alternatives to the neoliberal world order. Perhaps spending more time in the academy will someday convince me otherwise. But I hope not.

The following passage from *Disciplining Feminism*'s final chapter, "Playing by the New Rules," opens up a formidable juncture from which to rethink the argument that theoretical inquiry negates political practice. Messer-Davidow writes:

> What went wrong for progressives [including feminists] in the academy [was this:] We made . . . ourselves vulnerable by internalizing to academic discourses what we set out to analyze and change in society. Despite our professed concern with societal problems, our scholarly practices have recast them as discursive artifacts. The "problems" we now address get fabricated at the sites where esoteric theories collide, abstract categories rupture, and arcane knowledges avalanche. . . . [W]e became too driven by the imperative to criticize, too engrossed in particularizing identities and issues, and too busy sustaining our organizations on scant resources to keep the gradually shifting conditions of social change in view. And, sure enough, the gritty routine of doing all that work exhausted our energies, eclipsed our vision, and insulated us.[29]

Messer-Davidow argues that academic discourse makes what feminist scholars "set out to analyze and change in society" "internal" to the scholarly enterprise. At the same time, Messer-Davidow holds that "the gritty routine of doing all that work" forecloses other genuine political opportunities. In view of these divergent claims, it would appear that two different logics run simultaneously through Messer-Davidow's argument. Messer-Davidow figures academic discourse as both politically powerful (in terms of the damage it has done to feminism) and politically ineffective (as a means for positive political transformation). Further, she says that theoretical abstraction not only drives feminism toward political disaster, but does so in the service of nothing other than a "discursive artifact." For Messer-Davidow, what is especially distressing is that an "artifact"—a term commonly defined as "a product of *artificial* character"—has been the cause of so much "real" political damage. Implying that the political power of academic discourse is artificial, Messer-Davidow treats academic discourse as an analogue for academic feminism. She posits academic feminism as politically artificial, in other words, even while she focalizes academic discourse as a powerful institution of political influence.

What is instructive about these competing logics is that they highlight precisely the problematic implications of what Messer-Davidow preeminently endorses. That is to say, these logics expose the problems attendant to Messer-Davidow's recommendation that women's studies and feminism should reject the practices and traditions of theoretical inquiry. Indeed, these logics effectively demonstrate, against Messer-Davidow's stated argument, that there continues to be a *pressing political need for theoretical reflection and immanent critique across diverse forms of feminist scholarship and activism.*

Against the Neoliberalization of Women's Studies

Varieties of feminist theory and practice must reckon with the possibility that, like any other discursive practice, they are marked and constituted by, even as they constitute, the field of their production.
        Gayatri Spivak, *A Critique of Postcolonial Reason: Toward a History of the Vanishing Present*

In place of doing theory, Messer-Davidow recommends that feminist scholars ought to work toward aligning women's studies and feminism more broadly with structures she finds more capable of instituting political change, namely, the state and capitalism. Throughout the last third of *Disciplining Feminism,* Messer-Davidow compares academic feminism's discursive "abstractions" with conservative organizations' more concrete "machineries of their movement and [alliances with] the State" and capital.[30] Against this backdrop, Messer-Davidow calls on feminists to develop "a hard network" of progressive associations that integrate the techniques of state and market management with the academy, civil society, and the nonprofit sector.[31]

Messer-Davidow is worried, quite correctly, I believe, about conservative organizations' power to control dominant institutions of change. But Messer-Davidow also appreciates, in a critical way, conservative organizations' political effectiveness. Commenting on the Women and Poverty Project, the National Abortion Rights Action League, the National Institute for Women of Color, and the Older Women's League, she writes, "Although they [have] ranked up many achievements [these] feminist organizations impressed me as lacking the long-range vision, robust purpose-fulness, and coherent agenda I saw at conservative organizations."[32] "Conservatives, but not feminists," she explains, "[have] mastered the techniques of capitalization—direct-mail solicitation, endowment funding, and foundation support" for cross-sector networking, fund-raising, grant making, lobbying, and policy making.[33] Encouraging feminists to rethink their political priorities and strategies in light of conservatives' more successful methods, Messer-Davidow implies that women's studies ought to join with activist associations and move in the directions of corporatization, NGOization, and direct participation in state governance.

Many, if not most, academics and activists would probably acknowledge that activities like networking, fund-raising, grant making, lobbying, and policy making are central to myriad forms of feminist praxis, be they in the academy, in activist groups, or other venues. But when Messer-Davidow urges feminists and feminist scholars to dedicate themselves to these activities by embracing a paradigm shift toward "master[ing] the techniques of capitalization" and diving into the legislative process, she does not seem to register how the above activities also constrain political praxis. Under the parameters of contemporary neoliberalism, NGOs and nonprofit organizations are regulated by states, international associations (like the United Nations), and extra-national groups (such as the WTO, the World Bank, and the IMF). Meanwhile, states are regulated by international associations, extra-national groups, and financial markets. Unregulated organizations like the WTO, the World Bank, and the IMF—owing precisely to their unregulated status—are able to assert tremendous political and economic influence on all these other bodies. In this context, if women's studies was to incorporate itself into the form an NGO-, corporate-, and/or state-based organizational structure, such reorganization would not challenge the contemporary configuration of the international state-system and late capitalism which enables national, international, and extra-national bodies to work in complicity with corporate market aims to secure transnational exploitation on a global level. In other words, it is unclear how Messer-Davidow's proposals for changing women's studies could be directed, as she says they could, toward what she calls "distributive justice."[34]

Like Messer-Davidow, I believe that students and scholars of women's studies, as well as feminists at large, need to engage with the state and with capitalism in order to contest inequalities and injustices. But unlike Messer-Davidow, I would argue that a more subversive strategy of engagement is to radically challenge the state and capitalism via an insurgent, oppositional politics (such as that deployed by counter-globalization activists and USAS and cited above). Though Messer-Davidow compellingly argues against U.S. conservatism's "inequitable distribution of economic, social, and political goods," her strategy for making contemporary feminism more politically effective turns neither to Marxist nor to transnational feminist theories as critical resources.[35] It is exactly this absence of a radical critique of the nation-state and capitalism in contemporary globalization that opens up her proposals for prospective co-optation by what Wendy Brown has called, after Michel Foucault, neoliberal governmentality.[36]

In her final chapter, "Playing by the New Rules," this opening toward the potential neoliberalization of women's studies emerges when Messer-Davidow formally subsumes the question of the political status of women's studies under a consideration of the question of the future of "progressivism." In concluding this way, I would like to suggest that Messer-Davidow in effect covertly switches objects of study and conflates what are actually distinct entities. Or, put in de Manian terms, her analysis becomes ideological rather than critical insofar as it substitutes the linguistic reality of social movement politics for the phenomenal reality of academic feminism, a phenomenal reality her book had been up until this point centrally concerned with analyzing. Women's studies thus ends up taking the political backseat in her argument in more than one sense.

The final lines of *Disciplining Feminism* read thus: "Progressive scholars have paid a steep price for our achievements. While concentrating on our struggles to launch new knowledge projects in the academy, we became bystanders to the political struggles for everything else in the social field. Now that we have institutionalized these projects, isn't it time to call the question: knowledge for what? The answer is, as it has always been, up to each of you. But I hope this book convinces at least some of you to put progressive organizations and knowledges to work in the struggle over the nation's future."[37] In this passage Messer-Davidow's postulation of the cardinal fracture between "knowing change and doing change" reappears. Presuming this fracture to be the foundational result of institutionalization,

Messer-Davidow figures the academy as fundamentally separated from "political struggles for everything else in the social field." As I argued earlier, this universalizing logic prevents Messer-Davidow from recognizing academic feminism's intimate presence in a variety of locations across the social spectrum. Messer-Davidow overlooks the wide-ranging roles that academic feminism has played in international NGOs and establishments like the Ford Foundation and the Rockefeller Foundation; United Nations, World Bank, and IMF "development" projects; international groups such as Women in Black and Women Waging Peace; academic-activist collaborations like SIROW (Southwest Institute for Research on Women) at the University of Arizona and Barnard College's Center for Research on Women; organizations like NOW (National Organization for Women) and the Feminist Majority Foundation; as well as queer feminist activist groups like DAM! (Dyke Action Machine!) and the Lesbian Avengers. Bypassing the robust supplementarity between academic feminism and such groups, Messer-Davidow's totalizing vision makes it seem as if academic feminists somehow lived entirely in a world of their own making.

In forwarding this argument, Messer-Davidow's rhetorical strategy, like her critique of theory and her strategy for re-politicizing feminism, takes on a "disciplinary" quality in Wiegman's sense of the term. When Messer-Davidow uses the phrase "steep price" to refer to what progressive scholars have supposedly "paid" for their achievements, she implies that these "achievements" are not politically legitimate. However, Messer-Davidow's analysis of these achievements presumes that the language of social movement politics is the privileged idiom for evaluating progressive scholarship's political status. In making this presumption, it would appear that Messer-Davidow's argument relies on prescriptive rather than critical logics.[38] What I call prescriptive logics are forms of thought which supplant a normative idea of what (a given ideological position posits) *should be the case* in place of a critical questioning of what *might be the case*. Prescriptive logics prescribe or discursively project the appearance of what they retroactively designate as already established fact. What I find most troubling about Messer-Davidow's analytic, rhetorical, and political strategies is that the disciplinarity of their prescriptive dimension systematically forecloses the substantial history of the feminist critique of liberalism, the state, and capitalism—while at the same time suggesting in a precritical way that such institutions are exactly those to which feminists and practitioners of women's studies should ally themselves.[39] Though she does cite some feminist analyses of liberalism, the state, and capitalism, Messer-Davidow doesn't critically grapple with this body of scholarship's implications in any substantial way. Perhaps Messer-Davidow refuses to do so because, as she suggests in chapter 5, "Proliferating the Discourse," she finds such critiques to be overly critical and thereby divisive of cross-sector feminist solidarity. The kind of cross-sector feminist solidarity Messer-Davidow supports, however, would seem to be mostly that of the liberal variety.

When Messer-Davidow finally says that it is "time to call the question: knowledge for what?" and responds, "The answer is, as it has always been, up to each of you," I am thus left feeling the slight burn of what feels like a disingenuous neoliberal ideologeme. This claim entirely fails to account for the unequal conditions of access to representational technologies within women's studies, the academy, feminism as a heterogeneous international formation, and within the vastly uneven conditions of the globalizing world more broadly. Messer-Davidow would seem here to have "each of you" believe that institutional power does not mediate the production of feminist knowledges such as her own, when, in fact, the strongest argument of *Disciplining Feminism* is the suggestion that *it does* and powerfully so.

In her new book *The Twilight of Equality?* Lisa Duggan describes this sort of move as characteristic of a specific kind of neoliberal ideological practice wherein political neutrality is claimed ("The answer is, as it has always been, up to each of you") as a way to obscure actually existing political commitments.[40] Confusing reference with phenomenalism, this move appropriates democratic rhetoric in a context wherein neoliberalism may mean, as both Duggan and Brown suggest, the end of liberal democracy. From this perspective, it may be worth contemplating whether appeals to the transparency of the "political" enact a disciplinarity of their own, disciplining not only feminism or women's studies, but the possibilities of political praxis at large.

Conclusion: Toward the Radical Politicization of the "Political"

If feminism is set forth as a demystifying force, then it will have to question thoroughly the belief in its own identity.
      Trinh T. Minh-ha, *Woman, Native, Other: Writing Postcoloniality and Feminism*

Like Wiegman, I think that defining "academics" as apolitical does the long and complex history of feminist struggle a disservice. It does a disservice not only to women's studies but also to feminism in general. It denies the monumental challenges feminists overcame, which Messer-Davidow skillfully charts, as they worked tirelessly to transform the university into a positive space for the study of women and gender and for the cultivation of feminist knowledges. Indeed, in writing off the value of feminism as a knowledge project, defining women's studies as apolitical obscures the fact that knowledge continues to be a formative site of political struggle.

While it remains ever more crucial, as Messer-Davidow suggests, to make questions of social justice central to feminist scholarship, it also seems important to remember that women's studies, as Wiegman contends, is not entirely synchronic with or equivalent to a social movement project. When Wiegman writes in her essay "Feminism's Broken English" that *"'academic feminism' is not the solo referent for feminism as a political discourse and world-building force,"*[41] she implies that the politics of women's studies as a field *and* the politics of feminism as a social movement may, to borrow a phrase from Tani E. Barlow, "neither be reduced to a common denominator nor excluded from consideration when uncritically mobilized into story form."[42] When it comes to the relation between women's studies and the feminist movement in general, the difficult thing to recognize today is that though their politics are differentiated, their politics are not therefore ontologically discreet unto themselves either. Rather, their politics exist relationally and in relation to the politics of other entities and exigencies, in complex determinations that resist any attempt at either total unification or total dissociation.

Perhaps a more productive approach, then, would be for contemporary women's studies to pursue the radical "politicization of the political."[43] If political analysis is by definition based on situated judgment and is therefore always to some degree prescriptive, it would seem to be a pressing practical necessity for women's studies to theorize the "political" as a category of multiple deployments and significations. Indeed, women's studies needs to investigate the different deployments of the political so that it can more effectively deploy its own politics—which is to say, so that it can do two things. First, following Schmitt, so that it can more adequately distinguish its "friends" from its "enemies"; but also, moving beyond Schmitt, so that it may interrupt and intervene in and, if necessary, displace rather than reify that very determination.

From the perspective of this demanding work, women's studies may well need to rethink some allegedly straightforward components or suppositions of its political vocabulary, those which, in fact, turn out to be anything but straightforward or guaranteed in advance. What constitutes a "friend"? What constitutes an "enemy"? What happens when affirming one friend means turning a different friend into an enemy? What happens when a friend is also an enemy? What happens when the line between friend and enemy becomes hazy, illegible, or unintelligible? What happens to politics and political analysis when the fluidity of these categories is disclosed or effaced? What would happen if neither friendship nor enmity were a condition of identity or belonging? Beyond friends and enemies, would there still be politics?

The "political," it would seem, is a distinction that can never be completely fixed or stabilized. But yet, the political moment consists in the imperative toward that distinction's partial stabilization. So while the political remains a useful category when it comes to analyzing and challenging inequality and injustice, in its very usefulness it actually reproduces the structure of the friend/enemy distinction that, one would think, practitioners of women's studies, feminists, and others would want to question and challenge as well.

To conclude, I would like to suggest that the paradox of the "political" ought not to be understood as politically disabling. On the contrary, the paradox of the political is precisely what enables politics to continue happening—in spite of everything else. According to the late Pierre Bourdieu, what neoliberalism comes down to at its most basic is the desire to finally put politics to rest. For this reason, he ironically termed neoliberalism "the utopia (becoming a reality) of unlimited exploitation."[44] In the face of the hegemony of this nightmare, wherein no politics can claim a neutral relation to neoliberalism since its globalization admits no outside, perhaps an urgent task for women's studies will be to keep the paradox of the "political" both incessantly animated and immanently contested.

Notes

This essay is dedicated to a teacher and an institution: Tani E. Barlow, who originally inspired me to take up the question, and the Women's Studies Department at the University of Arizona, for pushing my thought beyond. For their enduring generosity and persistent critique, my deepest gratitude goes to Miranda Joseph, Sandra Soto, and Charlie Bertsch. For their teaching and commentary, thanks are also due to Diane Wiener, Laura Briggs, Barbara Babcock, Eric Hayot, Kari McBride, Suresh Raval, Kathleen Powers, and the *Women's Studies for the Future* team, especially Elizabeth Kennedy and Agatha Beins. Finally, I thank Juliet Ceballos, Solan Jensen, and Joshua Wilson, without whom my work would be an impossibility.

1. Robyn Wiegman, "Feminism's Apocalyptic Futures," *New Literary History* 31, no. 4 (2000): 805–825; "Academic Feminism Against Itself," *NWSA Journal* 14, no. 2 (2002): 18–37; and "Feminism's Broken English," in *Just Being Difficult? Academic Writing in the Public Arena*, ed. Jonathan Culler and Kevin Lamb (Stanford: Stanford University Press, 2003), 75–94.
2. Ellen Messer-Davidow, *Disciplining Feminism: From Social Activism to Academic Discourse* (Durham: Duke University Press, 2002).
3. Mary Jo Buhle, introduction to *The Politics of Women's Studies: Testimony from 30 Founding Mothers*, ed. Florence Howe (New York: Feminist Press, 2000), xv–xxvi.
4. Marilyn Jacoby Boxer, *When Women Ask the Questions: Creating Women's Studies in America* (Baltimore: Johns Hopkins University Press, 1998).
5. Wiegman, "Academic Feminism against Itself."
6. Bill Readings, *The University in Ruins* (Cambridge: Harvard University Press, 1996).
7. The following discussion draws on Michael A. Peters, *Poststructuralism, Marxism, and Neoliberalism: Between Theory and Politics* (New York: Rowman & Littlefield Publishers, 2001); Jean Comaroff and John L. Comaroff, eds., "Millennial Capitalism and the Culture of Neoliberalism" (special issue), *Public Culture* 12, no. 2 (2000); and Andriana Vlachou, ed., *Contemporary Economic Theory: Radical Critiques of Neoliberalism* (New York: St. Martin's Press, 1999).
8. Wendy Brown, "Neo-liberalism and the End of Liberal Democracy," *Theory & Event* 7, no. 1 (2003): http://muse.jhu.edu/journals/theory_and_event/v007/7.1brown.html.
9. Different accounts of these transformations can be found in Fredrick Jameson and Masao Miyoshi, eds., *The Cultures of Globalization* (Durham: Duke University Press, 1998); and Miranda Joseph, "Family Affairs: The Discourse of Global/Localization," in *Queer Globalizations: Citizenship and the Afterlife of Colonialism*, ed. Arnaldo Cruze-Malave and Martin F. Manalansan IV (New York: New York University Press, 2002), 71–99.
10. Walter D. Mignolo, "Globalization and the Geopolitics of Knowledge: The Role of the Humanities in the Corporate University," *Nepantla: Views from South* 4, no. 1 (2003): 97–119.
11. Carl Schmitt, *The Concept of the Political*, trans. George Schwab (Chicago: University of Chicago Press, 1996).
12. Ernesto Laclau and Chantal Mouffe, *Hegemony and Socialist Strategy: Toward a Radical Democratic Politics* (London: Verso, 1985).
13. Donna Haraway, "Situated Knowledges: The Science Question in Feminism and the Privilege of Partial Perspective," *Feminist Studies* 14, no. 3 (1988): 575–599.
14. Paul de Man, "The Resistance to Theory," in *The Resistance to Theory*, by Paul de Man (Minneapolis: University of Minnesota Press, 1986), 3–20.

15. Messer-Davidow, *Disciplining Feminism,* 287.
16. See Nancy A. Naples, *Community Activism and Feminist Politics: Organizing Across Race, Class, and Gender* (New York: Routledge, 1997); and Jean O'Barr, *Feminism in Action: Building Institutions and Community Through Women's Studies* (Chapel Hill: University of North Carolina Press, 1994).
17. Chandra Talpade Mohanty, "'Under Western Eyes' Revisited: Feminist Solidarity through Anticapitalist Struggles," *Signs* 28, no. 2 (2003): 499–535 (reprinted in this volume).
18. Joan W. Scott, Cora Kaplan, and Debra Keates, eds., *Transitions, Environments, Translations: Feminisms in International Politics* (New York: Routledge, 1997).
19. On this topic, see Judith P. Zinssler, "From Mexico to Copenhagen to Nairobi: The United Nations Decade for Women, 1975–1985," *Journal of World History* 13, no. 1 (2002): 139–168.
20. Elizabeth Hanssen, "A Meridians Report on MADRE: The War on Iraq," *Meridians: feminism, race, transnationalism* 4, no. 1 (2003): 132–141.
21. See the contributions to "International Feminism, Human Rights and the Women's Studies Curriculum: A Conference at the Nexus of Pedagogy and Activism," ed. Laura H. Roskos and Andrea L. Humphrey, *Meridians: feminism, race, transnationalism* 4, no. 2 (2004): 87–198.
22. On the privatization of the public sphere, see Teivo Teivainan, *Enter Economism, Exit Politics: Experts, Economic Policy, and the Damage to Democracy* (London: Zed Books, 2002).
23. On this question, see Colin Hines, "Time to Replace Globalization with Localization," *Global Environmental Politics* 3, no. 3 (2003): 1–7; and Nita Rudra, "Globalization and the Decline of the Welfare State in Less-Developed Countries," *International Organization* 56, no. 2 (2002): 411–445.
24. Sabine Lang, "The NGOization of Feminism" in *Transitions, Environments, Translations,* ed. Scott et al., 101–120.
25. On nonprofit activism and micro-credit, see Miranda Joseph, "Not for Profit? Voluntary Associations and the Willing Subject," in *Against the Romance of Community,* by Miranda Joseph (Minneapolis: University of Minnesota Press, 2002), 69–118. On "structural adjustment," see Pamela Sparr, ed., *Mortgaging Women's Lives: Feminist Critiques of Structural Adjustment* (London: Zed Books, 1995).
26. Messer-Davidow, *Disciplining Feminism,* 13.
27. Ibid., 207, 209, 213.
28. Liza Featherstone and United Students Against Sweatshops, *Students Against Sweatshops* (London: Verso, 2002).
29. Messer-Davidow, *Disciplining Feminism,* 287.
30. Ibid., 269.
31. Ibid., 288.
32. Ibid., 222.
33. Ibid.
34. Ibid., 270.
35. Ibid.
36. Brown, "Neo-liberalism and the End of Liberal Democracy."
37. Messer-Davidow, *Disciplining Feminism,* 288–289.
38. My theory of prescriptive logics is indebted to and inspired by Tani E. Barlow, "'green blade in the act of being grazed': Late Capital, Flexible Bodies, Critical Intelligibility," *differences* 10, no. 3 (1998): 119–158; Saidiya Hartman, "Seduction and the Ruses

of Power," in *Between Women and Nation: Nationalisms, Transnational Feminisms, and the State*, ed. Caren Kaplan, Norma Alarcón, and Minoo Moallem (Durham: Duke University Press, 1999), 111–141; and Miranda Joseph, "Analogy and Complicity: Women's Studies, Lesbian/Gay Studies, and Capitalism," in *Women's Studies on Its Own*, ed. Robyn Wiegman (Durham, Duke University Press, 2002), 267–292.

39. Examples of the kinds of critiques Messer-Davidow sidesteps include Wendy Brown, *States of Injury: Power and Freedom in Late Modernity* (Princeton: Princeton University Press, 1995); Lauren Berlant, *The Queen of America Goes to Washington: Essays on Sex and Citizenship* (Durham: Duke University Press, 1997); and Aihwa Ong, *Spirits of Resistance and Capitalist Discipline: Factory Women in Malaysia* (Albany: State University of New York Press, 1987).

40. Lisa Duggan, *The Twilight of Equality? Neoliberalism, Cultural Politics, and the Attack on Democracy* (Boston: Beacon Press, 2003).

41. Wiegman, "Feminism's Broken English," 86, Wiegman's emphasis.

42. Barlow, "'green blade in the act of being grazed,'" 136.

43. I owe the phrase "politicization of the political" to Miranda Joseph, who helped me theorize the idea during several formative discussions.

44. Pierre Bourdieu, "Neo-liberalism, the Utopia (Becoming a Reality) of Unlimited Exploitation," in *Acts of Resistance: Against the Tyranny of the Market*, trans. Richard Nice (New York: New Press, 1998), 94–105.

The Institutionalization of Women's and Gender Studies in Mexico

ACHIEVEMENTS AND CHALLENGES

LORENIA PARADA-AMPUDIA

In this essay I shall look at some aspects of the emergence and development of university centers and departments that promote feminism and gender studies in Mexico. Some of their achievements and limitations will be analyzed through a brief historical overview of the relations between feminism and women's studies. I will also outline some of the present conditions and challenges they face.

There are a number of features (often contradictory) common to the creation and consolidation of these units. For example, while nobody can deny the achievements the centers enjoy, they are also bound by the gags and straightjackets imposed by the alienating dynamics, cultures, and discourses prevailing in the educative institutions. Despite their limitations, these centers have contributed to the advancement of gender equity in society and have provided new learning environments for women.

Women's studies and gender studies in Mexico are the fruit of more than twenty years of personal and collective efforts by feminists to generate spaces in institutions of higher education. A number of factors have influenced the development of centers for women's and gender studies. Among them we can list the following:

The social impact of the feminist movement.

The relationship of some sectors of the feminist movement with the grassroots social movements.

The government and international agencies' policies toward women's and men's equity.

The particular origins and characteristics of each program.

The identity crisis of social sciences and humanities that opened possibilities for new issues of research and interdisciplinary work.

The specific structures of each university.

The long-term commitment of public higher education in Mexico to research, teaching, and service to society.

Changes in priorities in state policies toward education.[1]

In this overview I will focus on the energy of feminists and the constraints imposed by capitalist/patriarchal institutions.[2]

The 1970s

The new wave of Mexican feminism was strongly influenced by the 1968 student movement's worldwide claims for democracy, freedom, and justice and its criticism of the alienating and exploitative character of capitalist structures and institutions.[3] It was largely composed of leftist women, professionals, students, academics, and intellectuals. Despite their ties to political parties, working-class organizations, and other counter-cultural movements, feminists organized their own separate groups in their desire to not repeat those structures' inequalities in abusing power in relationships, in alienating the self and other beings. In their search to not have hierarchies that would subordinate or exploit others, they created organizations with no structures or at the most they chose horizontal ones. Being independent from any other existing organization was important in the construction of their identity. It provided them with the space and the time for critical reflection on their own thoughts and actions. They sharply debated the issue of political and organizational autonomy throughout this period.

The groups financed their activities with their own resources, including personal contributions and collections on the streets and public transport. They adamantly rejected collaboration with the government and were justly suspicious of international agencies. The feminist movement regarded the state as its adversary in its struggle for legalized abortion, day care, and effective legal protection against domestic violence and rape.[4] Not until the late 1970s were formal links established in a national front with trade unions and left parties. The National Front for Women's Rights and Liberation (Frente Nacional por la Liberacion y los Derechos de las Mujeres), founded in 1979, always discussed the need to maintain the political autonomy of the women's movement. It launched mass campaigns consisting basically in the broad dissemination of feminist demands.

This new movement did not restrict itself during the 1970s to specific demands; rather, it also criticized and debated everyday life, sexuality, power relations, the patriarchal family, and the very nature of human existence. Feminists contributed toward a new ideological, political, and cultural current for a change toward a more just, free, and egalitarian society for women and for all. Feminists in those times, according to Cristina Gonzalez, tended to exceed the limits of the existing order: "The possibilities for change of social movements are dependent upon their condition as collective actions, which tend to exceed the limits of the existing order, unlike others that are merely conflictual."[5]

At this point there were very few courses on women's studies; these were not required and almost underground courses in Mexican universities. As Tarrés Barraza asserts, feminists discussed women's conditions within the context of their own informal study and consciousness-raising groups, outside what they regarded as the essentially patriarchal institutions of higher education.[6]

The 1980s

This movement underwent changes in its mode of organizational expression during the 1980s. Feminist groups began to defrost the chilly relationship that they had with institutions as they decided that it was time to expand their scope of influence and to directly participate in grassroots community organizations, political parties, the mass media, and universities.

During the 1980s, a large part of the feminist movement formed NGOs (nongovernmental organizations) with international financing as a means of setting up programs that would provide services to women, particularly those in working-class neighborhoods. This produced transformations that presented challenges that unfortunately in most cases were not made explicit, shared, and collectively discussed. Among some groups, the horizontal structures shifted to more vertical ones. For example, less democratic decision-making processes took place where often the criteria used to evaluate were not open or transparent; the unpaid activist character of their participation changed to a professional, paid one, adding greater complexity by introducing work relationships to the existing political ones. The continuity of the organizations and their salaries depended on the grants they received from the international agencies.[7] A new arena of competition for economic resources and money among these NGOs was created, with non-explicit and non-discussed criteria and implications. What started as a political movement was transformed, with little introspection, into part of a new professional labor market.[8]

During this decade Mexican feminists broadened their horizons to include participation in international conferences sponsored by the United Nations and international women's networks that were organized around specific issues. Consequently, feminists began to lobby more actively with the government to respect the agreements and conventions to which it had subscribed. Both government and non-government sectors were forced to deal with women's political demands. The legitimacy of feminist issues was buttressed by increased financial support by international agencies funding projects promoting women's rights and organizing local, national, and international meetings.

Also, during this time Mexico experienced one of its worst economic crises. As part of its program of structural readjustment, the government decreased its annual expenditure on social development by 6.2 percent between 1983 and 1988. During this same period it reduced its expenditure on education by 29.6 percent. It decreased its expenditure on higher education by a whopping 38 percent from 1982 to 1987.[9] Mexican universities increasingly sought alternative sources of financial support.

It is precisely within this context that women's studies programs were formally established within Mexican universities. In sum, these were the following:

Growing availability of international funding for women's studies;

Shrinking government expenditure on higher education; and

Increasing recognition of the legitimacy of women's issues.

In 1983, the Interdisciplinary Women's Studies Program (Programa Interdisciplinario de Estudios de la Mujer) of El Colegio de México and the research unit Women, Identity, and Power (Mujer, Identidad y Poder) of the Metropolitan Autonomous University, Xochimilco branch, were founded. In 1984 the Center for Women's Studies (Centro de Estudios de la Mujer) was inaugurated at the Psychology School of the National Autonomous University of Mexico (UNAM). At the end of this decade, graduate certificate programs in women's studies were initiated at El Colegio de México and the Metropolitan Autonomous University, Xochimilco.[10] During this period these programs mainly focused on the following topics: family, employment, sexuality, violence, literature, mass media, maternity, and domestic labor. However, the topic of education, particularly higher education, was almost virtually ignored in Mexico as a research and teaching issue.[11] This would in part explain why up to the present there is a lack of scrutiny about feminist issues, values, principles, and strategies for mainstream curricular change and transformation of the educational system.

The 1990s

During the 1990s, new women's and gender studies programs were begun and existing ones were consolidated. A few disappeared completely; others were placed on the back burner as projects to be developed in the future. A notable difference in this period was the establishment of women's studies programs in public universities located in various states of the country. By 1999 there were thirty-five academic groups, although only nineteen were formal programs or centers in women's studies in Mexican universities nationwide.[12]

In general, the appearance of new centers responded to government and NGO demands for experts in this field. Research and teaching topics changed as well;[13] these now had shifted to reproductive health, the feminization of poverty, sustainable development, the environment, and masculinity. Worth noting is that international funding agencies explicitly considered these topics as priorities for research (mainly directed to diagnosis) and action-oriented projects. This pragmatic trend in women's studies also characterized the feminist movement. By the end of this decade it had largely been converted to NGOs, which rarely subjected the collaboration with government, international agencies, and political parties to reflection or criticism.

During the 1990s feminists also channeled their efforts toward the "dissemination" of feminist thought and research. For example, there are at least two specialized libraries in institutions of higher education; approximately 40 percent of the holdings are in English and the rest almost exclusively in Spanish.[14] Two of the centers also have their own publishing programs in order to support teaching and research in the field either with translations of texts from other languages or locally produced works. In 1990 *debate feminista,* a semi-annual journal that attempts to build a bridge between the feminist movement and women's studies, first appeared, although not from an academic center; since then it has become one of the most important feminist journals for the Spanish-speaking world. In 1994, the Women's Studies Center of the Universidad de Colima began to edit the journal *GénEros,* and the following year the Gender Studies Center of the Universidad de Guadalajara, a public university, published the first issue of *La ventana.*

The 1990s also witnessed the proliferation of women's studies continuing education courses and graduate programs. These included the following:

> Continuing education courses and programs at the State Universities of Michoacán and Colima and the National Autonomous University of Mexico.

> A graduate certificate program in gender and education at the National Teacher Training University (Universidad Pedagógica Nacional, 1998).

> An MA in gender and psychology at the University of the Americas (1991).

> An MA in women's studies at the Metropolitan Autonomous University (1998).

> Minors in women or gender studies in graduate programs (MA in rural studies, Colegio de Posgraduados, 1994; PhD in social science, Metropolitan Autonomous University, 1992).

All of these institutions were public except for the University of the Americas. This has been important for their social influence because in Mexico the immense majority of research is done in public universities and the majority of professionals are trained there.

By the end of this decade over one hundred persons held degrees in women's studies, thus providing an important pool of human resources for NGOs, governmental offices, and universities. However, the economic crisis also made it difficult to generate tenure-track jobs that would guarantee the future of these programs at universities.

Institutional Legitimacy, Collaboration, and Conflict

The fact that these centers have managed to keep going for more than fifteen years has won them a degree of institutional legitimacy; at the same time, such legitimacy is contingent upon the centers day-to-day relations with international agencies, NGOs, and government programs. Immersed in the organizational and political culture of higher education, they live in constant collaboration and conflict. While they enjoy having a basic budget and/or a place inside the academic and administrative structures, at the same time this makes them part of less democratic, strongly hierarchical, and heavily bureaucratic structures that still promote discrimination by class, ethnicity, and gender; this also makes them participants in evaluation systems that alienate individuals and groups. Among other things, efficiency is measured by quantity of activities instead of quality and most of the time evaluation criteria for the assignation of money and resources are not explicit and open. Their participants have to resolve the demands of traditional dynamics and structures of the universities while at the same time searching for the acceptance of new ways of working and new relationships among colleagues. Feminists in these institutions live most of the time exhausted in a creative tension of marginality versus institutional legitimacy.[15] In this way, the women involved have often lost sight of their personal and collective desires and utopias as feminists.

From Academic Legitimacy to the Transformation of Education

While the legitimacy of women's studies in certain disciplines of the social sciences and humanities (such as history, literature, anthropology, and demography) has been achieved, much remains to be accomplished to transform the educational system from, among other things, the individualizing environments of teaching and learning to ones more centered in the building and support of the community; from the anti-democratic and polarized modes of governance to more democratic, culturally diverse, and transparent styles; from the fragmented perspectives of the self to the integration of body, mind, and spirit; and, finally, from the teaching and learning perspectives centered in the intellect to ones that include the diversity of human experience, such as body-knowledge, knowing-intuition, creative expression, and spiritual insight.

Institutional Collaboration, Benefits, and Constraints

The fact of belonging to public universities collaborating with other institutions, such as the government and international bodies, has benefits for feminist development and dissemination. Nevertheless, at the same time this also imposes constraints. For example, participating in existing networks of power means that decisions are made and resources are allocated based on friendships, influences, and class privileges; it means they are part of objectives and priorities where they have little room, energy, time, and resources for addressing and following their own interests. Then their priorities often switch to developing the activities and projects that will bring acknowledgment and money for the institution. This creates a certain dependency on international bodies on account of the grants they have provided, while at the same time less economic support is given from university budgets.

With the passing of the years, the subjects of interest for feminism in Mexico have been enriched by the gradual incorporation of new areas of concern; yet, it is undeniable that this external support is having a determining influence on the orientation of the subjects addressed by feminism in the academic world. For example, according to the interviews with academics of women's and gender studies in Mexico, during the last ten years there was little financial support for research, especially in issues such as power relations, education, change and transformation, language, body, and spirituality, among others.[16] The more-developed issues were the ones found in the priorities of the international cooperation agencies, such as reproductive health, domestic violence, feminization of poverty, masculinity, and the environment. The discrepancy that may appear between the goals of feminism in a particular country and those of the international bodies calls for the establishment of collective strategies for negotiation that may yield greater benefits for the interests of feminism in the academic world. Since the early 1990s, some international agencies that financially supported women's and gender projects in Mexico had meetings to discuss their information and criteria for supporting projects and institutions. In 2001 the few national meetings of university centers and programs hardly ever presented and discussed information or criteria regarding their financial issues. Sharing information, discussing challenges, and creating collective strategies for negotiating with international agencies and other institutions could create a breakthrough against the underground competition for resources and produce better conditions to support feminist priorities in universities.

One of the risks faced by feminism today is the risk of becoming dissolved in its relations with the institutions, whether academic, political, financial, or any other kind. The principal challenge it faces, regarding both in its nature as a movement and its mission within the academic institutions, is to maintain its critical posture and to ensure the development of autonomous thinking oriented toward its own agenda, aimed at a new way of seeing, living, and building the world.

Some challenges for the near future include the following:

> To create different networking activities where criticism, transparency, reflection, and discussion can be maintained, "in order to be responsible and self-conscious in the choices we make regarding institutionalization and funding."[17]

> To maintain a critical posture toward ourselves and the women's and gender studies institutions where we work.

> To develop more inclusive perspectives and integral approaches to learning and research, ones that integrate the fragmented body, mind, and spirit in human potentiality. This means we need to include neglected dimensions such as the somatic, the creative, and the spiritual.

> To acknowledge and foster multiple ways of learning and teaching.

> To analyze the mainstream curricula.

> To integrate women's and gender studies approaches in the curriculum at all levels of the educational system.

To establish teacher training inside and outside women's and gender studies units.

Keeping our critical eye open and being more diverse and less fragmented in our practices and perspectives could create more grounded, integrated, and enjoyable ways of life that invite more younger women to join this path and create their own new agendas for the future.

Notes

This essay was originally presented to the Future of Women's Studies: Foundations, Interrogations, Politics, a meeting at University of Arizona, Tucson, October 20–21, 2000. I want to thank Mary Goldsmith and Dora Cardaci for their invaluable support.

1. See Maria Luisa Tarrés Barraza, "Notas sobre los programas de estudios de género y de la mujer en el México de los noventa," a paper presented to the VI Coloquio de Estudios de Género en la UNAM organized by PUEG, 1992.

2. I will speak from my own experience as a participant in the feminist movement as well as founder of two of its programs and centers; as promoter of two networks of university institutions in women's and gender studies, a national one in Mexico, since 1997, and the second one for Latin America, since 1992; and as a participant in a research project to analyze the emergence, development, and present situation of women's and gender studies university centers and programs in Mexico. See Dora Cardaci et al., "Los programas y centros de estudios de la mujer y de genero en México," in *Feminismos en México,* ed, Griselda Gutiérrez Castañeda (Mexico: PUEG-UNAM, 2002).

3. For research on the Mexican feminist movement, see Ana Lau Jaiven, *La nueva ola del feminismo en México* (Mexico: Grupo Editorial Planeta, 1987); Gabriela Cano, "Feminism," in *Encyclopedia of Mexico: History, Society, and Culture,* ed. Michael S. Werner (Chicago: Fitzroy Dearborn Publishers, 1997), 1: 480–485; and Gabriela Cano, "Revolución, feminismo y cuidadanía en México, 1915–1920," in *Historia de las Mujeres en Occidente,* ed. Georges Duby and Michelle Perrot (Madrid: Taurus, 1991), 5: 685–695; Marta Lamas, "Algunas características del movimiento feminista en la Cd. De México," in *Mujeres y Participación política avances y desafíos en América Latina,* ed. Magdalena León (Bogotá, Colombia: Tercer Mundo, 1994); Esperanza Tuñon, *Mujeres en escena: de la tramoya al protagonismo (1982–1994),* (Mexico: PUEG-UNAM/El Colegio de la Frontera Sur/Grupo Miguel Angel Porrúa, 1997); Cristina González, *Autonomia o alianzas: el movimiento feminista en la ciudad de México, 1976–1986* (Mexico, PUEG-UNAM Editions, 2001).

4. In the early 1970s the Mexican government, as a preliminary measure in the run-up to the UN-organized conference marking International Women's Year, began framing legal provisions in this area in order to clean up its international image. See Maria Antonieta Rascón, "Movimientos feministas y partidos políticos," 1971 report drawn up for the UNESCO; and Carmen Lugo, "El impacto del movimiento feminista en el cambio jurídico social," both cited by González, *Autonomia o alianzas,* 53.

5. González, *Autonomia o alianzas,* 18.

6. Tarrés Barraza, "Notas sobre los programas."

7. "International agencies" refers to institutions, some national and some international, that deal with the cooperation for development trough funding projects in the less-industrialized countries—such as the Ford Foundation, the John and Catherine T.

MacArthur Foundation, the Friedrich Ebert Foundation, NOVIB, Pan Para el Mundo, etc.

8. For more details on this processes, see Gloria Careaga et al., "Es la cooperacion para las mujeres," in *Mujeres y pobreza,* ed. Grupo Intersdisciplinario Mujer, Trabajo y Pobreza (Mexico: GIMTRAP/El Colegio de Mexico, 1994); González, *Autonomia o Alianzas;* and Marta Lamas, "Algunas caracateristicas"; Lorenia Parada-Ampudia, "Reflexiones sobre la independencia económica y la autonomía del movimiento feminista en México: una visión," in *La Mujer latinoamericana ante el reto del siglo XXI,* ed. Instituto Universitario de Estudios de la Mujer, Universidad Autónoma de Madrid (Madrid: Instituto Universitario de Estudios de la Mujer, Universidad Autónoma de Madrid, 1993).

9. Data from Friedman, Lustig, and Legorini (1997), quoted by Dora Cardaci, "Salud y género en programas de estudios de la mujer," draft of doctorate dissertation.

10. The origins, characteristics, and objectives of these programs and centers were diverse. The one at El Colegio de México and the one at the UAM-Xochimilco, although different in origin and structure, focused on research and developed postgraduate teaching programs, and these continue to the present. The third, at the UNAM, which focused on research and dissemination activities, was closed in 1991; in 1992 its library and two of its academics become part of the University Program on Gender Studies (Programa Universitario de Estudios de Género) at the same university. The Colegio de México is a private institution, while the UAM and the UNAM are the most important public universities in Mexico.

11. For a bibliography on this issue in Mexico, see Mercedes Blanco et al., "La docencia universitaria sobre la problemática femenina: facilidades y obstáculos," in *La docencia universitaria sobre la problemática femenina. Posibilidades y obstáculos,* ed. Mercedes Carreras Benedicho (México: UNAM/CISE, 1989); Olga Bustos Romero, "Las tesis sobre estudios de la mujer (y de genero) en la UNAM," in *Estudios de genero y feminismo I,* ed. Patricia Bedolla Miranda et al. (Mexico: Editorial Fontamara, 1989); Tarrés Barraza, "Notas sobre los programas"; Marisa Belausteguigoitia and Araceli Mingo Caballero, comps., *Géneros Prófugos: feminismo y educación* (Mexico: Paidos-PUEG/UNAM, 2000). It would seem—from the bibliographies that exists on the subject in Latin America—that this has been expressed in different ways in the countries of South and Central America and the Caribbean, regions where the conditions in which these studies have arisen and been produced have been different. Most progress has taken place in the study of the relations between feminism and higher education in countries such as Argentina, Brazil, Puerto Rico, the Dominican Republic, Costa Rica, and the English-speaking Caribbean. See works by Marcia Rivera, "El Caribe, los movimientos de mujeres y los estudios de género," in *Estudios de la Mujer en Puerto Rico: Marginalidad creadora vs. Agotamiento institucional la investigación sobre la Mujer en América Latina. Estudios de género y desafíos de sociedad,* ed. Marcia Rivera (Santo Domingo: INSTRAW-CIPAF, 1993); Yamila Azize Vargas, "Estudios de la Mujer en Puerto Rico: Marginalidad creadora vs. agotamiento institucional," in *Antologia latinoamericana y del caribe: mujer y genero: Periodo 80–90,* vol. 1, comp. Ivonne Siu Bermudez, Wim Dierckxsens and Laura Guzman, 115–136 (Managua, Nicaragua: Universidad Centroamericana, UCA); Yamila Azize, "Mujeres latinoamericanas y educación en el fin de siglo," in *Estudios Básicos de Derechos Humanos IV,* ed. Laura Guzmán and Gilda Pacheco (San Jose, Costa Rica: Instituto Interamericano de Derechos Humanos, 1999); Gloria Bonder, "Los Estudios de la Mujer en Argentina," in *Estudios de la Mujer en América Latina,* ed. Gloria Bonder (Buenos Aires, Argentina:

OEA, 1998); and Gloria Bonder, "Los estudios de la mujer y la crítica epistemológica a los paradigmas de las Ciencias Humanas," in *Antologia latinoamericana y del caribe,* vol. 1, comp. Bermudez, Dierckxsens and Guzman, 197–212.

12. For more information on these, see Dora Cardaci et al., "Los programas y centros de estudios."

13. For a thoughtful analysis on research agendas and methodological approaches in women's studies in Mexico, see Tarrés Barraza, "Notas sobre los programas," 13–16.

14. To date, the PIEM at El Colegio de México possesses a stock of 588 books, 80 journal titles, and a database with 28,039 documents, and at the UNAM the PUEG has a collection of 3,110 books, 392 journal titles, and 4,559 documents in its database.

15. As Marcia Rivera mentions in the subtitle of her book (*Estudios de la Mujer en Puerto Rico*) on women's studies in Puerto Rico: *Marginalidad creadora vs. agotamiento institucional.*

16. See Dora Cardaci et al., "Los programas y centros de estudios."

17. These are the words of an anonymous outside reader of the first version of this essay. I thank that reader and also the other two readers very much for their very useful, helpful, and enthusiastic comments.

Practicing What We Teach

JULIA BALÉN

$\mathbf{F}$eminist scholars exist in paradox. For those who inhabit this position, negotiating the paradoxes can be something of an art form. We teach about oppression in the midst of privilege, fight for greater recognition even as it often means greater co-optation, and teach about the construction and politics of identities in order to empower as well as to deconstruct the categories produced. Feminist scholars operate within and inevitably in support of capitalism, classism, racism, sexism, ableism, heterosexism, elitism, imperialism, etc., while working to undermine their operations and effects. We work for change within institutions while in the process of "becoming" the institutions—being produced by them. In material terms, we find ourselves caught between a desire for better lives for ourselves—surely a mark of improvement in the world—and the knowledge that our own privilege is gained at the expense of others within current systems of power. We negotiate between the demands of the institution and our desire for greater social justice. While thinking paradox might feel enlightening, living paradox often produces discomfort.

Resisting the many oppressive practices about which we teach requires that feminist scholars acknowledge our inevitable participation in oppressive practices, strategically working to mitigate them in the present, while also working to change our institutions over the long term. This presents serious challenges when administering women's studies programs. There are no ideal solutions—only provisional strategies in specific contexts. More than eight years of women's studies administrative experience has not shown me any easy answers. But the fact that ideal solutions are not possible cannot be an excuse to become comfortable or to suspend critical thinking when faced with administrative issues. If we actually hope to make feminist scholarship worth anything more than the paper it is written on, it seems to me that we must use the same critical tools that we teach our students whenever we are engaged in institutional interactions and decision-making processes. At the very least, we need to pose questions that interrogate our own positions of relative power and privilege and follow through with mitigating actions—however provisional.

What does the institution make of feminist scholars, relatively new members of academe, and vice versa? If part of the project of women's studies and feminist scholars more broadly is to transform our institutions to produce greater social justice, then how are we going about that and to what effects? Who and how might we be the institution differently? For some, transformation may merely mean more women in higher ranks. For me, it means developing and enacting personal and institutional practices that question all assumptions of power and all processes by which we deny social benefit to some for the aggrandizement of others, while working to remedy inequities. It means strategic use of the paradoxes of our current positions to shift the considerable resources of our universities in the direction of actively producing greater social justice throughout.

In her argument against privileging feminist social movement as the proper object of women's studies, Robyn Wiegman notes that the "urge to return to social movement to counter the forces of institutionalization" is a move that effectively disciplines the production of feminist knowledge too narrowly.[1] I agree with her call for feminists to support a full range of feminist knowledge production even in forums of relative privilege like academe. But I believe that this "urge" functionally displaces responsibility for movement. Limiting the proper object of the field to feminist or progressive social movement is like U.S. feminist attempts to intervene on behalf of women globally on issues like veiling or female genital cutting while at the same time failing to address problems like reproductive freedom for all women or welfare in the United States. Any privileging of social activism beyond academe as the "proper object" of women's studies displaces the focus outside of the scope where movement might more effectively be engaged by those making the claim—in our own institutions. Rather than objectifying activism or narrowly disciplining scholarship in the service of producing some personal comfort with the paradoxes of being feminist scholars, I suggest we engage the full range of feminist knowledge to more richly inform our institutional practices. Using administrative examples, I will consider a few of the paradoxes, limits, and possibilities of implementing feminist knowledge institutionally.

I articulate these concerns as I take up the project of helping to build a brand new university, California State University Channel Islands, after serving as associate director of a large women's studies department and as a founding member of LGBT studies at the University of Arizona, a Research I institution. These questions and suggestions are based as much on my scholarship on embodiment, subjectivity, and organizing for social change as they are on my early training in democratic group processes. I articulate these conundrums as much to keep myself conscious in my own actions, especially now that I enjoy the relatively privileged position of the tenure-tracked, as to encourage others to better integrate knowledge with practices in hopes that we all might improve our personal and institutional practices. I don't want to lose insights gained about institutional inequities from years of working "as if" faculty: serving as both BA and MA program director, chairing both committees, teaching, advising, hiring and supervising adjuncts, and managing research while serving in a year-to-year, twelve-month administrative position earning less than junior faculty. My analysis is based upon insider experience in positions of leadership usually taken by tenured faculty, but as seen by one who did not share the privileges of the tenure-tracked. I pose these challenges based on how I succeeded and failed, picked up the pieces and tried again, as well as from watching others struggle to creatively engage the knowledge we taught. I write this in the interest of offering some insight and hopefully useful questions to consider as we continue developing feminist scholarship and working for institutional change.

Administrative Opportunities

To begin, I want to briefly explore two concrete examples from the University of Arizona of administrative practices with which I was involved and from which we can begin to examine how we might better practice what we teach. The first is about developing Chicana studies as a concentration in the BA program, and the second is how the department came to revise its admissions and funding practices for the MA program.

Developing Chicana Studies

In the face of the university's dismal failures at recruiting and retaining faculty and students of color generally—specifically Mexican American, given local demographics—women's studies decided to develop a focus in Chicana studies by hiring in that area and developing a Chicana studies concentration within the major. It took the department over seven years of continual work to achieve some success: after several hiring failures and after a couple of promising hires were unsuccessfully retained, the department eventually hired two junior Chicana studies faculty, in 2001 and 2003, and a senior Chicana studies faculty member for fall 2004. The department learned a great deal, some the hard way, about the forces of institutionalized racism and the challenges of producing an environment conducive to supporting women of color on a predominantly white campus; this proved useful in developing the concentration.

As chair of the Undergraduate Committee, it was my job to steer the process of developing the Chicana studies concentration and revising the major accordingly. Faculty seemed to generally agree on the need to resist tendencies to tokenize, but that meant rethinking a constellation of classes that were largely born out of white, middle-class experience. The department also worked to recognize the leadership of junior Chicana studies faculty while not leaving the responsibilities for change primarily to them. We held retreats on curriculum development and met with faculty in Mexican American studies to discuss many possibilities, including shared curriculum, co-teaching, and how this might affect workloads. The committee researched what the concentration should consist of and which classes already taught in various programs might serve to fulfill concentration requirements. Some of the most challenging questions involved how major requirements supported or failed to support Chicana studies. Did our lower-division courses prepare students for an integration of race, ethnicity, and class throughout the curriculum? How well did the curriculum in general address these intersections? A sticking point that required the most negotiation was, if we required the Chicana Feminist Theories class as part of the concentration, how would it relate to Feminist Theories, the gateway course to upper-division course work upon which the logic of the major hinged. We wrestled with all these questions, discussing several different proposals.

We approved a four-course concentration that includes optional courses not cross-listed with women's studies. We also reconstructed the major to better support the concentration throughout by restructuring the general requirements: doing away with the tokenizing cross-cultural perspectives requirement and revamping the introductory course to integrate race more broadly throughout, with plans to do the same with the rest of the curriculum. While Feminist Theories remains the gateway course to upper-division course work, it is more clearly defined as a foundation for a second tier of courses in feminist thought that includes Chicana Feminist Theories. The department continues this project of curriculum development on several fronts: developing new core classes within the major and concentration; evaluating syllabi of non-cross-listed classes of possible interest for the concentration, to offer students in Chicana studies greater options; considering expanding the focus to Chicana/Latina studies; continuing evaluation of currently cross-listed courses with an eye to how well they support the concentration; and offering colloquia to intellectually engage affiliated faculty in pedagogical development of cross-listed courses that better support these changes.

While this work was fraught with all the paradoxes outlined above (especially producing identity categories even as we work to deconstruct them) and remains a fragile accomplishment given the forces working against its long-term success, it seems a good example of practicing what we teach in the moment and to the degree that the department assessed an institutional inequity; developed a strategic plan that marshaled resources to change it; engaged feminist, anti-racist knowledge against the grain of the current context to think through the issues; built tentative alliances across departmental boundaries and identity differences with other programs and individual faculty; and rendered the department identity more fluid, complicating what constitutes women's studies generally and institutionally by accepting classes that are not cross-listed with the department for the major. White faculty generally worked to understand their responsibility to address issues of race within women's studies and the institution more broadly and worked alongside faculty of color to produce opportunities for students and faculty that do not exist elsewhere. If white faculty continue to ask the questions that challenge their comfort, which is so necessary for producing a space for Chicana studies to flourish, the department might slowly change a part of the institution by creating institutional space for voices and knowledges that remain largely silenced. As they do, they will also need to keep asking what women's studies and Chicana studies mean in changing contexts.

Improving Graduate Funding Processes
Administrative issues rarely receive the same kind of intellectually rigorous attention as curriculum development. Not directly related to faculty research

interests and not perceived as producing a legacy in the same way that curriculum building does, they therefore do not tend to receive the same level of analysis or action from faculty without pressure. Fortunately for movement toward greater social justice, students often produce that pressure by applying what they learn in class to their own critiques. Some women's studies MA students rebelled against what they perceived as inequitable funding and admission practices in the face of department failures to adequately articulate a feminist funding policy. While they were reacting to a specific year's funding decisions without benefit of program history, their rage pressed the department to evaluate and codify the process.

As chair of the Graduate Committee for the MA program's first seven years, I oversaw the process of admissions and funding beginning with the second group of students admitted. As with any new program, there was no policy. When I first chaired the process, I facilitated committee discussion about what qualities were important to consider. In addition to academic excellence and knowledge of the field, given the lack of diversity in the first class, the committee agreed to include it for consideration. In my second year as chair, wanting to move the program closer to developing more feminist admissions and funding practices, I presented the criteria that the previous committee had agreed to and raised the question of considering need as part of the funding process, but, as one faculty member put it, "I feel qualified to assess academic abilities, but I don't feel I have the information to adequately assess need." While we did not directly consider need, we did implement a more general sense of balance in spreading funding more evenly. In my first three years as chair, while inevitably one to four students received all or some percentage of fellowship monies, the rest of the resources were generally spread more equally than not. We increased diversity for several years in a row through outreach, more active personal recruitment, and my negotiations with deans to increase funding packages.

As competition from the increase in graduate programs in the field grew, so did faculty frustration as we lost desirable candidates to other programs that could afford to give them better packages and/or offered PhD programs. The conjunction of frustration about losing these candidates and the desire to develop a highly ranked program in a competitive Research I environment combined to produce a committee that, against my arguments for maintaining a more equitable distribution, insisted on trying for one year giving the fullest possible funding to one or two "top" applicants at the expense of others in the interest of keeping those candidates. Under these conditions, my methods for maintaining a sense of fairness in funding, imperfect and limited as they were, were rendered useless. In the end, while as director of the MA program I took much of the brunt of the backlash that came, the student ire made palpable for the whole department the need to codify more equitable practices.

After much painful discussion between faculty and graduate students, we improved upon what we had already been doing for the majority of the program's history. The policy, now tested over several years, distinguishes between the admissions and funding processes and includes financial need as a factor in the funding decisions such that all students are admitted on equal footing rather than being ranked, and funding is determined by a list that prioritizes students based on four factors: academic excellence, community work, affirmative action, and financial need. Because the financial aid office never has FAFSA numbers soon enough for admissions, we developed a financial statement supplement that asks students about the level of education of their parents, how they funded themselves through their BA, what kind of support they currently have, and how many people depend on them for financial assistance. In addition, students must place themselves, socially, in their admissions essay. These elements together offer a picture of what students might actually require to join the program from which the committee works to strike a more equitable balance. Moreover, while the committee retains some flexibility in how it doles out the limited resources, no student is given a full fellowship out of departmental funds without also serving as either a teaching or research assistant. It is an art, not a science: I spent sleepless nights over how to weigh these factors. Nevertheless, since we institutionalized these practices, making them clearly available to students from the start, there has been substantially less rancor about funding.

This has not been a perfect system, but insofar as it has balanced, to a small degree, the issue of material differences between students, it puts in action what we teach. Like the Chicana studies concentration, this is a fragile work in progress. Faculty members can either choose to continue to engage the knowledge we teach in program decisions and actions or give way to institutional pressure to reproduce inequities. In the process of developing this policy, the faculty had to face the effects of inequitable meritocracy. The current system does not produce full equity, but it renders the process more transparent and requires faculty to challenge assumptions about what constitutes merit to produce somewhat more equitable decisions.

Notes on Feminist Knowledge in Practice

With these examples in mind, I would like to consider some key concepts that in the past four decades of feminist movement and knowledge production feminist scholars have developed, but that in my experience we do not often engage as productively as we might. There are many feminists from whose work I have deepened my understanding of feminist principles in action. Though they undoubtedly would emphasize and structure these concepts differently, those most directly influential here include Audre Lorde, Chela Sandoval, Donna Haraway, Janet Jakobsen, and Monique Wittig.[2] My purpose is not to develop the full complexity of either the knowledge that I assume feminist scholars are teaching, which we might better apply to administrative practices, or even to fully explore the paradoxes involved in attempting to do so, but rather to articulate feminist knowledge and administrative practices in relationship to each other and to encourage more conscious and ongoing articulation of the two. I develop some pertinent aspects of six important, interrelated concepts with some generalized examples based on not only my experiences, but those of other program administrators with whom I have discussed these problems—examples that augment the more specific examples described above.

1. We teach that identity, like all meaning, is constructed in each moment in any relating between social actors and therefore is intrinsically neither static nor natural and that this liberatory potential of identity production as process must function within a context of hegemonic social practices that relentlessly reproduce static identities into which we are all pressed to fit.

The constructedness of identity suggests the need for questioning all identity production—especially that which gives us stature. While academic ideals support deep questioning, university structures and history have not. For feminist scholars, the tension between the liberatory possibilities that new knowledge/meaning production enables and the oppressive normative practices that have served to keep the university a predominantly white, male, heteronormative, middle-class institution poses identity conundrums. For example, in some contexts merely claiming the position of feminist scholar still requires constant resistance while in other contexts such a position is one of power and privilege. In both cases, taking up the position provisionally can offer resistance to oppressive processes of identity production, but how many of us are willing to live in such provisional spaces interminably? Yet, becoming comfortable or identifying with any such position (e.g. oppressed feminist scholar or powerful feminist scholar) produces stasis, reproducing oppressive normative practices. Moreover, as the limits of liberatory practices become increasingly obvious and as we learn our own personal daily limits in terms of resistance, in my own experience, there is a tendency to increasingly desire the comfort of someplace we can feel known and belong. There is also a tendency to grow comfortable with what privilege we have managed to gain—always already problematically earned or unearned—without an ongoing conscious effort to figure out how that privilege might be exercised differently. As soon as we are allowed a place at the table, we are generally loathe to question at whose cost we enjoy the privilege.

Because negotiating identity is fundamental to how we are able to interact with others at all, it seems absolutely necessary that we practice as much kindness and generosity as possible with ourselves and our allies as we struggle for greater social justice. Failing to do so produces burnout and a consequent loss of potential for resistance and change. And yet, it is equally important to support ourselves and each other in remaining present with the discomfort that oppression produces and that resisting oppression seems to require. Resisting the desire for comforting definitions, we need to question our own identification with the privileges and powers conferred by our academic standing. How often do we critique our own identification with hegemonic values rather than just going along with the way it has always been done—whether the issue is graduate funding, program development, or labor practices—resisting our own comfort in the institution? If we are to practice what we teach, we need to keep all levels of identity consciously provisional and negotiable.

Administratively, we need to keep identity as process to the fore even as we work in departments or programs within larger institutions that structurally limit such possibilities. Developing the Chicana studies concentration was an exercise in this practice insofar as the department took the knowledge developed through critiques, largely by women of color, of practices that tokenize, reviewed the department's curriculum through that lens, and asked what needed to change in order to support and integrate Chicana studies. In the process it challenged women's studies core faculty to examine their intellectual identities, which required some level of acknowledgment of personal participation in racism. It was not an easy process, but to the degree that we were able to make it a thoughtful and generous process—intellectually and personally—faculty were better able to open up to produce space that goes a step beyond merely tokenizing.

2. Unity, when functionally a disciplinary demand placed upon individuals in order to be identifiable as a power block, renders movement static because it denies the complexity of differences between actors in order to be recognizable within dominant paradigms. Unity can only be liberatory when articulated in a moment of coming together with and through the complexity of our differences to produce new paradigms that allow for them all.[3] For example, any insistence that materially less privileged women, women of color, and/or lesbians accept their own erasure for the greater good of "women" or "women's studies" is a sure way to fragment and stall movement, contrary to the fears and claims of those who make such demands.

The paradoxes of administering interdisciplinary programs within discipline-based institutions exist at every level. Engaging "both/and" models within systems that repeatedly insist on "either/or" requires extra work and challenging choices. For example, many programs in their early development are happy to have as many courses and faculty affiliates as possible to substantiate fledgling programs and offer students more options for fulfilling degree requirements. Moreover, the felt need to remain cohesive in the face of institutional lack of support or outright hostility often produces relationships, if not institutional identities, that focus on working together for survival in ways that override intellectual differences—sometimes foreclosing for the sake of unity the challenges that new knowledge production might pose. Yet, as programs become departments with their own core faculty and administration, several shifts occur that pose conflicting challenges that might include the following: increasing division between core and affiliated faculty; core faculty in conversation among themselves about visions for program development that sometimes leaves affiliates both intellectually and structurally out of the loop; growing gaps between core faculty articulations of the field and how affiliates housed in traditional disciplines articulate the field, gaps that reinscribe the institutional schism between disciplinary and interdisciplinary foci; frustration on the part of students, who find such differing articulations of the field difficult to negotiate.

In both cases, attempts to maintain a sense of unity at the expense of acknowledging the complexities of intellectual diversity can lead to a piecemeal curriculum, while the desire to control the vision and development of the curriculum—the field's identity—can lead to damaging relationships with faculty who may have played important roles in the program's development. My previous department devised a multilayered approach to develop greater articulation of the complexity of intellectual diversity, specifically in relationship to the development of the Chicana studies concentration and the desire to resist any tokenizing. Strategies included creative intellectual forums to directly engage affiliates in discussions about specific changes in the program, particularly around integrating issues of race, that would encourage their assessment of their own courses in relationship to department changes; development of more specific cross-listing protocols aimed to allow flexibility across a multitude of differences while maintaining a new level of integrity for the curriculum, with regular review of cross-listed courses. While these strategies help keep communication open, they remain piecemeal. It seems important to keep asking what values we enact in these relations.

3. Alliances are necessary for movement. Creating alliances requires being an ally, which requires a willingness to understand and engage with the problems of identity and unity in movement in ways that inevitably challenge any sense of comfort or safety about one's own position. Anzaldúa's call for *mestizaje,* Haraway's call for cyborg consciousness, and Sandoval's hermeneutics of love are all attempts to articulate models for taking on the challenge that relational processes require.[4] Each in different ways calls for a radical fluidity of identity in relationship.

Such potential fluidity is particularly challenging in institutional settings defined by competitive territoriality. Given institutional imperatives to stake out positions that produce limited, recognizable identities, both intellectual and departmental, alliances are largely discouraged especially where money is concerned. From the hyper-individualized, entrepreneurial scholar to the institutional framework that rewards departmentalization, academic institutions discipline against strategic alliance building across units. But for scholars whose purposes are, at least in part, fundamentally challenging oppressive institutional practices to imagine something better, such alliances are foundational. (See Janet Jakobsen's chapter in this volume.)

An example of this inevitably provisional process of alliance building has been the development of lesbian, gay, bisexual, and, eventually, transgender (LGBT) studies on the University of Arizona campus. From the start over ten years ago there were discussions about what it means to develop another identity-based program. Undoubtedly largely due to the substantial role played by Janet Jakobsen in its development, we formed a committee that has resisted both any simplistic identity formation and standard institutionalization while increasing resources through alliance building both on and off campus. Instead of developing the standard academic programs or even a research center housed within a college or department, the committee functions directly under the provost and is supported by deans across campus enough to support a director and several research assistants and teaching assistants for LGBT projects and general education classes. While this structure is more flexible, it also requires more conscious attention to alliances; because its strength is in the diversity of its funding sources, every time there is a new dean or provost the committee must renegotiate. Since there is no permanent funding, the committee is not answerable to a single entity and can work more creatively across institutional and community boundaries.

Committee members have continually developed curriculum, indeed, the committee decided to develop a sexuality studies concentration within women's studies that parallels Chicana studies, but the primary focus has been programming the annual Lesbian Looks film series, a yearly speakers series, the activist collaboration project, and the Rockefeller Humanities Fellowships on Sex, Race, and Globalization—all of which have called for developing more conscious alliances. Given the state's conservative history, the committee's emphasis on programming that engages and integrates community concerns in more than token ways seems to have been an effective strategy because the committee withstood recent attacks from state officials while its programming and funding have expanded. Such creatively resistant management of university resources through alliances to better serve academe's highest ideals requires questioning all of the identities, structures, and ideologies that would contain movement toward greater social justice.

4. There is no subject position fully "outside" the system; only provisional opportunities for resistance within specific contexts exist. No one is free of the operations of oppression—internalized and/or externalized—and, therefore, each of us inevitably reproduces oppression in every moment that we are not actively resisting on every level.

Some might perceive such a claim as hopeless, but it actually produces more honest and strategic possibilities for effectively intervening in and resisting oppressive practices. If we acknowledge the full impact of hegemonic discipline, especially as regards our own unearned privileges, we can release guilt and get to work with a clearer idea of what we face, better able to assess strategies for addressing social injustice in ways that are less likely to reproduce oppression.

To do this, we need to acknowledge and own our power and privilege as well as our oppression because ignoring either leaves us dealing with only half the problem while also leaving us less able to creatively engage the power at our disposal for better purposes. Privilege tends to be blinding. While to those who enjoy less privilege, the blindness of those who have more is obvious, such blindness is also true for those from oppressed groups because we often develop identities that assume we lack privilege and, therefore, tend to deny what power and privilege we do have. Both the privilege and the oppression are true and our failure to remove the blinders that come with what privilege we do have will surely produce more oppression.

The graduate funding problem discussed above offers one example of what happens when we fail to acknowledge our relative privilege. Faculty make decisions that affect material conditions of students' lives with no personal consequences, which renders the need to codify the process less pressing for faculty. But within a context that encourages questioning privilege, students have a framework for questioning the failure to define processes that materially affect their lives.

Another example of the blinders of privilege is in the treatment of non-tenure-track faculty and administrators. Too many women's studies units, caught up in the increasing financial challenges of program development, can be just as ruthless in personnel matters as other departments—perhaps even more so due to implicit sororality, ignoring that power operates between feminists. A serious conundrum develops when the best interests of the program or the institution work against the best interests of the individual, as inevitably they must for those not eligible for tenure. For example, producing positions wherein the non-tenure-tracked are expected to act as if they are tenured or tenurable in terms of responsibilities and collegiality without comparable privileges puts them at a serious disadvantage. All of their work counts for the good of the department, while little to none may count toward their own career development. Indeed, such positions can count against one's career development. I urge feminist faculty to resist producing such oppressive positions at all, even against institutional pressure to do so. If we must hire non-tenure-track faculty/administrators, they should not be asked to take up program-building responsibilities without mentoring in relationship to their own career goals and clarity about how such work may help or hamper them. Similarly the non-tenure-tracked should not bear a service load that increases the privilege of the tenured and tenure-eligible. We must ask on whose backs we are building the prestige of our programs and departments. Who pays the price?

5. Meritocracies without full social justice are problematic at best and must always be regarded critically—including the ones we have successfully negotiated.

Valuing ourselves for being successful within institutional systems is a sure way to replicate institutional inequities. The whole academic enterprise is based on "merit"—the value of which has been studied and critiqued extensively for its replications of institutionalized oppression, but the application of this knowledge has usually lead to token efforts at best. The tendency has been to address these problems on the large scale of antidiscrimination laws, but to all but ignore them as they play out on micro levels.[5]

Even though we might be familiar with problems with meritocracies, there is a tendency, having named and analyzed oppressive systems, to act as if we no longer participate in them, especially if we identify as oppressed. As professionals in universities concerned with national rankings and "excellence," we may feel confident about judging quality within the narrow confines of our fields of study, but to what extent do we ask how those very judgments or qualities are based upon social inequities? If we are going to judge merit, we need to make serious efforts to assess to what degree unearned and problematically earned privileges produce the appearance of "merit." For example, to what degree does upper-class training to assume that one has the right to privileges automatically look meritorious? How does social training from economically lower classes automatically appear subservient and, therefore unmeritorious in academic circles? To what degree is merit based on sameness with those in power? To what extent does anxiety about adequately fitting into the institution—the need to prove the value of feminist scholarship—work to halt productive questioning of meritocracy? We need to better value our own scholarship by applying it to our own practices to develop concepts of merit that resist the reproduction of social injustice.

6. Silencing is a primary mode of oppression; producing greater social justice requires practices that counter this tendency at every level.

Feminist pedagogy has been at the forefront of changing standard educational practices that silence dissenting voices in the classroom, but as we move up the academic food chain it seems we are more willing to accept and participate in greater silencing of ourselves and others. As we gain greater privilege, we need to continue asking what cannot be said in different contexts to find out whose interests and knowledge production are being served and whose denied. Who might we be silencing in the process?

There are many practical ways to resist tendencies to silence ourselves and each other. The most simple include open and transparent decision-making processes—setting meetings at times when all parties can attend or making ways for people to participate if that is not possible; getting clear agendas and meeting minutes out in a timely fashion; making sure that everyone has explicit and reasonable opportunities to have their say on issues important to them.[6] If these are employed with special attention to all of the issues raised above, they can go a long way to producing more equitable environments for all parties involved.

Women's studies programs and departments face particular challenges in the increasingly corporatized university environment. Interdisciplinarity within highly discipline-oriented structures requires extra labor. Many universities are downloading central administrative labor to departments and programs without offering any additional support to employ people to do the extra work involved. Backlash against women's studies as a field and universities in general continues to erode public support. States are strapped and many failed to increase budgets when they had the money. In this context, the pressure to identify with the powers that be can seem overwhelming. If we have critiques of power in the classroom that are not applied in the faculty meetings, on committees, in departmental processes, or in the vision and goals of the department, then the disconnect is bound to produce anxieties in ourselves and our students. From my experience, employing feminist knowledge as represented by the concepts discussed above can help us improve our institutions and avoid becoming another set of cogs in machines that oppress us all.

Notes

1. Robyn Wiegman, "Academic Feminism Against Itself," *NWSA Journal* 14, no 2 (2002): 18–37.
2. Audre Lorde, *Sister Outsider: Essays and Speeches* (Berkeley: Crossing Press, 1984); Janet Jakobsen, *Working Alliances and the Politics of Difference: Diversity and Feminist Ethics* (Bloomington: Indiana University Press, 1998); Donna Haraway, *Simians, Cyborgs, and Women: The Reinvention of Nature* (New York: Routledge, 1991); Chela Sandoval, *Methodologies of the Oppressed* (Minneapolis: University of Minnesota Press, 2000); Monique Wittig, *The Straight Mind and Other Essays* (Boston: Beacon Press, 1992).
3. See Janet Jakobsen's *Working Alliances and the Politics of Difference* for a full development of these concepts.
4. Gloria Anzaldúa, *Borderlands/La Frontera* (San Francisco: Aunt Lute, 1987); Donna Haraway, *Simians, Cyborgs, and Women*; Chela Sandoval, *Methodologies of the Oppressed*.

5. Stephen J. McNamee and Robert K. Miller Jr., *The Meritocracy Myth* (Lanham, Md.: Rowman & Littlefield Publishers, 2004).

6. My own work in progress—currently entitled "Roberta's Rules: Practical Meeting Practices"—spells out democratic processes and practices in detail and should be available late 2005.

PART V

How Has Feminist Pedagogy Responded to Changing Social Conditions?

Antifeminism and the Classroom

LISE GOTELL AND BARBARA CROW

It is by now a familiar refrain that feminist politics and their institutionalized, academic expression in women's studies programs exist within a context of backlash. This generalized backlash has, however, entered into a new phase with the terrorist attacks on America and the new war on "terrorism." In the United States, Christian fundamentalist leaders blamed the terrorist attacks on the "feminists," "gays," and "civil libertarians" who have undermined the moral foundation of the nation.[1] Shortly after September 11, 2001, at a Canadian feminist conference on violence against women, a professor who is a woman of color and a Muslim feminist dared to speak out condemning the new war, calling attention to the blighted record of U.S. foreign policy, to the effects of Western domination for Third World women, and to the necessity of feminist opposition to the U.S. military effort.[2] In response, she was vehemently denounced in the national media. A criminal "hate speech" complaint was launched against her and the women's studies program in which she teaches received a barrage of hostile e-mails.[3]

All of this functions as a harsh reminder of the precariousness of the spaces that we as feminists have managed to carve out within the academy and within public discourse. But it also directs our attention to the space of the women's studies classroom as a site of resistance and dissent, not cut off from but instead inserted within a wider political context. The opportunities for antifeminist invasion of the classroom, we suggest, multiply in the wake of an intensified cultural backlash. Antifeminist interventions seeking to dismiss the diverse contributions of feminism and close down the space of the classroom need to be distinguished from student dissent and resistance, which are inevitable features of any process of knowledge production. This is an essay about dissent and antifeminism within classrooms and how to respond to them.

Women's studies frequently pushes students to the "frontiers" of critique. Its activist and engaged approach challenges students to reinterpret experiences and contexts. Indeed, as Leora Auslander comments, "[At] their best, . . . Women's Studies courses have productively minimized hierarchies, been systematically interdisciplinary, been responsibly open to new pedagogical strategies and effectively made connections between the academy and other social institutions and structures."[4] But what happens when antifeminist expression in the classroom thwarts this potential? How do we deal with what Annette Kolodny labels antifeminist intellectual harassment while at the same time maintaining an open pedagogical style?[5] As we have stressed elsewhere, a sense of "open boundaries" is essential to feminist teaching.[6] The space of the women's studies classroom is ideally a terrain of contestation, accommodating diversity, dissent, and the right to question. It must be consciously self-critical, recognizing the power inherent even in processes of knowledge production that profess emancipation. Our normative commitment to openness is, however, challenged when students use the space of the women's studies classroom as a forum for mounting antifeminist positions.

This essay will critically analyze some of the literature on feminist pedagogy. It will argue that feminist pedagogical approaches conceiving the women's studies classroom as a unified emancipatory space fail to provide necessary scope for dissent and thereby confirm the now familiar refrain of feminist teaching as a practice of political correctness. After defending the rationales for a feminist pedagogy of difference, the essay moves onto a discussion of student resistance. When we present feminism as a range of conflicting positions and encourage the articulation of multiple perspectives, do we leave ourselves with no basis to defend the intellectual space of our classrooms from antifeminist positions? Drawing upon our own experiences as women's studies professors, as well as some of the existing literature on antifeminism in the classroom, we seek to establish a careful distinction between student resistance and antifeminist intellectual harassment. We will develop the metaphor of the women's studies classroom as "public space" as a way of negotiating the limits of openness and distinguishing at a philosophic and ethical level the difference between debate and violation.

Pedagogical Reflections: Constructing a Feminist Pedagogy of Difference

A consideration of feminist pedagogy is a necessary beginning point for any discussion of the feminist classroom; this is because pedagogy forces an ethical and normative consideration of the kind of space that we as women's studies instructors seek to create. As Robert Hariman contends, "pedagogy should be construed less as an interesting application of theory and more as a means of reconstructing the arena of intellectual debate."[7] As we will argue, modernist variations of feminist pedagogy, with their emphasis on the women's studies classroom as site for the transmission of feminist Truth, fail to acknowledge their own dominating effects. These pedagogical approaches are thus inadequate to the objective of democratizing the classroom and fostering critical debate within it.

As many theorists now acknowledge, there is not one feminist pedagogy. It is even difficult to identify common grounds among feminist pedagogical approaches. Patricia Welch suggests that all feminist pedagogies share three fundamental principles: striving for egalitarian relationships in the classroom, valuing all students as individuals, and making use of the experience of students as a learning resource.[8] Kathleen Weiler goes further, arguing that feminist pedagogy is not only about questioning the authority of the teacher and valuing personal experience; it rests, most fundamentally, upon a vision of social transformation.[9]

One predominant variation of feminist pedagogy focuses upon the emancipatory function of the feminist classroom. Growing out of feminist consciousness-raising, this approach emphasizes feminist teaching as a practice of liberation. Underpinning the emancipatory approach to feminist pedagogy is the view that the oppressed consent to hegemonic meaning systems, locking their consciousness into the dominant ideology.[10] The function of the feminist teacher is thus to act as a transformative intellectual, releasing students from "false consciousness." Deploying an ontology of discovery, this modernist form of feminist pedagogy assumes that there is some order in the world that stands on its own.[11] The liberatory feminist intellectual must play a role in peeling away the disguises that distort reality, uncovering for her students the Truth of women's oppression.[12] As Jennifer Gore argues, "this is a modernist political project rooted in a view that individuals can be moved to recognize ideological and material domination by the Patriarchy and, in so recognizing, can struggle toward conditions and relations which give meaning to the principle of equality, liberty and justice."[13]

This emancipatory discourse of feminist pedagogy conceives power as both monolithic and repressive. While the locus of power may be contested (for some it resides in patriarchy, for others in capitalism, patriarchal capitalism, or racialized patriarchy), modernist feminist discourses are founded upon epistemological commitments to revealing the Truth of women's oppression. This Truth can be discovered through feminist methods rooted in the privileged epistemic gaze afforded by standpoints of marginality. Thoroughly enmeshed in the modernist conceptions of reason, in which reason is opposed to power, modernist feminist discourses seek legitimation of feminist Truth through its relation to worldly powerlessness.[14] In emancipatory versions of feminist pedagogy, then, feminist teaching is above all a political practice challenging a domination that resides elsewhere. In the process of revealing to students the character of their oppression, students become empowered in an atmosphere of "creative community energy."[15]

This vision of feminist pedagogy advocates an educational practice built upon "feminine ways of connecting with the world" and "women's distinctive, empathetic nurturing capacities."[16] The imagined classroom as nurturant space, rife with images of the feminist teacher as maternal symbol, risks inscribing our pedagogic practices in a confining image of femininity—the mother who has no desires, no needs of her own, except for the desire to empower and nurture her student children.[17] This vision also seems very far removed from the feminist classrooms we have inhabited as well as those we seek to foster, ignoring the inevitability of power even in those spaces we construct as liberating. As Gore contends, the feminist teacher cannot simply dispense with her authority "by maintaining an experiential realm in which shared narratives are assumed to equalize participants" or erase the "repressive potentials of her authority with a rhetoric of commitment to democratic relations."[18] Attempts to do so reflect a modernist conception of power as held, power which can simply be done away with.

The vision of the feminist classroom as an emancipatory space ignores its location within the disciplinary power of institutionalized pedagogy. Defined by university rules demanding organized curriculums, methods of evaluation, and the production of standardized mark distributions, the power of the teacher over the student is always present. Indeed, as Sneja Gunew insists, drawing upon the Foucauldian conception of the knowledge/power nexus, power structures are reproduced at every point where someone who knows is instructing someone who does not know.[19] This power is a form of surveillance circulating within the feminist classroom as it does elsewhere in the university. An emancipatory feminist pedagogy that calls for the "empowerment" of students very often fails to acknowledge this, with teachers imparting "knowledge"—supposedly neutral, impartial—to "empower" their students.[20] This discourse of feminist pedagogy ignores its own functioning as a regime of Truth, just as it obscures the self-discipline it demands of its students.[21]

The implied authority of the feminist teacher's understanding remains unproblematized within this pedagogical approach. Like the method of feminist consciousness-raising with which this approach shares epistemological ties, the feminist teacher acts as a theoretical midwife to the production of a true subjugated knowledge rooted in women's experience of subordination.[22] Emancipatory feminist pedagogy presumes that good, true, innocent knowledge—a form of feminist knowledge whose Truth is rooted in its "powerlessness"—will emerge in the liberatory space of the classroom. But as critics have argued, shared and homogenous experiences gain recognition within this practice whilst dissonant voices are silenced.[23] As Elizabeth Ellsworth asks, "What diversity do we silence in the name of liberatory pedagogy?"[24]

This is a question that those of us who inhabit the feminist classroom have been called upon to deal with in our day-to-day practice of teaching. The construction of the women's studies classroom as a homogenous, nurturing space has been critiqued because it privileges a singular form of experience, the experience of white middle-class women, as the basis for the construction of feminist knowledge. Our more recent efforts to present a complex account of women's lives in our classrooms has been the result of the well-founded critiques of feminist essentialism mounted by, among others, women of color and native feminists demanding acknowledgment of how race, class, and colonization have marked, shaped, and refracted gendered realities (see the introduction to this volume). Deconstructing the category "woman" and the idea of a universal experience of oppression is now a central objective of the women's studies curriculum.

But for many of us, our efforts to embrace difference within our practices of feminist pedagogy extend beyond the recognition of diverse experiences and interlocking forms of oppression. As Joan Scott argues, "experience is always an interpretation and always in need of interpretation."[25] In other words, given that experience itself only becomes meaningful through interpretation, context, and history, experience, even complex experience, cannot provide a ground for feminist Truth. When we recognize the role of interpretation in making meaning out of experience, we are forced to grapple with the role of the normative that always and necessarily intervenes between events and our understanding of events. The existence of interpretation, decision, and normative contestation cannot simply be exorcised from the classroom. When it is, as imagined by emancipatory versions of feminist pedagogy, dissent tends to be discouraged. When this occurs, as Patricia Lather puts it, "students in classrooms learn to produce correct answers, to follow a kind of 'group think' that repositions them within a sisterhood of oppressed women unified in their newly discovered outrage at the patriarchy."[26] While this uniformity is comforting and might seem to empower us against external enemies, it also operates to erase debate. Wendy Brown asks, "What is it about feminism that fears the replacement of Truth with politics, philosophy with struggle, privileged knowledge with a cacophony of unequal voices struggling for position?"[27]

Audrey Fisch, reflecting upon the experience of engaging her students in a difficult conversation about race and racism, has argued passionately about the importance of valuing conflict within the classroom. She argues, "I wanted my students to grasp that they, like the critics they read, might not always agree. . . . I wanted them to appreciate that passionate scholarly dialogue may not always end in neat resolutions and may be painful."[28] Conflict resides in the feminist classroom, just as it does within feminist movements. In classrooms where space is made for conflict, students can learn to live with the "uncomfortable awareness that others see things radically differently than we do."[29]

In our pedagogical practices, we have tried to work from the premise that feminist Truth must not be allowed to trump feminist politics. What this has meant is presenting feminism to our students as a historically evolving and culturally differentiated praxis that has always been a site of debate and difference. This is not to reduce feminism to an opinion or point of view. Instead, by introducing students to contending feminist perspectives and providing them with the analytical tools to dissect assumptions, compare interpretations, identify strengths, weaknesses, and inevitable ambiguities, we are providing a space where students think on their own behalf. In so doing, we are trying to "democratize" the space of our classrooms in a manner that is distinct from emancipatory feminist pedagogies. Our efforts are not motivated by a view of the feminist classroom as a site free of power. Instead, we try to acknowledge and interrogate the discursive power that exists even in our feminist teaching. In part we seek to negotiate power by engaging students in a feminism of difference; that is, a feminism that not only recognizes how power operates within the category "woman" but also recognizes the existence of multiple frameworks of interpretation. The kind of democratic praxis of teaching we try to build is one that takes into account the very real disciplinary power of our pedagogy and of our positions as feminist teachers. We do this by questioning our own preferred interpretations and bringing into our teaching the Foucauldian insight that there is no position free of power. Feminism and feminist teaching must engage in critical self-reflection, bringing the interpreter back into the narrative, embodied and invested in a variety of often contradictory privileges and struggles.

An Experience of Antifeminism in the Classroom

An analysis of the literature on feminist pedagogy allows for an ethical and normative reflection on feminist teaching practices. We must admit, however, that for both of us this is a recent intellectual endeavor. Placing ourselves within the rich debates that have developed in the field of feminist pedagogy has been a kind of backward journey, provoked by day-to-day and sometimes troubling classroom experiences. But as we have come to recognize through this project, "difficult and ambiguous pedagogical moments" can productively promote critical reflection.[30]

When the Chilly Climate Walked into My Classroom (by Lise Gotell)

In 1999, when I first met my introductory class of forty-five students, I was not surprised and not at all concerned to find that there was a male student in the class (I will call him Howard). Those of us who teach women's studies have all had many male students. I have found that, like women, men tend to enroll because they want to learn about feminist critical thinking and research; and, even when enrolled to fulfill degree requirements, male students have contributed to a respectful and productive classroom dynamic. The situation in my introductory class that year was anything but productive and respectful. This is because Howard seemed intent to halt the progress of the class.

I will give you some examples of his comments, comments that were interjected frequently in each class he attended:

"You feminists, you just want to silence debate!"

"Men have overwhelming sex drives; rape should be legalized; we should not criminalize nature."

"Young women use their sexuality to exert power over men."

"No one is holding a gun to women's heads to make them marry. How can they complain about the double day? It's their choice!"

A performance, not speech—Howard displays a pornographic magazine open on his desk during class.

You might imagine what happens. The other students are outraged. Some leave the class in tears. Many students respond angrily in class, engaging in a series of unproductive debates framed by Howard's interventions. The lecture topic is abandoned and we fall behind. Students line up at my office to complain about Howard.

I respond by calling him in to talk to me. With the supportive advice of my chair and the associate dean, I focus our meeting on his disruption of the classroom and his utter lack of respect for his classmates. He responds predictably by saying that we (the other students and I) are trying to silence his views. I write him a letter, copied to two associate deans, invoking our Code of Student Behavior sections on classroom disruption—all the while keeping my response focused on the theme of scholarly environment.[31] In other words, I emphasize the manner of his interventions, not their content and implications.

I become convinced it is my "open pedagogical style" that permits this violation of my classroom. Although I am (at this time) untenured and terrified of the possible repercussions of my actions, I move to silence Howard. This proves surprisingly easy. In response to his sweeping generalizations about feminism, I tell him that his comments do not address the specific topic of the lecture. I ask Howard to focus his commentary on the course readings, and I underline how these articles represent a variety of positions. After a few classes, he stops attending.

I learn, shortly afterwards, that Howard has a criminal record for assault and that he is being investigated in the sexual assault of a fourteen-year-old girl. Campus security has shared this information with the associate dean. While there is concern that Howard is taking feminist classes to "stalk potential victims," no one has alerted me. Although Howard has not appeared in class for several weeks, he frequently wanders through the halls of the Women's Studies Program and has not formally withdrawn from my course. Nervous and, finally, scared, I request that campus security attend the final exam for our course to ensure that the students are able to write their exam in a secure environment without having to worry about being harassed. Thankfully, Howard does not come to the exam. At the end of term, he is asked to withdraw from his program on grounds of academic performance.

The cost of this for me?

A course where we are forced to cut topics to make up for the class time wasted on Howard;

Many, many hours of anxiety;

More spent on documenting what happened, consulting with associate deans;

Time and energy taken away from my research, from my young son.

And all the while, I lived with the persistent feeling that I had failed as a feminist teacher.

This story is admittedly anecdotal. But when it has been recounted it resonates powerfully with feminist colleagues. When student resistance reaches rejection and silencing, threatening to stall the very process of learning, we are called upon to critically reflect upon our pedagogical commitments. Even for those of us committed to inhabiting the women's studies classroom as a site of contestation, there is a strong impetus to run back into the arms of the Truth claims on which the emancipatory feminist classroom is erected. This reaction parallels feminist critiques of postmodern theory. According to Nancy Hartsock, for example, interpretive Truth is necessary to justify feminist claims.[32] Without this Truth, she argues, we are left groundless on a hostile terrain. We might reframe this dilemma:

When we dispense with the emancipatory feminist classroom in favor of a pedagogy of difference, do we leave ourselves groundless in the face of student rejection and hostile antifeminism?

Situating Antifeminist Intellectual Harassment, Defining Resistance

In the space of such difficult pedagogical moments, it is important for us to draw out some distinctions between antifeminism and student resistance or dissent. Admittedly, the lines between antifeminism and student resistance are permeable and necessarily contextual. Nevertheless, we believe that it is essential to understand antifeminism in the women's studies classroom as a systemic practice, linked to and empowered by a wider social, political, and cultural context. As Marilyn Boxer reminds us, "antifeminism is as old as the 'woman question,' as is the history of denunciation of movements advocating women's rights as separatist, man-hating, and decadent."[33] Many social theorists have argued that antifeminism is a countermovement that needs to be understood in relation to the anxieties about changes that have been brought about through feminist activism, including advances in reproductive freedom, sexual autonomy, workplace equity, and family law.[34] Antifeminism distinguishes itself from sexism (although this is part of its analysis) by revealing the ways in which feminism has been "harmful," "hurtful," and "unfair" to existing relations between men and women. As a systemic practice, antifeminism's thrust is to undercut the modest progress of feminism both inside and outside the academy and to reaffirm unequal gender relations. Antifeminism's sense of entitlement comes from its ability to draw on dominant Western ideological practices entrenched in neoliberalism, neoconservatism, and an individualistic and abstracted conception of "liberal democracy."[35] Hence, its supporters can trump the individual and his or her freedoms at the expense of collective norms, in particular, a commitment to equality. This context makes it particularly pernicious for feminist scholars/teachers: How do we balance the uniqueness of the individual and the crucial importance of normative differences while at the same time acknowledging a complex context of hierarchal practices and policies that continue to subordinate?

As Pam Blake contends, until the late 1980s, students still tended to see feminism as being a part of their times, whereas by the turn of the millennium students were not so sure.[36] This shift can be attributed to the fact that the current political context within which academic feminism exists is one overshadowed by the backlash of the political right.[37] With the new ideological hegemony of neoliberalism, feminism, along with other equality-seeking political and intellectual movements, has been increasingly constructed as being outside of, if not antithetical to, a public good defined by the ideals of market efficiency, minimal government intervention, and individual self-sufficiency. The tendency to place feminism outside the realm of legitimate public and intellectual debate was starkly visible in the aftermath of the September 11, 2001, attacks on the United States. When Canadian professor Sunera Thobani made a well-reasoned speech that was harshly critical of Canadian support for the U.S.-led military action, the outcry was unprecedented, even though her position had been widely argued by other academics.

To an audience of feminist activists attending a conference on violence against women, Thobani condemned the violence of American-sponsored coups and military interventions, citing, among other examples, Chile, El Salvador, Nicaragua, and Iraq.[38] She drew attention to the "blood" of the victims of U.S. foreign policy, in the effort to bring the blood of the "other" into public consciousness alongside the blood of the victims of 9/11. This hard-hitting speech was greeted with thunderous applause by feminists attending the conference. But the vehemence of political and media reactions to Thobani's critique was completely unparalleled. Her speech was called "hateful," a "rant," "febrile misandry," and "hysterical,"[39] and Thobani was referred to as an "idiot" in the national newspaper, the *Globe and Mail.*[40] Her critique of American foreign policy was, in effect, cast into the realm of the hysterical, paralleling the gendered dualism of male equals rational and female equals emotional. Based upon the misrepresentation that Thobani had labeled the American *people* bloodthirsty, a criminal "hate speech" investigation was initiated. In editorial cartoons, Thobani was depicted as cloaked in the "costume" of the Taliban. Drawing on racist, antifeminist, and anti-immigrant currents circulating just beneath Canadian public discourse, the media constructed her as an ungrateful immigrant. Both the federal minister of defense and the premier of British Columbia, Thobani's home province, felt the need to publicly condemn her remarks and used this occasion as a way of discrediting feminism. In the midst of this, Thobani's Women's Studies Program (and other programs across the country) began receiving hate mail and she was forced to request that security be posted at the door of her classroom.[41]

The pillory of Sunera Thobani might, on one level, be seen as evocative of the neo-McCarthyism of the current political context, in which dissent has been silenced and cast outside the hegemonic construction of the "civilized nation." On another level, however, these events are a manifestation of a broader backlash against feminist, antiracist, antihomophobic, and other pedagogies of social change, pounding on the doors of the classroom and providing a context for antifeminist expression within it. In countless publications, women's studies and other identity studies are identified as a central culprit in the destruction of the intellectual environment of the university.[42] Antifeminism, wrapped in the popular slogan of "political correctness," has taken aim at the institutional progress of feminism and other critical social movements in the academic and intellectual life of North America. What is astonishing, especially given the competitiveness of academic publishing, is the uniformity of these attacks. In a now familiar refrain, the university has been politicized and political correctness has replaced the search for truth and objectivity as the mission of higher education. "Black activists, militant homosexuals and radical feminists," lumped together hyperbolically, are condemned for "politicizing curricula," enforcing "intellectual conformity sometimes by intimidation," and "turning whining into a science of victimization."[43] What this critique fails to acknowledge is the always situated character of knowledge and the manner in which the so-called cannon has been erected upon the silences of many. Abstract and decontextualized defenses of academic freedom tie these charges together. Of course, the academic freedom that is defended is a concept forged without the participation of women (especially feminists), people of color, native peoples, and gays and lesbians. Having played no part in defining academic freedom, the intellectual products of these groups are understood to be protected only so long as they conform to dominant paradigms.[44] Feminist critical discourse is cast as intrinsically political with no possible place in the construction of "objective" knowledge and public debate.

An absolutist conception of freedom of expression underpins this traditional conception of academic freedom, rooted in a specific liberal ideology privileging individualism and the uncritical adoption of a marketplace of ideas. Within such an absolutist conception, limits on academic expression are constituted as always unjustifiable; freedom of expression is conceived of as an unbounded right. For example, in his attack on "political correctness" in Ontario universities, Heinz-Joachim Klatt defines academic freedom in the following unlimited way: "We defend, therefore, the right to certain types of speech and academic expression which, in fact, we do not condone, and in some cases deplore. This includes the right to defend one another. It includes the right to express—the right of access to intellectual materials which express—racially, ethically or sexually discriminatory ideas, opinions or feeling. . . . It also includes the right to make others uncomfortable, to injure, by expression, anyone's self-esteem, and to create, by expression, atmospheres in which some may not feel welcome or accepted."[45] In this view, there are no boundaries on academic discourse; academic freedom is a concept defined in the absence of responsibility. The crucial importance of wide participation in intellectual debate is dismissed. The "rights" to exclude, silence, and harass are instead privileged, and implicit here is the privileged participation of those who would discriminate and injure through their contributions to academic debate. As Patricia Williams observes, this dominant view of academic freedom would protect "even the grunt of a Nazi" because it is speech, but would quickly condemn "hissing" from feminist instructors "because it's censorship."[46] A women's studies professor's right to engage in critical debate about the war against terrorism, for example, clearly falls outside of this conception of academic freedom defined from the center, as it becomes transformed into "hate speech" or even "hysteria."

The wide circulation of such views and the attention they receive in the media provide the external context for antifeminism within the space of the women's studies classroom. As Blake contends, given the pervasiveness of the political correctness critique, many students are predisposed to think that feminism is a "selfish special interest group steered by a cabal of male-bashing elites"; women's studies is viewed as lacking intellectual rigor, with feminist teaching descending to the level of "group therapy," providing a forum for professors "to indoctrinate students into a monolithic worldview."[47] This caricature, while resting on misrepresentation, does elicit, albeit in a grossly exaggerated manner, some of the problems that we have identified in emancipatory versions of feminist pedagogy. Yet, even when instructors consciously attempt to move from the conception of teaching as a practice of consciousness-raising, even when critical reflection is actively encouraged, this caricature persists. In the story told earlier, "Howard" frequently called upon the central texts of the "academic freedom" brigade in his efforts to silence the views of other students and dismiss the course materials. His insistence that he was being silenced through the practices of feminist political correctness provided a legitimizing narrative for his antifeminist interventions.

Antifeminism in the classroom can take a variety of overt and subtle forms, including intellectual devaluing and ridiculing of feminist ideas, political baiting of feminists, and at times physical threats.[48] As Kolodny defines it, antifeminist intellectual harassment is a practice of silencing, antithetical to intellectual debate and to the production of feminist knowledges. It occurs when

> (1) any policy, action, statement and/or behavior has the effect of discouraging or preventing women's freedom of lawful action, freedom of thought, and freedom of expression; (2) *or* when any policy, action, statement, and/or behavior creates an environment in which the appropriate application of feminist theories or methodologies to research, scholarship, and teaching is devalued, discouraged, or altogether thwarted; (3) *or* when any policy, action, statement, and/or behavior creates an environment in which research, scholarship, and teaching pertaining to women, gender, or gender inequities are devalued, discouraged, or altogether thwarted.[49]

Repeated dismissals of feminist perspectives writ large, the justification of violence against women and coercive sexuality, repetitive victim-blaming as a means of erasing the structural characteristics of oppressive systems, all justified by the appeal to an abstract conception of freedom of expression, interrupt the pursuit of knowledge in the feminist classroom, and intimidate other students into an angry silence. This is not merely disruption, even though this is the discursive framework that we as instructors are often forced through institutional pressures to deploy. To construct this kind of harassing action as "disruption" is to individualize and decontextualize, erasing its specific content and harmful effects. This is why the concept of antifeminist intellectual harassment offered by Kolodny is so useful. Behaviors and words that devalue and thwart the process of knowledge construction in the feminist classroom have systemic and harmful effects that are both linked to and legitimized by the broader backlash against feminism in our universities.

Resistance, by contrast, is dissent that may challenge feminist interpretations but does not seek to close down the intellectual space offered by feminism. Indeed, as we have tried to argue in our discussion of feminist pedagogy, any pedagogical practice, any claim to knowledge, even those with liberatory objectives, inevitably exerts power and produces dissent. As Gore, Lather, and Ellsworth have all insisted, our teaching practices necessarily exert a kind of disciplinary power on our students, of which resistance is an expected product.[50]

Resistance represents itself in the classroom in a variety of ways. Resistance can take aim at the course content, instructor, lectures, and/or pedagogy. It appears in particular kinds of behavior in the classroom, such as "body language conveying

silent dismissal, angry outbursts, caustic remarks, disruptive questions, loud whis-
pers, and so on," and quite frequently as comments in course evaluations.[51] In our
many years as feminist instructors at four different universities, we have encountered numerous instances of resistance, often the result of a perceived dissonance
between personal experience and questions raised by feminist, antiracist, and
antihomophobic perspectives. This dissonance arises, in part, because we teach a
generation of students who have enjoyed the benefits of feminism but are often
oblivious to feminism's role in achieving change and to the need for continued
struggles.[52] The following represent some of the forms of resistance that manifest
in the feminist classroom:

> 1. Refusal to acknowledge structural relations of power and privilege: *There
> is no sexual division of labor. I can be anything I want. Single mothers
> on welfare should use birth control. Muslim women shouldn't wear the
> veil when they live in Canada. Don't some women say no when they mean
> yes? I find this all so overwhelming.* The classroom very often generates
> profound discomfort as instructors encourage students to see their own
> positions within structural relations of power. Students challenged by criti-
> cal discussions of power relations may react with discomfort. They may
> express forms of the dominant ideologies that are grounded in a profoundly
> individualized understanding of social problems and in racist, sexist, ho-
> mophobic, and classist beliefs.[53] Students sometimes resist what they see
> as the ideological pressure to adopt a feminist analysis, particularly when
> they feel as though they are being characterized as victims, without any
> agency.[54]
>
> 2. The discomforts of critical thinking: *But what do you think is the right
> feminist perspective on pornography? Which is the best feminist theory?
> What do we need to know for the exam?* Dispensing with the banking
> model of teaching, in which students receive knowledge that they are then
> expected to reproduce, can be profoundly unsettling. The feminist class-
> room exists within a regime of institutionalized pedagogy, with pressure
> to perform framing many students' assessments of their courses. Critical
> thinking may sometimes be seen as messy, with right answers elusive. Dif-
> ferences from the banking model of education can be perceived as weak-
> nesses.[55] The effort to teach students that all knowledge claims are situated
> and to deconstruct the claim to objectivity can be misinterpreted as rela-
> tivism.
>
> 3. Resistance to theory: *The readings are too difficult. There are too many
> readings. There's too much theory in this course.* Both the emancipatory
> version of feminist pedagogy and, ironically, the political correctness bri-
> gade construct the feminist classroom as an experiential realm. Drawing
> on these images of the feminist classroom, students often exhibit a pro-
> found hostility to theory, which they see as being the project of patriar-
> chal theory. Students would not make the same comments about their

economics or philosophy courses, and they often resist the effort to situate experience within a theoretical context.[56] This could also be represented as a form of anti-intellectualism reflecting a tension that has been characterized as the activism/accessibility and intellectualism/inaccessibility in women's studies (see Robyn Wiegman, this volume).

This is by no means an exhaustive list of forms of resistance, but these forms repeat themselves in our experiences of teaching courses. Yet moments of resistance can be used to promote critical conversations in classroom situations. Strategies can be employed to manage resistance and to increase the potential that its expressions can evolve into productive learning, without stifling dissent in the classroom. For example, as Lather has demonstrated, student resistance to feminist teaching is accentuated by approaches that position students as passive victims of both structural forms of power and the learning process.[57] Attention to the achievements of feminist struggles, class discussions in which students are encouraged to debate strategies of resistance, and an analytic emphasis on agency can all work to subvert the fatalism that often accompanies the recognition of structural forms of power.[58] Techniques that foster agency and engagement with course materials can be deployed in the classroom and in course design. One important technique is a journal-writing assignment with personal evaluation of the course readings and discussions; this assignment can involve students in a process of critical reflection, where they can interrogate why they have accepted some knowledge claims but resist others.[59] We have also used assignments like the "outrageous act" assignment, where students are asked to perform a personal or political act of resistance and then share this action with the class. Assignments through which students are encouraged to embody or enact theory can work to subvert alienation from theory and make theoretical analysis more tangible and relevant. For example, in an effort to get students to understand and engage with the poststructuralist feminist insistence that both sex and gender are enacted through repetitive performances, a colleague has used techniques like classroom drag shows and gender workshops.[60]

These methods of enhancing student agency promote a creative learning environment where contestation is valued, not silenced, and where feminist claims are opened to critical debate and not closed down. But as we argued, if contestation, dissent, and resistance are inevitable, if not valuable, features of a feminist pedagogy of difference, antifeminist intellectual harassment is not. Antifeminist intellectual harassment exceeds dissent and resistance. Instructors need to exercise their authority from the beginning of every class to define the range of debate and set out ground rules for discussion. However, when disrespect, persistent attempts to silence other students, and the dismissal of course content interrupt the feminist classroom, instructors cannot be left alone to formulate a response. Antifeminism in the classroom defies the limits of our pedagogical practices, no matter how well thought out. Empowered by antifeminist and political-correctness backlash discourses, antifeminist intellectual harassment in the classroom requires institutional responses that specifically acknowledge its harms and defend feminist knowledge construction.

Conclusion: Classroom as a "Public Space"

In attempting to construct responses to "antifeminist intellectual harassment" that are at the same time consistent with the feminist pedagogy of difference, we are drawn toward the idea of "public space" as a metaphor for the classroom. The value of this metaphor is that it seeks to reconcile diversity and openness with respect. In a public space such as a park, people may be side by side doing entirely different things; a picnic lunch with children, demanding physical exercise, and sexual cruising can all peacefully coexist. This is because the rule that governs our interactions in public space is common regard, common respect. We do not need to be the same as one another, something suggested by the metaphor of "community" that underpins emancipatory feminist pedagogy, but we do need to coexist with regard to our fellow public-space occupants.[61] And it is this principle of equal respect and regard that antifeminist intellectual harassment violates when the conduct of its classroom proponents repeatedly dismisses the course content or devalues the input of other students. It is this principle that is violated when sexual aggression is justified within earshot of someone who has experienced rape. And it is this principle that not only feminist instructors but also our institutions are called upon to enforce in our classrooms.

Of course, the behavior of students enrolled in our universities should be held to an even higher standard than the metaphor of public space allows. Each student has made a decision to participate in a learning environment in which respect for others is a central foundation of intellectual debate. Women's studies students have made decisions to learn about feminist scholarship and struggles. When hostile dismissal undermines the learning environment for fellow students, institutional responses are demanded. As we have argued, the practice of a feminist pedagogy of difference is complex and often a struggle where student resistance is expected. Antifeminist intellectual harassment goes beyond the boundaries of dissent through its practices of silencing. Through its guerilla warfare–like tactics it seeks to halt feminist critique on a course-by-course basis.

To the extent that universities have responded to antifeminist intellectual harassment, it is quite often by squeezing this problem into frameworks that deny its specific nature and harmful effects. To return to the two examples that have grounded this discussion—an experience of antifeminism in an introductory course and the public pillory of a Canadian women's studies professor—institutional responses left the problem of antifeminist intellectual harassment unacknowledged. In the case of a very deliberate attempt to halt the progress of learning in a feminist classroom, university administrators defined the actions of the student as an instance of "disruption" under a behavior code. In this way, the antifeminism of the student's actions was obscured, as events were transformed into a depoliticized instance of misbehavior. This code, like many others, included provisions on both discrimination and harassment. If the student's actions had been categorized as discriminatory or harassing, there would have been much greater scope to contextualize both the actions and their effects. In the case of Professor Thobani, University of British Columbia academic vice president Barry McBride publicly defended her speech by appealing to abstracted conceptions of academic freedom and free speech.[62] Yet university administrators failed to specifically condemn the antifeminism and racism that were the basis of Thobani's pillory. Nor did they offer any defense of the important role of women's studies as a site for the production of critical knowledges, including as a source of expertise on foreign policy. The authority of feminist inventions in public debate, fostered by the institutionalization of women's studies, remained both unacknowledged and suppressed by a university response that leaned upon an empty appeal to free academic debate.

The public space of the women's studies classroom is one over which we are guardians and which feminist intellectuals struggled to create. And yet, its outermost boundaries are not ours to defend; this is the responsibility of our institutions. It is obvious to us that a more nuanced and power-sensitive conception of academic freedom, one which recognizes the vital role of critical knowledges, will need to be forged as a basis for this responsibility. Academic discourses whose thrust is to silence, exclude, and harass should no longer be the fundamental concern of defenses of academic freedom. Institutional policy responses to antifeminist intellectual harassment must proceed from the foundation of a power-sensitive conception of academic freedom. These responses must recognize the connections between antifeminism in the classroom and the larger social and political context of antifeminism and avoid treating antifeminist intellectual harassment as isolated cases of disruption, misbehavior, or, more perniciously, as the legitimate exercise of free speech. In both Canada and the United States, there are a variety of existing university policy mechanisms that could be used to create an effective response to antifeminism in the women's studies classroom, including so-called speech codes as well as provisions on discrimination and gender (and racial and homophobic) harassment in codes of student conduct. Institutional responses should embrace mechanisms that move the level of analysis from the individual to the creation of collective actions and responses.

Notes

1. John F. Harris. "God Gave US 'What We Deserve,' Falwell Says," *Washington Post*, September 14, 2001, C3.
2. Mary Vallis and Mark Hume, "Thobani Rant Called Hateful: B. C. Premier, Liberal Senator Voice Disgust," *National Post*, October 3, 2001, A3.
3. Hayley Mick, "Critics Question Media Coverage of Thobani's Speech," *UBC Journalism Review: Thunderbird Online Magazine* 4, no. 2 (2001). http://www.journalism.ubc.ca/thunderbird/2001-02/december/thobani.html (August 2, 2002).
4. Leora Auslander, "Do Women's + Feminist + Men's + Lesbian and Gay + Queer = Gender Studies," *differences* 9, no. 3 (1997): 2.
5. Annette Kolodny, "Paying the Price of Antifeminist Intellectual Harassment," in *Antifeminism in the Academy*, ed. Veve Clark et al. (New York: Routledge, 1996).
6. Barbara Crow and Lise Gotell, eds., *A Canadian Women's Studies Reader* (Toronto: Prentice-Hall, 2000).
7. Robert Hariman, "The Rhetoric of Inquiry and the Professional Scholar," in *Rhetoric in the Human Sciences*, ed. Herbert Simons (London: Sage, 1989), 226.
8. Patricia Welch, "Is Feminist Pedagogy Possible?" in *Changing the Subject: Women in*

Higher Education, ed. S. Davis et al. (London; Bristol, Pa.: Taylor and Francis, 1994), 156.

9. Kathleen Weiler, "Friere and a Feminist Pedagogy of Difference," *Harvard Educational Review* 61, no. 4 (1991): 449–450.

10. Patricia Ann Lather, *Getting Smart: Feminist Research and Pedagogy with/in the Postmodern* (New York: Routledge, 1991), 137.

11. Kathy Ferguson, *The Man Question* (Berkeley: University of California Press, 1993), 10.

12. Jennifer Gore, *The Struggle for Pedagogies: Critical and Feminist Discourses as Regimes of Truth* (New York, London: Routledge, 1993), 121.

13. Ibid., 122.

14. Wendy Brown, "Feminist Hesitations, Postmodern Exposures," *differences* 3, no. 1 (1991): 76.

15. Carolyn Shrewsbury draws on Carol Gilligan's work to constitute the feminist classroom as the embodiment of a feminine ethic of care. Carolyn Shrewsbury, "What Is Feminist Pedagogy?" *Quarterly* 15, no. 3–4 (1987): 9; Carol Gilligan, *In a Different Voice* (Cambridge, Mass.: Harvard University Press, 1993).

16. Jennifer Laurence, "Remembering That Special Someone: On the Question of Articulating That Genuine Feminine Presence on the Classroom," *History of Education Review* 20, no. 2 (1991): 53–54.

17. Gina Mercer, "Feminist Pedagogy to the Letter: A Musing on Contradictions," in *Knowing Feminisms*, ed. Liz Stanley (London: Sage, 1997), 42.

18. Gore, *The Struggle for Pedagogies*, 125–126.

19. Sneja Gunew, "Feminist Knowledge: Critique and Construct," in *Feminist Knowledge: Critique and Construct*, ed. Sneja Gunew (London: Routledge: 1990), 23.

20. Elizabeth Ellsworth, "Why Doesn't This Feel Empowering?: Working through the Repressive Myths of Critical Pedagogy," *Harvard Educational Review* 59, no. 3 (1989): 297–324.

21. Gore, *The Struggle for Pedagogies*.

22. Lather, *Getting Smart*, 137.

23. Carol Smart, *Feminism and the Power of Law* (London: Routledge, 1989), 172.

24. Ellsworth, "Why Doesn't This Feel Empowering," 301.

25. Joan Scott, "Experience," in *Feminists Theorize the Political*, ed. Judith Butler and Joan Scott (New York: Routledge, 1992), 25.

26. Lather, *Getting Smart*, 139.

27. Brown, "Feminist Hesitations, Postmodern Exposures," 73.

28. Audrey Fisch, "On the Discomforts of Teaching," *Feminist Teacher* 12, no. 1 (1998): 40.

29. Ibid., 44.

30. Sandra Bell, Marina Marrow, and Evangelia Tastsoglou, "Teaching in Environments of Resistance," in *Innovative Feminist Pedagogies in Action*, ed. Maralee Mayberry and Ellen Cronan Rose (New York: Routledge, 1999), 24.

31. University of Alberta (1999–2000) "Code of Student Behaviour." http://www.ualberta.ca/~unisecr/policy/sec30a.html#3 (August 2, 2002).

32. Nancy Hartsock, "Foucault on Power: A Theory for Women?" in *Feminism/Postmodernism*, ed. Linda Nicholson (New York: Routledge, 1990), 171.

33. Marilyn Jacoby Boxer, *When Women Ask the Questions: Creating Women's Studies in America* (Baltimore, Md.: John Hopkins University Press, 1998), 223.

34. Moira Ferguson et al., "Feminism and Antifeminism: From Civil Rights to Culture Wars," in *Antifeminism in the Academy*, ed. Veve Clark et al. (New York: Routledge, 1996).

35. Ibid., 48–49.
36. Pam Blake, "Theory, Critical Thinking, and Introductory Women's Studies," *Feminist Teacher* 12, no. 2 (1998): 120.
37. Ibid.; Ferguson et al., "Feminism and Antifeminism."
38. Sunera Thobani, "War Frenzy—Sunera Thobani Responds" (sunera-legalsize.pdf), October 22, 2001. http://print.indymedia.org (July 17, 2002).
39. Mick, "Critics Question Media Coverage of Thobani's Speech."
40. Margaret Wente, "Two Reasons to Thank Sunera Thobani," *Globe and Mail*, October 4, 2001, A19.
41. Mick, "Critics Question Media Coverage of Thobani's Speech."
42. Christina Hoff Somers, *Who Stole Feminism? How Have Women Betrayed Women* (New York: Simon and Schuster, 1994); Daphne Patai and Noretta Koertge, *Professing Feminism: Cautionary Tales for Inside the Strange World of Women's Studies* (New York: Basic Books, 1994); Alan Charles Kors and Harvey A. Silvergate, *The Shadow University: The Betrayal of Liberty on America's Campuses* (New York: Free Press, 1998).
43. Patricia Williams, "Talking about Race, Talking about Gender, Talking about How We Talk," in *Antifeminism in the Academy*, ed. Clark et al., 70.
44. Kolodny, "Paying the Price of Antifeminist Intellectual Harassment," 8–9.
45. Heinz-Joachim Klatt, "Regulating 'Harassment' in Ontario," *Academic Questions* 8, no. 3 (1995): 48–59.
46. Williams, "Talking about Race," 77.
47. Blake, "Theory, Critical Thinking, and Introductory Women's Studies," 120.
48. Ferguson et al., "Feminism and Antifeminism," 48.
49. Kolodny, "Paying the Price of Antifeminist Intellectual Harassment," 9.
50. Gore, *The Struggle for Pedagogies;* Lather, *Getting Smart;* Ellsworth, "Why Doesn't This Feel Empowering."
51. Jordan J. Titus, "Engaging Student Resistance to Feminism: 'How Is This Stuff Going to Make Us Better Teachers?'" *Gender and Education* 12, no. 1 (March 2000): 22; Dale Bauer and Katherine Rhoades, "The Meanings and Metaphors of Student Resistance," in *Antifeminism in the Academy*, ed. Clark et al.
52. Titus, "Engaging Student Resistance to Feminism," 22.
53. Bell, Marrow, and Tastsoglou, "Teaching in Environments of Resistance," 25; Titus, "Engaging Student Resistance to Feminism," 26.
54. Lather, *Getting Smart*, 143.
55. Bell, Marrow, and Tastsoglou, "Teaching in Environments of Resistance," 43.
56. Ibid., 31–32.
57. Lather, *Getting Smart*, 143.
58. Titus, "Engaging Student Resistance to Feminism."
59. Lather, *Getting Smart*, 127–128.
60. Dr. Heather Tapley, Assistant Professor, Women's Studies, University of Alberta, uses these techniques in her introductory course.
61. Davina Cooper, "Regard between Strangers: Diversity, Equality, and the Reconstruction of Public Space," *Critical Social Policy* 18 (1998): 465.
62. Vallis and Hume, "Thobani Rant Called Hateful," 3.

Imagining Our Way Together

INEZ MARTINEZ

I was making little headway composing this piece about diversity and the women's studies PhD when I had a dream.[1] In this dream a number of women I know, a rainbow of feminists, were sitting around talking. They were one after another agreeing that they were disappointed with the graduate education they had received. I had to admit that I was, too.

Of course, I don't think my dream captures the universal experience of feminists who have received graduate education in America. It just gave me a clue about what aspect of my experience I could offer that might be useful in our thinking about the emerging PhD in women's studies and the challenges posed by diversity.

As I ruminated the next few days over why I had been disappointed in my graduate education, I happened upon an illuminating passage from Carl Jung's *Memories, Dreams, and Reflections.* Jung is narrating his encounter with a Native American from New Mexico:

> [In Taos] for the first time I had the good fortune to talk with a non-European, that is, to a non-white. He was a chief of the Taos Pueblos, an intelligent man between the ages of forty and fifty. His name was Ochwiay Biano (Mountain Lake).

> "See," Ochwiay said, "how cruel the whites look. . . . Their eyes have a staring expression; they are always seeking something; they are always uneasy and restless. We do not know what they want. We do not understand them. We think they are mad."

> I asked him why he thought the whites were all mad.

> "They say that they think with their heads," he replied.

> "Why of course. What do you think with?" I asked him in surprise.

> "We think here," he said, indicating his heart.[2]

I cannot claim to be a blood Pueblo, although I may, in fact, be so blessed, nor do I claim that Ochwiay Biano's words represent the beliefs of all Pueblos. In fact, one point I want to stress about diversity is that no writer or thinker is representative of any whole group because no whole group is homogenous in its beliefs or time-bound in its culture. Nevertheless, what Ochwiay says about identifying knowing with what happens in our heads seems to me the source of my disappointment with my graduate education.

I cannot tell you how validated I feel when I read of research that indicates that a kind of knowing occurs in other areas of the body. Studies done by Dr. Antonio Damasio and Dr. Hanna Damasio, for example, indicate that visceral reactions are a form of "covert awareness" that helps people make decisions. When access to these visceral reactions is blocked through injury, people are unable to display any reaction to scenes of suffering such as "children burned alive or people cut into pieces."[3] If one thinks of knowing as including emotions, then our linguistic habit of assigning some sort of cognitive status to "gut feelings" appears to have some basis in our biology.[4]

The idea that parts of our bodies (in addition to our brains and spinal cords) participate in our "knowing" illuminates what otherwise seems quite inexplicable in my experience. I have since childhood found my most numinous moments of understanding not to be just concepts. Rather, when I have experienced what I shall call "consciousness," my ideas were accompanied by my imagination, my feelings, my body, and a sense that what I was grasping could lead to change—in me and often in the world. Indeed, I have come to distinguish what we normally call "cognition" from "consciousness" by whether ideas are all that we are experiencing when we know something (cognition) or whether our experience of knowing includes our bodies, feelings, and imaginations (consciousness). By imagination I mean the psychological capacity to create images of visions and narratives that one has not oneself experienced in the external world—and to respond emotionally to them. I also mean the arising from within of ideas one has never had before, usually after a period of time of giving attention to a problem or question.[5]

These experiences of thinking, imagining, feeling, embodied recognizing, and a sense of relevance were most powerful in me when I was reading imaginative literature. That is why I wanted to major in literature, teach it, and, if I could, write it.

At graduate school, studying imaginative literature was subordinated to learning current critical discourses, each to be discarded when the new intellectual fashion appeared, providing new fields of possibility for interrogation and, not insignificantly, publications for each emerging generation of professionals. Much was required of the head, but little of the heart or the imagination. Nor was there much concern over the effect of what was being learned on either me or society.

Women's studies is now offering graduate education, and whether it shall repeat, indeed, emulate, isolating head knowledge as the purpose of graduate work is for me the pivotal question. Must women's studies, at least in its guise as graduate studies, "professionalize" in the sense of equating "rigorous" knowledge with knowing with the head, or may it continue to try to transform our understanding of knowledge itself by not succumbing to the academic prejudice that rigorous knowledge consists only of hard data, replicable experiments, abstruse theory, and critique?

A recent anthology exploring the implications of institutionalizing women's studies, *Women's Studies on Its Own,* provides grounds for fearing that leading women's studies practitioners believe the answer to that question is "professionalize." The book's emphasis on criticism as opposed to vision and personal and social transformation signals that knowledge is being limited to cognition. In her introduction, the editor, Robyn Wiegman, specifically notes the "tension" between women's studies' "visionary labor of the past" and an "academic commitment to critique."[6] The thrust of Wiegman's argument and of the majority of the essays she included in the anthology is that the crucial work in women's studies is that of critique: critique of the constraining limits of its visionary past on knowledge production; critique of its limited analyses of nationalism, capitalism, and political purposes of women of color; critique of its political and economic activities in the academy; critique of its own self-narration as a progressive, liberating enterprise. The very frequency with which the words "criticism" or "critique" occur in Wiegman's introduction convey her commitment to the idea that critique is the foremost function of academic inquiry. She herself raises the issue of how academic critique affects the activist utility of an idea, such as identity as a "woman." In her words, "'The Progress of Gender' [her essay] reflects . . . my critical concern with . . . what happens as an identity rubric becomes refracted through the lens of academic critique, especially when identity has had such enormous utility in organizing social transformation in various parts of the world in the twentieth century."[7]

What scholar would argue against the value of analysis and critique? What person in pursuit of consciousness would not—eventually—have at least a grudging gratitude for examples of how one's framework is limiting one's understanding? Analysis and critique are effective and indispensable tools of the scholar's trade insofar as a scholar is seeking knowledge of the head. If one is seeking transformational knowledge, they are still necessary but, when alone, can also be inhibiting. They specifically train one to separate out (or deny) one's feelings. To the degree that feelings are the basis of values, analysis and critique thereby drain the heart-motivations for making change. Analysis and critique are excellent for identifying what is wrong but can be immobilizing as they dishearten. They need to be accompanied by hope and by imagination seeking alternatives.

The difference between Wiegman's hopes for knowledge production in women's studies and my own can be seen in the areas where we emphasize lacunae in women's studies' historical analyses. Wiegman is critical of "presentism," that is, looking at a subject matter in terms of current concerns rather than in terms of its historical contexts. Building on Jane O. Newman's essay,[8] Wiegman argues that this focus limits the possible significance of data to its expedient political relevance and limits interpretation to a framework of current progress. I have no quarrel with the idea that looking at historical data in terms of the discourses of the period yields useful knowledge, although I refuse the conclusion that looking for relevance in historical data to present circumstances is intellectually dubious. I would, however, argue (1) that whether one can hope for progress is inherent to knowing from the heart and (2) that any focus yields partial knowledge. There is, however, a crucial focusing question that I see missing from our historical analyses. I would like to extend our inquiry into the past into the dimension of the unconscious. I would like us to inquire about our psychological past fixed in unconsciousness and evidenced, among other ways, in violent social eruptions. Let me try to explain.

Women's studies emerged in a context of political movements for social justice—civil rights, the antiwar movement, the women's movement. It accordingly distinguished itself from most academic fields in its overt commitment to social changes intended to lead to societies in which women as well as men and people of all nations, races, and ethnicities could have the opportunity to realize their potential as human beings, societies in which bigotries would be replaced by the harvesting of differences.

Here in America, even in our women's studies communities, we have not succeeded in creating such a society—nor has any other people. I believe that to work toward that end we need to educate not only to inform, but actually to *transform*. I do not think that we can do so without grasping the psychological dimensions of what we are trying to transform. Grasping that complexity requires not only realizing that individuals are moved by that of which we are unconscious, but realizing that groups and societies also behave out of shared unconscious motives. In the last few years, we have seen how historical conflicts—the Balkans, Islam and Christianity, enmities in central Africa, to name a few—do not disappear because of the passing of time or the long enjoyment of victory by one of the parties. Conflicts that are resolved by physical power live on as long as their descendants live on. They live on psychologically, which means both consciously and unconsciously. It is as if conflicts that are not dealt with conscientiously but are stifled by successful impositions of power become cultural embodiments of human stuckness, a level of fixation that will not go away and will not even significantly change until human imagination, consciousness, and conscience intervene in some way to alter the dynamic.

The dynamic in its simplest terms consists of you or me and in its simplest terms must be changed into you and me, a transition that involves an imaginative, emotional, kinesthetic grasp of the humanity of the other and the actuality of the other's experience.

What might such an intervention look like? Totally unpredictable—but I believe one historical example is passive resistance. In 1966, when I was working at Sacred Heart University in Bridgeport, Connecticut, I heard a white priest speak of having been part of a sit-in in a café in a southern town. The café had a sign in the window: "no coloreds." Both black and white men entered the crowded café and sat at the counter. It took only an instant for the others present to understand the challenge to segregation. The civil rights workers, all of whom had been trained to tolerate verbal abuse and physical punishment, were dragged outside and beaten. They were kicked and punched again and again, and they did not resist. The priest said he caught a glimpse of the face of the restaurant owner as he watched from inside the café. The latent violence through which segregation functioned was made brutally, bloodily visible, and recognition of the horror of it electrified the owner's face. Finally, the police arrived and arrested the civil rights workers. When they were eventually released, the priest returned to the café. The sign was gone. Two black men sat at the counter. The café was integrated. The priest told this story as an illustration of what he called "the moral jiujitsu" that passive resistance could work on those white people who lived in denial of the evils of segregation (not those who justified them). While a complete transition to "we" was not accomplished, its beginnings were, as the restaurant owner kinesthetically experienced the violence that he was colluding in inflicting on others. Actually seeing the violence underlying the racial segregation he had been supporting worked a moral shift. The hard truth, I am afraid, is that such moral shifts occur only one or a few at a time. We have centuries of our group hatreds upon which to reflect and work.

Imagining such moves as passive resistance requires ideas, but it requires more than ideas. We in America have had access to excellent ideas about how to struggle against racism, ideas put forth by many thinkers. In our own time, women and men of color have pointed us, both whites and people of color, to next steps we could take: perceiving as the outsider within, as Patricia Hill Collins has directed;[9] being willing to endure conflict for its creative possibilities, as Audre Lorde has advised;[10] finding the voice within us and not "selling it for a handclap or our name in print," as Gloria Anzadúa urges;[11] learning to travel playfully and lovingly between the worlds of people we have been taught to think of as not real, as Maria Lugones explains;[12] trying to learn what it means to think from the heart, as the epistemologist Mountain Lake, referred to earlier, takes for granted.

If we are serious about transforming race relations in the United States, we will have to learn to acknowledge the ignorance—and value the knowledge of—the heart. By ignorance of the heart I do not mean unawareness of its desires. I am referring to those desires that wish aggrandizement of the self and harm to others. To the degree that our hearts are so driven, we are ignorant of the reality and suffering of others. That is, we do not experience them imaginatively. Ignorance of the heart underlies not only all the cruelty of which we humans are capable, but also the state of psychological fixation in unresolved historical conflicts such as racism. In this country, for example, Americans have taken the land that supported the lives of Native Americans. Although Americans have enjoyed the victory of that usurpation for centuries, the fact of it psychologically has not gone away. Even as I write, the Dann sisters, Shoshones, fight in Nevada for the right to use land enjoyed by their ancestors.[13] Nor has the fact of the enslavement of people from Africa or the displacement of Spanish cultures, themselves products of imperialism, in the American South and Southwest vanished from the American psyche. Not only the material, but the psychological and moral consequences of these disempowerments persist, providing us the challenge of attempting to imagine ways to evolve through them.

All culture has been imagined. Any of it can be reimagined. That is the hope for human psychological evolution. We need to be able to imagine redemptive acts that could lead to transformation of the psychological states remaining from patterns of cultural oppression, including racism. I use the word "imagination" quite purposefully, because I believe such inspirations arise from the unconscious. Of course, the imagination, like the heart, can be put to destructive purposes. The destruction of the World Trade Center, for example, was an act of realized imagination that was stupefying in its completeness and effectiveness. I suspect that a major cause of the depression that followed for so many of us was the unarticulated sense that our materialistic, rationalistic culture has not psychological force to equal it. It is our challenge as human beings to incubate acts of imagination as redemptive in effect as the attacks on the World Trade Center were expressive of resolution to destroy.

Let me clearly acknowledge that neither "the heart" nor imagination are simply sources of good. We hate from the heart and can be sadistic and genocidal from the heart. Nor is imagination inherently conscientious. The holocaust had to be imagined. Hiroshima and Nagasaki had to be imagined. But if our feelings and imaginations are excluded from the educational process as negligible, what hope have we of helping students learn empathy for others, of helping them reimagine their lives and world in ways that lead to increased consciousness and conscience, to more realized social justice? In other words, how can we hope to make our aspirations of realizing our diversity in life-enhancing ways a reality?

As educators, we in women's studies are particularly well placed to attempt this psychological work on a daily basis, but our practice has been constrained by our limited understanding of what it is to know. The approach most of us have taken toward education of students' feelings and imaginations has been to try to get them to recognize aspects of their socialization. Philosophically, we do not communicate a vision of an existing unconscious psyche that we share, that can evolve or regress, and that contains unrealized possibilities for conscious human psychological development or horror. A vision of human history as revelatory of collective psychological capacities for conscientious social life could root our efforts toward social justice in matter's evolutionary movement toward consciousness.[14] It could provide a unifying framework for recognizing that "being" consists of unique instances of common stardust. Fundamental identity underlies inevitable difference.

An epistemology that includes the imagination, feelings, and the body along with cognitive knowledge in the definition of consciousness has pedagogical implications. We do not normally ask students to integrate the ideas they're learning into their bodies, feelings, and imaginations. We don't for a number of reasons:

We conceive of knowledge as of matter of intellect, ideation, language;

We hesitate to teach what we cannot measure, and we do not know how to measure learning that occurs in imaginations, feelings, and bodies; and

We do not honor the timing rhythms of the body.

We ask students to cram in more material and to turn out more work than their bodies, feelings, and imaginations have time to integrate. One of my favorite images of this dilemma describes a farmer who sneaks out every night to yank at the young plants in order to speed them along. Let me make the obvious point that the restlessness Ochwiay describes prevents the kind of knowing that comes from being still—nurturing the development of our unconscious psyches by taking time for the integration of ideas, feelings, and experience. Can we create programs that give priority to that kind of time?

I am suggesting that our approach to knowing is too exclusively heady to have much effect on human dilemmas such as racism. I think that this one-sidedness comes from our graduate education's cultural origins in Europe, specifically from the idea of the university, developed in Germany, that focused on "impartial" research.

Women's studies has in a number of ways distanced itself from that "value-free" aspiration, including by asking students to bring to consciousness the possible social implications of the knowledge they produce. In that sense, it has practiced knowing from the heart.

What else might we be able to do within the structures where we work? Although the best way to bring contents of the unconscious to consciousness is reflecting on our dreams, I do not believe that approach can be used in an educational institution. A more workable approach to nurturing students' imagination is to ask them to study art, particularly imaginative literature, for what it reveals about the unconscious psyche.[15] Also, more of our institutions could consider accepting products of the imagination as work worthy of degrees. We could also nurture the unconscious by structuring our programs so that students have time to integrate their feelings and sensations with their ideas, time to treat their bodies respectfully in terms of labor, time to watch as the unconscious psyche unfolds and manifests. We could start that process by modeling it ourselves, for our students learn what it means to be professional scholars from watching us.

Helping the collective psyche evolve requires individual development from each of us. I would like to see our concern for diversity extend to the psyche of each individual. No two human beings from any group have the same potentialities. Trying to create space and conditions for each person to develop into the realized, conscientious human being she or he is capable of becoming is the fundamental challenge to living with diversity in a socially just way. In this vision of a *socially responsible* individualism, space must be made for the existence (not the domination) of each individual's sense of reality, including that person's weaknesses and horrors, not that they might inflict them on others but that they may own and learn to deal with them responsibly.[16]

In the classroom, the most challenging moments occur when a student expresses bigoted, violent, or otherwise destructive psychological realities. A teacher's first impulse, I think, is to use power to repress these expressions, e.g., "You may not call another student by that name in this classroom!" an impulse I certainly have had to resort to upon more than one occasion. Usually, when an exchange has reached this point, it has already deteriorated from a conversation seeking understanding to pure power assertions of respective realities. It is, on the level of language, the handling of differences by imposing power, and similarly results in psychological fixation rather than change.

Over the years I have worked toward keeping the classroom discussion on the level of conversation that permits people to express even taboo ideas as long as they are not directed toward denigrating anyone present. Once an idea, such as the ascribed inherent evil of a group, is articulated, it can be addressed, particularly if the worth of the speaker is not attacked. Evidence and counter-evidence can be introduced. A range of anecdotes can be expressed. Parallels between negative ascriptions to various groups not enjoying cultural dominance can be pointed out. Questions about what is gained by groups enjoying cultural dominance making such ascriptions can be asked.

These and other such rational techniques can often work to contain and subordinate the expression of destructive psychological realities without refusing them room to exist, although such rational approaches rarely seem to shift anyone's beliefs on the spot. Being allowed to have one's beliefs be part of a conversation does seem, however, to be a condition for re-evaluating them, a process that can occur almost unnoticed over a period of many conversations.

I recently had a student, for example, who felt free to articulate his version of "Social Darwinism," a guiltless "me over you" position. Class members began to call him names, and I intervened, saying I wanted to hear him explain his position. My responding in terms of argument rather than putdown led the students to respond similarly. There were a series of such exchanges over the semester. The moment of recognizable change occurred when the student entertained Ralph Ellison's scathing depiction of the ethically corrosive effects of racism on white men in "Battle Royal" in *Invisible Man* as worth considering.[17] In spite of this breakthrough, when I last spoke to him, he still embraced the idea that "if survival is between you and me, it's going to be me" as grounds for supporting President Bush's preemptive policy. Deep change usually takes time.

Without creation of psychological space for destructive attitudes of the heart to be expressed and addressed, however, I cannot imagine cultures, including our own, stopping the use of difference as excuse to subordinate, deprecate, physically violate, and even maim and kill others. The good part about trying to create space for each person's psyche to manifest is that it can be attempted by each of us individually as teachers in the classroom. It can, at times, actually educate, that is, lead out the students so that their gifts and those latent in their culture can be lived out in society.

A gratifying example of this kind of culmination—all too infrequent, I'm afraid, in my experience—occurred when I was co-teaching a graduate seminar in women's studies, a rare opportunity for a community college teacher. I brought to the task, particularly through my written responses to student journals, an emphasis on the students' subjective responses, an emphasis that one learns in working with nonacademically oriented community college students. One of the most brilliant and hard-working students in the seminar had working-class origins about which she had not spoken in class. Influenced by our exchanges via the journal, she finally on the last day of class introduced them into her presentation. She told us that she had never before been able to bring this basic aspect of herself into her academic work and that she realized her personal experience of working from childhood and all through her academic career gave her an angle on the material that our conversations needed, an angle she then demonstrated through illustrative questions. I believe that she had been suffering a graduate education conceived solely as a matter of cognition and was able that day to acknowledge the role of her emotional and material life in her experience of "knowing."

Let me use her moment of transformation to plead against institutionalizing graduate women's studies as a replica of other graduate programs in the sense of defining knowledge as exclusively a matter of the head. Let us, instead, continue our efforts to transform, beginning with expanding our understanding of knowledge as we imagine how to educate our students. Gloria Bowles pointed out, in her concluding commentary on *Women's Studies on Its Own,* that students typically say the most important thing that has happened to them in women's studies courses is that they have developed confidence.[18] Useful as that result is, I would hope that the next generation of our graduates would have deeper answers. I would want them to say that their teachers and curriculum taught them not only data and theory about power relations. I would want them to say that they had learned how knowing can enable empathy and imagination, can be the grounds for a conscientious life in pursuit of a world in which ever more people live fulfilled lives in societies seeking social justice.

I am asking, then, that our PhD programs—those most vulnerable to being fully absorbed into the dehumanizing aspects of academe because they are most prestigious and most committed to producing a culturally defined elite—be examined in terms of how they help students integrate their ideas with their feelings, bodies, imaginations, and sense of social responsibility. I think such integrated knowledge has a chance to help us gradually through the centuries transform the psychological responses to injustices transfixed in history, to do so in our lives with one another. Diversity as the realized wealth of human potential personally and culturally—that is the educational vision I would like to see guiding the development of the PhD in women's studies.

Notes

1. This essay is a revision of a talk delivered during the first national conference on the PhD in women's studies, held at Emory University in Atlanta, Georgia, October 12–14, 2001.
2. Carl Jung, *Memories, Dreams, Reflections* (New York: Vintage Books, 1965), 247–248.
3. Sandra Blakeslee, "Complex and Hidden Brain in Gut Makes Bellyaches and Butterflies," *New York Times,* January 23, 1996, C8.
4. See Michael Gershon, *The Second Brain* (New York: Harper/Collins, 1998).
5. For a theoretical underpinning of the idea that the body and imagination are fully involved in cognition, see Mark Johnson, *The Body in the Mind: The Bodily Basis of Meaning, Imagination, and Reason* (Chicago: Chicago University Press, 1987).
6. Robyn Wiegman, "Introduction: On Location," in *Women's Studies on Its Own*, ed. Robyn Wiegman (Durham: Duke University, 2002), 2.
7. Ibid., 11.

8. Jane O. Newman, "The Present and Our Past: Simone de Beauvoir, Descartes, and Presentism in the Historiography of Feminism," in *Women's Studies on Its Own,* ed. Weigman, 146–148.

9. Patricia Hill Collins, "Learning from Outsider Within: The Sociological Significance of Black Feminist Thought," in *(En)Gendering Knowledge: Feminists in Academe*, ed. Joan E. Hartman and Ellen Messer-Davidow (Knoxville: University of Tennessee Press, 1991), 40–65.

10. Audre Lorde, "The Master's Tools Will Never Dismantle the Master's House," in *Zami, Sister Outsider, Undersong,* by Audre Lorde (New York: Quality Paperbook Book Club, 1993), 111.

11. Gloria Anzaldua, "Speaking in Tongues: A Letter to Third World Women Writers," in *This Bridge Called My Back: Writings by Radical Women of Color,* ed. Cherríe Moraga and Gloria Anzaldua (Watertown, Mass.: Persephone Press, 1981), 173.

12. Maria Lugones, "Playfulness, 'World'-Travelling, and Loving Perception," in *Making Face, Making Soul, Haciendo Caras: Creative and Critical Perspectives by Femininsts of Color,* ed. Gloria Anzaldua (San Francisco: Aunt Lute Books, 1990), 390–402.

13. Charlie LeDuff, "Range War in Nevada Pits U.S. against 2 Shoshone Sisters," *New York Times*, October 31, 2002, A18.

14. See Thomas Berry, *The Dream of the Earth* (San Francisco: Sierra Club Books, 1988), 91–92.

15. For an illustration of how imaginative literature can illuminate for collective consciousness aspects of what lives unconsciously in psyche, see my article, "Reading for Psyche, Kate Chopin's *The Awakening*," *Harvest: International Journal for Jungian Studies* 50, no. 2 (December 2004): 104–117.

16. See Carl Jung's comments on projection of evil and integration of one's own negative aspects in his *Psyche and Symbol: The Collected Works of C. G. Jung* (Princeton: Princeton University Press, 1991), 121, and *Man and His Symbols* (Garden City, N.Y.: Doubleday, 1964), 83.

17. Ralph Ellison, *Invisible Man,* 2nd ed. (New York: Vintage International, 1995), 15–33.

18. Gloria Bowles, "Afterword: Continuity and Change in Women's Studies," in *Women's Studies on Its Own*, ed. Weigman, 458.

Distance Education

A MANIFESTO FOR WOMEN'S STUDIES

LAURA BRIGGS AND KARI BOYD MCBRIDE

Internet-based distance education pre-
sents feminists with some of the same paradoxes that Donna Haraway first articulated in her groundbreaking "Manifesto for Cyborgs."[1] The Net is a technological
medium invested with the values of the military (and now, the worst of transnational
capitalism as well), but nested within it is a digital world that carries radically democratizing potential. For too long, feminist debate about distance education has
relied on simple, predictable dualisms of technophobia and technophilia. The Net
can be anything but woman friendly, but it is a contradictory medium that also
creates new possibilities for feminism. On the one hand, the Net engenders hyper-
heterosexualized, exploitative identities that seem to call out for a Dworkinite anti-
pornography campaign; at the same time, it gives rise to chaotically undisciplined
subjects and identities. The complex questions that the Net poses and the challenges it raises for progressive scholars may be easily set aside by a feminism that
associates women with purity, blood, milk, and the moon. But Donna Haraway's
claim that technology creates a world of cyborgs rather than goddesses—mythic
hybrids of machine and organism, creatures whose sexuality, gender, and bodies
refuse simple categorization—invites a more complex and creative response.[2] In
this essay and in our pedagogy, we try to work from within the conundrums to see
new possibilities, neither minimizing the intrinsic difficulties of using the Net to
extend higher education to the vast numbers of people who are underserved by
traditional pedagogical modes and media, nor relying on simplistic accounts of
technology as "male" or "elitist." By taking a lesson from models at the margins,
we hope to learn how to make the Net serve our pedagogical goal of reaching out
to rural, homebound, and incarcerated women with a high-tech feminist curriculum. We look to Web sites and programs developed by educators in the Third World
(among others) for inspiration as we think about creative, innovative, and radical
ways to develop e-education at our own institution, the University of Arizona. We
hope that what we create here can be a model for programs at other First World
institutions that seek to teach across the digital divide.

While both of us basically like instructional technology and use it widely in
our classes, we do not see it as the simple solution to questions of globalized pov-

erty, educational inequality, and institutionalized sexism and racism, as some of its most optimistic proponents—on both left and right—have proposed. We are wary of the kind of e-welfare educational plans that would get the underclass online (à la Newt Gingrich) while preserving intact the structure of neocolonialism in which the Net is imbricated. Secretaries in low-wage, dead-end jobs, "phone actresses" selling virtual sex, and laborers in offshore circuit-board factories all use high-tech equipment in their work, but they do not escape exploitation and low wages; merely knowing how to use technology is not intrinsically liberating. With these lessons in mind, we want to put at the forefront of our project questions about the long-term and global implications of e-education. To what extent will the Net, in general, and distance education, in particular, simply place more resources (information, capital, production capacity, skills, etc.) in the hands of the global "haves"? In what ways might it offer the potential to put resources in the control of the "have nots"? The contrast between the egalitarian ideals of many hackers and other "netizens" (especially before the dot-com explosion of the mid to late 1990s), who saw the Net as a utopian medium in which information just wanted to be free, and the real limitations of access for most of the world, even the affluent West, continues to haunt the Net and, now, insistently, distance education.

Even within academic disciplines, the old hierarchies of race, gender, ability, nation, and ethnicity have been much in evidence from the beginning of the short life of the Net, perhaps in educational sites in particular, which initially archived the most traditional and canonical of materials. For instance, the online database Past Masters claims to offer "the largest collection of full-text electronic editions in philosophy in the world," but it's all dead white guys, all the time: the site includes no works by women or by authors outside the narrowest understanding of the Euro-American philosophical tradition.[3] Similarly, feminist literary historians who led the recuperative feminist project of the 1970s to explode the canon might well feel that the task has to be taken up all over again, as elegant Shakespeare and Interactive Dante Web sites (with links to "the complete works") proliferate, while the works of women authors and people of color continue to be represented by homespun sites, the design equivalent of the mimeographed copies of the works of Aphra Behn and her literary sisters that once circulated in literature departments alongside artful anthologies of Renaissance or Romantic poets (all, evidently, male). At the same time, it is important to note the very existence of these less well funded sites and all the personal and community home pages that proliferate on the Web. Markers of gender, race, class, nation, language, ability, and age are in some ways made hyper-visible on the Net, but the old protocols of "publication" are, if not gone, then reconfigured; even those who are marginalized can have a Web presence.

Nonetheless, many women's studies programs and much feminist writing display a profound resistance to distance learning and instructional technology in general. Some have gone so far as to argue that the Net is an essentially male domain, that enacting feminist pedagogy is dependent on the construction of a community of learners in a "woman-friendly" space that honors women's experience and women's voices.[4] But to conceive distance education and the Net in terms of gender dualism—or class or national divide—is to mistake the problematic. If we view the Net as the same old enemy, we will miss the exigent struggles as well as opportunities it presents for progressive scholars, teachers, scientists, philanthropists, and, yes, even progressive corporations. Perhaps in this context it is useful to recall the genealogy of the Net, a system developed by and for the military of a dominant Western imperial power, a system designed to have no center, no single nexus whose destruction could bring down the whole structure.[5] Those founding principles continue to inform the Net's presence in the world. Yes, it is a medium for global capital and U.S. military dominance.[6] But its lack of a center and its diffuse structure make it resistant both to "outside" attack and "inside" control. Perhaps more than any other medium of mass communication, the Net has shown itself to be available to what Michel de Certeau calls "le quotidien, or "the practice of everyday life," the vision of users as "nomads poaching their way across fields they did not write."[7] The Internet may still assist in military operations, but it has also, for example, connected progressive activists from across the United States and around the world who are opposed to twenty-first-century U.S. wars. The e-mail forum Professors for Peace, which emerged during the war against Afghanistan, used not only the system of the (military-designed) Internet, but the computing and networking infrastructures of universities all over the country—universities that are funded in great part by global capital and the military industrial complex—to disseminate news reports and news analyses critical of the propaganda that presently dominates and eviscerates U.S. media, which is, of course, also funded in great part by global capital.[8] (More recently, a multitude of Web sites like Truthout.org and Salon.com have taken up this critical work, providing an alternative to the corporate monopolies that provide what passes for "news" in the United States.) This is living as a subversive art, the practice of everyday life. Our observations about the paradoxes of the Net and technology are not new; indeed, it is axiomatic in historical studies of science that new technologies simultaneously produce new social relations and reproduce old ones.[9] But we believe that acknowledging the contradictions in the intentions and effects of the Net may provide us with a way to remap the world and to reassess old binaries.

We come to these reflections on the politics of the Net from our attempt, as yet unrealized, to develop an e-certificate in women's studies and Internet computing for those on the wrong side of the digital divide. The program we envision would be offered entirely through Web-based distance learning for people who are in prison, who are rural or homebound, or who may live in urban Arizona, perhaps within blocks of a university, but who are underrepresented in our classrooms and degree programs. In Arizona, the scenarios in which people become marginalized in relationship to education are myriad. To name only some examples:

1. Outside of a handful of wealthy suburbs in the Phoenix and Tucson areas, Arizona's public school are profoundly underfunded and, as a result, simply do not prepare very many students for college.
2. A related fact is that the communities served by impoverished schools are

disproportionately Chicano and Native American as well as low income, an effect of the uneven distribution of poverty in the United States.

3. People in rural communities are not well served by the community college system, whose facilities, while extensive, are concentrated in more populous areas.

4. Those with the least access to education in urban areas are the homebound, people who for reasons of disability or caregiving responsibilities for young children or ill or elderly relatives cannot seek educational opportunities.

5. Most caregivers are women, who may be further restricted by a network of social and cultural norms and expectations that confine them to the home and limit their ability to take advantage of education and training programs.

Our desire to develop a distance education program is an attempt to address some of the inequities built into access to higher education, even in a state that has three (relatively) inexpensive and high-quality public universities and numerous community colleges.

We envision reaching underserved students through distance education because that is the best way we know to solve the problems of access posed by geography, disability, work, or familial restrictions in this large and highly rural state. People in rural communities must go to a tremendous amount of trouble to share in what we have to offer through traditional modes. In addition, we think that distance education also has the potential to reach those who find our classrooms inaccessible for more subtle cultural reasons, people who sometimes are made to feel like "illegal aliens" on our campuses. To serve these students, we imagine creating a program with women's studies content that empowers them to think critically about their place in society and culture and with tech-rich assignments that teach them a variety of skills, from word processing to spreadsheets to Web design. We think that this unusual combination of medium and message could provide students with an effective bridge to more traditional university study while opening the door to better-paying employment in the meantime—or in the long term.

Thinking of distance education as a strategy for empowering those without easy access to higher education or technological literacy sets our project apart from most distance education efforts and most community education projects in the United States. Distance education, whether designed and marketed through the private sector or by universities, has most often been conceived along the lines of the University of Phoenix, that much-written-about model of for-profit education that primarily targets business people who want to upgrade their credentials and are happy to pay to do so.[10] Outreach plans for education, on the other hand, have largely focused on expanding community college systems, either by opening more satellite campuses or using cable channels to broadcast course content. While we are admirers of the community college system, we think we could supplement it and perhaps even reach students that community colleges cannot.

In order to imagine what the specifics of such a program might look like, we need several kinds of help. First, the technology experts from our campus must be full partners in designing and teaching the curriculum. Second, we need two kinds of people involved from outside the university: those community groups already active in youth and community education projects whose members might help us develop curriculum and business people who can help us get students jobs, build or support community computer centers, fund scholarships, and provide computer hardware and software. With respect to the former, we can benefit immensely from the Chicano movement's focus on youth and the teaching of Chicano history and culture; among the groups that have expressed preliminary interest in our project is the local chapter of Chicanos por la Causa, and we hope to initiate similar dialogue with tribal councils of local Indian nations. We have already hosted a mini-conference that brought together women's studies faculty from around the state, tech gurus from the University of Arizona Faculty Center for Instructional Innovation, and representatives of local community organizations. We plan ongoing interaction that will connect us with a wider range of community leaders and with local business leaders willing to support this project by funding some hardware and scholarships and helping us to identify what skills they are looking for in workers.

Our goal in this project was to harness the Net's potential for decentralizing power and producing new social formations, for reaching a new student population and bringing them the best of feminist pedagogies and feminist research. While we had initially looked to traditional models for distributing our program, thinking that perhaps we could simply offer what were essentially our regular courses in a Web format, substituting technology but not adapting pedagogy, we discovered that was precisely what most U.S. universities were doing: offering very traditional materials in higher-tech formats, with LCD (liquid-crystal display) standing in for printed words, monitors for codex books, and keyboards for pencils, but the same old student-as-empty-vessel-to-be-filled teaching style. Even the ubiquitous talking heads of community college and elite university televised courses that haunt the night airways employ a version of authoritarian "sage on the stage" pedagogy that replicates the worst features of mega-lecture-hall university education and have done little either to accommodate or take advantage of the potential offered by broadcast media. The more we looked, the less we liked these formats. As we started looking farther afield for similarly subversive projects, we were startled to learn that not only was our conception of how to do this un-original, but we were way behind the curve. Educators throughout the Third World have been working on such projects for a long time. We found a global array of transgressive models for distance education, among which we took most inspiration in the Committee for the Democratization of Information (CDI) and their "virtual favelas" in Brazil, the African Virtual University (AVU), rural education models from the Philippines and Malaysia, and the "web-back" online performance pieces of Guillermo Gómez-Peña. We were especially curious about how these various projects recruit and (hyper)textually imagine their students and what models of virtual education and empowerment they create.

First, we turn to the work of CDI in Brazil's favelas: In 1994, the group that was to become CDI opened a computer center in the Santa Marta favela, one of Brazil's infamous shantytowns that have virtually no schools and only irregular electrification, water, utilities, and other services.[11] The project was the brainchild of Rodrigo Baggio and an ever-expanding corps of volunteers; within a few years they had created ten centers/schools with no budget, just volunteers and donated equipment. The goal was to teach children and adults computing and Internet skills, to expand their employment prospects, and to connect the favelas' often socially and politically isolated residents to each other and to the wider world.[12] Today CDI is running diverse programs, including preschools, projects for people with disabilities, over two hundred schools in thirty cities, and an online newspaper, with sponsorship from corporations like Microsoft and Esso. An initiative inspired by CDI in Brazil, called CDI Americas, has now opened offices in Colombia, Mexico, and Uruguay and seeks to expand activities to other countries of Latin America and the Caribbean.

What we like about this model is the extent to which it assumes neither hardware access nor computer experience of its students but rather makes providing those things its first task. We have had to think in these terms to imagine how to involve students in some of the largest rural areas of Arizona, Indian reservations, as many of those areas do not have phone service. And this is a crucial issue worldwide; the Philippines, to take one example that is neither particularly good nor particularly bad, has nine phones per one hundred residents. Part of the privilege and responsibility of being at a university or corporation is that we have some power and financial resources to change these kinds of realities. Northern Arizona University, for example, has been at the forefront of efforts to insist that the vast areas of land in our state that are federal Indian reservations get access to being "wired." The other piece this has forced us to think about is how to set up throughout the state proctored computer labs that would enable people to have access to computers that they need not personally own, where we could provide "just-in-time teaching" for Internet computing skills.[13]

We are also intrigued by the distance learning model developed by the African Virtual University.[14] Since its founding in 1997, the AVU has offered computer classes in English and French to students in learning centers in fifteen African countries. Faculty in media studios around the world offer classes that are then beamed by satellite to the learning centers, which are equipped with at least fifty computers and an on-site moderator. Students in the program, who are given free e-mail accounts, have the opportunity to interact in real time via e-mail and phone with the professor and with other students through a "crossroads" threaded discussion list. The AVU paradigm encourages us to think broadly about our resources in imagining and producing course material: our brick-and-mortar universities need not define our faculty, our guest lecturers, or our interlocutors. And it challenges us, in our profoundly place-based model, to be open to the possibility that the "rural" students we target may be in India or Kenya as well as in Why or Snowflake, Arizona.

Another important model for rural education is provided by CEBU: Philippines Secondary Education Distance Education Project and Universiti Sains Malaysia.[15] These are projects that have relied on the print, paper, and pen resources that they give to students to do most of their coursework.[16] Students then have the opportunity to e-mail faculty with questions. In other words, it is decidedly low-tech and in many ways not much different from extension programs, particularly agricultural extension programs as they have been running in the United States and elsewhere since the 1930s. Low-tech programs like CEBU also resemble the university-without-walls plans that have been available since the 1970s, albeit with the important difference that e-mail now allows for communication without the time lag of mail or traveling (though in places with low technological density, it is possible to overstate how instantaneous virtual communication is). While after some consideration we decided that packet and pencil delivery systems were not what we were after, it is important to keep these kinds of models in mind lest we think we have invented the world anew with e-education or that Web-based learning is the best paradigm for all settings.

From Guillermo Gómez-Peña and his "virtual barrio" and "web-back" Net performance pieces, we accept the challenge of thinking about how the imagined utopias of the Net can feel like the same old disempowering, discouraging, lonely, racist, and hostile places to those historically excluded from political power and cultural authority in European and American public and civic spaces.[17] He pushes us to ask, Are cyborgs white? What does it mean that English has become the lingua franca of the Web? Things like courseware and Web design tell a story of whom we expect (and want) to find in these spaces. How do we re-encode them as less hostile without engaging in condescending practices of assuming that some people—read: women, people of color, people inhabiting or migrating from the global South—are somehow culturally disabled when confronted with IT? When Gómez-Peña writes of "low-riding through the interneta" on his laptop with a 3-D Virgin of Guadalupe sticker on it, he may be describing precisely what all of us, in fact, do—bring our wholly racialized, gendered, place-specific selves to the practices of Internet computing.

Gómez-Peña's barrio vernacular is highly specific. A "low-rider," of course, is a very cool car, rebuilt with hydraulics to lift and drop, an expression of individuality and artistry, and the police believe everyone who drives one is a criminal. To "low-ride" is to engage in an extremely hip, hypermasculinized, usually harmless activity that nevertheless subjects you to police harassment. The Virgin of Guadalupe is a dark-skinned incarnation of the Virgin Mary who first appeared in Mexico during the Conquest, who has become the patroness of Mexicans and their descendents, protector, nationalist symbol, and even emblem of the Zapatista uprising. "Interneta" is Spanglish, that proud, edgy, postmodern, transnational language invented by Spanish-speakers in the United States, especially youth; Spanglish irritates parents, teachers, English-only policy-makers, and all humorless defenders of pure languages and identities alike. Gómez-Peña's point is crucial to how we invite students to use the Internet, to appropriate it, engage it, challenge it, and transform it in their full, funky, troubling selves. Far from entertaining conceptions of the Net as a genderless, raceless, disembodied place, a cyberspace of pure digital stream and binary logic, we need to conceive of it as having a culture—obviously: why else do we have words like "netizens" and "netiquette"?—albeit a culture that conceives of itself as neutral, as simultaneously mainstream and endlessly multi-sited, the "culture of no culture," in Sharon Traweek's phrase.[18]

We also need to acknowledge the other problem that Gómez-Peña's and all of these projects point to: not all people are equally netizens. Well-to-do and middle-class white men in urban areas of wealthy countries dominate in techno-logical knowledge and learning. Forty-one percent of all Internet users are in the United States, but even within the United States, blacks, Latinos, and Native Ameri-cans are underrepresented. Women now make up more than 50 percent of all U.S. Internet users, but they continue to lag numerically as designers and developers of software and hardware. This is partly a function of access: white, urban men in the global North make up the demographic group most likely to have jobs or be in educational settings that allow them to learn how to use the toys while being paid or as part of the normal course of their education. They are also the group most likely to have the disposable income to spend on private access to technol-ogy. Though girls and women in technologically saturated societies like the United States, Japan, and Sweden grow up with similar (although not identical) house-hold and educational access to technology, they rarely find their way into com-puter engineering programs; indeed, their numbers in such programs are falling.[19] Black and Latino students show similar patterns of disenfranchisement with re-spect to the Net compared to white students in the same classrooms. Gómez-Peña's model suggests something of why: some of us experience ourselves as aliens in the world of the Web.

A large caveat is in order here: this is a leaky generalization, with plenty of exceptions in the behavior of individual women, girls, men, and boys; we make no claims about the predictive power of this generalization into the future. We as-sume that gender-divergent behavior with respect to technology has nothing to do with innate abilities or biology, but rather derives from gender-dimorphic social-ization and acculturation. (As the thirteen-year-old daughter of one of us said, "I never thought I'd like computer games, because they're for boys. But I do!") Simi-larly, we assume that racial differentials in computing have to do with access and expectations, not intelligence or ability.

With the goal also of increasing employability for historically disenfranchised groups, we aim to create a more flexible learning environment. When flexible learn-ing "increases the learner's control over [her] own learning and enables [her] to develop increased responsibility and independence in [her] . . . study," then we will be continuing to uphold our responsibilities as educators.[20] As we develop our e-certificate, the concept of flexible learning has consequences both for the form of our program and for its content. We like the flexibility implied in an educa-tional "marketplace," especially as that concept encourages us to think outside the traditional degree program composed of three-unit courses, but we want to resist the notion of "education as e-commerce" where forms of learning curriculum be-come purely commodities.[21] We do not rejoice in the notion that "customer pull (student demand) will obtain effective influence over a market that for 600 years has been shaped only by the producer push (instructor offerings)."[22] Our sense is that "instructor offerings" have in fact been largely (to use Althusser's language)

ideological state apparatuses over much of that period; what universities have offered has always functioned as a "commodity" in that sense.[23] At the same time,
the notion of academic freedom has always had the potential (sometimes realized)
to prevent scholarly work from merely echoing the banalities of empire and capital. Insofar as our proposed e-certificate attempts to reach students on the wrong
side of the digital divide, we think it carries on that tradition.

In addition, our experience as professors teaches us that most students are
remarkably passive about their learning. We suspect, in fact, that "student demand"
ventriloquizes the desires of global capital and that "customer pull" is a stand-in
for short-term corporate labor needs. And yet this gesture to students seems to be
one place where universities and corporations might find some common ground.
While students are unlikely to "demand" opportunities for critical thinking if allowed to shop the educational marketplace unsupervised, those skills are what the
best teaching offers and also what the most viable industry needs. Rather than wish-
ing to turn universities into wholly owned subsidiaries of global corporations, CEOs
and boards of directors should be doing everything they can to ensure that truly
independent education not only survives, but thrives.

At the same time, those of us who are inside universities need to set aside
some of our disdain for the corporate world to engage the project of educating for
fulfilling work outside the ivory tower. In this context, it is useful for us to think
about the curriculum initially imagined for our e-certificate by participants at a
2001 mini-conference we hosted. We rather optimistically designed six three-credit
courses, whose descriptions we include below:

1. Place, History, and Identity: Life Stories. By connecting personal life stories with the stories of other times and places, all of us can rewrite history
   to include our lives and experiences. Students will explore voices and silences in historical documents, asking why history so rarely tells the stories
   of working-class people, people of color, rural people, lesbians and gay men,
   and women in general.
2. Acting Up, Making Change. This course encourages students to become active agents of social change by examining the ways in which people have
   mobilized for social change in a variety of locations on a range of issues. It
   will provide tools and opportunities for analyzing contemporary problems,
   making links across communities and borders, and participating in organized
   struggles for social justice.
3. Feminisms. This class will explore feminist ideas and movements around the
   world, including activism that promotes women's rights but not under the
   banner of feminism. One of the tasks of this course will be to explore the
   meanings of feminism in different times and places.
4. Laboring Women: At Home and in the Work Force. This course will explore
   women's paid and unpaid work experiences. Topics to be covered include
   housework, labor unions and organizing, the global economy, maquiladoras,
   stratification of the labor force, sexual harassment, reproductive labor, racism,
   pay equity, occupational safety and health, government policies, and welfare.

5. Feminism and Gender Issues in Chicana/o Communities. This course will explore the history of activism by Mexican American women and Chicanas; their participation in creating and questioning cultural values, with a special look at religion, motherhood, family, and sexuality; new Chicana theories and paradigms for political, social, and academic transformation; the specific challenges facing Chicanas in the workforce; and literature created by and about Chicanas.

6. Women, Health, and Society. This course will offer critical perspectives on a number of issues and practices including hormones, breast cancer, diabetes, body image, childbirth, child development, hypertension, the pill and contraception, domestic violence, psychotropic drugs, drug use and abuse, prison health, HIV/AIDS, SIDS, STDs, women's empowerment, women's health organizing, HMOs, environmental racism, neglect of women in research, women versus men in research, reproductive politics, maternity care, reproductive technologies, and sexuality.

These courses offer the very kind of material that can make students critical thinkers and give them a sense of agency about their place in history and contemporary culture. It wasn't until recently, however, that the Net began to be seen as more than a transparent delivery system for the course content that might then lead students to pursue traditional degree programs at the university. We have come also to realize that the competencies our students will gain in the process of participating in the program—the computer and Internet skills they will need merely to complete course requirements—will provide them with a significant measure of immediate employment advancement and security right away;[24] that kind of economic empowerment may be every bit as radical and subversive as any of our course materials. In other words, we need to emphasize the *e* in the e-certificate, making it not simply an alternative program in women's studies (however desirable we may hold that to be), but a program that carries credible certification in marketable skills. We need to make the computing experts at the university not simply "tech support" but full partners in teaching and certifying a program that explicitly combines critical thinking about the individual and society with computing skills, what Han and Gilbert call a "holisitic" approach.[25] Approaching our e-certificate from this perspective will also, no doubt, lead us to reflect creatively on our pedagogy, which has been designed to serve classroom "goddesses" rather than cyborgs.[26] Students who have earned an e-certificate that effectively integrates computing as both skill and content have a shot at earning the kind of money that would allow them to pursue a bachelor's degree in any number of fields. Or not. Either way, we will have done the kind of radical work that represents the best in university education.

We do not underestimate the task ahead of us if university faculty are to remain players in twenty-first-century education. And we become even more daunted when we realize that many of our colleagues have not yet even learned to read and write in this new language, while much of the corporate world and, increasingly, our on-campus students look to the Web as their first resource for learning.

We often feel trapped between the agendas of funding agencies and administrators looking for glitzy distance education programs that will serve the well-wired upper middle class and a conviction that our work must take us out of this vicious educational circle to teach and learn from those students whose taxes pay our salaries at public universities, but who will never see the inside of a traditional classroom until universities start to do things differently. Figuring out how to bridge these digital divides is now the challenge, and it will take all the wisdom and political commitment of strong feminist thinking to get it right.

Notes

Early versions of this essay were given at SSGRR (Scuola Superiore G. Reiss Romoli) 2002w: International Conference on Advances in Infrastructure for Electronic Business, Education, Science, and Medicine on the Internet, L'Aquila, Italy, January 23, 2002, and at Technotopias: Texts, Identities, and Technological Cultures, University of Strathclyde, Glasgow, Scotland, July 11, 2002. A short exposition of our argument also appeared in *IEEE Computer,* October 2002, 108, 106–107.

1. Donna J. Haraway, "A Cyborg Manifesto: Science, Technology, and Socialist Feminism in the Late Twentieth Century," in *Simians, Cyborgs, and Women: The Reinvention of Nature,* by Donna J. Haraway (New York: Routledge, 1991), 149–182.

2. This is a challenge which other feminists have taken up, as well; one such argument can be found in Pamela Whitehouse, "Women's Studies Online: An Oxymoron?" in *Women's Studies Quarterly* 3–4 (2002): 209–225.

3. InteLex Corporation, Past Masters. http://www.nlx.com.

4. See, for instance, Susan Herring, "Gender Differences in Computer-Mediated Communication: Bringing Familiar Baggage to the New Frontier," keynote address for Making the Net*Work*: Is There a Z39.50 in Gender Communication? American Library Association Annual Convention, Miami, Florida, June 27, 1994, http://www.cpsr.org/cpsr/gender/herring.txt; and Laurie Fink, "Women: Lost in Cyberspace?" Enhanced Learning Project, Denison University and Kenyon College, http://enhanced-learning.org/prox/paper5.htm.

5. On the origins of the Internet, see Barry M. Leiner et al., *A Brief History of the Internet,* version 3.32, Internet Society, December 10, 2003. http://www.isoc.org/internet/history/brief.shtml.

6. See Donna J. Haraway, *Modest_Witness@Second_Millennium.FemaleMan©_Meets_ OncoMouse™* (New York: Routledge, 1997).

7. Michel de Certeau, *Arts de Faire [The Practice of Everyday Life],* trans. Stephen Rendall (Berkeley: University of California Press, 1984), 174.

8. Professors for Peace. http://groups.yahoo.com/group/professors_for_peace.

9. See especially Bruno Latour, *The Pasteurization of France [Microbes]* (Cambridge, Mass.: Harvard University Press, 1988).

10. See, for instance, Brian Knestout and Alison Stevenson, "Teachers Pet," *Kiplinger's Personal Finance,* October 2002, 58–59.

11. CDI: Comitê para Democratização da Informática. http://www.cdi.org.br.

12. Daniela Katzenstein Hart, "Combating Technological Apartheid in Brazilian Favelas," *Disability World* 3 (June–July 2000). http://www.disabilityworld.org/June-July2000/Tech&Access/Apartheid.htm/.

13. Just-in-time teaching, or JiTT, refers to the pedagogical method that delivers skills and

information to students based on their immediate needs. It was first developed by Gregor Novak; see http://webphysics.iupui.edu/jitt/jitt.html.

14. AVU: The African Virtual University. http://www.avu.org.

15. CEBU: Philippines Secondary Education Distance Education Project and Universiti Sains Malaysia. http://www.usm.my.

16. Pureza Veloso et al., "Infrastructure for E-Education on the Internet: Response to Total Access to Philippine Education via Distance Learning." SSGRR 2001s: ICAI, L'Aquila, Italy, August 2001, CD-ROM.

17. Guillermo Gómez-Peña, "The Virtual Barrio: The Other Frontier (or, the Chicano Interneta)." http://www.telefonica.es/fat/egomez.html#paper.

18. Sharon Traweek, *Beamtimes and Lifetimes: The World of High Energy Physics* (Cambridge, Mass.: Harvard University Press, 1988).

19. See Dale Strock, "Women in AI," *IEEE Expert* 7, no. 4 (1992); and Vanessa Davies and Tracy Camp, "Where Have Women Gone and Will They Be Returning?" *CSPR Newsletter* 18, no. 1 (2000), http://www.cpsr.org/publications/newsletters/issues/2000/Winter2000/index.html.

20. Pat Halloran, "'Thinking outside the Square': A Strategic Approach to Learning," SSGRR 2000w: ICAI, L'Aquila, Italy, January 2000, CD-ROM.

21. On curriculum design, see Gill Windall et al., "Design Patterns for E-Education," SSGRR 2000w: ICAI, L'Aquila, Italy, January 2000, CD-ROM.

22. Beverly Park Woolf et al., "A Digital Market Place for Education," SSGRR 2000w: ICAI, L'Aquila, Italy, January 2000, CD-ROM.

23. Louis Althusser, "Ideology and Ideological State Apparatuses: Notes Towards an Investigation," in *Lenin and Philosophy*, trans. Ben Brewster (London: New Left Books, 1971), 127–186. For a short tutorial on Althusser, see Dino Felluga, "Modules on Althusser: On Ideological State Apparatuses," in *Introductory Guide to Critical Theory* (Purdue University, November 28, 2003). http://www.purdue.edu/guidetotheory/marxism/modules/althusserISAs.html.

24. Motilal Sharma et al., "Information Technology for Poverty Reduction," SSGRR 2001w: ICAI, L'Aquila, Italy, January 2001, CD-ROM.

25. Chia Y. Han and Juan E. Gilbert, "A Smart E-School Framework," SSGRR 2000s: ICAI, L'Aquila, Italy, August 2000, CD-ROM; D. Garrison, "Distance Education for Traditional Universities: Part-Time Professional Learning," *CADE* 13 (1998), http://cade.athabascau.ca/vol13.2/garrison.html.

26. Lucia M. M. Giraffa and Michael da C. Móra, "Virtual Classes Instead of Traditional Classes: Is It True? Is It Possible? Is It Desirable?" SSGRR 2000s: ICAI, L'Aquila, Italy, August 2000, CD-ROM. See also Michael Collins, "The Importance of Electronic Communications in Successful Web-Based Courses," SSGRR 2000s: ICAI, L'Aquila, Italy, August 2000, CD-ROM; Leon L.Combs, "Web-Based Education Utilizing Learner Styles," SSGRR 2001w: ICAI, L'Aquila, Italy, January 2001, CD-ROM; Carol Young Carver, "The Application of Pedagogy and Technology to E-Education: An Analysis of Factors Affecting Success and Failure," SSGRR 2001s: ICAI, L'Aquila, Italy, August 2001, CD-ROM; K. D. Blum, "Gender Differences in Asynchronous Learning in Higher Education: Learning Styles, Participation Barriers, and Communication Patterns," *Journal of Asynchronous Learning Networks* 3 (1999): 46–66; and Karen Evans, "Barriers to Participation of Women in Technological Education and the Role of Distance Education," in *Commonwealth Heads of Government* (Vancouver, Canada), *The Commonwealth of Learning*, 1995, http://www.col.org/barriers.htm.

CONTRIBUTORS

JULIA BALÉN, assistant professor at California State University's new Channel Islands campus, has a PhD in comparative cultural and literary studies with a focus on issues of embodiment and power relations and has published numerous articles on topics ranging from feminist humor to activism and pedagogy. She is currently finishing a book, to be titled "Roberta's Rules," on feminist decision-making practices and has two new projects in various stages of development: a collection of essays on the central project of Monique Wittig's work and a study of the international LGBT choral movement.

AGATHA BEINS received an MA in Women's Studies in 2003 and is currently an MFA student in creative writing, with a concentration on poetry, at Eastern Washington University. Her interest in popular cultural texts and the interconnections between discourse and materiality has been influenced particularly by postmodern, poststructural, queer, and Marxist theories, as well as the field of cultural studies. As a composition instructor, she has also been exploring the practical and theoretical aspects of critical, feminist, and cultural studies pedagogies in the classroom.

NAN ALAMILLA Boyd has a PhD from Brown University, and she currently teaches in the Women's and Gender Studies Department at Sonoma State University. In 1994 and 1995 she was a Rockefeller fellow at CLAGS, the Center for Lesbian and Gay Studies, and from 2000 to 2002 she was at the Institute for Research on Women and Gender at Stanford University. She has published widely in queer studies, and her book *Wide Open Town: A History of Queer San Francisco* was published by the University of California Press in 2003.

LAURA BRIGGS is the author of *Reproducing Empire: Race, Sex, Science, and US Imperialism in Puerto Rico* (University of California Press, 2002). She works on reproduction, race, and imperialism and has published on science fiction, forced sterilization, and hysteria. Her current interests include eugenics, reproductive technology, and transnational adoption. She teaches courses on the cultural contexts of science, eugenics and reproduction, gendered race and raced gender, the history of sexuality, and feminist postcolonial studies and critical race theory.

MONICA BROWN is an associate professor of English at Northern Arizona University, where she teaches Latino/a literature, U.S. multiethnic literature, women's literature, and feminist theory. She is the author of *Gang Nation: Delinquent Citizens in Puerto Rican, Chicano, and Chicana Literature* (University of Minnesota Press, 2002) and an illustrated children's book, *My Name Is Celia/Mi Nombre es Celia* (Rising Moon, 2004).

MIROSLAVA CHÁVEZ-GARCÍA is an assistant professor of Chicana/o history in the Chicana/o Studies Program at the University of California, Davis. She received her doctorate in history from the University of California, Los Angeles, and she has published articles on gender, patriarchy, and the law in nineteenth-century California. She teaches courses on Chicana/o history, Latina/o history, U.S.-Mexico border relations, and Chicana politics and community activism. Her current research interests focus on gender, race, ethnicity, and juvenile delinquency in the late nineteenth and early twentieth centuries.

BARBARA CROW is an associate professor in communication studies and women's studies at York University. Her research interests are women's studies, technology, and feminist theory. She is the editor of *Radical Feminism: A Documentary Reader* (New York University Press, 2000) and coeditor, with Lise Gotell, of *Open Boundaries: A Canadian Women's Studies Reader* (Prentice Hall/Allyn and Bacon, 2000). She was president of the Canadian Women's Studies Association, 2002–2004.

MARY JO TIPPECONNIC FOX, a Comanche, is the director/chair of American Indian Studies and associate to the president for American Indian Affairs at the University of Arizona, Tucson. She earned her doctorate in higher education from the University of Arizona in 1982 and has over twenty-five years of teaching and administrative experience. Her scholarly activity focuses on American Indian higher education, especially American Indian studies and American Indian women's issues.

ESTHER FUCHS is professor of Judaic studies and Near Eastern studies at the University of Arizona. She has published widely on modern Hebrew literature, biblical literature, Jewish studies, and gender. Her most recent books are *Israeli Mythogynies: Women in Contemporary Hebrew Fiction* (State University of New York, 1987), *Women and the Holocaust: Narrative and Representation* (Oxford and Lanham, 1999) and *Sexual Politics in the Biblical Narrative: Reading the Hebrew Bible as a Woman* (Sheffield Academic Press, 2000). She is coeditor of *Wisdom on the Cutting Edge: The Study of Women in Biblical Worlds* with Jane Schaberg and Alice Bach (Continuum, 2003). Currently she is at work on *Israeli Women's Studies: A Reader* (forthcoming, Rutgers University Press).

LISE GOTELL is an associate professor of women's studies at the University of Alberta. She researches and writes in the area of gender, sexuality, and law. She is a coauthor of *Bad Attitude/s on Trial: Feminism, Pornography, and the Butler Decision* (University of Toronto Press, 1997), the coeditor of *Open Boundaries: A Canadian Women's Studies Reader* (Prentice Hall/Allyn and Bacon, 2000), and has written several journal articles and book chapters. She is currently working on a Social Science and Humanities Research Council–funded research study, "Canadian Sexual Assault Law and the Contested Boundaries of Consent: Legal and Extra-Legal Dimensions." This study assesses the recent impacts of sexual assault law reform.

BEVERLY GUY-SHEFTALL is founding director of the Women's Research and Resource Center (since 1981) and the Anna Julia Cooper Professor of Women's Studies at Spelman College. She is also an adjunct professor at Emory University's Institute for Women's Studies, where she teaches graduate courses in its doctoral program. She has published a number of texts within African American and women's studies, including the first anthology on black women's literature, *Sturdy Black Bridges: Visions of Black Women in Literature* (Doubleday, 1979, with Roseann P. Bell and Bettye Parker Smith); her dissertation, *Daughters of Sorrow: Attitudes toward Black Women, 1880–1920* (Carlson, 1991); *Words of Fire: An Anthology of African American Feminist Thought* (New Press, 1995); and *Traps: African American Men on Gender and Sexuality* (Indiana University Press, 2001, with Rudolph Byrd). Her most recent publication is *Gender Talk: The Struggle for Equality in African American Communities* (Random House, 2003, with Johnnetta Betsch Cole).

EVELYNN M. HAMMONDS, a Spelman College alumna, is professor of the history of science and of African and African American studies at Harvard University. She was co-organizer of the historic national conference "Black Women in the Academy: Defending Our Name, 1894–1994," held at the Massachusetts Institute of Technology in 1994. She has written widely on the epidemic of HIV/AIDS among African American women, including "Gendering the Epidemic: Feminism and the Epidemic of HIV/AIDS in the United States, 1981–1999," in *Science, Medicine, and Technology in the Twentieth Century: What Difference Has Feminism Made?* edited by Angela Creager, Elizabeth Lunbeck and Londa Schiebinger (University of Chicago Press, 2000). She is also the author of the widely cited article "Black (W)holes and the Geometry of Black Female Sexuality," which appeared in *differences: A Journal of Feminist Cultural Studies* (1994). She is currently completing a reader on race and gender in science and medicine and a monograph on the history of race in science and medicine in the United States. In 2004, Spelman College awarded her an honorary doctorate of humane letters.

JANET R. JAKOBSEN is director of the Center for Research on Women at Barnard College. She is the author of *Working Alliances and the Politics of Difference: Diversity and Feminist Ethics* (Indiana University Press, 1998), coauthor, with Ann

Pellegrini, of *Love the Sin: Sexual Regulation and the Limits of Religious Tolerance* (New York University Press, 2003), and coeditor, with Elizabeth Castelli, of *Interventions: Activists and Academics Respond to Violence* (Palgrave, 2004). She is currently working on a book project, "Sex, Secularism, and Social Movements: The Value of Ethics in a Global Economy." Before entering the academy, she was a policy analyst and lobbyist in Washington, D.C.

MIRANDA JOSEPH is associate professor of women's studies at the University of Arizona. She is the author of *Against the Romance of Community* (University of Minnesota Press, 2002) as well as several essays, including "Analogy and Complicity: Women's Studies, Lesbian/Gay Studies and Capitalism," in *Women's Studies on Its Own,* edited by Robyn Wiegman (Duke University Press, 2002).

ELIZABETH LAPOVSKY KENNEDY is professor of women's studies at the University of Arizona, Tucson, with affiliated appointments in history and anthropology, having served as the head of the Department of Women's Studies from 1998 to 2003. Kennedy was a founding member of women's studies at the State University of New York at Buffalo, where she taught for twenty-eight years. She is coauthor of the prize-winning book *Boots of Leather, Slippers of Gold: The History of a Lesbian Community* (Routledge, 1993, with Madeline Davis) and *Feminist Scholarship: Kindling in the Grove of Academe* (University of Illinois Press, 1985, with Ellen DuBois et al.). In 2003–2004 she was a fellow at the National Humanities Center.

INEZ MARTINEZ, professor emerita of English, served as co-director of women's studies at Kingsborough Community College from 1995 to 2003. She has just completed a manuscript, "Reading for Psyche," an exploration of imaginative literature through the Jungian concepts of ego, self, numinosity, shadow, and psychological freedom.

VIVIAN M. MAY is assistant professor of women's studies at Syracuse University. She has published articles about the literary and philosophical contributions of writers such as Shani Mootoo, James Baldwin, Anna Julia Cooper, and Melvin Dixon. She has also published essays exploring the politics of interdisciplinary methods and critical pedagogies. In addition to coediting a special issue of *Womanist Theory and Research,* she has coauthored essays in the field of feminist disability studies. Currently, she is working on a book exploring the philosophical innovations and political implications of Anna Julia Cooper's life work.

KARI BOYD MCBRIDE is associate professor and undergraduate director in women's studies and director of the Group for Early Modern Studies (GEMS) at the University of Arizona. She publishes on early modern literature and culture and instructional technology. With Laura Briggs, she has explored the problems of establishing a certificate in women's studies and Internet computing through distance education.

CHANDRA TALPADE MOHANTY is professor of women's studies and dean's professor of the humanities at Syracuse University. Her work focuses on transnational feminist theory, cultural studies, and antiracist education and has been translated into German, Dutch, Italian, Spanish, Chinese, Russian, Swedish, Thai, and Japanese. She is author of *Feminism without Borders: Decolonizing Theory, Practicing Solidarity* (Duke University Press, 2003) and coeditor of *Third World Women and the Politics of Feminism* (Indiana University Press, 1991) and *Feminist Genealogies, Colonial Legacies, Democratic Futures* (Routledge, 1997). She edits a series called Comparative Feminist Studies for Palgrave/Macmillan.

SHEILAH E. NICHOLAS, a Hopi, is a doctoral candidate in American Indian studies at the University of Arizona. She is currently completing her dissertation on the role of Hopi language among contemporary Hopi youth. Her academic interests in American Indian women, Indian education, and indigenous languages has afforded her the opportunity to work on a diversity of projects for and with schools and tribal communities. She received her BA in special education and MA in American Indian studies from the University of Arizona.

LORENIA PARADA-AMPUDIA was born in Sonora, Mexico, and has lived in Mexico City for the last thirty years. She studied in areas including social psychology, gender and development, Latin American studies, and body and sexuality. She has been a feminist activist since 1978. She is the founder of a feminist autonomous group of university students (GAMU, 1978–1982); a founder, staff member, and professor of the first Women's Studies Center at the National Autonomous University of Mexico (1984–1991); and a founder and staff member of the University Program for Gender Studies (Programa Universitario de Estudios de Genero: PUEG/UNAM, 1992–2003).

PRITI RAMAMURTHY is an associate professor in the Department of Women's Studies, University of Washington, Seattle. In recent essays, published in the journals *World Development, Cultural Anthropology,* and *Feminist Studies,* she has theorized feminist commodity chains as analytics of power constituted materially and culturally, mediated by social relations, difference, and politics, and as likely to rupture as to connect. A core member of the Modern Girl Around the World collaborative research project (http://depts.washington.edu/its/moderngirl.htm), her current research is on the modern girl in India, 1920 to 1950.

DAVID RUBIN, who recently earned master's degrees in comparative cultural and literary studies and in women's studies at the University of Arizona, works in the areas of feminist, poststructuralist, Marxist, and queer theory as well as on questions of the praxis and politics of contemporary counter-globalization, LGBT, and transnational feminist movements.

SANDRA K. SOTO is an assistant professor of women's studies and an affiliated faculty member with English and with the Center for Latin American Studies at the

University of Arizona. She is completing her manuscript, "Queering Aztlan: The Challenge of Racialized Sexuality in Chicana/o Literature," and launching a new study that examines the relationship between the study of U.S. domestic differences and transnational feminist studies. Her principal research interests are Chicana/o literary and cultural studies, queer theory, and contemporary feminist theories. She is co-coordinator of the Chicana/Latina Studies Concentration in the Department of Women's Studies at the University of Arizona.

BANU SUBRAMANIAM is an assistant professor of women's studies at the University of Massachusetts, Amherst. Her research interests lie in the relationships between gender, race, colonialism, and science. Primarily trained as a biologist, she is interested in interdisciplinary work between the natural sciences and the social sciences and the humanities. She is coeditor of *Feminist Science Studies: A New Generation* (Routledge, 2001).

ALYS EVE WEINBAUM is an associate professor of English and an adjunct associate professor of women's studies at the University of Washington, Seattle. She is the author of *Wayward Reproductions: Genealogies of Race and Nation in Transatlantic Modern Thought* (Duke University Press, 2004). Currently, she is working on an edited collection, "W.E.B. Du Bois and the Gender of the Color Line" (co-edited with Susan Gillman), and on a project on contemporary reproductive cultures and politics, "Rethinking Reproductive Labor in Transnationalism." She is also a member of the Modern Girl Around the World collaborative research group.

ROBYN WIEGMAN is the Margaret Taylor Smith director of women's studies and an associate professor of women's studies and literature at Duke University. She is the author of *American Anatomies: Theorizing Race and Gender* (Duke University Press, 1995) and the editor of a number of anthologies, the most recent of which is *Women's Studies on Its Own* (Duke University Press, 2002). Her book *Being in Time with Feminism* is forthcoming from Duke University Press.

BONNIE ZIMMERMAN has been a professor of women's studies at San Diego State University since 1978. She served as chair of the department and graduate advisor as well as chair of the University Senate. She was active in the National Women's Studies Association until 2003 and considers her 1998–1999 term as president as one of the highlights of her career. She is the author of *The Safe Sea of Women: Lesbian Fiction, 1969–1989* (Beacon Press, 1990) and editor of *Professions of Desire: Lesbian and Gay Studies in Literature* (Modern Languages Association, 1995), *The New Lesbian Studies* (Feminist Press, 1996), and *Lesbian Histories and Cultures: An Encyclopedia* (Garland Publishing, 2000). In addition, she has published numerous articles and book reviews, including the oft-reprinted "What Has Never Been: An Overview of Lesbian Feminist Literary Criticism." She is currently associate vice president for Faculty Affairs at San Diego State University.

INDEX

academia. *See* higher education

Ackerman, Lillian, 172, 173, 180

Acklesberg, Martha, 166

activism, 1, 17–19, 21, 23–24, 70–71, 81–83, 88, 89–93, 99, 135, 137, 144, 145, 157, 219, 245–284, 322; anarchic pluralisms, 166; and conscientization, 187–188; feminist, 17, 34, 45, 70, 71, 84, 92, 93, 250–251, 256, 263–264, 294; grassroots organizing, 106, 166, 272; and HIV/AIDS, 103; place-based, 82, 92; relation to theory, 13, 17, 18, 21, 22, 23, 36, 41–44, 46, 56, 70–71, 73, 78, 127–128, 144–145, 157, 166, 200, 223, 224, 245, 246, 250–252, 253, 255–256. *See also* feminism; Jewish feminist studies; politics; social justice movements

administration. *See* women's studies administration

Africa: African Virtual University, 318, 319

African American studies, 8, 11, 61, 64, 66, 67, 69, 191, 222. *See also* black women's studies

African American women. *See* black women

Aguilar-San Juan, Karin, 105–106

Alarcón, Norma, 117–118, 218

Alexander, M. Jacqui, 218

Allen, Judith, 14

Allen, Paula Gunn, 176, 178

alliance. *See* politics of alliance

Althusser, Louis, 125

American Indians, 304, 317, 318, 319; American Indian studies, 4, 11, 12, 13, 172, 180, 222, 319; colonization of, 171, 178, 308; gendered division of labor, 172, 176, 178–179, 180; gender ideologies, 172, 175, 177, 178; tribal cultures and practices, 170, 172, 174–178. *See also* indigenous struggles

American Indian women, 80, 102, 150, 170–181; cultural representations of, 170–171, 173, 174, 176, 180; feminism, 170, 176, 178, 290; indigenous knowledges, 80, 81; roles in tribal societies, 170, 171, 172–173, 174–176, 179–180; scholarship about, 13, 171–174, 177, 180; scholarship by, 176, 180; silencing of, 170, 178; tribal perspective, 13, 173, 304; and women's studies, 12, 13, 150

American Studies, 4, 102, 115, 121; internationalization of, 11, 112–113, 114, 123n6

analogy, 220–221; and subject formation, 199, 222, 227n47; and women's studies' identity, 196, 197, 198, 199. *See also* community; politics of difference

Anita Hill/Clarence Thomas hearings, 68

anti-globalization movements, 9, 18, 23, 79, 80, 82, 83–93, 251, 252, 255. *See*